MW01258217

AMERIND STUDIES IN ANTHROPOLOGY

Series Editor, **Christine R. Szuter**

AMERIND STUDIES
IN ANTHROPOLOGY

FLOWER WORLDS

RELIGION, AESTHETICS, AND IDEOLOGY IN MESOAMERICA AND THE AMERICAN SOUTHWEST

EDITED BY
Michael D. Mathiowetz and Andrew D. Turner

THE UNIVERSITY OF
ARIZONA PRESS
TUCSON

The University of Arizona Press
www.uapress.arizona.edu

We respectfully acknowledge the University of Arizona is on the land and territories of Indigenous peoples. Today, Arizona is home to twenty-two federally recognized tribes, with Tucson being home to the O'odham and the Yaqui. Committed to diversity and inclusion, the University strives to build sustainable relationships with sovereign Native Nations and Indigenous communities through education offerings, partnerships, and community service.

ISBN-13: 978-0-8165-4232-1 (hardcover)
ISBN-13: 978-0-8165-4847-7 (paperback)

Cover design by Leigh McDonald
Cover photo: Ancestral Pueblo, 1300–1400. Fourmile Polychrome bowl with flower and hummingbirds. Ceramic and paints, 11.43 × 25.4 × 25.4 cm. Catalog number 1988.100.FA, Dallas Museum of Art, Foundation for the Arts Collection, anonymous gift. Photo by Brad Flowers. Typeset by Sara Thaxton in 10.5/14 Adobe Caslon Pro and Trade Gothic LT Std

Publication of this book is made possible in part by the proceeds of a permanent endowment created with the assistance of a Challenge Grant from the National Endowment for the Humanities, a federal agency.

Library of Congress Cataloging-in-Publication Data
Names: Mathiowetz, Michael D., 1973– editor. | Turner, Andrew (Andrew David), editor.
Title: Flower worlds : religion, aesthetics, and ideology in Mesoamerica and the American southwest / edited by Michael D. Mathiowetz and Andrew D. Turner.
Other titles: Amerind studies in anthropology.
Description: Tucson : University of Arizona Press, 2021. | Series: Amerind studies in anthropology | Includes bibliographical references and index.
Identifiers: LCCN 2020046910 | ISBN 9780816542321 (hardcover)
Subjects: LCSH: Uto-Aztecan Indians—Religion. | Visual metaphor. | Spirituality. | Anthropological linguistics.
Classification: LCC E99.U85 F55 2021 | DDC 978.004/9745—dc23
LC record available at https://lccn.loc.gov/2020046910

To the memory of Jane H. Hill

CONTENTS

FOREWORD

When Michael and Andrew planned a symposium on the flower world in the Southwest and Mesoamerica, they invited Jane Hill to serve as the primary discussant with some assistance from me as Jane was unwell and unsure if she could travel. Jane's participation was much anticipated because she defined the central concept discussed here, the Uto-Aztecan Flower World. In 1992 Jane published her definition of these sets of ideas on floral imagery expressed in song across most communities who speak Uto-Aztecan languages. Her article, "The Flower World of Old Uto Aztecan," was well received, and shortly after it was published, Jane invited me to explore expressions of the flower world in material culture. We published "The Flower World in Material Culture: An Iconographic Complex in the Southwest and Mesoamerica" in 1999. Michael, Andrew, and I hoped that Jane and I would craft our comments together. Jane really wanted to find out how her 1992 article influenced scholars to carry on research that brought archaeology, ethnology, and linguistic anthropology together to help us understand the long-term histories of Uto-Aztecan-speaking communities and their neighbors. But she lost her battle with health challenges on November 2, 2018, six months before the initial symposium was convened at the Society for American Archaeology meeting in Albuquerque. She would have enjoyed that session and even more the subsequent intensive seminar at the Amerind Museum, not far from her home in Tucson.

In this preface, I want to explain a little bit about Jane's research interests and intentions as I understand them from my small role in her explorations of the flower world. I'll relate a short history of how I got involved in Jane's project and then speculate about what we might have done differently if we knew then what we know now.

Jane H. Hill was a linguistic anthropologist born and raised in California. She earned her PhD from the University of California, Los Angeles, with a dissertation on Cupeño grammar (Philips 2019). The Cupeño are an Indigenous community in Southern California, and their language is classified in the Takic branch of the Uto-Aztecan language family. Jane met and married her husband, Kenneth C. Hill, while at UCLA. Ken is also a linguist specializing in Uto-Aztecan languages, especially Hopi. They both went on to study Nahuatl (Mexicano), and Ken coedited the monumental *Hopi Dictionary* (Hopi Dictionary Project 1998). Jane and Ken worked in Michigan for many years and then relocated to the University of Arizona in 1983, the same year I began my graduate program in archaeology there, having also relocated from Ann Arbor and Detroit. Jane's Arizona decades are perhaps best known for two books, *Speaking Nahuatl* (1986) and *The Everyday Language of White Racism* (2008). Her last project, together with Ken, was a comparative grammar of the Takic languages. In all of their work, the most important point was to encourage revitalization of Indigenous languages by providing communities with useful linguistic resources, and to help anthropologists—even archaeologists!—understand the multifaceted importance of language and speech as living, strategic, and expressive.

Jane was working on her flower world article while I was working on my dissertation in the late 1980s. Emory Sekaquaptewa and Ken Hill were beginning work on the *Hopi Dictionary* at that time. I was taking Hopi language class with Emory and working on the Homol'ovi archaeological project, analyzing pottery from ancestral Hopi sites. For my dissertation, I was comparing decoration of early painted pottery in the Four Corners area with other media. Jane was on my doctoral committee, and we enjoyed many conversations about art, language, culture, and science. In 1992 I completed and defended my dissertation, and Jane published her flower world article in the *Journal of Anthropological Research*. I graduated and moved to Flagstaff to work as a pottery analyst for the Navajo Nation Archaeology Department. Some UA faculty told me I was "wasting" my PhD and disrespecting the time they had "invested" in me by signing on as a tribal CRM archaeologist instead of applying for academic jobs. In contrast, Jane had always supported community-engaged anthropology, and she supported me, as did Emory, Ken, my committee chair J. Jefferson Reid, and some others.

In her flower world article, Jane recommended a follow-up study to look for flower world imagery in material culture. She got a grant to fund a literature and collections search. I think in part to show her continued support for my research and career choices, she hired me for the project. The income was welcome as I struggled to pay back student loans. But more important, this study allowed us both to continue research that we found fascinating.

Our initial question was, can we find the verbal flower world ideas in material culture using archaeological evidence? Flower world iconography was obvious in the material culture of Yaqui Easter celebrations in Tucson, which we both enjoyed attending, but mostly in perishable media. Had material expressions survived from ancient times? If so, what is the time-space distribution of flower world imagery? Would we have anything interesting to say about it? To start, we had to narrow Jane's flower world criteria to a sort of checklist and then produce a matrix of associations—not just presence/absence but cooccurrences. We knew that no matter what we found, our sample would be too small for statistics. Any classification of imagery and any 3D matrix of time, space, and medium would be oversimplified. As in any archaeological project, we knew data would be incomplete and sometimes inaccurate (e.g., we now know about flowers in Hohokam rock art, and the Hohokam pottery that we highlighted probably dates somewhat later than we said it did).

Then came the fun part—once I had compiled a structured data set, Jane and I got to kick around all the ideas you see in our article: diffusion, gender, relationships between verbal and visual arts, and so on. We floated our preliminary results at the 1996 Southwest Symposium in Tempe, which I helped organize along with Michelle Hegmon and others (Hays-Gilpin and Hill 2000). To my surprise and relief, we found a supporter in George Cowgill, one of the leading Mesoamerican archaeologists of our time. George piqued my interest in learning a little more about Mesoamerican archaeology, especially the mural paintings of Teotihuacan.

Our first draft of the material culture article was much more speculative than the published version (Hays-Gilpin and Hill 1999). *JAR*'s peer reviewers split—one thought the manuscript was innovative and interesting, but the other seemed annoyed about it. True, it was data rich but short on conclusions. And at that time, many archaeologists were nervous about the humanities—a science versus humanities split had been raging since the early 1980s, and by the late 1990s the "science-only" advocates were on the retreat (as were the radical relativists). When the review came in, I had just accepted a tenure-track job at Northern Arizona University and was for the first time worried about professional reputation and peer-reviewed journal articles. Jane told me "this is how academia is" and advised me to develop "the hide of a rhinoceros" and keep at it. Larry Strauss, *JAR*'s editor, supported us. Jane resolved that we would focus our manuscript more tightly. For one thing, we took a firmer stand on the question of time depth even though we could not "prove" our conclusion. Was the flower world ancient in the Southwest as well as Mesoamerica, or did it diffuse northward in the 900s or so? We decided to go with the former stance, but what you will read in this volume challenges this position. With either temporal framework, Jane and I suggested that the flower world was a primarily linguistic phenomenon that emerged into material culture at various times and places because of local circumstances for various reasons, including shifting gender ideologies. In this volume, you will discover some other probable reasons for florescence (pun intended) of these related sets of imagery at certain times and places.

My work on iconography continued to annoy a few archaeologists who think that, as one faculty member in Albuquerque once told me in the late 1990s, "science and humanities DO NOT INTERDIGITATE." They do interdigitate in linguistic anthropology, as Jane and others have long shown us, so why not archaeology if we are indeed all anthropologists? Recent decades have been more kind to those of us working on archaeologies of imagery and meaning. The influence of Claude Lévi-Strauss has not faded after all, as Peter Whiteley (1998, 2018), John Ware (2015), Severin Fowles (2013), Scott Ortman (2012), and others show here in the Pueblo world. The authors in this volume demonstrate the exciting productivity of working across disciplines—linguistic anthropology, epigraphy, iconography, archaeometry, ethnobotany, ethnology, archaeology, art history, ethnohistory, advanced digital recordation and imaging. We pull methods and theories from an expanding universe to focus on questions that deepen and change the more we work on them.

What would we do differently now? I can only speak for myself, not Jane. I would put more emphasis on diversity in deployment of images. In our original article, we stressed that the flower world is not one thing or one place or one essential set of images. We wrote, "The Flower World complex should not be interpreted as a 'religion' or 'cult' in its own right. Instead, the complex constituted one of several 'part ideologies' or a set of symbolic tools that remained available, either separately or in combination, to the ritual practice and thought of Southwestern people over a long period of time." I would emphasize this point more today than we did then, and I would cite Fredrik Barth's (1987) *Cosmologies in the Making*. One of the strengths of archaeology is our time depth and attention to change and the social, political, and economic contexts of long-term change—just what we see in most of the chapters presented here. We were then, and mostly are now, using long-standing anthropological and historical methods, very much in a Western scientific (and humanities) framework.

We might instead (or in addition) try to move to a more Indigenous ontology, if we can do so respectfully and not appropriate Native authority. Instead of talking about metaphor, "this flower stands for that concept," we could put aside the Western dichotomy and look to Indigenous monism and pantheism. You will see this approach demonstrated in this volume in chapters by Sandstrom, Neurath, and Molina and Shorter.

I would incorporate more consultation with artists and Native-language speakers in descendant communities, as many of the authors in this volume do. Emory Sekaquaptewa's help was invaluable, of course, but what I know now is that each Hopi Mesa, each village, each clan, and each ritual society has its own history, its own roles in a very complicated ideological system and ritual calendar. The older ethnographies don't do justice to the diversity of Hopi verbal and visual art. I've pursued some of our original questions in a modest way with a handful of Hopi artists from different mesas, notably Michael Kabotie (Second Mesa). Dorothy Washburn and I have had enlightening conversations with Phillip Tuwaletstiwa (Third Mesa). But in the end, I know less than I used to about Hopi philosophy and layers of meaning in the imagery that we are studying. And that's OK. What both Mike and Phillip have stressed is that the flower world isn't a thing or a place but a state of mind. To the extent that it's a place, it's a place "where men's and women's spiritual lives can become manifest," according to Phillip. It's part of the Katsina Society's world and practice, but that is only half the Hopi ritual cycle. The other half is more esoteric. Phillip also says, "ask ten Hopis and you will get ten answers." Probably that is true in Nahua, Zuni, Pima, and Huichol communities, and others. It's true of archaeologists, art historians, anthropologists, and linguists as well, and our diversity of approaches and views enriches our discussion. Actively encouraging, including, and taking seriously Indigenous participation in our research and reporting is not just a suggestion but an imperative.

Finally, I'd step outside the Uto-Aztecan-speaking world and expand the linguistic, temporal, and spatial scope of investigations and comparisons even if doing so makes this fuzzy topic even fuzzier. It may be that "the Uto-Aztecan Flower World" is only part of the story and not even the original chapter in that story.

The chapters in this volume advance our understanding of flowery worlds in the deep history and contemporary Indigenous and mestizo communities throughout the southwestern United States, Mexico, and beyond. More important, they demonstrate interdisciplinary research methods that can be applied widely to enrich and enliven our understanding of past lives and connections across time and cultures. I think Jane would have been pleased. We honor her work and her memory with what follows in this volume.

Kelley Hays-Gilpin

REFERENCES

Barth, Fredrik. 1987. *Cosmologies in the Making: A Generative Approach to Cultural Variation in Inner New Guinea*. Cambridge Studies in Social Anthropology. Cambridge, Mass.: Cambridge University Press.

Fowles, Severin M. 2013. *An Archaeology of Doings: Secularism and the Study of Pueblo Religion*. Santa Fe, N.Mex.: School for Advanced Research Press.

Hays-Gilpin, Kelley, and Jane H. Hill. 1999. "The Flower World in Material Culture: An Iconographic Complex in the Southwest and Mesoamerica." *Journal of Anthropological Research* 55(1):1–37.

Hays-Gilpin, Kelley, and Jane H. Hill. 2000. "The Flower World in Prehistoric Southwest Material Culture." In *The Archaeology of Regional Interaction: Religion, Warfare, and Exchange Across the American Southwest and Beyond*, edited by Michelle Hegmon, 411–28. Boulder: University Press of Colorado.

Hill, Jane H. 1992. "The Flower World of Old Uto-Aztecan." *Journal of Anthropological Research* 48(2):117–44.

Hopi Dictionary Project. 1998. *Hopi Dictionary: Hopìikwa Lavàytutuveni; A Hopi-English Dictionary of the Third Mesa Dialect*. Tucson: University of Arizona Press.

Ortman, Scott G. 2012. *Winds from the North: Tewa Origins and Historical Anthropology*. Salt Lake City: University of Utah Press.

Philips, Susan U. 2019. "Jane H. Hill." *Anthropology News*, January 25, 2019. https://www.anthropology-news.org/index.php/2019/01/25/jane-h-hill/.

Ware, John A. 2015. *A Pueblo Social History: Kinship, Sodality, and Community in the Northern Southwest*. Santa Fe, N.Mex.: School for Advanced Research Press.

Whiteley, Peter. 1998. *Rethinking Hopi Ethnography*. Washington, D.C.: Smithsonian Institution Press.

Whiteley, Peter, ed. 2018. *Puebloan Societies: Homology and Heterogeneity in Time and Space*. Santa Fe, N.Mex.: School for Advanced Research Press.

PREFACE

This volume came to fruition through a collective desire to bring together a group of scholars whose ongoing research focuses on the subject of Indigenous flower worlds—a diverse set of related ideas and ethical values found among Indigenous groups ranging across a broad swath of the Americas from the American Southwest to Central America. We owe a debt of gratitude to Jane Hill, Kelley Hays-Gilpin, and Karl Taube, whose work as pioneers in flower worlds research made this volume possible. This volume grew from a session at the 84th Annual Meeting of the Society for American Archaeology (SAA), which was held in Albuquerque, New Mexico, in April 2019. We thank the selection committee of the SAA Amerind Seminar Award, who gave us the opportunity to convene an extended seminar at the Amerind Foundation facilities in Dragoon, Arizona, in September 2019, where we could further explore some of the key issues raised during the SAA session. All of the seminar participants and volume contributors deserve our gratitude for contributing their unique insights that made the session and seminar so intellectually and emotionally fulfilling. We are especially grateful to Kelley Hays-Gilpin for all of her additional help in ensuring the success of both the seminar and the volume. We extend our deepest gratitude to Christine Szuter, Eric Kaldahl, and the Amerind staff for their wonderful hospitality, which provided order and a great space for productivity in the daily workshops. Christine also deserves much credit and thanks for helping ensure that this project remained on track and on schedule. We would like to thank Kathryn Conrad, Allyson Carter, Scott De Herrera, and C. Steven LaRue of the University of Arizona Press and the press staff, all of whom in their work and guidance brought this volume to publication in a timely and easy manner. Will Russell and Mauricio Díaz García provided excellent illustrations, and Will expertly prepared maps. Two anonymous reviewers graciously provided critical evaluations of each chapter that led to an overall improvement and focus of the volume.

FLOWER WORLDS

Flower Worlds

A Synthesis and Critical History

Andrew D. Turner and Michael D. Mathiowetz

The identification of flower world as a floral spiritual domain represents one of the most important breakthroughs in the study of Indigenous belief systems in Mesoamerica and the American Southwest. Nearly three decades of scholarship devoted to this topic have demonstrated that while many of the cultures of both regions share in fundamental aspects of these beliefs, there are also key differences among a plurality of flower worlds. Furthermore, as these realms are multisensory and reach back at least 2,500 years, efforts to understand them extend well beyond the capabilities of any particular academic discipline and require the collaboration of scholars and religious specialists who bring a variety of perspectives. Far more than religious movements or cults, flower worlds form vital and dynamic cores of the cosmologies, histories, rituals, and everyday lives of Indigenous peoples of Mesoamerica and the Southwest, past and present.

In her influential 1992 article "The Flower World of Old Uto-Aztecan," Jane Hill noted prevalent patterns of floral metaphors and chromatic symbolism in the oral canons, particularly songs, of Uto-Aztecan speech communities and their neighbors (including the Zuni and Tzotzil Maya) ranging geographically from Arizona to Chiapas (maps 1, 2). According to Hill, this suite of linguistic metaphors evokes a spirit land or paradise, often a land of the dead, that is "a timeless world, parallel to our own" (Hill 1992:127). She coined the term *Flower World* to describe the sacred landscapes referenced and invoked in this cross-cultural and cross-historical phenomenon, which includes *sea ania* of the Yoeme (Yaqui); Tamoanchan, Tlalocan, and the Sun's Heaven of the Mexica (Aztecs);

and Wirikuta of the Wixárika (Huichol). Within this linguistic complex, flowers invoke not only the flower world but a constellation of concepts including song, the human spirit, and vital forces (such as blood and hearts, fire, and often "male strength and spirituality") (Hill 1992:122). Hill (1992:136–38) suggested that these concepts originated with an ancestral "Old Uto-Aztecan" speech community that spread from north to south with Uto-Aztecan linguistic expansion, but she also raised the possibility that a "flower world complex" could have originated in Mesoamerica and spread north with maize agriculture.

In 1992 Louise Burkhart also published an article in which she noted similar patterns of floral metaphors in early colonial Nahua Christian literature, especially Fray Bernardino de Sahagún's *Psalmodia christiana* (1993 [1583]) and the *Cantares mexicanos* (Bierhorst 1985). Burkhart points out that the process of conversion to Christianity in postconquest Mexico was also a process of mutual accommodation in which Spanish friars and Nahua interpreters sought parallels between Indigenous conceptions of paradise and the Christian heaven and Eden. Nahua converts aestheticized and translated the otherwise remote heaven and Eden into their own terms as paradise gardens accessible through ritual and song (Burkhart 1992:90). Within this context, Nahua conceptions of flower world not only survived but thrived and in turn modified New World Christianity.

Pursuing questions raised by Hill's (1992) original study, Kelley Hays-Gilpin and Jane Hill (1999, 2000) expanded on the flower world as a linguistically based phenomenon to encompass material culture by investigating its historical spread into the Southwest through ancient iconographic motifs. The authors associated imagery such as butterflies, flowers, rainbows, and colorful birds with the flower world, noting that evidence is particularly prevalent in the Southwest after A.D. 1300. They add that rather than a cult or religion, flower world "constituted 'part ideologies' or a set of symbolic tools that remained available, either separately or in combination, to the ritual practice and thought of Southwestern peoples over a long period of time" (Hays-Gilpin and Hill 1999:16).

Karl Taube (2004) provided the first in-depth study of the flower world in ancient Mesoamerica. Focusing primarily on the Classic Maya, Taube discussed conceptions of breath, jewels, flowers, music, the soul, and a celestial solar paradise, including how these notions place humans

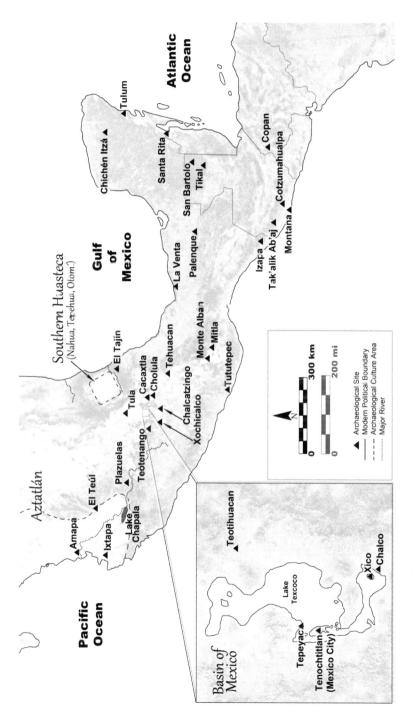

Map 1 Regional map of Mesoamerica. Drawing by Will Russell.

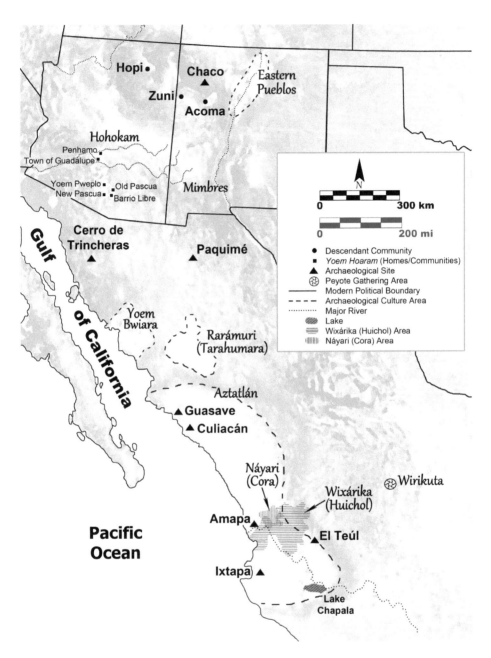

Map 2 Regional map of west Mexico, northern Mexico, and the American Southwest. Drawing by Will Russell.

in relation to the life-giving environmental forces of wind, rain, and sun that promote agricultural abundance (Taube 2004:91–93). Through analysis of artwork in relation to ethnographic and ethnohistoric sources, Taube (2004:79–91) drew attention to Flower Mountain, a place of origin and celestial ascent of the sun and apotheosized ancestors and found parallels in the cosmologies of Teotihuacan, the contemporary Tzutu-jil Maya (Carlsen and Prechtel 1991) and Hopi, among other cultures. The emergence of the first people, often aided by deities, from a Flower Mountain or Flower Mound, is a central theme in origin stories of Meso-america and the American Southwest (Saturno et al. 2005:48–50; Taube 2010b:111–18; Taube, this volume). Taube noted the early appearance of flower world imagery among the Middle Formative (900–400 B.C.) Olmec, exposing the deep roots of flower world concepts in Mesoamer-ica (Taube 2004:90). In focusing on the Classic Maya, this work also demonstrates that, while strongly prevalent among Uto-Aztecan speak-ers as Hill (1992) observed, the flower world is not tied to a particular language group.

Building on Hill's (1992) original recognition and description of the flower world and the foundational works that demonstrated its resil-ience and flexibility in times of social upheaval (Burkhart 1992), its cor-relates in visual culture (Hays-Gilpin and Hill 1999), and its antiquity and pervasiveness among the cultures of Mesoamerica (Taube 2004), we continue to refine and add nuance to our understanding of the flower worlds of past and present cultures of Mesoamerica and the American Southwest. Oswaldo Chinchilla Mazariegos (this volume) urges us to consider a plurality of flower worlds, as multiple distinct floral realms coexist within certain traditions and, while sharing important charac-teristics, the various manifestations of this phenomenon are distinct and culturally and environmentally situated. Since Hill's (1992) assessment of the geographical range of this phenomenon as extending from Arizona to Chiapas, subsequent studies have recognized its presence at the east-ernmost boundaries of Mesoamerica. However, while widespread and diverse in representation, flower worlds are not present among all cultures at all times in these regions. What follows is a brief historical sketch of the development of the flower worlds of Mesoamerica, west Mexico, northern Mexico, and the American Southwest based on current under-standings and the contributed chapters of this volume.

OLMEC AND MAYA FLOWER WORLDS

Notions of chromatic and aesthetically pleasing realms of ancestors, precious objects, and agricultural abundance are deeply rooted in Mesoamerica, with the earliest evidence appearing in Olmec material culture. Taube (2004:90) notes that floating flowers, jewels, and visible breath elements in front of the faces of certain figures, as well as anthropomorphic personages with butterfly wings (Figure I.1a), suggest that conceptions of a floral paradise were well developed by the Middle Formative period (900–400 B.C.). The latter butterfly-winged figures, carved in lustrous jadeite, recall much later Mesoamerican beliefs that ancestors could be manifest as butterflies, birds with precious feathers, and radiant jewels (Mendieta 1980:97). As such, these Olmec jewels, and other lustrous objects including nacreous shells, may be physical embodiments of ancestors, rather than simply representations of them (Turner, 2020). According to Taube (2004:90, 2010b:79–82), Monument 1 from Chalcatzingo (Figure I.1b), a petroglyph carved on a probable Flower Mountain, renders visible the relationship between flower world, ancestors, breath, rainmaking, and agricultural abundance. On the monument, a probable ancestor sits within the mouth of a zoomorphic cave that exhales wind, giving rise to rainclouds that in turn fertilize the surrounding landscape laden with plants and floating jewels. Taube (2004:90) considers the spread of flower world beliefs to have accompanied the adoption of maize agriculture, directionalism, and the valuation of jade as part of a ritual complex originally promulgated by the Middle Formative Olmec (see Taube 2000a).

The Late Preclassic Maya North Wall mural at San Bartolo, Guatemala (100 B.C. to A.D. 100) reflects continuity and further elaboration of flower world themes (Saturno et al. 2005). Much like the earlier Chalcatzingo Monument 1 (Figure I.1b), the San Bartolo mural (Color Plate 1) portrays a Flower Mountain with a zoomorphic cave maw as a source of wind and agricultural abundance. In the scene, the cave—covered with plants and fierce animals—exhales a serpent with yellow blossoms on its back, which foreshadows the feathered serpents of later Mesoamerican traditions that were manifestations of breath and wind. Ancestral figures, including the Maize God and his consorts, emerge from the cave along

Figure I.1 Images portraying aspects of Olmec and Classic Maya flower worlds. (a) Olmec jade butterfly figure (after Taube 2004:Figure 18c). (b) Figure seated within a zoomorphic cave that exhales wind volutes with rainclouds above, Chalcatzingo Monument 1 (after drawing by Carlo Gay). (c) Face of Classic Maya anthropomorphic wind god exhaling a breath blossom (after Taube 2004:Figure 4d). (d) Detail of an ancestral figure (Chan Bahlum) on the side of Pakal's sarcophagus, Palenque (after photo by Merle Greene Robertson). Drawings by Andrew D. Turner.

the floral path bringing a water-filled bottle gourd and tamales—the sustenance that makes human survival possible. Themes of ancestral emergence and primordial sustenance in the San Bartolo murals resonate with later Mesoamerican and Southwestern flower world traditions (Saturno et al. 2005:48–50; Taube 2010b:111–18).

For the Classic Maya (A.D. 100–900), flower world as both an afterlife destination and aesthetic ideal is linked to rulership and royal lineage. Although Maya commoners may have been destined for a dark, dreary, and terrifying underworld, often referred to as Xibalba and comparable to the Mictlan of Central Mexican traditions, deceased Maya elites could ascend Flower Mountain to be apotheosized as solar and lunar deities that dwell in a celestial paradise of floating jewels and flowers (Taube 2004). In addition to celestial beings, other deities that were distinctly associated with flower world and elite aesthetic ideals include an anthropomorphic wind god who embodied music, breath, and the idealized human soul (Figure I.1c; Taube 2004:73–78) and the Classic Maya Maize God, the embodiment of agricultural fertility, regeneration after death, and elite beauty (Taube 1985, 2004).

Floral imagery is central to Classic Maya conceptions of beauty, the soul, and the afterlife. The animate breath soul, related to sweet aromas and song, could be portrayed as jade beads, pearls, or blossoms hovering in front of the faces of anthropomorphic figures (Figure I.1c; Taube 2004:72–73; Turner, 2020), the latter probably representing the "white flower breath" referred to in Classic Maya texts (Houston et. al 2006:143). Classic Maya temples, many of which housed elite tombs, could also be conceptualized as Flower Mountains. David Stuart noted that certain temples were referred to as "5 Flower Mountain" (cited as personal communication in Taube 2004:81), and temple façades, especially in the Río Bec, Chenes, and Puuc regions, were often constructed as zoomorphic Flower Mountain cave maws (Taube 2004:83–85). As an expression of the floral soul and dynastic succession, royal ancestors could also be envisioned as fruit-laden trees, as portrayed on the sides of Pakal's sarcophagus at Palenque (Figure I.1d). Cameron McNeil (2006, this volume) bridges iconographic, ethnohistoric, and ethnographic perspectives with archaeobotanical analysis of pollen samples collected in the floors of royal tombs at Copan to reconstruct the role of flowers—and which species were significant—in Classic Maya funerary ritual.

MILITARISM, SACRIFICE, AND THE FLOWER WORLDS OF CENTRAL MEXICO

Conceptualizations of flower worlds follow two distinct trajectories in Mesoamerica. While an emphasis on sensory pleasure and agricultural abundance is present across Mesoamerican flower worlds, the flower worlds of ancient Central Mexico were inextricably bound with militaristic ideologies, probably originating with the Teotihuacan state. Over the last century, several scholars (e.g., Berlo 1983; Beyer 1965; Headrick 1999, 2007; Nielsen 2016; Seler 1990–1998:5:39; Taube 2000b, 2005, 2006; von Winning 1987:1:115–17) have argued that the prevalence of butterflies in conjunction with martial and mortuary imagery at Teotihuacan indicates that fallen warriors became apotheosized as butterflies and birds, as they did in later Aztec imperial ideology, and that both cultures shared beliefs in specific afterworld realms (e.g., Caso 1942). Butterfly imagery occurs frequently in the art of Teotihuacan beginning around the third century A.D. (von Winning 1987:1:115), and mural scenes painted thereafter evoke flower world through such elements as flowering speech scrolls and scenes of paradise teeming with blossoming trees, birds, and butterflies (Hays-Gilpin and Hill 1999:16). Figurines that represent enthroned mortuary bundles (Headrick 1999:76; Taube 2000b:306) often wear butterfly headdresses with upturned snouts and drooping feathery antennae (Figure I.2a), linking nectar-drinking insects to the deceased. The mortuary bundle, when burned, is comparable to a chrysalis that releases the warrior's soul as a butterfly (Taube 2000b:309), and in this way, Teotihuacan state ideology employed a metaphor drawn from nature to liken the fiery transformation of deceased warriors to the butterfly's metamorphosis (Nielsen 2016). By contrast, butterfly imagery is scarce in Classic Maya art (Taube 2020), and unlike those of the Maya, Teotihuacan flower worlds do not appear to emphasize royal lineage. A unique manifestation of the flower world is prominently portrayed in the artwork of Late Classic (A.D. 600–900) Cotzumalhuapa, on Guatemala's Pacific coast (Chinchilla Mazariegos 2013, 2015). Like Classic Maya flower worlds, Cotzumalhuapa Flower World imagery emphasizes music, solar deities, floating jewels, and blossoming plants while lacking overt butterfly imagery, but it is unique in its distinct focus on human sacrifice that likens heart extraction and dismemberment to the harvest of fruit,

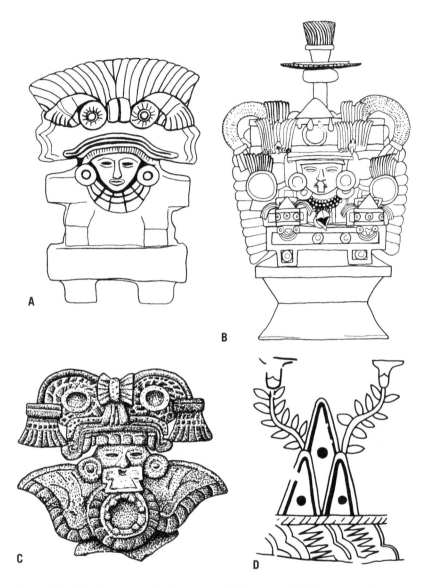

Figure I.2 Teotihuacan-style flower world imagery. (a) Figurine in the form of a mortuary bundle with a butterfly headdress. (b) Theater-style censer in the form of a mortuary bundle from La Ventilla, Teotihuacan. (c) Teotihuacan-style censer lid with butterfly wings, headdress, and nose ornament from coastal Guatemala (after von Winning 1987:1:9:Figure 2f). (d) Toponym representing Flower Mountain from stuccoed tripod vessel, Yale University Art Gallery. Drawings by Andrew D. Turner.

especially cacao. To date, there is evidence of flower world themes in the Classic-period Gulf Coast that warrants further investigation (Taube 2005; Turner, this volume), and the presence or absence of flower world has not been assessed among the Classic Zapotec of Oaxaca.

Like the enthroned figurines, theater-style censers from Teotihuacan and Escuintla, Guatemala (Figure I.2b–I.2c), appear to represent the mortuary bundles of deceased warriors (Taube 2000b:308–9). In addition to monstrous butterfly headdresses, many appear surrounded by flowers, quetzals, butterflies, and glittering mica. These colorful and radiant symbols, along with the aroma of burning incense, would have evoked the flower world through the senses, while clouds of smoke pouring out of the censers reenacted cremation and the metamorphosis of the deceased. Some censers appear as Flower Mountain, a location that is also specified in Teotihuacan artwork by a toponym representing a mountain flanked by blossoms (Figure I.2d; Taube 2005, 2006). The centrally located Temple of Quetzalcoatl of Teotihuacan also may have been constructed as a Flower Mountain ornamented with feathered serpents swimming through a shell-filled sea and emerging through blossom-like portals on its façade (Taube 2004:88–90, 2006:162, 2010a:182).

From the perspective of Teotihuacan, situated in Highland Central Mexico, the Maya Lowlands to the east appear to have been conceived as a lush, tropical paradise of the dawning sun and abundant wealth in the form of jade, cacao, and precious bird feathers (Taube 2005:38). According to Taube (2005, 2006), Teotihuacanos situated Flower Mountain in that very region as they expanded their political and economic grasp to the Maya Lowlands and the Pacific coast of Guatemala. Oswaldo Chinchilla Mazariegos (this volume) explores how Teotihuacanos living within that region conceptualized flower worlds. While discussion of Teotihuacan-style censers and butterfly imagery has tended to revolve around male notions of warfare, he questions whether Teotihuacan Flower Worlds were inherently masculine domains, pointing to the association of feminine figures in conjunction with flower world imagery.

Although it is clear that the Mexica drew inspiration from the city of Teotihuacan and even emulated and collected its artwork (López Luján and De Anda Rogel 2017; Umberger 1987), relatively few studies have considered how flower world themes developed in Central Mexico following the collapse of Teotihuacan around A.D. 600 and the founding of Tenochtitlan in 1325. Andrew Turner (2016, this volume) explores how Epiclassic polities such as Xochicalco and Cacaxtla adapted, modified, and spread flower world ideology, rooted in Teotihuacan, in response to new sociopolitical and economic changes that influenced the whole of Mesoamerica. Headrick (2018) and Taube (2020; Taube et al. 2020) have investigated the ways that Teotihuacan-inspired militarism and Maya conceptions of paradise merged in the flower worlds of the Early Post-classic (A.D. 900–1200) Toltecs of Tula and Chichén Itzá, ultimately giving rise to those of the Mexica.

Among the Mexica (A.D. 1325–1521), the realms of Tamoanchan, Tlalocan, and Tonatiuh Ilhuicac were distinct yet complementary forms of paradise (López Austin 1997). These places of origin also were places of return in which one's manner of death (rather than life) determined the soul's destination, unlike in Christian notions of paradise introduced by the Spanish. The Aztec Empire famously glorified death on the battlefield or sacrificial stone in the form of "Flower Wars" against rival polities. At the same time, Aztec poets composed songs that praised fallen warriors and chromatic afterworlds that have survived through the writings of Spanish friars (e.g., Bierhorst 1985). Despite a rich corpus of ethnohistoric literature composed during the early colonial period, relatively few studies have considered the clear link between flower world and state-sponsored violence among the Mexica and how it was manifest in the material culture and built environment of their imperial capital. Ángel González López and Lorena Vázquez Vallín (this volume) analyze offerings found in the Templo Mayor and chambers and mosaic pavements at its base, arguing that the Templo Mayor was a Flower Mountain that harkened back to the divine hearth at Teotihuacan that gave rise to the deities of the Aztec pantheon and provided ideological justification for militaristic conquest and human sacrifice.

FLOWER WORLDS AND SOCIAL TRANSFORMATIONS IN MESOAMERICA

Flower world themes proliferated across Postclassic Mesoamerica through long-distance exchange of prestige goods and pilgrimage to religious centers (Mathiowetz 2011; Patel 2012; Pohl, this volume; Taube 2010a). A Late Postclassic "international" art style drew on shared conceptions of flower worlds that linked cultures across Mesoamerica (Taube 2010a). Rather than the overt militaristic ideologies of Teotihuacan and the Mexica, multiethnic confederacies—particularly those centered in Puebla and Oaxaca—celebrated revered ancestors, codified alliances, and promoted exchange through flower world ritualism devoted to the "Flower Prince" Xochipilli (Pohl, this volume). Scribes from this region also produced some of the most exceptional sacred manuscripts that survive that, according to analysis by Davide Domenici (this volume), evoked and physically embodied "flower and song" through both their content and the materials from which they were made.

Following the Spanish invasion of Mexico, flower world became deeply imbedded in early-colonial Mexican Catholicism through the mutual accommodation of overlapping Indigenous and Spanish conceptions of paradise (Burkhart 1992; Forde 2020). Central Christian figures entered flower world: Christ was likened to a solar deity (Burkhart 1988), and the Virgin of Guadalupe miraculously appeared amid falling flowers (Córdova, this volume). Flowers, which continue to activate altars and express the beneficent aspects of an orderly universe (Sandstrom, this volume), along with the plumage of colorful birds, acquired additional layers of meaning through Christian ritual and symbolism (Alcántara Rojas 2011, 2015; Burkhart 1992; Córdova, this volume). Cloisters became gardens where Nahua and Christian paradise converged (Peterson 1993). However, despite efforts to concentrate and control access to flower worlds in pre-Hispanic temples (González López and Vázquez Vallín, Pohl, and Turner, this volume) and colonial churches and monasteries, flower worlds exist in the landscape—revealed or "unconcealed" to those who are prepared to experience them (Molina and Shorter, Neurath, and Sandstrom, this volume).

FLOWER WORLDS IN THE AMERICAN SOUTHWEST AND NORTHERN MEXICO

Following Hill's (1992) and Hays-Gilpin and Hill's (1999, 2000) initial assessments of flower worlds in greater Mesoamerica and the American Southwest, surprisingly few scholars in the northern regions have taken up the mantle by further analyzing the past and present social, political, and economic implications of these sets of related ideas for people who adopted, adapted, or engaged these worldviews either peripherally or as the central organizing principles of societies. Early studies on the archaeology of flower world and related ritualism in the American Southwest proposed hypotheses for (1) an origin at the onset of maize agriculture (e.g., Taube 2001, 2010b), or (2) the possibility that flower world ideologies either accompanied maize agriculture or were always present as a shared cosmology that was retained in oral canons but only periodically appeared in late pre-Hispanic material culture (Hays-Gilpin and Hill 1999, 2000; Hill 1992). Much of the material or symbolic evidence for flower world presented in these early studies, however, dates after A.D. 900 with only sparse to no evidence of flower world associations in earlier material culture.

Some recent case studies contend that flower world is quite ancient in the Southwest. For example, McNeil and Shaul (2018) proposed an interpretation arguing for the presence of cloud, maize, and katsina symbolism in San Juan Anthropomorphic Style petroglyphs of the Western Basketmaker II period (800 B.C.–A.D. 400) in southern Utah and northern Arizona. They contend that this ideology was brought northward by immigrant maize farmers during the Early Agricultural period (ca. 2000 B.C.) who later merged with ancestral Hopi foragers during the Basketmaker II period (800 B.C.–A.D. 400) and in time came to identify as Hopi southern clans. Other scholars and Hopi collaborators specifically associate these ancestral rain, cloud, and maize concepts with flower world, and these ideas and their visual manifestation are generally considered to be evident in the Southwest no earlier than A.D. 1000 in limited Mimbres examples and most intensively after A.D. 1300 across the western to eastern Puebloan regions (see below). Although flower world terminology is not explicitly invoked in McNeil and Shaul's (2018) article, they link these postulated southern origins of a maize-related cosmology to well-documented Hopi Palatkwapi clan migration traditions that involve immigrants from Mexico arriving with new religious practices during the pre-Hispanic era. Among other issues, their interpretation of an Early Agricultural origin for this flower world–related maize-agricultural cosmology is complicated by the fact that the generally accepted date for the arrival of Hopi southern clans from Palatkwapi (and by extension Mexico) to the Hopi mesas with new religious beliefs and practices is around the late 1200s to 1300s A.D. (Bernardini

2005:177; Mathiowetz 2011:1016–91), over eight centuries after the latest Basketmaker II dates.

On the other hand, Boyd (2016) proposed an apparently omnipresent flower world ideology in her interpretation of Archaic period (2700 B.C.–A.D. 600) Pecos River Style rock art in the White Shaman rock shelter (400 B.C.–A.D. 400) of southern Texas. The interpretation of these scenes, created by nomadic hunter-gatherers, draws on specific flower world themes that were first identified for ancient Mesoamerica by Karl Taube, including Flower Mountain (the birthplace of the sun in the east) and Flower Road (the floral path of the sun). Uto-Aztecan ethnohistorical and ethnological data of the Mexica (Aztec) and Huichol were cited almost as a verbatim road map to interpret the Pecos River pictograph scenes as an apparently universal flower world cosmology (Boyd 2016). At the center of the interpretation of the White Shaman pictographs is what Boyd considers to be a flower world–related "birth of the sun" narrative tied to accounts drawn directly from contemporary Huichol ethnological accounts of the peyote pilgrimage journey of ancestor gods to the east to observe the first birth of the sun (Neurath, this volume).

Two issues complicate this interpretation. First, while flower world concepts do date back to Olmec agriculturalists in Formative Mesoamerica, the specific "birth of the sun" narrative that Boyd cites for the White Shaman shelter (400 B.C.–A.D. 400) in fact dates no earlier than Classic-period (A.D. 250–600) Teotihuacan in highland Mexico (Taube 2000a) and is not likely to have spread across Mesoamerica until after the collapse of Teotihuacan around A.D. 600 (González López and Vázquez Vallín, and Turner, this volume; Taube 2000b) where it later became evident in Postclassic Toltec, Mixtec, and Aztec symbolism. Second, the "birth of the sun" narrative reported in Huichol ethnology probably also only dates after A.D. 850/900 in the Aztatlán (i.e., ancestral Huichol) region of west Mexico when explicit solar and floral symbolism first occurs in material culture related to Xochipilli/Piltzintli ceremonialism, the young solar god of dawn whom Huichol and Cora people both recognize (Mathiowetz 2011, 2019a, 2019b, 2020, 2021). There is no iconographic or material evidence that the named Huichol deities—whom Boyd ascribes to the Archaic-period White Shaman shelter imagery—existed in west Mexico during this era. In other words, the flower world–related "birth of the sun" narrative and associated ritual practices first linked to Teotihuacan apparently were not present in west Mexico or highland Mexico at the time that the White Shaman pictographs were created around 400 B.C. The historical dynamics of flower world expressions documented by multiple authors in this volume instead indicate that flower world themes are neither pan-Mesoamerican nor pan-southwestern (i.e., universal) but instead appear at particular times within particular historical contexts and were often disseminated (and thereby are traceable) as historically contingent intellectual lineages.

The clearest evidence of flower world material culture and symbolism in the Southwest—including flower depictions, shell trumpets, scarlet macaws, cacao, copper ornaments, and other items—occurs after A.D. 850/900, an era that coincided with heightened evidence of Mesoamerican (west Mexican) connections (Mathiowetz, this volume). Some Hohokam scholars consider various geometric designs to be flower world–related plants and flowers on Hohokam ceramics dating perhaps as early as A.D. 450 (Evans and Lail 2015). One often-cited Hohokam bowl with floral depictions dates to A.D. 750–850, the latter date correlating with the earliest flower world imagery in west Mexico (Figure I.3a). Others recently proposed the presence of flower world in some limited regard at Hohokam petroglyph sites clustered around Tucson, Arizona, after A.D. 950 (e.g., Hernbrode and Boyle 2017). Hohokam cosmology often is considered distinct from Ancestral Pueblo, Mogollon, and Pueblo IV cosmologies, and many of the flower world–related concepts linked to ancestral katsina ritualism appears to be largely absent in Hohokam cosmology. In general, Hohokam representations of potential flower world themes are spare.

Although Chaco (A.D. 850/900–1150) and Mimbres (A.D. 1000–1130) flower worlds were observed to share similar thematic elements, Chacoan floral expressions are limited to a single cache of wooden flower objects (Figure I.3b). Mimbres floral expressions primarily appear as figurative representations in the interior of Black-on-White bowls often found in mortuary contexts. The expression of emergence traditions linked to cicada also factor into flower worlds at this time, particularly in Mimbres bowl imagery (Taube, this volume). People in the Chaco and Mimbres regions and other locales imported copper crotals from west Mexico probably because of flower world associations (Hosler 1994). Similarly, the Chacoan Flower World also involved the use of cacao likely obtained from west Mexico (Mathiowetz 2011, 2019a, this volume; see Weiner 2015). Expressive culture and the sensory aspects of musical instruments, performance, and iridescent items were key elements in Chacoan Flower World ideology. Performative rituals utilizing the above-noted Mesoamerican material items along with foot drums, wooden flutes, bone whistles, rattles of walnut and deer hooves, and the strategic use of natural landscape acoustics at ritual locales were key (Brown 2014; Weiner 2015). While Chaco and Mimbres ideologies and ceremonialism involved varying degrees of flower world symbolism, the question of how flower world related to political, social, and economic organization and the nature of hierarchies (or lack thereof) at Chaco and Mimbres sites and their connections to Mesoamerican social dynamics remains unclear. Later kiva murals with birds and possible flowers in the Pueblo III–era Gallina and Mesa Verde regions and cave caches of wood and leather floral and avian objects in the Kayenta region (A.D. 1200–1300) of Arizona evince some connecting thread to flower world in the post Chacoan and Mimbres era, however sparse, before an intensification of flower world symbolism developed after A.D. 1300 (Figures I.3c, I.3d; Hays-Gilpin and Hill 1999).

Perhaps the first scholar to apply Jane Hill's ideas to the archaeological record of the American Southwest was Patricia Crown (1994), who contended that the flower world was an aspect of designs on fourteenth- to fifteenth-century Salado polychromes in southern Arizona and New Mexico, which she characterized as "The Southwestern Cult," linked to rain, fertility, and ancestors. Although Salado scholars have not continued Crown's investigations on this subject, it may be worth reconsidering this view given that Salado origins are linked to the Kayenta diaspora (where aspects of flower world were known) while the southeastern Salado region overlapped with part of the Casas Grandes region with its flower world ritualism (see below).

Taube (2000a, 2001, 2010b, this volume) similarly found inspiration in Hill and Hays-Gilpin's work and made comprehensive comparative analyses that resulted in the identification of significant shared characteristics of flower world (e.g., wind, breath, cloud, flower, and maize ritualism) ranging from Mimbres to the Pueblo IV period to the present, which provided new data on the historical dynamics of cross-cultural and interregional interactions. Taube's work, along with significant additional

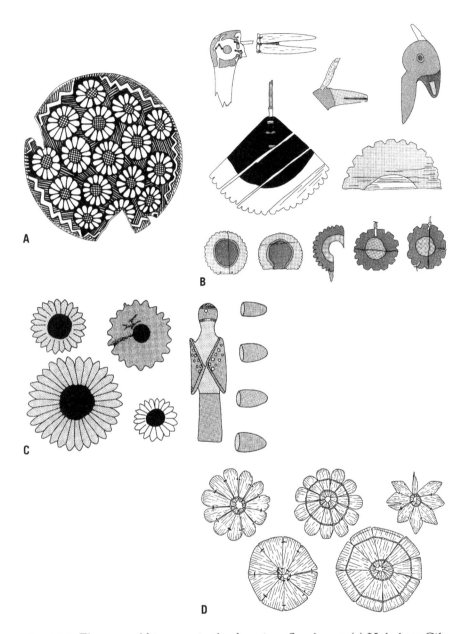

Figure 1.3 Flower world imagery in the American Southwest. (a) Hohokam Gila Butte Red-on-Buff bowl with flowers, Hardy site, Arizona. (b) Painted wooden ritual regalia of birds and flowers, Chetro Ketl, Chaco Canyon, New Mexico. (c) Kayenta painted wooden ritual regalia of birds and flowers, Sunflower Cave, Arizona. (d) Kayenta painted wooden ritual regalia of flowers, Bonita Creek Cave, Arizona. Drawings by Ronald Beckwith, courtesy of Kelley Hays-Gilpin.

contributions by others (e.g., Hays-Gilpin et al. 2010; Sekaquaptewa and Washburn 2004), includes the identification of flower world–related scenes in Pueblo IV (post-A.D. 1300) kiva mural scenes at Awat'ovi on the Hopi mesas and Pottery Mound in New Mexico (Color Plate 2). Research on Hopi expressions of flower world and in Pueblo IV symbolism highlights the significance of the range of conceptual metaphors imbued in pictorial traditions that record histories and serve as mnemonic devices for bringing flower world into existence through oral canons such as songs during ritualized performance (Washburn, this volume). Flower world symbolism occurs in multiple media in the Southwest, including various pre-Hispanic ceramic types with portrayals of butterflies, flowers, scarlet macaws and feathers, clouds, and other designs such as those on Rio Grande Glaze Wares and other types (Mathiowetz 2018a, 2021). While some scholars identify flower world themes in analyses of petroglyphs of the Pueblo III to Pueblo IV periods (e.g., Jones and Drover 2018), explicit floral depictions in rock art are typically rare in the Southwest. Considering that flower world in highland Mexico is linked to war and martial themes, it is notable that the intensified visual expression of flower world in the Puebloan region after A.D. 1300 also coincided with a heightened florescence of Venus-related warfare symbolism in kiva murals and rock art (e.g., the Rio Grande Rock Art Style) that was probably related to the similar expression of flower world and related Venus warfare themes in the Aztatlán region of west Mexico (Mathiowetz 2011; Mathiowetz et al. 2015; Schaafsma 2000). It is probable that the coincidence of martial and flower world themes reflects the complementary dualities that exist wherein warfare begets fertility.

Until recently, most analyses of Casas Grandes (A.D. 1200–1450) religion and symbolism in northern Mexico avoided assessments of the presence of flower world, which is typically mentioned in studies only briefly despite these populations being likely Uto-Aztecan speakers. Indeed, significant aspects of flower world are present in iconography on Chihuahuan polychromes; in the Mesoamerican ball game; in the abundance of shell jewelry, copper bells, scarlet macaws, and musical instruments; and in the appearance of a new form of solar, rain, and maize ritualism. What distinguishes the Casas Grandes version of flower world from other southwestern expressions is that hierarchical political offices linked to flower world probably first became evident in the office of Sun

Priest (or Sun Chieftaincy), where ritual leaders at Paquimé embodied a solar deity as a living intermediary and probably fulfilled the role of sun watcher and agricultural calendrical keeper, a political office later documented in the ethnohistory and ethnology of the Pueblo region (Mathiowetz 2011, 2018a, 2018b, 2019a, 2021). This Sun Youth ceremonialism reflects clear connections to far west Mexican Flower World traditions, particularly the analogous solar deity Xochipilli worshipped by Aztatlán peoples and the political office of "Sun King" documented along the Pacific coast of west Mexico and centered in Nayarit (Mathiowetz 2019a, this volume). A new form of flower world–related maize ceremonialism in the Casas Grandes region was adopted from west Mexico after A.D. 1200 and subsequently adapted across the Pueblo IV world (Mathiowetz 2021). Flower world at Paquimé and related sites also appears connected to feasting events as a major component in the regional integration of the Casas Grandes polity, as is also evident in the Aztatlán, Nahua-Mixteca, and Maya regions and in the "feasting landscapes" among Pueblo IV communities in the Southwest where related Sun Youth–oriented flower world ritualism became manifest (Mathiowetz 2011). How Casas Grandes Flower World ideology (as encoded on ceramics) intersected with the cosmologies of people at sites in adjoining cultural regions where Chihuahuan polychromes were recovered, such as Cerro de Trincheras, Sonora, remains undetermined. Nevertheless, the Casas Grandes Flower World appears to have had a major influence on southwestern social transformations after A.D. 1200/1300.

One of the most significant contributions of Hill, Hays-Gilpin, and Taube's pioneering flower world research—exemplified in this volume—is the demonstration that science and the humanities do indeed "interdigitate," as Hays-Gilpin notes in the foreword of this volume. Breakthroughs in understanding the archaeological expressions and meanings of flower worlds simply could not be accomplished without integrating knowledge and histories embedded in the ethnohistorical and ethnological record of these cosmologies in conjunction with the Indigenous oral traditions, ritual practices, and lived experiences of descendant communities who continue to engage the flower worlds, as is evident in the work of Hopi collaborators and anthropologists (Washburn, this volume). Similarly, the ethnographic and emic detail that informed early flower world research— such as deer songs linked to the Yoeme Flower World, or *sea ania* (e.g.,

Evers and Molina 1987)—carries through today in the collaborative work of Felipe Molina and David Delgado Shorter (this volume). Their work illustrates a key point that Indigenous histories and identities are embedded in the natural landscape within multidimensional and interconnected worlds/realms along with the plants, animals, and ancestral beings that inhabit them. Performance and song as forms of collective sacrificial labor are critical acts at the intersection of these worlds to bring them into presence, which involves collective remembrance that is critical to identity formation. Elsewhere in northern Mexico, Rarámuri (Tarahumara) scholars in northern Mexico also have incorporated the flower world into emic insights on ecology and Indigenous perceptions of the environment, landscape, and plant world and their role in it, which provides new analytical approaches to ethnobotanical research (Salmón 1999). This approach has implications for interpretations of plant use and human-environmental interactions evident in the archaeological record.

FLOWER WORLDS IN WEST MEXICO

Compared with the American Southwest, northern Mexico, and broader Mesoamerica, research on flower worlds in west Mexico remains in its infancy. Inspired by Jane Hill's analyses, Johannes Neurath (2005, this volume) incorporated a Flower World framework into interpretations of Wixárika (Huichol) cosmology and worldview, a perspective that has been expanded recently to include the ethnology of the Náyari (Cora) of Nayarit (e.g., Benciolini 2014; Mathiowetz 2011). The identification of flower world among the Wixárika, particularly in relation to their peregrination to San Luis Potosí to observe the first birth of the sun at Reu'unaxi, or Cerro Quemado—a Flower Mountain—evokes a solar origin narrative that has been traced back to Teotihuacan, as noted earlier. Neurath's research (this volume) demonstrates that the Wixárika Flower World is actively created through mutualistic relations between the living and deceased and through ritual obligations that are simultaneously manifested on a grand scale in sacred landscapes and within a microcosm on the dance patio and in gourd bowls. While flower world has been documented among the contemporary Huichol and Cora, evidence of flower world has not been identified among other west Mexican cultures such as the Postclassic and historic-period Tarascans of Michoacán.

To date, flower worlds have not been securely identified in the ar-chaeological record of west Mexico before A.D. 850/900, including in Epiclassic-period La Quemada and Alta Vista material culture. Perhaps the earliest scholarship on a possible pre-Hispanic manifestation of flower world in west Mexico before this era is Christopher Beekman's (2003) study of the Late Formative to Early Classic Teuchitlán tradition. He contends that the radial layout of the *guachimontón* public architecture—which is made up of rectangular structures arranged in a circle around a plaza—may relate to the cross section of a maize cob or a radial flower. It is notable, however, that Teuchitlán ceramics and material culture do not contain any identified floral, rain/cloud, or solar imagery typically linked to Flower World. The maize agricultural *mitote* rites in the Gran Nayar region often linked to Teuchitlán architecture and ceremonialism may actually date no earlier than the Postclassic period (Mathiowetz 2011, 2021)—a topic that deserves further study.

Perhaps the best evidence in pre-Hispanic west Mexico for a cos-mology linking a solar and floral realm of deceased ancestors as rain to the maize-agricultural ceremonial cycle (*mitotes*) is found among the Postclassic-period Aztatlán culture (Mathiowetz 2011, 2021), an era when copper bells were used to evoke this floral and solar domain (Ho-sler 1994). Current evidence indicates that the initial presence of flower world in west Mexico and the concomitant social transformations that occurred during this era relates to historical processes involving the spread of maize-oriented Xochipilli (Piltzintli), Venus, and feathered serpent ritualism from highland and southern Mexico to the Aztat-lán region after A.D. 850/900. The new Aztatlán Flower World ide-ology appears to have driven changes in technologies, industries, and shifts in human-environmental relations—such as cacao cultivation/consumption and the intensification of cotton production and related weaving activities that contributed to reshaping social relations at the individual, household, and community levels (Mathiowetz 2011, 2019a, 2019b, 2020, 2021, this volume). These studies indicate that much like for groups in the Gran Nayar region of west Mexico, flower worlds both in antiquity and in the present can be created through the intersecting domains of domestic and ritual activities, which we may consider here to be indistinguishable. For example, in a complex set of interrelated conceptual metaphors, the act of gendered weaving activities among

Wixárika (and earlier Aztatlán) households places into the hands of the individual weaver the ability to instigate the birth of the sun, to facilitate the arrival of the ancestral clouds and rain, and to create the flowering landscape. Comparable links between weaving and flower world are known for other regions of Postclassic Mesoamerica (Patel 2012), although the extent to which these ideologies relate to other economic industries remains unclear. These conclusions intersect with both Neurath's and Molina and Shorter's (this volume) assertions that ritual labor is a form of self-sacrifice that is critical to bringing the flower world into presence.

Finally, the recognition that ideology and cosmology play significant roles in driving social change, much as ideologies shape social change today, should factor into a shift in focus from exclusively environmental-driven processual models of social change commonly proposed in archaeological case studies, such as the southward depopulation of the Four Corners region in the American Southwest, a dramatic demographic shift that occurred just as flower world imagery became most evident in the macroregion to the south (Mathiowetz 2011). How might the processes of flower world–related ideological florescence and dissolution tie into other notable societal transformations on a macroregional scale? In the Mesoamerican world, for example, given the link between flower world and political legitimization, how might shifts in flower world tenets or legitimization strategies relate to the collapse of Classic Maya polities and their reorganization during the Postclassic Period, a historical process that to date has almost exclusively been linked to drought, intersocietal conflict, and environmental degradation? Addressing the questions of how flower world ideologies transformed technologies, industries, societal organization, and social relations should remain a key research endeavor in the future of Mesoamerican and southwestern studies.

THE ORGANIZATION OF THIS VOLUME

This volume stresses the importance of contemporary emic perspectives and experiences by opening with studies of living traditions that are informed by discussions and observations shared between community members and cultural anthropologists. These studies tell us that today, flower worlds are expressed in everyday work and lived experiences. They are embedded in sacred geographies of interconnected local and distant landscapes. They are ritually practiced and engaged both individually and in communities. And they frame and reinforce social relationships and obligations of the individual to society (chapters by Molina and Shorter, Neurath, Sandstrom, and Washburn). Many ways through which flower worlds are revealed—such as the rhythms of speech, music, and dance, the aroma of flowers and incense, the smoke that carries prayers, and the personal and societal meanings invested in the landscape—are ephemeral, accessible only to those who experience them firsthand.

Archaeological and historical perspectives are by nature limited to interpretation of patterned material traces and extant visual representations that are informed by ethnological and ethnohistorical viewpoints. Contributors to this volume employ a varied methodological palette, including analysis of pollens and pigments (Domenici and McNeil), iconography and artwork (Chinchilla Mazariegos, Córdova, González López and Vázquez Vallín, Mathiowetz, Pohl, Taube, and Turner), architecture (González López and Vázquez Vallín, Pohl, and Turner) and the distribution of material culture (Mathiowetz and Pohl). Chapters in the second section of the book are arranged in rough chronological order, rather than by method or geography, to stress the historical trajectories of flower worlds in their diverse manifestations and the development and deployment of the central themes and concepts that we use to define them.

Nearly three decades after Hill's (1992) initial definition of the flower world as a series of interrelated cross-cultural phenomena, we are better positioned to address issues such as the social and historical conditions that may have guided the wholesale or partial adoption, rejection, modification, and spread of flower world concepts; how they may have been appropriated by elites to legitimize political ideologies or to undermine them; and how everyday behaviors and quotidian tasks serve to embody and materialize overarching cosmological principles in individuals' daily lives as lived experiences. The convergence and interplay of multidisciplinary analyses in this volume reflect richly nuanced and complementary endeavors that are at once historical, humanistic, experiential, and qualitative as well as scientific and quantitative. A key point evident to the editors and contributors to this volume is that multidisciplinary collaborations—which are at once scientific and humanistic and emphasize Indigenous voices—are essential to the future explorations of flower worlds and their links between living communities and past societies in the Americas.

REFERENCES

Alcántara Rojas, Berenice. 2011. "*In Nepapan Xochitl*: The Power of Flowers in the Works of Sahagún." In *Colors Between Two Worlds: The Florentine Codex of Bernardino de Sahagún*, edited by Louise Waldman, 106–32. Florence: Kunsthistorisches Institut in Florenz, Max Planck Institut, Villa I Tatti, and the Harvard University Center for Italian Renaissance Studies.

Alcántara Rojas, Berenice. 2015. "Of Feathers and Songs: Birds of Rich Plumage in Nahuatl *Cantares*." In *Images Take Flight: Feather Art in Mexico and Europe 1400–1700*, edited by Alessandra Russo, Gerhard Wolf, and Diane Fane, 145–55. Trento: Hirmer.

Beekman, Christopher S. 2003. "Fruitful Symmetry: Corn and Cosmology in the Public Architecture of Late Formative and Early Classic Jalisco." *Mesoamerican Voices* 1:5–22.

Benciolini, Maria. 2014. "Iridiscencias de un mundo florido: Estudio sobre relacionalidad y ritualidad cora." Unpublished Ph.D. dissertation, Instituto de Investigaciones Antropológicas, Universidad Nacional Autónoma de México, Mexico City.

Berlo, Janet Catherine. 1983. "The Warrior and the Butterfly: Central Mexican Ideologies of Sacred Warfare and Teotihuacan Iconography." In *Text and Image in Pre-Columbian Art: Essays on the Interrelationship of the Visual and Verbal Arts*, edited by Janet Catherine Berlo, 79–117. British Archaeological Reports International Series, vol. 180. Oxford: British Archaeological Reports.

Bernardini, Wesley. 2005. *Hopi Oral Tradition and the Archaeology of Identity.* Tucson: University of Arizona Press.

Beyer, Hermann. 1965. "La mariposa en el simbolismo Azteca." In *El México Antiguo: Tomo X*, edited by Carmen Cook de Leonard, 465–69. Mexico City, Mex.: Sociedad Alemana Mexicanista.

Bierhorst, John. 1985. *Cantares mexicanos: Songs of the Aztecs.* Stanford, Calif.: Stanford University Press.

Boyd, Carolyn E. 2016. *The White Shaman Mural: An Enduring Creation Narrative in the Rock Art of the Lower Pecos.* Austin: University of Texas Press.

Brown, Emily J. 2014. "Music of the Center Place: The Instruments of Chaco Canyon." In *Flower World: Music Archaeology of the Americas*, vol. 3, edited by Matthias Stockli and Mark Howell, 45–66. Berlin: Ekho.

Burkhart, Louise M. 1988. "The Solar Christ in Nahuatl Doctrinal Texts of Early Colonial Mexico." *Ethnohistory* 35:234–56.

Burkhart, Louise M. 1992. "Flowery Heaven: The Aesthetic of Paradise in Na-huatl Devotional Literature." *RES: Anthropology and Aesthetics* 21:88–109.

Carlsen, Robert S., and Martin Prechtel. 1991. "The Flowering Dead: An Inter-pretation of Highland Maya Culture." *Man* 26:23–42.

Caso, Alfonso. 1942. "El paraíso terrenal en Teotihuacán." *Cuadernos Americanos* 6:127–36.

Chinchilla Mazariegos, Oswaldo. 2013. "The Flower World of Cotzumalhuapa." In *The Maya in a Mesoamerican Context: Comparative Approaches to Maya Studies; Proceedings of the 16th European Maya Conference, Copenhagen, December 5–10, 2011*, edited by Jesper Nielsen and Christophe Helmke, 79–92. Acta Mesoamericana, vol. 26. Markt Schwaben: Anton Saurwein.

Chinchilla Mazariegos, Oswaldo. 2015. "Sounds in Stone: Song, Music, and Dance on Monument 21 from Bilbao, Cotzumalguapa, Guatemala." *PARI Journal* 16(1):1–12.

Crown, Patricia L. 1994. *Ceramics and Ideology: Salado Polychrome Pottery*. Albu-querque: University of New Mexico Press.

Evans, Victoria R., and Warren K. Lail. 2015. "The Representation of Plants in Hohokam Pottery Design." *Kiva* 81:247–63.

Evers, Larry, and Felipe S. Molina. 1987. *Yaqui Deer Songs/Maso Bwikam*. Tucson: University of Arizona Press.

Forde, Jamie E. 2020. "Broken Flowers: Christian Spolia in a Colonial Mixtec Household." *Colonial Latin American Review* 29(2):195–222.

Hays-Gilpin, Kelley, and Jane H. Hill. 1999. "The Flower World in Material Culture: An Iconographic Complex in the Southwest and Mesoamerica." *Journal of Anthropological Research* 55(1):1–37.

Hays-Gilpin, Kelley, and Jane H. Hill. 2000. "The Flower World in Prehistoric Southwest Material Culture." In *The Archaeology of Regional Interaction: Re-ligion, Warfare, and Exchange Across the American Southwest and Beyond; Pro-ceedings of the 1996 Southwest Symposium*, edited by Michelle Hegmon, 411–28. Boulder: University Press of Colorado.

Hays-Gilpin, Kelley, Elizabeth Newsome, and Emory Sekaquaptewa. 2010. "*Siitálpuva*, 'Through the Land Brightened with Flowers': Ecology and Cos-mology in Mural and Pottery Painting, Hopi and Beyond." In *Painting the Cosmos: Metaphor and Worldview in Images from the Southwest Pueblos and Mexico*, edited by Kelley Hays-Gilpin and Polly Schaafsma, 121–38. Museum of Northern Arizona Bulletin 67. Flagstaff: Museum of Northern Arizona.

Headrick, Annabeth. 1999. "The Street of the Dead . . . It Really Was: Mortuary Bundles at Teotihuacan." *Ancient Mesoamerica* 10(1):69–85.

Headrick, Annabeth. 2007. *The Teotihuacan Trinity: The Sociopolitical Structure of an Ancient Mesoamerican City*. Austin: University of Texas Press.

Headrick, Annabeth. 2018. "The Osario of Chichen Itza: Where Warriors Danced in Paradise." In *Landscapes of the Itza: Archaeology and Art History at Chichen Itza and Neighboring Sites*, edited by Linnea Wren, Cynthia Kristan-Graham,

Travis Nygard, and Kaylee Spencer, 198–225. Gainesville: University Press of Florida.

Hernbrode, Janine, and Peter Boyle. 2017. "Broad Distribution of Flower World Imagery in Hohokam Petroglyphs." In *American Indian Rock Art*, vol. 43, edited by Ken Hedges and Mark Calamia, 75–83. San Jose, Calif.: American Rock Art Research Association.

Hibben, Frank C. 1975. *Kiva Art of the Anasazi at Pottery Mound.* Las Vegas, Nev.: KC Publications.

Hill, Jane H. 1992. "The Flower World of Old Uto-Aztecan." *Journal of Anthropological Research* 48(2):117–44.

Hosler, Dorothy. 1994. *The Sounds and Colors of Power: The Sacred Metallurgical Technology of Ancient West Mexico.* Cambridge, Mass.: MIT Press.

Houston, Stephen D., David Stuart, and Karl A. Taube. 2006. *The Memory of Bones: Body, Being, and Experience Among the Classic Maya.* Austin: University of Texas Press.

Jones, Bernard M., Jr., and Christopher E. Drover. 2018. "Flower World Iconography and Metaphor of the Southern Colorado Plateau: The Puerco and Little Colorado Watersheds." In *Rock Art Papers*, vol. 19, edited by Ken Hedges and Anne McConnell, 135–51. San Diego, Calif.: San Diego Rock Art Association.

López Austin, Alfredo. 1997. *Tamoanchan, Tlalocan: Places of Mist.* Niwot: University Press of Colorado.

López Luján, Leonardo, and Michelle De Anda Rogel. 2017. "Teotihuacan en Mexico-Tenochtitlan: Descubrimientos recientes, nuevas perspectivas." *Estudios de Cultura Náhuatl* 54:17–60.

McNeil, Cameron L. 2006. "Maya Interactions with the Natural World: Landscape Transformation and Ritual Plant Use at Copan, Honduras." Unpublished Ph.D. dissertation, Department of Anthropology, Graduate Center, City University of New York.

McNeil, Lynda D., and David L. Shaul. 2018. "Western Basketmakers: Social Networking Among Uto-Aztecan Foragers and Migrant Farmers on the Colorado Plateau." *Kiva* 84(2):203–36.

Mathiowetz, Michael D. 2011. "The Diurnal Path of the Sun: Ideology and Interregional Interaction in Ancient Northwest Mesoamerica and the American Southwest." Unpublished Ph.D. dissertation, Department of Anthropology, University of California, Riverside.

Mathiowetz, Michael D. 2018a. "From this Day Forward I Am Your Way of Life: The *Capitan* Icon on Rio Grande Glaze Wares in the Southwestern United States (AD 1300–1700)." *Journal of the Southwest* 60(3):699–752.

Mathiowetz, Michael D. 2018b. "The Sun Youth of the Casas Grandes Culture (A.D. 1200–1450)." *Kiva* 84(3):367–90.

Mathiowetz, Michael D. 2019a. "El hijo de Dios que está en el Sol: Autoridad política y personificación del Dios Sol en el antiguo Noroccidente de

México." In *Aztatlán: Interacción y cambio social en el Occidente de México ca. 850–1350 d.C.*, edited by Laura Solar Valverde and Ben A. Nelson, 287–312. Zamora: El Colegio de Michoacán.

Mathiowetz, Michael D. 2019b. "A History of Cacao in West Mexico: Implications for Mesoamerica and U.S. Southwest Connections." *Journal of Archaeological Research* 27:287–333.

Mathiowetz, Michael. 2020. "Weaving Our Life: The Economy and Ideology of Cotton in Postclassic West Mexico." In *Ancient West Mexicos: Time, Space, and Diversity*, edited by Joshua D. Englehardt, Verenice Heredia Espinoza, and Christopher S. Beekman, 302–48. Gainesville: University Press of Florida.

Mathiowetz, Michael D. 2021. "The Dance of the Sprouting Corn: Casas Grandes Maize Ceremonialism and the Transformation of the Puebloan World." In *Borderlands Histories: Ethnographic Observations and Archaeological Interpretations*, edited by John Carpenter and Matthew Pailes. Salt Lake City: University of Utah Press.

Mathiowetz, Michael, Polly Schaafsma, Jeremy Coltman, and Karl Taube. 2015. "The Darts of Dawn: The Tlahuizcalpantecuhtli Venus Complex in the Iconography of Mesoamerica and the American Southwest." *Journal of the Southwest* 57(1):1–102.

Mendieta, Gerónimo de. 1980. *Historia eclesiástica indiana*. Mexico City: Porrúa.

Neurath, Johannes. 2005. "Cosmogonic Myths, Ritual Groups, and Initiation: Toward a New Comparative Ethnology of the Gran Nayar and the Southwest of the U.S." *Journal of the Southwest* 47(4):571–614.

Nielsen, Jesper. 2016. "The Cave and the Butterfly: Thoughts on Death and Rebirth in Ancient Mesoamerica." *Contributions in New World Archaeology* 10:101–12.

Patel, Shankari. 2012. "Journey to the East: Pilgrimage, Politics, and Gender in Postclassic Mexico." Unpublished Ph.D. dissertation, Department of Anthropology, University of California, Riverside.

Peterson, Jeanette Favrot. 1993. *The Paradise Garden Murals of Malinalco: Utopia and Empire in Sixteenth-Century Mexico*. Austin: University of Texas Press.

Sahagún, Bernardino de. 1993 [1583]. *Bernardino de Sahagún's Psalmodia Christiana (Christian Psalmody)*. Translated by Arthur J. O. Anderson. Salt Lake City: University of Utah Press.

Salmón, Enrique. 1999. "Sharing Breath with Our Relatives: Rarámuri Plant Knowledge, Lexicon, and Cognition." Unpublished Ph.D. dissertation, Department of Anthropology, Arizona State University, Tempe.

Saturno, William A., Karl A. Taube, and David Stuart. 2005. *The Murals of San Bartolo, El Petén, Guatemala. Part 1: The North Wall*. Ancient America 7. Barnardsville, N.C.: Center for Ancient American Studies.

Schaafsma, Polly. 2000. *Warrior, Shield, and Star: Imagery and Ideology of Pueblo Warfare*. Santa Fe, N.Mex.: Western Edge Press.

Sekaquaptewa, Emory, and Dorothy Washburn. 2004. "They Go Along Singing: Reconstructing the Hopi Past from Ritual Metaphors in Song and Dance." *American Antiquity* 69(3):457–86.

Seler, Eduard. 1990–1998. *Collected Works in Mesoamerican Linguistics and Archaeology*, 6 vols. Edited by Frank E. Comparato. Culver City, Calif.: Labyrinthos.

Taube, Karl A. 1985. "The Classic Maya Maize God: A Reappraisal." In *Fifth Palenque Round Table, 1983*, edited by Merle Greene Robertson and Virginia M. Fields, 171–81. San Francisco: Pre-Columbian Art Research Institute.

Taube, Karl A. 2000a. "Lightning Celts and Corn Fetishes: The Development of Maize Symbolism in Mesoamerica and the American Southwest." In *Olmec Art and Archaeology: Social Complexity in the Formative Period*, edited by John E. Clark and Mary Pye, 296–337. Studies in the History of Art. Washington, D.C.: National Gallery of Art.

Taube, Karl A. 2000b. "The Turquoise Hearth: Fire, Self-Sacrifice, and the Central Mexican Cult of War." In *Mesoamerica's Classic Heritage: From Teotihuacan to the Aztecs*, edited by Davíd Carrasco, Lindsay Jones, and Scott Sessions, 269–340. Boulder: University of Colorado Press.

Taube, Karl A. 2001. "The Breath of Life: The Symbolism of Wind in Mesoamerica and the American Southwest." In *The Road to Aztlan: Art from a Mythic Homeland*, edited by Virginia M. Fields and Victor Zamudio-Taylor, 102–23. Los Angeles: Los Angeles County Museum of Art.

Taube, Karl A. 2004. "Flower Mountain: Concepts of Life, Beauty, and Paradise Among the Classic Maya." *RES: Anthropology and Aesthetics* 45:69–98.

Taube, Karl A. 2005. "Representaciones del paraíso en el arte cerámico del Clásico Temprano de Escuintla, Guatemala." In *Iconografía y escritura teotihuacana en la Costa Sur de Guatemala y Chiapas*, edited by Oswaldo Chinchilla Mazariegos and Bárbara Arroyo, 35–54. U Tz'ib, Serie Reportes, vol. 1, no. 5. Guatemala City: Asociación Tikal.

Taube, Karl A. 2006. "Climbing Flower Mountain: Concepts of Resurrection and the Afterlife at Teotihuacan." In *Arqueología e historia del Centro de Mexico: Homenaje a Eduardo Matos Moctezuma*, edited by Leonardo López Lujan, Davíd Carrasco, and Lourdes Cué, 153–70. Mexico City: Instituto Nacional de Antropología e Historia.

Taube, Karl A. 2010a. "At Dawn's Edge: Tulúm, Santa Rita, and Floral Symbolism in the International Style of Late Postclassic Mesoamerica." In *Astronomers, Scribes, and Priests: Intellectual Interchange Between the Northern Maya Lowlands and Highland Mexico in the Late Postclassic Period*, edited by Gabrielle Vail and Christine Hernández, 145–91. Washington, D.C.: Dumbarton Oaks Research Library and Collection.

Taube, Karl A. 2010b. "Gateways to Another World: The Symbolism of Supernatural Passageways in the Art and Ritual of Mesoamerica and the American Southwest." In *Painting the Cosmos: Metaphor and Worldview in Images from the Southwest Pueblos and Mexico*, edited by Kelley Hays-Gilpin and Polly

Schaafsma, 73–120. Museum of Northern Arizona Bulletin 67. Flagstaff: Museum of Northern Arizona.

Taube, Karl A. 2020. "In Search of Paradise: Religion and Cultural Exchange in Early Postclassic Mesoamerica." In *A Forest of History: The Maya After the Emergence of Divine Kingship*, edited by Travis W. Stanton and M. Kathryn Brown, 154–86. Boulder: University Press of Colorado.

Taube, Karl A., Travis W. Stanton, José Francisco Osorio León, Francisco Pérez Ruíz, María Rocio González de la Mata, and Jeremy D. Coltman. 2020. *The Initial Series Group at Chichen Itza, Yucatan: Archaeological Investigations and Iconographic Interpretations.* San Francisco: Precolumbia Mesoweb Press.

Turner, Andrew D. 2016. "Cultures at the Crossroads: Art, Religion, and Interregional Interaction in Central Mexico, A.D. 600–900." Unpublished Ph.D. dissertation, Department of Anthropology, University of California, Riverside.

Turner, Andrew D. 2020. "The Olmec Spoon Reconsidered: Material Meanings of Jade, Nacreous Shells, and Pearls in Ancient Mesoamerica." *Ancient Mesoamerica.* https://www.cambridge.org/core/journals/ancient-mesoamerica/article/abs/olmec-spoon-reconsidered-material-meanings-of-jade-nacreous-shells-and-pearls-in-ancient-mesoamerica/F0ACB777D0FA643A9D6658A777E736B0.

Umberger, Emily. 1987. "Antiques, Revivals, and References to the Past in Aztec Art." *RES: Anthropology and Aesthetics* 13:62–105.

von Winning, Hasso. 1987. *La iconografía de Teotihuacán: Los dioses y los signos.* 2 vols. Estudios y fuentes del arte en México. Mexico City: Universidad Nacional Autónoma de México.

Weiner, Robert S. 2015. "A Sensory Approach to Exotica, Ritual Practice, and Cosmology at Chaco Canyon." *Kiva* 81:220–46.

PART I

CONTEMPORARY FLOWER WORLDS

1

Flower World in the Religious Ideology of Contemporary Nahua of the Southern Huasteca, Mexico

Alan R. Sandstrom

Nahua people of Amatlán, a pseudonymous village in the southern Huasteca (Map 1), tell a narrative about how the world got to be the way it is. The account centers on a mountain they call Postectli, the most important prominence in their elaborate and complex conceptions of the sacred landscape. This ancient volcanic core juts straight out of the surrounding countryside to an altitude of nearly two thousand feet. In primordial times, it connected the celestial and terrestrial levels of the cosmos, but examination of its profile from certain angles reveals that it appears to be broken off at the top. The connection between sky and earth has been severed. How could this have happened? In the beginning, the story goes, *tonantzin*, "our honored mother" created a beautiful garden in the sky. It was filled with tropical flowers, beautiful birds including iridescent hummingbirds, and colorful butterflies, all illuminated by glorious sunshine. One day the earth mother noticed that leaf-cutter ants were climbing up the mountain and destroying her garden. She became enraged and sought the help of *sahuan*, the owner of water. *Sahuan* himself is the subject of myth, where it is revealed that he is a problematic character with an unstable personality. He provides the water so necessary for life, but he is like a rainy-season thunder storm, filled with pent-up violence, and he does not seem to know his own strength. For the safety of humanity his assistants have chained him to the bottom of the Gulf of Mexico. Once loosed by *tonantzin* he swept across the countryside, and in a great cataclysm of fire, molten rock, and smoke he broke off the mountain with his thunderbolts. *Tonantzin*'s garden paradise was saved, but humanity was cut off from the gods and condemned to live in the disorder of the earth's surface, teetering on the brink of chaos. In the Nahuatl language the name Postectli means "broken," and its central importance in Nahua myth shows that far more than a mountaintop was destroyed by the actions of *tonantzin* and *sahuan* on that critical day in the distant past. Humanity lost access to paradise and was set on a historical course filled with struggle and striving to regain its place in the cosmic order.[1]

In this chapter I address this fall from grace and attempt to answer the question of whether the Nahua of this region partake of a cultural feature found in certain Native American societies called chromaticism, a symbolic complex first identified by Claude Lévi-Strauss (1969) and elaborated in a seminal article by linguist Jane Hill (1992). Hill documents that speakers of Uto-Aztecan languages, including Nahuatl spoken by the Nahua, often exhibit a focus on "Colored flowers and other brightly colored and iridescent natural phenomena, including dawn and sunset, rainbows, hummingbirds, butterflies and other colorful and iridescent insects, shells, crystals, and colored lights and flames" (1992:117). According to Hill, these vivid phenomena act as metaphors or symbols of spiritual power or perhaps as entrances to spirit realms. Chromatic symbols "permit ordinary people to glimpse the Spirit Land, and of dreams and visions of the beauty of the Spirit Land" (1992:119). Flowers are the key element in this chromatic realm, and Hill calls the space created by these plant displays the "flower world." The Aztecs and their Nahua descendants exemplify this near obsession with the place of blossoms in the cosmic order (González López and Vázquez Vallín, this volume).

In Hill's view, the elaboration and distribution of the flower world concept indicates that it originated very early on in Uto-Aztecan speech communities (1992:117). Is *tonantzin*'s garden in the narrative of Postectli an example of this apparently ancient and widespread cultural phenomenon? I will argue that the Nahua of this region do have a strong cultural focus on chromatic phenomena with a particular interest in flowers of all types. Furthermore, several key myths they recount reference a garden-like lost paradise, an idea shared by other Native American groups (Molina and Shorter, Neurath, and Washburn, this volume). Finally, I want to emphasize the monistic philosophy and world view of the Nahua, contrast monism and dualism as distinct perspectives, and show how monism places them in a relationship with the flower world not imagined in Hill's original formulation. I suggest that for the Nahua, flowers and other colorful, shimmering, and luminescent phenomena directly embody or reveal deity to those sensitized to see it.

THE HUASTECAN NAHUA AND THEIR NEIGHBORS

The Nahua of northern Veracruz state (part of the southern Huasteca region) live in small communities scattered throughout the foothills of the Sierra Madre Oriental, and most people make their living through slash-and-burn horticulture. Despite their impressive expertise in dealing with the tropical-forest environment, the Nahua face uncertain conditions that render life precarious from year to year. Rainfall is unpredictable, violent storms often sweep through the region and destroy the standing maize, and disease or hungry animals can devastate a field. Added to all of this uncertainty, acts of disrespect on the parts of Nahua and non-Nahua alike can fracture the delicate equilibrium between human beings and spirit entities leading the latter to withhold key resources such as rain that the crops require (Washburn, this volume). Disrespect (or *axtlatlepanitta*) comes in many forms, and it always disrupts, pollutes, and threatens the perpetually fraught relations between people and the sacred powers. Farmers disrespect the earth when they burn it or plant in it without providing ritual compensation. Fighting, lying, stealing, or similar antisocial acts disturb cosmic balance. The two gravest forms of disrespect are envy and sorcery. In Nahua belief, envy disrupts the social order and undoes the work of others. Sorcery, often pursued because of envy, is a deliberate act of sending disease and death out of revenge or jealousy and sometimes for pay (Sandstrom and Sandstrom 2020).

It is clear that the surface of the earth (*tlaltepactli*) inhabited by the human community contrasts with *tonantzin*'s brightly lit, colorful garden in the celestial realm (*ilhuicactli*). Intimations of that paradise can be found in earthly flowers and terrestrial scenes of beauty, but they are not equivalent to the glory of the actual thing. The contrast could not be clearer between the sparkling beauty of the heavenly garden and the disturbed (and one could accurately say contaminated) existence on the earth. Color-infused realms of delight are not restricted to the sky. In addition to *tonantzin*'s garden we catch glimpses of other possible chromatic worlds in Nahua belief and myth. Water dweller (*apanchaneh*) is an aspect of *sahuan* who lives in bodies of water such as springs, lakes, and arroyos. She is often visualized by the Nahua as a siren, a kind of mermaid with a fish tail in place of legs. Her role is to receive water from the mountain dwarfs called "little old ones," *pilhuehuentzitzin*, who carry the precious liquid from *sahuan*'s realm in the Gulf to *apanchaneh*'s cave near the peak of Postectli, from which she distributes it to the milpas in the form of rain. One might think that she is a benevolent character because of her role in providing rain, but she is capable of striking out and destroying those who show her or her fish children disrespect. Here again is the Nahua monists' unwillingness to divide the world into strict categories of good and evil or beneficent and malevolent (Sandstrom and Sandstrom 2020). Her watery realm is called *apan*, or "water place"; people describe it as iridescent, clear, and beautiful, and it is there where she inhabits *atecpantzin*, "honored water palace." There are no flowers per se, but she is surrounded by strikingly colorful tropical fish, vivid aquatic creatures, bright-green water plants, and iridescent bubbles gliding to the surface; it is a place every bit as chromatic as *tonantzin*'s garden. Here water dweller gambols with her fish offspring, exudes precious salt from her body, and provides fish to eat for those who are respectful. The souls of people who die by drowning, by being struck by lightning, or from certain diseases are believed by many Nahua to travel to *apan* to enjoy a glorious afterlife in this aquatic place of delight. Souls of people who die normal deaths go to *mictlan*, "place of the dead," located beneath the surface of the earth notable for its dreary colorlessness, lack of sunshine, and gloomy atmosphere; *mictlan* is like an antiflower world.

Before expanding the scope of the investigation into behavioral patterns that may reveal evidence of the flower world, I would like to address two questions. First, how sure can we be that the Nahua flower world is Indigenous in conception? Could it not simply be a modified version of the Garden of Eden story brought by the Spaniards? Second, is this idea strictly local or is it shared by other Nahua or even non-Uto-Aztecan Native American groups in the Huasteca and elsewhere? The answer to the first question has been provided by Louise Burkhart, who establishes that the idea of a flowery paradise was definitely pre-Hispanic. For the Aztecs, however, it was not heaven where souls were rewarded for good behavior but rather an example of a place where the sacred cosmos reveals itself to all those open to see it. This flowery link between the physical and transcendent led early Nahua converts to employ a garden metaphor when trying to make Christian ideas comprehensible to the mass of people (Burkhart 1992a: 345–46; 1992b: 106). Gardens for the Aztecs evoked a deeper appreciation of the sacred cosmos itself.

Regarding distribution of the flower-world chromaticism, there is ample evidence that it is widespread throughout Mesoamerica and even extends into the North American Southwest, where it may have begun deep in prehistory (Chinchilla Mazariegos, Hays-Gilpin, McNeil, Mathiowetz, Taube, and Turner, this volume; Hays-Gilpin and Hill 1999). Anthropologist Catharine Good Eshelman found that Nahua from a Rio Balsas community in the state of Guerrero go on pilgrimage to a place called Oztotempan, which they describe as the "navel of the world" (Good Eshelman 2001:280). The site is a hole leading to a flowery paradise characterized by copious amounts of water, colorful birds, and cultivated fields with luxuriant flowers and plants. It seems clear that the sacred hole serves as a portal between the earth's surface and the flower world beneath.

Ideas of flower worlds in Indigenous Mesoamerican cultures certainly exist outside of the Uto-Aztecan family as well. Karl Taube's (2004) thorough examination of the flower world among the Maya is one example (see also Taube, this volume). The Tepehua of the southern Huasteca and the Totonac centered just south of the Huasteca have ideas of a flowery paradise occupied by important spirit entities. The languages of these two groups belong to the Totonakan family, unrelated to Uto-Aztecan (Kaufman 1994:37). Both groups have a belief in a place where the ancient ones are seated around two tables with iridescent tablecloths. These spirit entities are dressed in beautiful clothes and occupy decorated seats. Apparently, the Tepehua and Totonac have combined their version of the flower world with paintings or images they have seen of the Last Supper with Jesus and his disciples (Ichon 1973:162; Williams García 1963:198).

NAHUA RITUAL AND THE FLOWER WORLD

Flowers are central features of religious rituals among today's Nahua of the southern Huasteca. They are associated with the sun, growing corn, life-giving water, the bounty of the living cosmos, and ancestors who visit the homes of their relatives during Day of the Dead. For the contemporary Nahua, at least, flowers are far more than mere examples of beauty; rather they are evidence of a beneficent universe that is responsible for children, abundant crops, health, and the possibility of human existence even though that universe may at the same time be unstable and filled with the forces of chaos and destruction. One word in Nahuatl for ritual is *xochitlalia*, meaning "to put down flowers," and no ritual is ever held without the incorporation of copious blossoms in the altar or display (Color Plate 3). While we have little evidence of an elaborated, well-developed idea of a specific flower world among the contemporary Huastecan Nahua, we have documented the importance of flowers in many areas of their lives both within and outside of religious contexts. It is my contention that the privileged place of flowers in the narratives and metaphors of the contemporary Nahua goes beyond an obvious appreciation of beauty, instead offering a telling example of the ancient, widespread idea of a flower world, revealing the monistic philosophy shared by Indigenous groups throughout Mesoamerica (Neurath, this volume).

Intimations of flowery paradises can be found in Nahua behavior toward earthly flowers and terrestrial scenes of beauty. Strangers entering a shrine or encountering a ritual event could not fail to notice that greenery and tropical flowers are requisite altar embellishments. Ritual participants and helpers spend much time and effort gathering greenery and flowers and constructing the elaborate adornments required of any major offering (see España Soto 2018). Certainly colorful blossoms are appreciated by people all over the world, but the Nahua take their love of flowers to a whole new level. Flower allusions are found throughout the Nahua language: a shrine or *xochicalli* is a "flower house"; the male aspect of the corn spirit is *chicome xochitl*, "seven flower"; the female aspect of the corn spirit is *macuilli xochitl*, "five flower"; a garden is a *xochimilli*, "flower milpa"; sacred music is *xochisonis*, "flower sounds"; the ancestors' path to the Day of the Dead altar is a *xochiohtli*, "flower trail"; *aguardiente* is *xochiatzin*, "flower water," and a virulent but colorful disease-causing agent is called *xochiehecatl*, "flower wind." Nahua women embroider their traditional blouse designs with bold floral patterns. One can observe both men and women carrying around small flower bouquets, and people's house plots are festooned with a great variety of blossoming plants.

Jane Hill and Kelley Hays-Gilpin have identified a valid feature of the religious and aesthetic ideology shared by the cultures of Mesoamerica and the American Southwest. However, in Hill's symbolic anthropological approach, an interpretive procedure that is dualistic at its core, flowers *represent* the flower world, a garden is *a metaphor* for paradise, and bright colors *symbolize* that other realm. In this formulation, the signifier is distinct from what is signified. The dualism that permeates Euro-American thought is revealed by this analytical approach to the flower world. Dualist thinking is ubiquitous in the West, and we find it in the distinctions made between body and soul, mind and matter, a religious statue and the saint it represents, or the costumed dancer and the spirit entity portrayed. This dualistic perspective seriously underestimates and misrepresents the philosophy and world view of the Indigenous people who share conceptions of the flower world.

The world view of contemporary Nahua from the Huasteca is based on philosophical monism, a world view in which people regard every living being, inanimate object, and natural process as an expression of one single substrate or ground of existence. This substance, energy, or essential quality is all powerful, sacred, and omnipresent even though it remains largely invisible and thus difficult for people to discern in their daily lives. The Nahua of the Huasteca call this entity *totiotzin*, a word that can be translated as "our honored divinity," which is based on the Nahuatl root *teotl*, translated by the sixteenth-century friars as "God." What the friars failed to appreciate is that *teotl* was a very different idea of God when compared with their own theistic conceptions. Although not all experts agree, I am increasingly convinced that the solution to comprehending the monist universe of the Nahua of the Huasteca—and generally the ancient Mesoamerican pantheon as well—is to view these religious systems as pantheistic (Sandstrom and Sandstrom 1986:275ff.; Sandstrom 1991:238–39; Maffie 2014:79–92). The idea that Mesoamerican religions are pantheistic was first suggested in 1910 by Hermann Beyer (1965:398; see Monaghan 2000:27) and more fully developed by anthropologist Eva Hunt (1977). Monotheistic religions such as Christianity, Judaism, or Islam postulate an omniscient, omnipotent deity that created human beings and everything else in the universe. In pantheism, by contrast, the creation and the creator are one and the same, and the universe and every object and being in it are aspects of the single, sacred unity that is coterminous with existence. The different named spirit entities are temporary aspects or manifestations of this seamless totality.

Deities may seem on the surface to be organized into a polytheistic system, that is, a hierarchy of gods, each controlling a different domain of the universe. But for those studying the ancient Aztecs as well as ethnographers investigating contemporary Mesoamerican cultures, polytheism has always been problematic; the model never quite fit the data. The deities do not have stable identities and can proliferate and blend into one another; see, for example, the discussion of the Aztec rain deity Tlaloc by López Austin (1997:207–14). These features of Mesoamerican religion have forced researchers to extend and modify their definition of polytheism to the point that it becomes almost unrecognizable. For example, Leonardo López Luján (2005) lists eight general elements of Mesoamerica religion and includes as the sixth item the following: "According to Mesoamerican religious concepts, divine beings were omnipresent in the cosmos, and they were manifested in all the processes of nature as heterogeneous forces in conflict. This led to extreme polytheism. However, the divine personalities did not have sharp boundaries. They were thought to be capable of division and fusion" (López Luján 2005:32). An advantage of ethnography over historical sciences is that we can ask people what they think about their own culture. Here is how Abelardo de la Cruz, a young Nahua man from a small village in the Huasteca and currently an anthropology graduate student at the University at Albany, State University of New York, sees it: "A Nahua person is just a single piece of the Nahua universe. Each element of nature is connected to all the others. In the Nahua universe, all elements of nature are intertwined, and therefore what exists in nature belongs to a homogeneous whole. Christian elements may also be included in Nahua religion, but what happens in many cases is that at the time they were incorporated, these elements were given a divergent use and meaning from that of their religion of origin" (Cruz 2017:272). The statements of Cruz and López Luján are more consonant with pantheism than polytheism, no matter how conceived.

According to the Nahua, everything around us is an expression of *totiotzin*, yet it is difficult to perceive this overwhelming presence, much less summon it to receive a ritual offering. Simply getting the attention of this pervasive spirit presence is a preoccupation of ritual specialists, both ancient and contemporary. The lavish, highly elaborated, and seemingly near-continuous ritual occasions of the Aztecs in their capital city was an attempt to overcome this problem. Nahua rituals that I have witnessed are punctuated by fireworks explosions, bells ringing, and whistles blowing to gain the notice of the critically important but always aloof spirit entities. *Totiotzin*, however, can make itself known (or better, reveal itself) under certain circumstances. For those willing and able to observe it, elements of the landscape reveal *totiotzin*. Mountains, caves, ponds at or near the summit of major hills, or any anomalous geographic features are quintessential expressions of the great sacred unity. Properly arranged things (*tlamantli*, singular) similarly have the potential to reveal deity. A carefully composed piece of music expertly played also exposes *totiotzin*, as does a beautiful poem or exquisite artwork. Nahua ritual specialists and their helpers construct elaborate, finely tuned altars that express the layered structure of the cosmos where *totiotzin* is a living presence. The well-arranged altar in my estimation serves to concentrate *totiotzin*, making it a sacred space worthy of a ritual offering and thus the notice of the spirit entities. A properly cut anthropomorphic paper figure, a mainstay of Nahua rituals in this part of Mexico, reveals particular aspects or manifestations of deity that are then addressed in a ritual occasion. A paper figure of *apanchanch*, for instance, is designed to expose or unconceal that part of the cosmos that is water. The critical point is that the altar and paper figure do not represent, symbolize, or act as metaphors of the deity or the sacred; they embody it.

But what about the much-discussed dualism of classic Aztec religion and world view? It is common knowledge among experts that the Aztecs incorporated binary classification schemes in their understanding of the natural surroundings and social world. Examples of such dualistic principles include male–female, day–night, dry–moist, order–disorder, center–periphery, or birth–death. Doesn't this feature of Aztec thought exhibit a dualist philosophy thereby contradicting monism? Philosopher James Maffie calls this tension between opposing forces operating within a single pantheistic reality "agonistic inamic unity," by which he means "the continual and continuous cyclical struggle (agon) of paired opposites, polarities, or dualities" (2014:137). *Inamic* is a Nahuatl word that has been translated as "its correspondent," "its complement," "its complementary polarity," or "its match." Although he was concerned with explaining ancient Aztec philosophy, he could have been writing about the contemporary Nahua when he states, "The cyclical back-and-forth tug-of-war between inamic partners combined with the alternating, temporary dominance of one inamic over its partner constitutes and hence explains the genesis, diversity, movement, and momentary ordering of the cosmos. Each moment in this back-and-forth cosmic tug-of-war consists of the temporary dominance of one or the other inamic within a pair and therefore represents a temporary imbalance between the two" (Maffie 2014:138). All of these temporary states of being derive from the identical primordial substance and do not threaten a monistic philosophy.

If both the ancient Aztecs and the Nahua of today are understood to be philosophical monists, we must examine their ritual behavior in a whole new light. Ritual paraphernalia and actions can no longer be interpreted as metaphoric or symbolic in content; properly created, organized, and executed, these objects and acts must instead be seen as laying open to view what is normally hidden, exposing what is latent, disclosing the sacred substrate, demonstrating deity. The gods or spirits among the Aztecs and today's Nahua are not concrete beings but essentially embodiments in certain phenomena of the great unity revealed through ritual action and chanting. Following a ritual performance these apparently independent entities devolve back into the great unity and recede from human perception. Maffie writes that the named gods and deity pairs are best thought of as processes or orderly successions of actions that affect human beings:

> I believe the Aztecs singled out and emphasized specific processes and constellations of processes for ritual, practical, pedagogical, and artistic purposes. The various gods and goddesses of the Aztec pantheon . . . serve as conventional, shorthand handles or tags for specific constellations of processes. The use of these names no more entails that the Aztecs considered their referents to be perduring substantive entities than our calling a hurricane "Sandy" commits us to the view that hurricanes are substantive entities rather than processes. Names, after all, may refer to entities or to processes. (Maffie 2014:88)

In sum, the proliferation of identities and the way the spirits' functions overlap and merge into one another convinces us that these beings are best understood as temporary expressions of the single, sacred principle of *totiotzin*.

The Nahua I know express these philosophical principles in the structure of their rituals, in their chants addressing the spirit entities, in myths, and in the meticulous construction of ritual objects (Figure 1.1). They

Figure 1.1 Nahua participants in a pilgrimage to the sacred mountain Palaxtepetl construct bundles embodying Seven Flower and Five Flower, male and female aspects of maize. The highly chromatic bundles with their flowers and cloth wrapping reveal *totiotzin*, the sacred cosmos in their pantheistic religion. Photo by Alan R. Sandstrom.

illustrate through their actions and words what it means to be a Nahua and live in a world that is itself the deity. The theology of their religion is not written in books but is woven into their strategies for dealing with *totiotzin*. It is not deep discussions of religious principles that puts the world in order but actions that set things right.

NAHUA RITUAL OBJECTS

I will discuss briefly some of the ways the Nahua present the sacred cosmos in their rituals before returning to my conclusions regarding flowers and the worlds they create. It is clear from ethnographic research over the years that Nahua religion is organized around what Westerners would call ritual objects. This object orientation is shared throughout Mesoamerica by the Aztecs and other Indigenous groups both ancient and contemporary. Frances Berdan (personal communication, April 25, 2017) shared an unpublished ninety-four-page list titled "Material Dimensions of the 18 Monthly Ceremonies (Mexica)" she compiled from the ancient chronicles of ritual objects used by the Aztecs in their eighteen monthly ceremonies. Hundreds of items are included, ranging from paper banners to precious capes and feathers. Contemporary Nahua rituals include, among many other items, statuary, images of saints, crosses, decorated walking sticks, glowing beeswax and tallow candles, smoking incense braziers, coyol-palm leaf and marigold-blossom adornments, five-flower and seven-flower marigold wands, clay whistles, flowers tied at intervals onto vines, perfect maize-ear bundles, clothed images of seeds, and divination bundles containing maize kernels, coins, crystals, prehistoric figurines, and copper axes. The list does not count the abundance of ritual paper figures deployed during ritual offerings that are carefully manufactured and counted out, sometimes numbering in the tens of thousands. These objects and numerous other ritual implements are prominently on display during Nahua rituals held to mark the agricultural cycle throughout the year.

On offerings and ritual objects, Nahua anthropologist Arturo Gómez Martínez writes,

> The characteristics, derivation, and selection of the elements of the offering acquire important meanings in the logic of the ritual, depending on the goals expressed to the divinities. The offering not only integrates a grouping of things that are presented in the rite, they are gifts charged with messages and symbolism and allude to petitions, gratitude, commitments; by means of the objects, the link between humans and the sacred world is realized. (Gómez Martínez 2016:143, my translation)

The overall purpose of Nahua ritual is to recalibrate relations between forces in the universe and the human community. No matter how pragmatic or restricted in scope the immediate religious goals, participants view their efforts as a genuine attempt to reestablish the cosmic balance. Equilibrium is constantly threatened—whether from disrespectful behavior, neglect and failure to acknowledge the spirit entities, or the machinations of a sorcerer. It is almost as if, at any given moment, the universe is on the brink of dissolution and chaos. This state of affairs traces to the destruction of the sacred mountain Postectli and the severing of the link between earth and sky. For the Nahua, their immediate needs and the more abstract goals of maintaining balance and equilibrium are largely accomplished through the manipulation of objects. The strategy is clearly ancient, and we surmise it is related to the pantheistic nature of Mesoamerican religion (Sandstrom and Sandstrom 1986). We know that other pantheistic traditions such as sects of Buddhism and Hinduism are also highly object/image-oriented religions as well. In the end, the focus on tangible artifacts in Nahua rituals may be understood as a strategy to objectify and make more relevant for pragmatic ends the foundations of what we argue is a sophisticated and abstract religious and philosophical system. If a child is sick, rarefied thoughts about cosmic imbalance are of little comfort or help for distraught parents. The Nahua curer temporarily brings *totiotzin* into lived experience by cutting a paper figure of the disease-causing agent and through ritual means neutralizing it.

What is most important to remember about Nahua ritual objects (or even certain natural objects or special places in the landscape) is that they reveal or unconceal divinity, that is, they are object-subjects that are vehicles embodying aspects of *totiotzin*. They lead people to glimpse what lies beyond their own sense impressions. Far from being lifeless things, ritual objects disclose deity and are animated entities that are themselves agents. People can interact with created ritual objects because, if properly constructed, they are embodiments or manifestations of essential spiritual substance. The reason the Nahua cut paper figures in such profusion and load their altars with ritual items and food offerings is because they regard these entities as revealing of *totiotzin* and a focus of its energy. It is the unique knowledge of the ritual specialist coupled with the out-of-the-ordinary venue of the ritual itself that allow people to engage with ritual objects as a form of social activity. It is difficult for people of Western European cultural backgrounds to see objects as anything other than lifeless quantities of matter. The Nahua, by contrast, see all things as part of the fabric of a living cosmos that can impinge on human consciousness and act in congruence with or work against human interests and welfare.

Why then the proliferation of ritual objects? Why do Buddhists and Hindus surround themselves with statues, paintings, prayer wheels, bells, and incense? For the same reason that the Nahua venerate a Catholic saint's likeness, a festooned walking stick with ribbons the color of the sunrise, or the dizzying array of reduplicated cut-paper figures of a particular spirit entity: all reveal different aspects of *totiotzin*, providing a unique vehicle through which the sacred cosmos expresses itself. An altar laden with the proper objects properly arranged discloses more of the deity and increases the sacred value of the place of offerings. Ritual objects provide an additive function to the rituals. The greater the number and variety of objects, the more *totiotzin* is concentrated or focused: 10,000 sacred paper figures are 10,000 expressions of deity. It is precisely because of all of the objects they carry that Nahua altars are overwhelming power centers. The altar becomes a crucible where the energy of the cosmos converges.

For pantheists like the Nahua, *totiotzin* can be seen in natural objects that are colorful or that sparkle or glisten: the sun, the stars, lighted candles, the surface of the water, crystals, sea shells, mirrors, shiny colorful stones, and of course, flowers. To assemble objects that flash their qualities and shine vividly is to concentrate and focus the power of deity. *Totiotzin* can be seen as a tangible form of energy and lustrous or luminous things convey that power to the observer. Ethnographer Domingo España Soto recorded statements from Otomí ritual specialist Miguel Tolentino San Juan, who lives near Amatlán, that come very close to expressing the views presented in this chapter. The ritual specialist states, for instance that "they say that the flower is energy" when it is part of a ritual offering and that flowers are "the invention of light" (España Soto 2018:128; all translations mine). He says that is why "people always liked things that sparkle, things that call attention when making offerings to God" (2018:129). He goes on to state that "the sun is supposedly composed of various colors" (2018:129) and that the sun itself is "the presence of God" (2018:130). The ethnographer concludes that for the Otomí, "light is at the same time part of God, but also the same as God" (2018:130). In my view, people are attracted to luminescent things because they reveal *totiotzin* as a form of energy and make it possible to dedicate offerings to this elusive but critically important being. Viewed in this light it is interesting that the ancient Mesoamerican stone statues were painted in vivid colors much like ancient Greek sculptures (and temples too) (López Luján and Chiari 2012). Clearly the ancient Aztec artists were using colors to enhance the religious experience of the viewers of their efforts just as contemporary ritual specialists do today (Domenici, this volume).

CONCLUSION

In my view, this line of reasoning regarding the sacred explains a number of puzzling features of Mesoamerican culture and history. For example, it helps to illuminate the meaning of the stone caches that have been unearthed by archaeologists at the Aztec Templo Mayor site in Mexico City. These treasure boxes are filled with objects such as seashells, stingray spines, statuettes, colorful rocks and other objects, and even *amate* bark-paper placards with deities painted on them with rubber (Barrera et al. 2001; López Luján 2009, 2018). It seems that all of these objects concentrate the power of *teotl* and fix the Aztec capital as the religious center of the empire. It became a place where the deity dramatically revealed itself. In another example, one wonders if the clay figurines found so commonly in archaeological contexts in Mesoamerica are remnants of ancient attempts to embody the sacred principle for ritual purposes, similar to the use of cut-paper figures among the Nahua, Otomí, and Tepehua of the Huasteca and surrounding regions today. The anthropomorphic figurines embody aspects of *teotl* designed to address specific concerns of the households that employ them. Perhaps by this same reasoning we might offer an alternative explanation for the marvelous green serpentine pavements stacked one on top of the other beneath the courtyard at the Olmec site of La Venta (Map 1). Resembling the stacked plates of a storage battery, the construction embodied deity and thereby transformed the site into a concentrated center of religious power.

I think we can answer the question of why flowers and the worlds they create are so important to the Nahua: it is because they manifest *totiotzin* and provide a glimpse into a splendid reality normally concealed from people in their day-to-day lives. They are a living embodiment of what lies at the heart of existence. They do not symbolize the flower world: they give form to it. A garden is an ordered arrangement of plant life that allows people to experience directly the power and beauty of the seamless, sacred cosmos—a conception that for the Nahuas is *teotl–totiotzin*. Flowers are expressions of that cosmos, part of the whole, proof of the ordered beauty that transcends human beings' fragmented experiences of reality and shows the face of *totiotzin* to the people who believe and respect the things of this world.

NOTE

1. The narratives summarized here are publicly accessible at the Archives of the Indigenous Languages of Latin America (AILLA) at the University of Texas, Austin, Benson Latin American Studies and Collections, available after free registration at https://ailla.utexas.org/.

REFERENCES

Barrera Rivera, José Álvaro, Ma. de Lourdes Gallardo Parrodi, and Aurora Montúfar López. 2001. "La ofrenda 102 del Templo Mayor." *Arqueología Mexicana* 8(48):70–77.

Beyer, Hermann. 1965. "El ídolo azteca de Alejandro de Humboldt." In *Obras completas*, edited by Carmen Cook de Leonard, 1:390–401. El México antiguo 10. Mexico City: Sociedad Alemana Mexicanista.

Burkhart, Louise. 1992a. "The Amanuenses Have Appropriated the Text: Interpreting a Nahuatl Song of Santiago." In *On the Translation of Native American Literatures*, edited by Brian Swann, 339–55. Washington, D.C.: Smithsonian Institution Press.

Burkhart, Louise. 1992b. "Flowery Heaven: The Aesthetic of Paradise in Nahuatl Devotional Literature." *RES: Anthropology and Aesthetics* 21:88–109.

Cruz, Abelardo de la. 2017. "The Value of El Costumbre and Christianity in the Discourse of Nahua Catechists from the Huasteca Region in Veracruz, Mexico, 1970s–2010s." In *Words and Worlds Turned Around: Indigenous Christianities in Colonial Latin America*, edited by David Tavárez, 267–88, Boulder: University Press of Colorado.

España Soto, Domingo. 2018. "La historia de la flor en 'el costumbre' otomí = The Story of the Flower in the Otomí *costumbre*." *Anales de antropología* 52(2):123–40.

Gómez Martínez, Arturo. 2016. "Las ofrendas aritméticas entre los nahuas de la Huasteca veracruzana." In *"Convocar a los dioses": Ofrendas mesoamericanas; estudios antropológicas, históricos y comparativos*, corr. and augmented 2nd ed., Serie Antropológica 26, edited by Johanna Broda, 143–67. Mexico City: Universidad Nacional Autónoma de México, Instituto de Investigaciones Históricas.

Good Eshelman, Catherine. 2001. "Oztotempan: El ombligo del mundo." In *La montaña en el paisaje ritual*, edited by Johanna Broda, Stanislaw Iwaniszewski, and Arturo Montero García, 375–93. Mexico City: Instituto Nacional de Antropología e Historia; Universidad Nacional Autónoma de México, Instituto de Ciencias Sociales y Humanidades; Consejo Nacional para la Cultura y las Artes, Fondo de Cultura Económica.

Hays-Gilpin, Kelley, and Jane Hill. 1999. "The Flower World in Material Culture: An Iconographic Complex in the Southwest and Mesoamerica." *Journal of Anthropological Research* 55(1):1–37.

Hill, Jane H. 1992. "The Flower World of Old Uto-Aztecan." *Journal of Anthropological Research* 48(2):117–44.

Hunt, Eva. 1977. *The Transformation of the Hummingbird: Cultural Roots of a Zinacantecan Mythical Poem*. Ithaca, N.Y.: Cornell University Press.

Ichon, Alain. 1973. *La religión de los Totonacas de la Sierra*. 1st Spanish ed. Colección SEP-INI no. 16. Mexico City: Instituto Nacional Indigenista, Secretaría de Educación Pública. Originally published 1969 as *La religion des Totonaques de la Sierra: Etudes et documents de l'Institut d'Ethnologie*, Paris: Centre National de la Recherche Scientifique.

Kaufman, Terrence. 1994. "The Native Languages of Meso-America." In *Atlas of the World's Languages*, edited by Christopher Moseley and R. E. Asher, 34–41. London: Routledge.

Lévi-Strauss, Claude. 1969. *The Raw and the Cooked*. New York, N.Y.: Harper and Row.

López Austin, Alfredo. 1997. *Tamoanchan, Tlalocan: Places of Mist*. Mesoamerican Worlds. Niwot: University Press of Colorado.

López Luján, Leonardo. 2005. *The Offerings of the Templo Mayor of Tenochtitlan*. Rev. ed. Albuquerque, N.Mex.: University of New Mexico Press.

López Luján, Leonardo. 2009. "Aguas petrificadas: Las ofrendas a Tláloc enterradas en el Templo Mayor de Tenochtitlan." *Arqueología Mexicana* 16(96): 52–57.

López Luján, Leonardo. 2018. "The Codex Mendoza and the Archaeology of Tenochtitlán." In *Mesoamerican Manuscripts: New Scientific Approaches and Interpretations*, edited by Maarten Jansen, Virginia M. Lladó-Buisán, and Ludo Snijders, 15–44. The Early Americas: History and Culture, vol. 8. Leiden, Neth.: Brill.

López Luján, Leonardo, and Ciacomo Chiari. 2012. "Color in Monumental Mexica Sculpture." *RES: Anthropology and Aesthetics* 61/62:330–42.

Maffie, James. 2014. *Aztec Philosophy: Understanding a World in Motion*. Boulder: University Press of Colorado.

Monaghan, John. 2000. "Theology and History in the Study of Mesoamerican Religions." In *Supplement to the Handbook of Middle American Indians*, vol. 6, *Ethnology*, edited by Victoria R. Bricker and John D. Monaghan, 24–49. Austin: University of Texas Press.

Sandstrom, Alan R. 1991. *Corn Is Our Blood: Culture and Ethnic Identity in a Contemporary Aztec Indian Village*. Civilization of the American Indian Series,

vol. 206. Norman: University of Oklahoma Press; 2012 Internet Archive edition, https://archive.org/details/cornisourbloodcuoosand/, accessed January 4, 2020.

Sandstrom, Alan R., and Pamela Effrein Sandstrom. 1986. *Traditional Papermak-
ing and Paper Cult Figures of Mexico*. Norman: University of Oklahoma Press;
2012 Internet Archive edition, https://archive.org/details/traditionalpapeoo
sand/, accessed January 4, 2020.

Sandstrom, Alan R., and Pamela Effrein Sandstrom. 2020. "Sorcery and Counter-
Sorcery Among the Nahua of Northern Veracruz, Mexico." In *Mesoamerican
Sorcery*, edited by Jeremy D. Coltman and John M. D. Pohl. Boulder: Uni-
versity of Colorado Press.

Taube, Karl A. 2004. "Flower Mountain: Concepts of Life, Beauty, and Paradise
Among the Classic Maya." In *RES: Anthropology and Aesthetics* 45:69–96.

Williams García, Roberto. 1963. *Los Tepehuas*. Xalapa: Universidad Veracruzana.

2

Becoming Peyote, or the Flowers of Wirikuta

Johannes Neurath

To find an adequate way to understand native people of the Americas in their unity as well as in their diversity has proven challenging for anthropology. Cultural similarities can be detected, sometimes among very distant people (Lévi-Strauss 1964–1971), and scholars then sometimes develop a certain enthusiasm for comparison. However, because of lacunae in our sources and the limitations of archaeology and historical linguistics, the common history of Native American people is difficult to grasp. Even neighboring groups often show an astonishing degree of diversity. It is thus apparent that Native American people like diversity, and they appreciate being distinguishable from their neighbors. As a consequence, other scholars studying Native American cultures have developed a preference for particularism (eventually focusing on small regions) and cultivate skepticism about comparative approaches.

As most approaches seem to overstate either unity or diversity, what would a comparativist middle ground look like? Jane Hill's study on the chromatic "Flower Worlds" that appear in Uto-Aztecan and Mesoamerican ritual songs has proved to be one of the most inspiring proposals. It is a concept that can be useful to reconstruct the legacy of proto-Uto-Aztecan culture (Hill 1992; 2001), the common culture of northwest Mexico (Bonfiglioli et al. 2004), or historical and cultural connections between Mesoamerica and the North American Southwest (Hays-Gilpin and Hill 2000). It has also become part of efforts to construct a model for a shared Mesoamerican worldview, connecting Teotihuacan and the Classic Maya (McNeil, this volume; Taube 2004), as well as Late Postclassic Central Mexico and Early Colonial Christianity (Alcántara 2011; Córdova, González López and Vázquez Vallín, and Pohl, this volume). In a recent publication, Berenice Alcántara gives a definition of flower world: "The flower world was the upper realm of reality, a place full of light, heat, fire, war, singing, and dancing—a world in which forces and powers manifested themselves among humankind through colored flowers and other brightly colored and iridescent natural phenomena" (Alcántara 2011:121–22). Of course, it makes sense: Indigenous ideas about the luminous part of the cosmos fused with Christian notions about paradise. On the other hand, I think it is a pity Hill's flower world became almost indistinguishable from more commonplace Mesoamerican cosmovision studies. In this way, some of the potential of the original proposal may have been lost.

FLOWER WORLD REVISITED

In 1999 Jane Hill visited Mexico. I remember a seminar attended by many members of the new generation of graduate students and researchers working on Wixárika (Huichol), Cora, and Tarahumara topics (Map 2). We were inspired to create an online journal called *Flower World* with Philip (Ted) Coyle as editor. Not many numbers were published and, sadly, the journal is not available any longer.[1] Renewed interest in comparison materialized in books like *Por los caminos de maíz* (Neurath 2008) and the three volumes of *Las vías del Noroeste* (Bonfiglioli et al. 2006–2011).

The original proposal by Hill was largely inspired by the Yaqui (Yoeme) concept of *sea ania* (Evans and Molina 1987; Molina and Shorter, this volume). Other main ingredients were the songs of the Paiute, Shoshone, Cupeño, Pima, and Tohono O'odam as documented by different anthropologists; Classic Nahuatl sources studied by John Bierhorst and Miguel León-Portilla; and Maya texts from Chiapas and Guatemala. Although reference was made to textual sources in the Huichol language, Wixárika ethnography played an important role in the formulation of "Flower World." Hill mainly used Barbara Myerhoff's (1974) *Peyote Hunt*, a well-written, easy-to-read book that many of my colleagues (and I) do not take all that seriously. Allegedly it is based on only one week of fieldwork. This information, provided by Jay Fikes (1993) in his controversial book *Carlos Castañeda, Academic Opportunism, and the Psychedelic Sixties*, may be a bit exaggerated or perhaps not entirely true, but the writings of Myerhoff clearly belong to the "psychedelic phase of Huichol ethnography" (Galinier 2004:268–72). In the late 1960s and 1970s, there was a whole group of mostly American authors who wrote extensively on shamanism, *hikuri* (peyote, *Lophophora williamsii*), and similar topics. Critics call them "peyotecentrist" (Neurath 2002) or "shamaniac" (Klein et al. 2002). Most of them had close links to the countercultures of the late 1960s and took fieldwork rather easy (Jáuregui 2005). Hill did not quote better or more recent literature because in 1992 there was not much available. Without doubt, more information on Huichol rituals might have been useful for her theory. In this chapter, I would like to add some information on Wirikuta and the Wixáritari,[2] mainly to balance some aspects of Hill's conceptual framework or its reception in order to ward off the influence of cosmovision.

The Huichols are famous for their peyote rituals but also for their colorful art, a topic that I have written about extensively (Neurath 2013). The principal Wixárika communities are located in the southern Sierra Madre Occidental in rugged canyon lands that are divided between four states of the Mexican Republic: Jalisco, Nayarit, Durango, and Zacatecas.[3] The term *Wirikuta* refers to an area in northern San Luis Potosí that is actually quite far away from where the Huichol live today. The Wixáritari travel there to collect peyote and to visit some of their most important ritual sites that are located in this locale.

Is it correct to talk about flower world when talking about Wirikuta? *Tuutu*, "peyote flower," as well as *xuturi*, "paper flower" (as used in rituals), are terms used to refer to the peyote seekers. In speaking about the Huichol Flower World, we must discuss ritual actions and ritual agents. I have been studying Huichol culture for several decades, and I still haven't figured out a proper etymology for the term *Wirikuta*. Wixárika ritual terms are often enigmatic. In their own folk-etymological practice, the Huichol themselves often translate Wirikuta as *desierto floreado*, or "flowering desert," but linguistically this seems not to be the exact meaning of the term. But it is quite clear that whenever the Huichols talk about the flowers of Wirikuta, they refer to peyotes and peyote seekers.

In reading Hill's article, one may say that it somehow sounds a bit too "naturalistic," especially when she defines flower world as a realm of metaphoric and symbolic meaning. Is it appropriate to define flower world as an Indigenous conception of the desert? The Eurocentrism implied in such an argument has been criticized by, among others, Alfred Hallowell (1960), Roy Wagner (1981), Kenneth Morrison (1992), Bruno Latour (1993), Eduardo Viveiros de Castro (1998) and Philippe Descola

(2012). Those authors, often grouped together as "ontological anthropologists," try to take Indigenous concepts and practices more seriously, even literally, trying to "denaturalize" Western dichotomies on what is naturally given and what is culturally constructed. Obviously, when Jane Hill wrote her paper in the early 1990s, questioning "Western Naturalism" as just one of the possible epistemologies was not yet such a big topic in anthropology as it has become now.

Based on my own experience, I also want to contextualize Huichol peyote rituals as part of initiation and emphasize the ambiguity of the deities and the initiated people associated with flower world. In contrast to what is usually said, there are more sinister aspects as well. At least in the case of Wixárika ritual cosmology, the conception of flower world as a luminous realm opposed to darkness is a bit too simple. So I will try to get beyond the dualist worldview that Mesoamericanist scholars like to project on Native American people.

As Hill notes, the flowers of Wirikuta are "beautiful," and they have a dreamlike quality. But the flowery desert does not exist independently of ritual action. It is envisioned by the peyote seekers. In that experience, initiates become peyote, the "blue flowers" (*tuutu muyuyuawi*) (de la Cruz 1993). As "Hikuri-people" (*hikuritamete*; Spanish, *peyoteros*) they turn into peyote and into their own ancestors. They are able to perceive the world as peyotes and, therefore, envision the (first) sunrise (Color Plate 4).

However, it must be noted that transforming into deities is quite dangerous. The initiates have to be careful not to take the rituals too far. Some peyote seekers suffer from "bad trips," while others are unable to endure the physical hardships involved in participating in peyote rituals. On the other hand, peyote seekers face difficulties during their reintegration into the communities they had to leave behind during their "pilgrimages" and hunting trips. When they come back, they can become dangerous for the noninitiated. As deities, they also are pathogenic agents or even hunters of people. The ancestors may be enemies. Normally they only attack people when they feel neglected, but you never know what may happen when you deal with ancestral beings. The ordinary people who stayed at home and did not participate in the peyote hunt may get sick just from looking at the initiates. Thus, coming back from Wirikuta is the most complicated part of the whole ritual cycle. With regard to flower world, understanding the ambiguity of the "peyote-flowers" is a challenge.

ONTOLOGY AND ETHICS OF WIRIKUTA

One aspect of Wirikuta that cannot be overestimated is the emotions it evokes among those Huichol who have been there. They are intense memories and feelings, above all sentiments of generosity and compassion but also of nostalgia. It is a place of intense collective experiences where a lot can be learned and where inspiration can be found. People enjoy being there and, afterwards, they remember many details, including specific songs and visions. Such experiences may be recalled many decades later. I have met Wixárika artists working on yarn paintings that depict visions they had experienced many years before. Also, I know a famous Huichol musician who dreamed five books of songs. Until now, he has performed and released only a part of the songs that he already knows.

On the other hand, Wirikuta is an elusive place. You can't really get to Wirikuta until you die, so the experience of being in Wirikuta has to be partial. Simultaneously, you have to be there and not to be there. Listening to the syncopated, microtonal, largely improvised music of the Huichol *sones de peyote*, played with *xaweri* and *kanari* (small violins and guitars), provides an idea about what might be called the Huichols' "infinitesimal" approximation to Wirikuta. The same can be said about Huichol visual art, like yarn painting, with its fluid and ambivalent but always well-structured aesthetics (Neurath 2013).

Accounts of Huichols traveling to Wirikuta to collect peyote have become cliché. It is by far the best-known Huichol ritual, as it has been shown in several documentaries and vividly described by writer Fernando Benítez (1984 [1968]). In recent decades, Real de Catorce, the former mining town close to Wirikuta, has established itself as a hot spot for international psychedelic drug tourism (Kindl 2017). Understandably, in such a context many misunderstandings have been produced, and misrepresentations have been popularized.

What Huichol peyote seekers do is often called a "pilgrimage," a term I find to be somehow inadequate. The Huichol don't "adore" peyote, nor do they "visit" their gods. The whole ritual is about becoming peyote and becoming deities. In order to have a better understanding of what goes on in Huichol peyote rituals, it may be useful to have an understanding of certain quite fundamental differences from other religions. Sanctuaries of Christianity and Islam are places that are considered to have been in physical contact with a deity, a prophet, or a saint at some moment in time. In this sense they follow a logic of contagion as in the veneration of relics. Believers seek to be physically close to God or the sacred. Asian religions, too, are organized around places of pilgrimage. Temples are believed to be inhabited by deities, and humans have the obligation to visit them at their places. Huichol gods mainly exist in ritual contexts. Generally speaking, they are not beings that exist independently from humans and human ritual action. Peyote seekers become them. Talking about "pilgrimage" obscures this important aspect. For the same reason it is not adequate to talk about peyote as a drug or an "entheogen." In the case of the Wixárika, users turn into the drug they take.

Huichol peyote seeking is best understood as a collective initiatory vision quest. The final destination is Paritek+a, the "Place Under the Sunrise," where the Sun is born, a place also known as Burnt Hill, Reu'unaxi. Perhaps the only problem with the term *vision quest* could be not taking into account what might be called "sonic visions." *Peyote hunt* is an adequate term, too, because peyote seeking is actually experienced as a deer hunt. Huichol peyote seekers run behind the deer, but when they reach the desert, Our Elder Brother, the deer, gives in to the hunters and through this voluntary sacrifice obtains *nierika*, or "visionary ability," and transforms into peyote. As *hikuri* is actually a deer, peyote is hunted. As peyote seekers ingest the deer transformed into peyote, they turn into *hikuri* themselves.

Did I say desert? No, "Flower World" is not a desert. Wirikuta is full of colors and full of flowers. How should we understand that according to the Huichols, those colors and flowers are not just the result of a hallucinatory perception of an otherwise arid and barren landscape? The ontological status of Wirikuta is like certain relevant dream visions that are not just dreams. Such experiences refer to an actual reality, but it isn't a reality that is naturally given. In this sense, again following Roy Wagner's (1981) *Invention of Culture*, it is important to emphasize that from the Huichols' perspective, Wirikuta is not a "natural area" where one goes in order to collect specimens of *Lophophora williamsii*. Wirikuta and the psychotropic cactus are better understood as being artificial, as something made by the Huichols. In this context, peyote is understood as an ancestor who lives in the desert for ethical reasons. It is an austere vision seeker who practices self-sacrifice, setting an example for his younger brothers, the Wixáritari.

PARTIAL TRANSFORMATION

Participating in the peyote hunt means going through a whole range of practices of austerity, purification, and "self-sacrifice," such as fasting, sleep deprivation, and enduring long hikes through the desert. Initiates identify with peyote and/or deer because they embody the shamanic ideal of austerity. At some point, Peyote-Deer starts to sympathize with the peyote hunters. Here, the *hikuri* appears in front of the pilgrims like a deer that agrees to be killed by the hunters. It does so because, in the words of the pilgrims, "it feels sorry" for the hunters. According to other accounts, peyote grows from the trails of the deer while chased by the peyote hunters.

The effect of the hallucinogenic is the light of dawn. Learning to see like a peyote, the *jicareros* become "peyote-people," or *hikuritamete*. They put on special hats with feather decorations that look like—and are—peyote flowers. In a multinaturalist dynamic (similar to other cases studied by Viveiros de Castro [1998]), the *peyotero* takes the perspective of peyote, so he becomes peyote, and he becomes flowering peyotes, because he dresses as one.

The observation that peyote is not just a "drug" should direct our attention to a bigger cultural complex in relation to what Westerners call the Native American use of "psychoactive substances." In the South American Lowlands, the use of psychedelic or psychoactive plants follows the same logic of transformation. An example would be Pierre Déléage's account of the Sharanawa identifying *ayahuasca* and the anaconda and transforming into the anaconda when using *ayahuasca* (Déléage 2009).

Huichol identification with *hikuri* goes through a series of stages. First, peyote seekers identify with the deer allowing itself to be killed. Then, they learn to see like a peyote. They perceive the world differently, through peyote's eyes. That means, above all, they perceive a greater amount of light. In this state, they are able to envision the sunrise. Yellow face paint made of a root called *uxa* are the reflections of the rising sun and other visions on the faces of the peyote seekers. On the way back from Wirikuta they wear special hats featuring peyote flowers made of white turkey feathers. Now they are *hikuritamete*, "peyote people." Finally, they also envision the "cloud snakes"—the first rain, and thus the respiration (*iyari*) of the world. When they arrive back in their communities they transform into a giant cloud snake, and as such they appear during the big Peyote Festival. As a group, initiates turn into the first Huichols, that is, the original community of their own ancestors. In this sense, they are their own deities, the ones who are—and live at—the sacred spots of ritual landscape as well as in the temples and shrines of the ceremonial centers. They are powerful and dangerous, and for this reason not everybody welcomes them.

When practicing peyote initiation, it is important not to be an overachiever. In a way, transformation has to remain partial. A complete transformation would be irreversible and cause the initiate's death as a human. Occasionally, peyote seekers actually die of exhaustion during the rituals, and I was told that such deaths are often understood as a permanent transformation into a deity. Sleep deprivation is a central aspect of the Huichol vision quest and probably the hardest of all the exercises involved. After several days of consuming *hikuri*, initiates are often unable to sleep even if they would be allowed to do so. Together with isolation, dehydration, and exhaustion, such extreme sleep deprivation can be a serious health threat. So, participating in peyote initiation definitely has its risks, a fact that much of the "shamaniac" literature avoids mentioning.

FLOWER WORLD AS PART OF COMMUNITY ORGANIZATION

In order to avoid exoticizing misrepresentations of Huichol culture, it is important to contextualize flower world and peyote rituals. On one hand, Wirikuta is not the only sacred place with which the Huichols identify and visit. On the other hand, what we call "sacred places" are more than places. Sacred places are ancestors and, as such, they are living persons who are part of community organization and politics. Located in the geography, they are also part of the social hierarchy. The whole cosmos is a human "macrobody" with Wirikuta as the head or brain; other sacred spots correspond to other parts of the body (like the navel or the genitals), and water is identified with blood. The whole set of sacred spots is something like a "distributed collective self" of the Huichols obtaining initiatory visions.

Wirikuta is also a social category. Wixárika ritual is always focused on the reproduction and strengthening of community organization, or *kiekari*, a notion that includes not only Huichols' *rancheridad* but shared, animist humanity and the whole cosmos (Liffman 2011). The Wixárika deities have complex identities. They are artifacts, including gourd cups (*xukurite*) and arrows (*+r+te*), animals (many of them hunting humans), places distributed on the landscape, and actual people living in ceremonial centers called *callihuey* or *tukipa*, where they embody the original members of the community.

I have frequently heard that the ceremonial centers are the *kiete* or *rancherías* of the gods. A *ranchería* is the regional type of domestic unit of production and residence (Hinton 1974), and so a ceremonial center is a *ranchería* founded by the ancestors. In later times populations dispersed, and people founded more *rancherías*. However, in order to practice shamanic initiation and to serve in the religious hierarchy of the community, ordinary people go back to the original villages to be or to become the ancestors. During their incumbency, the cargo holders literally live in temples, using the names of the deities as their personal names.[4] In this sense, the ancestors continue living in the ceremonial centers.

The ones who are chosen to embody the deities are called the *xukuri'+kate*, or "holders of the gourd cups." In Spanish, which is widely spoken in the region beside the native languages, they are known as *jicareros*. For five years they are placed in charge of a set of ancient gourd bowls kept inside the temples of the ceremonial centers. Usually those gourds are wrapped in cloth, and it is quite impossible to have a look at them. As they are so "delicate" (*ma'iwe*), or "sacred," even the people in charge of them may not know how their gourd bowls look. Unsurprisingly, they have rarely been sold to collectors.

There seems to be a perfect system of correspondences and identifications connecting temples and deities, *jicareros* and *jícaras*, but there are subtleties to which we must pay attention. The gourd cups are the "mothers" or wombs from which the ancestral deities are born. So, until they finish shamanic initiation, the cargo holders are something like embryonic or baby gods. They embody the ancestors who are still common people because they have not yet been born as the deities. In every ceremonial center there is a limited set of sacred gourd cups and, ideally, there is one cargo holder for each cup. In the place I know best, Keuruwit+a in northern Jalisco, there are twenty-six *jícaras*. Occasionally a cargo holder may be in charge of two or even more cups, but this is considered an anomaly, and it is not well regarded because even a single cargo is considered difficult to fulfill.

The group of *jicareros* acts like a polygamic, hierarchized, extended Wixárika family composed of a great-grandfather (Tatutsi Maxakwaxi, Our Great-Grandfather Deer-Tail), a grandfather (Tatewarí, Our Grandfather, the fire), a grandmother (Takutsi, Our Grandmother), a father (Tayau, Our Father, the sun), several mothers (Tateiteime, Our Mothers of rain, clouds, or breath, and corn), and several elder brothers (Tamatsime, Our Elder Brothers, like deer, peyote, and wind). Additionally, there are *jícaras* for Kam+kime, the wolf, and for a group of five hunters (Awatamete) armed with rifles, bows, and arrows. They have to serve ten years and lead the groups of *jicareros*. Three singer-shamans—the *+r+k-wakame*, the *nauxatame*, and the *t+karimahana*, who are not *jicareros* any longer—act as the authorities of the ceremonial center.

All cargo holders are members of the community; most of them are young male adults, some are older men, some are females of different ages, and some of them are children. Even toddlers may be holders of a *jícara*. Their selection is a complicated process made up of several stages. First they are "dreamed" by the members of council of elders (the *kawiterutsixi*). Then they are proposed to the assembly and ratified. But the dreams of the elders may be rejected, so in this case they have to start over again.

Gender is an important factor. Women can only embody female ancestors, while men and male children can be in charge of any of the deities. So there may be a man called "Our Mother the Western Rain," or "Our Mother Corn," but no woman called "Our Grandfather Fire." Interestingly there is nothing humorous about a man called "Our Mother" despite the fact that the Wixáritari live in *machista* rural Mexico. After accomplishing a cargo for five years, a *jicarero* may be elected again, and in this case, they normally receive a more prestigious cargo. In order to become a *mara'akame*, "a person who knows to dream" (i.e., a ritual specialist such as a healer or a singer-shaman), normally one has to participate several times in groups of *jicareros*. Above all, initiation is always a matter of personal experience.

Specific Wixárika ancestral deities are identified with animals (e.g., deer), plants (e.g., corn), and elements of the cosmos (e.g., the sun, Morning Star, fire, wind, rain, certain lakes, rivers, springs, and waterholes). Because of the association between temples and sacred places, ancestral deities are also identified with landscape features. Huichol deities may be called "ancestor-toponyms" (Lira 2014), or "people-places," much like in Melanesian ethnography (Mondragón 2015:183–84). As deities are ambivalent beings, it is dangerous to visit their sacred places. One needs to practice purification and to acquire a special quality called *nierika*, which is, among other things, a "front shield" that allows approaching sacred spots and deities. *Nierika* is a polysemic term variously meaning cheek, face, mirror, picture, vision, visionary ability, and also shield (Kindl 2005; Negrín 1986; Neurath 2013).

Because of the identification of micro- and macrocosmos, rituals are celebrated on several scales. During the so-called pilgrimages, people actually travel to the sacred places. But during ceremonies celebrated inside the ceremonial center it is not much different. Participants permanently travel between the sea, the Place of Sunrise, and other spots just by dancing around the ceremonial center or walking up and down the stairways of the elevated shrines. Manipulating gourds and objects inside can also be understood as travels or "pilgrimages" in time and space (Coyle 2000).

PRACTICING EMERGENCE

According to my experience, Huichols do not see themselves as dependent on ancestral deities. Rather, they feel obliged to the ancestors, who are identified with the cargo holders and authorities. They feel responsible for carrying out the ongoing creation of a livable cosmos, and they are conscious of the importance of their own community organization and ritual system as the basis of their political autonomy—that is, everything they define as *kiekari*. Becoming an ancestor means emerging from a gourd bowl and turning into an "arrow-person." In order to be born from the gourds, the *jicareros* practice a vision quest, which should be an experience as similar as possible to what the ancestors underwent, according to Wixárika stories of origin. Basically, they emerge from the sea in the West (also identified with a gourd cup) and search for the Place of Sunrise to be discovered in the East. To find the dawn, or to "wake up," one must practice sacrifice and purification and refrain or walk away from anything having to do with the sea, the underworld, and darkness. One should not eat salt, but should refrain from "sin" (basically defined as extramarital sex), sleep as little as possible, and traverse the arid steppes of the Mexican highlands (which are quite far away from the coast). Because of the importance of vision quests, the "pilgrimage" to the place of sunrise is considered their most important ritual activity. But it is not the only one. During the five years that they live in the "*ranchería* of the gods," they cultivate a communal cornfield, renovate the buildings, and fulfill many other tasks.

At some moment, *jicareros* eventually conclude initiation, and one aspect of them turns into an "arrow-person" (+r+kate) or "grandfather" (*teukari*), a living ancestor, who manifests himself or herself as a little stone (sometimes a rock crystal) that is wrapped in cloth, attached to a votive arrow, and kept in a shrine belonging to a family or kinship group. An arrow-person manifests to a member of the community who already has accomplished initiation. Frequently, the little stone appears in a bowl of corn beer.

Finding someone's +r+kame is an act of recognition. A person who has manifested as an arrow-person is regarded as a *mara'akame*, "one who knows how to dream." But like *hikuritamete* (the homecoming peyote seekers), arrow-people are dangerous. Arrow-people are not clearly distinguished from other pathogens, are in the form of arrows that make people sick, and are often extracted in sessions of shamanic healing. Interestingly enough, the arrow-people belong to the small ceremonial centers (*xirikite*) of the *rancherías*, families, and kinship groups, which are considered to be far lower in hierarchy than the ceremonial centers of the communities. Ancestors who have not yet become deities live in the communal ceremonial center; the ones who turned into deities belong to the families and kinship groups.

THE HUICHOL AGAINST FLOWER WORLD

The most interesting phase in Huichol ritual is the moment when the peyote seekers' rituals of gift and sacrifice come to an end and general emphasis switches back to ritualized exchange, which happens at a crucial moment during the peyote dance Hikuli Neixa. This is the main event of the Huichol ritual year, and it is held at the communal ceremonial centers (*tukipa*) toward the end of the dry season. Lasting for five days and nights, this event culminates in the appearance of a feathered "cloud serpent" (Haiku), who descends from the Place of Sunrise (Paritek+a) located in the east. This is not unlike the serpent descending Flower Mountain in Classic Maya and Teotihuacan iconography as noted by Taube (2004).

During the Huichol peyote dance, the peyote people collectively transform into the cloud snake (Haiku), the breath of the world, now using the white feathers as part of their regalia. Haiku is composed of twenty-five to thirty-five homecoming peyote pilgrims, and its arrival on the dance ground is the arrival of the first rains. At the same time, they give out great amounts of peyote, corn, and calabash seeds to members of the community. In addition, each member of the group also embodies a specific ancestral deity, making the cloud snake a composite being containing all of the assembled ancestors. Because of the fact that all deified ancestors may be conceived as deer, during certain parts of the choreography the *peyoteros* jump around in imitation of deer and also mimic other forms of this animal's behavior. Throughout this dance, they frequently assemble in order to form a giant snake head which attacks imprudent bystanders.

Their peyote dancing is actually the last of a whole series of rituals that began several months earlier. After weeks of hardship—including travels to faraway places such as the semidesert of Wirikuta, the deer hunt, vision quest, all kinds of nocturnal ceremonies, fasting, reclusion, sexual abstinence, daily ingestion of peyote, and also hard work on cornfields— the dancers perceive their return to the ceremonial center as a triumph. As they are not yet fully reintegrated into the community, they are as dangerous as rattlesnakes. Some of them may have gone through ritual near-death experiences. Having obtained the visionary ability (*nierika*) of shamans (*mara'akate*), they now are the ancestral deities. As the ancestral deities they create and invent the world through their own self-sacrifice. They have managed to obtain visions and to transform themselves into the objects of their visions, like peyote and deer, rain snakes and sunlight. Giving out peyote and seeds during the final peyote dance is part of this generous giving away of themselves.

In terms of Maurice Bloch's (1986) theory of "rebounding violence," things are not always as neat during the final phase of initiation processes.

Huichol rituals are not really functional in reaffirming or creating social hierarchies. The peyote seekers (now turned into ancestors) cannot reconquer the community they had left as ordinary human beings. The people of the village, those who had remained at home, are reluctant to receive gifts of the peyote seekers. Even more, they do not treat them with much respect; rather, they make fun of them. Certain dances consist of non-*peyoteros* hunting *peyoteros* down like deer. Deer paradigmatically gives itself to the shamanic hunter, but here not much respect is shown for the captured deer-gods.

The *peyoteros* actually became the ancestors, but they are treated like impostors or as ordinary people pretending to be something special. They may even be called show-offs or *mamones* (in Spanish). Non-*peyoteros* receive the gifts of the returning peyoteros, but they oblige them to accept tiny tamales, cigarettes, or small coins as "payment." They do so partly to neutralize the *peyoteros'* dangerousness because initiated people tend to become all too powerful in communities. Religious and political power has to be brought under communal control.

CONCLUSION

The Huichol Flower World, as a realm of the "free gift," is productive in terms of world making. Knowledge, light, and time only exist because of the initiates' generosity and visionary experiences. On the other hand, shamanic power has to be limited to avoid the formation of centralized forms of traditional government, like *cacicazgos*. The distrust common people show for the shamans and the *peyoteros* has important political implications. As the creators of everything important, initiated people have an enormous potential to accumulate and to abuse power. Moreover, the beings whom initiates create in their visions are dangerous. Whenever those beings are neglected or otherwise not treated correctly in rituals, they may turn into pathological agents. The gifts of the gods and the shamans have to be tamed and incorporated into a framework of ritualized exchange. In this sense, and as a conclusion, it is important to point out that Wirikuta, the Huichol Flower World—which is presumably equivalent or comparable to the "time-spaces" of other North and Middle American Native people—should always be understood in its ontological and relational complexity.

NOTES

1. A couple of years later, another volume series called Flower World (edited by Arnd Adje Both) was initiated to focus on "music archaeology" in the Americas.

2. Plural of *Wixárika*.

3. My research on Huichol ritual (Neurath 2002) is based on ethnographic fieldwork with the community of Tuapurie in northern Jalisco.

4. Traditional civil-religious hierarchies of Latin American peasant and Indigenous communities are usually called cargo systems.

REFERENCES

Alcántara, Berenice. 2011. "In Nepapan Xochitl: The Power of Flowers in the Works of Sahagún. In *Colors Between Two Worlds.*" In *The Florentine Codex of Bernardino de Sahagún*, edited by Joseph Connors and Gerhard Wolf, 106–32. Florence: Kunsthistorisches Institut in Florenz, Max-Planck-Institut, Villa I Tatti, and the Harvard University Center for Italian Renaissance Studies.

Benítez, Fernando. 1984 [1968]. *Los indios de México.* Vol. 2, *Los huicholes.* Mexico City: Editorial Era.

Bloch, Maurice. 1986. *From Blessing to Violence: History and Ideology in the Circumcision Ritual of the Merina of Madagascar.* Cambridge: Cambridge University Press.

Bonfiglioli, Carlo, Arturo Gutiérrez, and María Eugenia Olavarría. 2004. "De la violencia mítica al 'mundo flor': Transformaciones de la Semana Santa en el Norte de México." *Journal de la Société des Américanistes* 90(1):57–92.

Bonfiglioli, Carlo, Arturo Gutiérrez, and María Eugenia Olavarría, eds. 2006–2011. *Las vías del noroeste: Una macrorregión indígena americana*, 3 vols. Mexico City: Universidad Nacional Autónoma de México.

Coyle, Philip E. 2000. "To Join the Waters: Indexing Metonymies of Territoriality in Cora Ritual." *Journal of the Southwest* 42(1):119–28.

De la Cruz, Xitakame Julio. 1993. *Wixarika N+awarieya: La canción huichola.* Guadalajara.: Universidad de Guadalajara.

Déléage, Pierre. 2009. *Le chant de l'anaconda: L'apprentissage du chamanisme chez les Sharanahua (Amazonie occidentale).* Paris: Société d'Ethnologie.

Descola, Philippe. 2012. *Más allá de naturaleza y cultura.* Buenos Aires: Amorrortu.

Evers, Larry, and Felipe S. Molina. 1987. *Yaqui Deer Songs/Maso Bwikam: A Native American Poetry.* Tucson: University of Arizona Press.

Fikes, Jay C. 1993. *Carlos Castañeda, Academic Opportunism, and the Psychedelic Sixties.* Victoria, BC: Millenia Press.

Galinier, Jacques. 2004. "Reseña de Neurath, Johannes, Las fiestas de la Casa Grande." *Journal de la Société des Américanistes* 90(1):268–72.

Hallowell, Alfred I. 1960. "Ojibwa Ontology, Behavior, and World View." In *Culture in History: Essays in Honor of Paul Radin*, edited by Stanley Diamond, 19–52. New York: Columbia University Press.

Hays-Gilpin, Kelley, and Jane H. Hill. 2000. "The Flower World in Prehistoric Southwest Material Culture." In *The Archaeology of Regional Interaction: Religion, Warfare, and Exchange Across the American Southwest and Beyond*, edited by Michelle Hegmon, 411–28. Boulder: University of Colorado Press.

Hill, Jane H. 1992. "The Flower World of Old Uto-Aztecan." *Journal of Anthropological Research* 48(2):117–44.

Hill, Jane H. 2001. "Proto-Uto-Aztecan: A Community of Cultivators in Central Mexico?" *American Anthropologist*, n. s., 103(4):913–33.

Hinton, Thomas B. 1974. "Northern Mexican Indian." In *Encyclopedia Britannica*, 15th ed., 245–49. Chicago: Encyclopedia Britannica.

Jáuregui, Jesús. 2005. "La región cultural del Gran Nayar y los estudios sobre su area septentrional: Tepehuanes del sur, mexicaneros y tepecanos." In *Las regiones indígenas en el espejo bibliográfico*, vol. 3, edited by Jesús Jáuregui and Aída Castilleja, 235–305. Mexico City: Instituto Nacional de Antropología e Historia.

Kindl, Olivia. 2005. "L'art du nierika chez les Huichols du Mexique: Un instrument pour voir." In *Les cultures à l'oeuvre: Recontres en art*, edited by Michèle Coquet, Brigitte Derlon, and Monique Jeudy-Ballini, 225–48. Paris: Éditions de la Maison des sciences de l'homme.

Kindl, Olivia. 2017. "Mostrar y ocultar ofrendas en el altiplano potosino." In *Mostrar y ocultar en el arte y los rituales: Perspectivas comparativas*, edited by Guilhem Olivier and Johannes Neurath, 293–338. Mexico City: Universidad Nacional Autónoma de México.

Klein, Cecelia, Eulogio Guzmán, Elisa Mandell, and Maya Stanfeld-Mazzi. 2002. "The Role of Shamanism in Mesoamerican Art: A Reassessment." *Current Anthropology* 43(3):383–419.

Latour, Bruno. 1993. *We Have Never Been Modern*. Cambridge, Mass.: Harvard University Press.

Lévi-Strauss, Claude. 1964–1971. *Mitologiques*. 4 vols. Paris: Plon.

Liffman, Paul. 2011. *Huichol Territory and the Mexican Nation: Indigenous Ritual, Land Conflict, and Sovereignty Claims*. Tucson: University of Arizona Press.

Lira, Regina. 2014. "L'alliance entre la Mère Maïs et le Frère Aîné Cerf: Action, chant et image dans un rituel wixárika (huichol) du Mexique." Unpublished Ph.D. dissertation. École des Hautes Études en Sciences Sociales, Paris.

Mondragón, Carlos. 2015. *Un entramado de islas: Persona, medio ambiente y cambio climático en el Pacífico Occidental*. Mexico City: El Colegio de México.

Morrison, Kenneth M. 1992. "Beyond the Supernatural: Language and Religious Action." *Religion* 22(3):201–5.

Myerhoff, Barbara G. 1974. *Peyote Hunt: The Sacred Journey of the Huichol Indians*. Ithaca, N.Y.: Cornell University Press.

Negrín, Juan. 1986. *Nierica: Espejo entre dos mundos; Arte contemporáneo huichola.* Mexico City: Museo de Arte Moderno.

Neurath, Johannes. 2002. *Las fiestas de la Casa Grande: Procesos rituales, cosmovisión y estructura social en una comunidad huichola.* Mexico City: Instituto Nacional de Antropología e Historia.

Neurath, Johannes, ed. 2008. *Por los caminos del maíz: Mito, ritual y cosmovisión en la periferia septentrional de Mesoamérica.* Mexico City: Biblioteca Mexicana, Consejo Nacional para la Cultura y las Artes, y Fondo de Cultura Económica.

Neurath, Johannes. 2013. *La vida de las imágenes: Arte huichol.* Mexico City: Artes de México, Consejo Nacional para la Cultura y las Artes.

Taube, Karl A. 2004. "Flower Mountain: Concepts of Life, Beauty, and Paradise Among the Classic Maya." *RES: Anthropology and Aesthetics* 45:69–98.

Viveiros de Castro, Eduardo. 1998. "Cosmological Deixis and Amerindian Perspectivism." *Journal of the Royal Anthropological Institute*, n. s., 4:469–88.

Wagner, Roy. 1981. *The Invention of Culture.* Chicago: Chicago University Press.

3

"The Living Beautiful Part of Our Present World"

The Yoeme *Sea Ania* (Flower World)

Felipe S. Molina and David Delgado Shorter

For many Yoeme people, the *sea ania* (flower world) is not imaginary or fantastical, nor is it located in distant history or the archaeological archive. The *sea ania* (like other *aniam*, "worlds") exists here and now, a beautiful part of our living world. In this essay, we first locate the Yoeme people (also known as "Yaquis") geographically and give some context to their worldviews, history, and culture. We pay particular attention to conceptions of *aniam* taken from our own experiences in the Yoeme communities. Next, we examine deer songs. One author, Felipe S. Molina, is a deer singer; he is most comfortable teaching Yoeme culture through deer songs. In the Yoeme context, deer songs provide precise interpretive access to the *sea ania*, or *sewa ania* in Yoeme song language.[1] We also use personal narratives to accentuate the vibrant, visceral, tangible, and beautiful aspects of the Yoeme flower world.

Yoeme communities span from their ancestral homeland, or *Yoem Bwiara*, in northern Mexico across the southwestern United States around Tucson and Phoenix in contemporary *Yoem Hoaram*, or Yoeme communities/homes (Map 2).[2] Oral tradition places their homeland around the *Hiak Vatwe*, or Yaqui River, winding through the Mexican state of Sonora. Precontact Yoeme lifeways appear in the stories of the *surem*, small proto-Yoemem living in complete unity with their environment. These ancestors, the original inhabitants of the *yoem bwiara*, communicated telepathically with all living beings. Yoeme people today speak of the *surem* specifically as fully interconnected in a shared, unified existence with plants, animals, and each other. Over time, this world would become differentiated into various *aniam*, which we will discuss later. Oral histories of the primary era recount that the world and all of life communicated without needing spoken language until a tree started making an unintelligible humming sound. After much confusion, a young woman translated the tree's prophecies that a group of people were coming over the ocean from the west; some of them would try to take the land; others would bring new technologies, missionaries, and subsequently a whole new way of living that would also include mortality. The prophecy led some *surem* to move into the hills and bodies of water where they could remain immortal, though they are able to cross from their world, now known as the *yo ania* ("enchanted world"), into our dimension. The rest of the *surem* (approximately half of them) stayed in the terrestrial *Yoem Bwiara* and grew to current human size, fought the invaders, and welcomed the Jesuits. As Shorter accentuated in chapter 3 of his book, *We Will Dance Our Truth: Yaqui History in Yoeme Performance* (2009), the *Konkista* (the real "conquest" in Yoeme history) took place as the community responded to the tree's prophecy by factionalizing. Yoemem significantly interpret their own people's historic disruption as internal, consciously denying European agency in contact.

Having defeated Spanish armies three times between 1533 and 1609, Yoemem, plural of "Yoeme," kept conquistadors at bay but invited two Jesuit missionaries to their pueblos in 1617. During this phase, Yoemem maintained control of their geographic and cultural boundaries while thousands of community members shaped new cosmologies, rituals, and stories in dialogue with Jesuit missionaries. This unique mission history presents us with a different colonial situation than that confronted by most Native Americans and many Indigenous peoples elsewhere. As Shorter wrote in *The Encyclopedia of Religion and Nature* (2005:1780), "Yoemem powerfully enforced and strategically maintained their territorial and cultural boundaries, allowing for self-management from pre-Columbian time up through Jesuit collaboration." This history must be considered when attempting to understand Yoeme spatial orientations, including their "worlds."

Over the seventeenth and eighteenth centuries, Yoemem sustained a very long, complex synthesis of their aboriginal ways of life with new forms of communication, modes of sustenance, Catholic ritual performances, and social structures. A metaphor that we learned together in the late 1990s remains appropriate, that of adoption. Yoemem across eight original pueblos adopted Catholic figures such as they adopted the Jesuits themselves: they adopted new rituals but primarily when those accentuated Indigenous values. We can find the resulting cultural hybridity in many areas of Yoeme pueblo life today. Even after the years of violent attempts to decimate the Yoeme community by Spanish slave raiding, outright warfare, decades of Mexico's debt peonage, and the continuing theft of their land and water, most Yoemem take considerable care with their religious responsibilities. Yoeme ceremony often involves maintaining good relations with Jesus, Mary, God, and the saints. But those saints also include Saint Horny Toad, Saint Lizard, and Saint Tortoise. Good relations undoubtedly extend to the land, animals, and all aspects of the English word *nature.* The calendar year contains Catholic holidays celebrated across the pueblos. And these pueblos, ceremonies, and people continually ground their knowledge, power, and healing through the aboriginal, precontact *aniam.*

KNOWING *ANIAM*

Yoemem in the southern pueblos demonstrate, sometimes implicitly, that their lives are multidimensional, composed of overlapping yet distinctive realms called *aniam.* These *aniam* are glossed well by "worlds," though we have found that we can usefully call them realms, dimensions, places of encounter, states of being, or fields of power. We talk about *aniam* as agentive to accentuate that they demonstrate will, intention, and ability. For example, we once traveled with some elders to Los Pilares, a rock formation known as a portal to the *yo ania* (enchanted world), to see an immortal Yoeme man who shows up at noon to speak with people. But the *huya ania* (wilderness world) tricked us, and we drove in circles for hours. According to the elders' consensus later, we had not asked the *huya ania* for permission/protection. On our drive, however, the *sea ania* showed itself to us and was quite beautiful (Color Plate 5). In these ways, Yoemem speak of *aniam* as having the ability to materialize or not (Shorter 2009:41, 42–45). In such cases, "worlds" might not always be the best translation unless we expand our understanding of "world" to include something (or someone) with the ability to appear or not.

In writing this essay, David Shorter felt compelled to provide another story of the *aniam.*

> I was nine years old, hiking by myself out in the mountains surrounding my small hometown in southern New Mexico. I was a

latchkey kid because of working, perhaps trusting, and otherwise preoccupied parents. My dad and stepfather taught me much about self-care in the woods and deserts: hunting, fishing, exploring, and surviving dangerous situations. I was climbing near a mesa with steep, almost vertical rock walls that provided only a sliver of shade in the midday sun. I sat down to drink some water from my dad's military canteen. I sat there noticing the little blooms on an unassuming groundcover plant nearby. In my nine-year-old brain, I reconciled the fact that the desert, from a distance, could look dry and brown, harsh and prickly. But up close, intimately, not only is the desert alive but thriving, offering up these little white and yellow flowers in a leafy green, low-lying plant. I heard the faint sound of music. I heard tinny, barely discernable sounds of music and what sounded like people socializing.

I moved up the side of *la mesita* in the direction of the noise, and the origin came into view: some sort of cave mouth, a hole just under two feet wide by about four feet tall opening into the mountain. I approached the opening and noticed that the ground at its mouth was a mix of sand and little tiny shells, like snail shells and shapes I recognized from once visiting a beach in California. But we were in southern New Mexico. And just inside the opening of the cave, reaching just a few inches below the edge of the mouth, was water, dark and flat, like a sheet of black glass extending into the dark cave. I pulled out my emergency kit to find my mirror (always in my kit to signal for help). I angled the sun's reflection into the cave. The light illuminated the back wall of the narrow opening about four feet away, and I could discern an opening leading to the left. The reflected light could not penetrate much into the dark water. Confoundingly, the faint sound of people mingling and playing music reached me from the back of the cave, as though I were hearing it peripherally. Their mood was lively, murmuring, social; their language undiscernible.

I was a nine-year-old boy born and raised within ten miles of this spot. I was both curious and afraid. I had failed my beginner swim test three times by this point, and I had no sense of the water's depth. Surely spiders and snakes retreated from the desert sun here. And who else might be lurking beyond my view? I still believed in monsters. This story remains one of my most perplexing memories. The experience felt like a state altogether different than normal waking life. I had experienced a shift in perspective from seeing the little flowers far from civilization, appreciating their beauty, hearing the sound of sociality, perceiving life inside a subterranean realm.

Most of us spend some portion of our lives walking around others in our communities; we are people walking in what might be called the *pueblo*, quotidian life. Here, we turn space into place through social structures, expected behaviors, and practiced habits. For some humans, this one realm is the sum total of their experiences. They do not consider very deeply the existence of other dimensions. Yoeme has a label for this group of people: *kaa tetekiakame* or "ones without ceremonial duties." Molina emphasizes that the label carries no negative connotations. And, in contrast, some people venture into the other realms of relating.

Some of us know that other ways of being are possible when we move outside of societal structure into the wilderness, desert, or mountains. That realm, in Yoeme, is called the *huya ania*, or "wilderness world." The *huya ania* has been called the "natural world" because *huya* can designate those areas outside of civilization. The *huya ania* is where we hike, walk in the hills, get away from civil life. The *huya ania* might be thought of as the space of human/plant/animal relations, neither the city nor the other realms of Yoeme indigeneity described below. In some ways, the *huya ania* is the entry way or connection to other dimensions. One example might prove illustrative.

On one auspicious trip to Potam Pueblo, Shorter had a remarkable dream and casually relayed it to his collaborator, Guillermo Flores Sombratuka'u, over breakfast.[3] During his lunch break from work, Guillermotuka'u returned with an elder, asking Shorter to retell the dream. At dinner, three more elders came by to hear David tell the dream again, asking him specifics about the animals and how they acted in the dream. Little did Shorter know, his dream was one of a set of recognized dream tropes that convey messages from the *huya ania*. The elders met later on that week to determine that while (1) they were generally hesitant to share "deep" cultural knowledge with Shorter, (2) they understood the dream as coming from the *huya ania*, which somehow overrode their humancentric concerns. As we understand that pivotal moment in Shorter's work with certain Yoeme families in Potam, the *huya ania* instructed the elders through the *tenku ania* (dream world) to speak with Shorter about the *aniam*. The *aniam* made Shorter's research possible. The *aniam* have agency, and that agency also seems clear from other stories we have heard about these spaces (Shorter 2009:40, 51–55).

We have traced approximately nine *aniam* in our years of talking with Yoemem about this interdimensionality. People have particular encounters, ways of relating and knowing, in the night world, or *tuka ania*. Some people understand the dream world, or *tenku ania*, as having other possibilities. Oceans, rivers, or any naturally occurring body of water provide another realm of relations, called the *vawe ania*. Witches and power people are sometimes capable of accessing a world of witchery, called *nao ania*, or "corncob world." A *moreakame* (healer) cautioned Shorter to guard that information. Some Yoemem refer to the *kawi ania*, or "mountain/hill world," as having distinct features that do not duplicate those of the *huya*, *sea*, or *yo aniam*. The combination of wilderness, altitude, the wider visual perspective available and the possibility of worlds located underneath raised topography all lead to perceptions of a mountain/hill world as unique.

Some Yoemem also relate to Christian spaces such as heaven, hell, and purgatory. Yoeme oral traditions occasionally refer to places under particular hills or mountains where some people are punished after death or where other-than-human persons reside (Shorter 2009:123–26). Shorter (2009:46–50) suggests that Christian realms are temporally accessible (after death, during certain days of the year) whereas the precontact realms described above are spatially accessible (through geography, ritualized space, or ceremony). But none of these other spaces appear as frequently in the stories, mythology, and body of ritual songs as the *yo ania* (enchanted world) and *sea ania* (flower world). Along with the *huya ania* (wilderness world), the *yo ania* and *sea ania* deserve primary focus.

We imagine any interpretation of Yoeme worldviews would necessarily recognize the fluidity between the *huya ania*, *yo ania*, and *sea ania*. As we learned among the pueblos, "many Yoemem say that the *sea ania* and *yo ania* are thought of as emerging within the *huya ania*" (Shorter 2009:36). Since the *surem* lived in a unitary world, the *yo ania* seems the earliest space, a world from which power and ancestral knowledge still venture outward into contemporary Yoeme life. Some Yoemem tell stories of the *yo aniam* being accessible by mountain caves that open to the west. Because of the tendency for Indigenous communities who engaged missionaries to create moral hierarchies in which precontact ways of life are framed as pagan, or worse satanic, we feel that the *yo ania* is the realm most shaded by scholarly doubt and misrepresentation. When interviewed by Muriel Thayer Painter for her collection of Yoeme perspectives (1986), many people gave intentionally misleading descriptions of the *yo ania*. Or they spoke in terms that they thought Painter would understand, whether anthropological language or Christian concepts. But in Shorter's research, when Yoeme elders wanted to share reliable knowledge, they designated the *yo ania* as the most respected and indigenous of Yoeme places.[4] Linguistically, a respected elder is called *yo'owe*, and, in these contexts, *yo* may itself be translated as "respected because of experience." Most elders refer to the *yo ania* as "the enchanted world," and we retain that usage in this essay. But especially when used with *ania*, *yo* suggests not just "old" but oldest, ancient, primordial. The *yo ania* is an ancient world, a place outside of historic time and space where many oral traditions, song content, extraordinary power sharing, and cosmogenic histories take place. The *yo ania* can also be present in the most immediate way. *Yo*, then, refers to the essential and originative quality of being Yoeme.

The *yo ania* embodies the most ancestral ways of life for Yoemem. Wanting to avoid Judeo-Christian concepts that burden our interpretations with ineffective and in some cases detrimental dichotomies (sacred/profane, holy/mundane, spiritual/physical), Shorter has many concerns about the use of words that connote imaginary or unreal qualities (Shorter 2016). Worried that "enchanted" might play into common associations with the "magical," we have discussed between ourselves as authors and interpreters the use of "respected" versus "enchanted" to translate *yo ania* in English. Often at odds over which is best, we use "enchanted" in our coauthored writing, but we do not mean to suggest that the *yo ania* is anything less than real, knowable, and actual.

SINGING DEER SONGS TO RE-MEMBER *ANIAM* IN THE PRESENT

As a cosmological dimension that shows up in our perceptual reality, the *yo ania* is also connected to the art of dancing deer and *pahko'ola* (ceremonial hosts; called *pascola* by many), since the *yo ania* provides some people their power and talent to perform the rituals. In ways similar to vision quests in other southwestern Indigenous cultures, some Yoemem have been known to seek the *yo ania* in order to gain abilities like singing and dancing or to find success in life. Molina noted that "when someone has ability from the enchanted homes and the enchanted world, he can dance well" (Evers and Molina 1987:101). Shorter (2009:40) has noted previously that

> Yoemem may stumble upon the *yo ania* by virtue of having a good heart, out in the wilderness, at the right time, in the right place. Some Yoemem have told stories of reaching the *yo ania* by achieving a proper state of mind. . . . These *yo ania* experiences tend to be the most important and most efficacious examples of true encounter and power exchange in their lives.

We can also understand how the worlds are interrelated by listening to what is always the first song of the *pahko* (ceremony), "Sewailo Malichi." Translated by Molina, the deer singers sing, "flower-covered fawn went out, enchanted, from each enchanted flower, wilderness world, he went out" (Evers and Molina 1987:88). The first verse of the first song, at every *pahko*, creates a space for the deer to be born, a space in the wilderness among the flowers. Bringing all three worlds together (the *huya ania*, *sea ania*, and *yo ania*), the deer singers introduce the deer and his worlds to the ceremonial participants and audience. Since the deer dancer brings the lyrics to life, Yoemem perform the deer dance to reestablish relations to these worlds. The performance is at once an act of memory and a ritualistically performed sharing of identity grounded in remembering and re-membering (bodying again) the places of their ancestors.[5] In the starkest terms, they are making old new again.

The importance of the deer dance in Yoeme cultural continuity is continually emphasized by Yoeme cultural leaders, community members, and ethnographers. Yoeme families host deer dances for special occasions, such as weddings and death ceremonies, community meetings, and the high point of the ceremonial calendar, their Easter rituals. Stemming from hunting rituals, the deer dance entails musicians accompanying the percussive dancing of the *maaso* (deer) and clown-like "friends of the deer" called *pahkola* (ceremonial hosts). The deer dance provides Yoeme

communities a reliable repertoire of cultural sustenance since the instruments, deer song language, costumes, ritual logic, and cosmological
references all draw from precontact origins (Shorter 2009:210–51). In
both the death ceremony and Easter forms of the deer dance, the events
can take days and days of preparation, involve hundreds of laborers and
attendees, and run from one day into the next morning.

In a previous essay (Molina and Shorter 2015), we wrote that the *yo
ania* and *sea ania* present themselves in certain caves, in stories, or through
other *aniam* such as the dream or night world, but nowhere do they more
obviously manifest themselves than in songs. Deer singers are not representing an external reality in their songs as much as they are engendering
that reality in the present moment and space. The singers literally open
the doors of the worlds through which the deer passes into the dance area,
thereby making the dance area the flower world, the *sea ania* (or, in song
language, *seyewailo*). For this reason, we rely heavily on deer songs as the
explanatory mode of *ania* research. To know and sense the *aniam* and the
flower world particularly, we rely on the same evidence that Yoeme do:
the language itself, the stories told, and the songs sung. For this essay, we
take a standard ethnographic approach to formulating our interpretation
and seek to find social meanings that make sense in the community's
language, in what we see of their behavior and habits, and also in how
they explain their own behavior.[6] Deer songs are always performed in
the Yoeme language (*yoem noki*), the ceremonial attendants demonstrate
flowering behavior, and the deer singers evidence Yoeme values.

In terms of Yoeme worldviews, the *sea ania* is of fundamental importance, since most community members in the southern pueblos understand flowers, *seewam*, as actualizing sacrifice and the nurturing acts of
giving. The concepts related to flowers are too numerous to list here, but
some of the most nurturing elements of the world—such as streams,
lakes, clouds, and rain—are considered to be evidence of the *sea ania*.
Many Yoemem understand the deer as living in the *sea ania*. He does
not leave the *sea ania* when he joins us to dance; he brings the *sea ania* to
our dimension. Yoeme elders explained the actuality of deer and *sea ania*
presence to us clearly. In singing the deer songs, Yoemem are not only
commemorating the first song sung in the *sea ania*, they are also opening
the doors of the world through which *saila maaso* (little brother deer)

passes into the dance area, making the dance area the *seyewailo*. The *sea ania* can be thought of as the *huya ania* in bloom, a perfect image of the beautiful outside world. Located by most Yoemem in the east, beneath the dawn, the *sea ania* refers to the world of flowers, the beginning of life, and the result of hard work. The *sea ania* is the home of the actual embodiment of sacrifice, the deer (Shorter 2009:36).

In both song and story, many Yoemem use flowery language to describe deer dancing and affiliated ceremonies. For example, when deer are killed, they are said to be laid "atop a bed of flowers." Hunters must have *seatakaa*, or "flower body," to hunt deer successfully. Flowers adorn the deer dancer's antlers and skirt as well as the necklaces, hair, and masks of the deer dancers' ritual coperformers, the *pahko'olam*. Even the spectators often have flowers embroidered on their shirts, skirts, handkerchiefs, and shawls. Paper flowers are often woven into the *carrizo* walls, mats, and ceilings. These paper flowers make cherished and effectively powerful gifts to keep in the car or on an altar at home.

In their book-length study of deer songs, Larry Evers and Felipe Molina (1987) write that the most common words found in the songs are Yoeme terms for flowers. Molina notes with Evers and in our conversations that the main purpose of the songs is to bring the deer's voice from the *sea ania* to the ceremony. He adds that "almost every piece of regalia and every instrument used in deer dancing and deer singing may be called '*seewa*' or '*sea*' as well" (Evers and Molina 1987:52). The deer and the *sea ania* have an additional contribution to Yoeme communities in that they contribute to health, both individually and collectively. Talking with elders in the Yoeme communities, Shorter learned that deer were considered the healers of the animal world. They knew which plants to chew together to create poultices and digestible medicines for themselves and other animals. Their songs bring comfort to listeners since their perspectives remind Yoeme listeners of their relatedness.

Felipe considers deer songs, especially the songs appearing here, shared with us by Guadalupe Molinatuka'u, to be exceedingly insightful into understanding the flower world. Receiving these songs, we are hearing songs distilled from Yoeme experiences among the *aniam*. We are reading and sharing (again and again) knowledge that is distinctly Yoeme. Felipe recounts the song as follows:

Sewa yotume, sewa yotume sewa
    Growing flower, growing flower went with the
machi hekamake siika
    flower enchanted dawn wind
Machi hekamake wesime
    Going with the dawn wind
Yo machi hekamake siika
    Went with the enchanted, enchanted dawn wind
Ayamansu seyewailo huyatanaisukuni
    Over there in the center of the wilderness world
Taa'ata aman wechew
    Where the sun sets
Kalalipalipati ansime
    Going sparkling brightly
Sewa yotume, sewa yotume sewa
    Growing flower, growing flower
Yo machi hekamake siika
    went with the flower enchanted dawn wind
Yo machi hekamake sika
    Went with the enchanted, enchanted dawn wind.

Guadalupetuka'u said that this song is sung a little after midnight. The song speaks with anticipation of the coming new day. The dawn wind is pushing the night to the west; the night sparkles as it goes. If you are new to deer songs, you will see immediately that the song starts with "sewa," emphasizing the central descriptive role that flowers have in deer songs. As the night is going into the morning, all the collective sacrifice (cooks, singers, spectators, etc.) enlarges the flower. The "flower" in the second line is used to modify the "enchanted dawn wind." The flower references the *sea ania* of course: the flower world is growing more present. The wind blows from the *yo ania*, the most respected and powerful of the various worlds. We have, then, a song that begins with immense power and beauty, weaving recognition of collective labor with the powerful worlds of Yoeme identity.

Using a word not often found in Yoeme speech, *kalalipalipati* (sparkling), this song's beauty is striking. *Kalalipalipati* is a bit like "shimmering," as when the light dances off the top of a body of water's surface.

The word can also be used for the twinkling of the stars. In both cases the play of light is something the water and stars are doing, and the sparkle itself is not understood as an illusion but very real. The word is often used in conjunction with *aane* to emphasize that the *kalalipalipati* is present here and now. Much of ontological theory rests on the phenomenological reality of Indigenous lifeways, positing an alternative to objectified positivism. Many Yoeme elders are quite explicit about their truth claims in speeches and songs, emphasizing that they speak literally, not figuratively. The singers know they might be misunderstood on the issue of the "really real" and often proactively assert the "true," "real," and "present" meanings of what they say and sing.

The second verse of this song begins with a common Yoeme term *ayamansu* meaning "over there." Speakers often use "over there" in oral performances to distinguish between dimensions, such as the worlds from which deer, *pahkola*, or masked dancers come during Lent. We have also heard elders use the phrase "over there" to say where translucent snakes come from to materialize in powerful places, an example of *kawi ania* (hill world) overlapping with the *yo ania*. "Over there" in Yoeme oral performance contrasts with the "here" where the singing is taking place, a social setting within the pueblo (most likely a deer dance). The "here" of society is contrasted with the "over there" in the *huya ania*, which is indicated to be in the west but is now, through the ceremony of the deer dance, brought to life on the dance patio. And the collective labor, the sacrifices made by everyone to conduct the ceremony, manifests as a flower, one that is both growing and sparkling bright.

What a wonderful image. That flower of collective labor rides the respected wind as the night passes, allowing dawn to come. Yoemem historically used *lutu'uria* as a word for "truth," but it more accurately conveys the social performance of knowledge; they are dancing truth in ceremonies. Flowers permeate ways of knowing and being. Flowers in the wind are a common reference to "grace" and "blessings." When taking off their cowboy hats, men often set them upside down so as to catch any falling blessings, conceptualized as flowers. In their Passion Play, Jesus's cross is hoisted upright in the church plaza covered with a sheet; flowers previously in the sheet fall down around the cross, appearing as blooms rather than blood. At the end of Easter ceremonies, people throw flowers to defeat the challengers to the Church.

Guadalupetuka'u was a very wise elder with a good memory for songs. He relayed one particularly beautiful song to Steve Armadillo and Felipe Molina in the late 1960s.[7] Sung in the morning, as the light is coming up over the horizon, the deer engenders the voice of all the people present for the ceremony:

> Empo sewa yo huya aniwa
>> You are a flower enchanted wilderness world
>
> Empo yo huya aniwa
>> You are an enchanted wilderness world
>
> Vaewa sola vooka, huya aniwa
>> You lie we see through freshness, wilderness world
>
> Empo sewa yo huya aniwa
>> You are a flower enchanted wilderness world
>
> Empo yo huya aniwa
>> You are an enchanted wilderness world
>
> Vaewa sola vooka, huya aniwa
>> You lie we see through freshness, wilderness world
>
> Ayamansu seyewailo huyatanaisukuni
>> Over there in the center of the little Brother/Sister flower world
>
> Senu yo machi hekamake uhyoisi vooka
>> With one enchanted dawn wind you lay beautifully,
>
> aniwa huya
>> wilderness world
>
> Empo sewa yo huya aniwa
>> You are a flower enchanted wilderness world
>
> Empo yo huya aniwa
>> You are an enchanted wilderness world
>
> Vaewa sola vooka, huya aniwa
>> You lie we see through freshness, wilderness world
>
>> (Evers 1980:196–197)[8]

Commonly, deer songs relate the deer's perspective, and deer singers are relied on to make the deer's voice understandable to listeners. Here the deer addresses the *aniam*, a "who," not a "what." As explained previously, *aniam* sometimes demonstrate agency, acting with will and intention. The deer addresses the *aniam* directly, naming the dimensions specifically as flower, enchanted, and wilderness: *sea*, *yo*, and *huya*. And the most respected of the worlds, the *yo ania*, is seen "through" the wilderness world. The deer not only accentuates that the *aniam* are other-than-human persons (a phrase we take from A. Irving Hallowell [1975], among others) but that the deer also puts us in relation with the *aniam*. The *sea ania* is not simply alive, but our relative, "the little Brother/Sister flower world" (embodying both genders). When asked whether the place being described is physical or immaterial, Molina explained, "Both. The deer is talking about the fresh dew on the grass and the plants he sees in the early morning." After a night of winter rain, plants are covered with dew and raindrops. When the sun starts rising in the east, you can see these drops sparkling and prismatic like a rainbow.

CONCLUSION

Kenneth Morrison's (1992) essay "Sharing the Flower" was a benchmark in the ethnographic Yoeme literature. Up until then, most outsiders understood Yoeme culture in categorical ways, reflecting perhaps the academic penchant for labels and taxonomic structures. Morrison noted that for Edward Spicer and Muriel Thayer Painter (two well-recognized anthropologists of Yoeme culture), their tribal collaborators lived in a bifurcated culture, split between sacred (church) and profane (clowning or hunting) activities. Through their own Christian lenses, the anthropologists saw hierarchical relations (God and the saints) more prominently than they saw horizontal ones (power sharing across the *aniam*).[9] They saw the deer dance as a metaphor for the life and death of Jesus rather than seeing how Jesus made sense to Yoemem because they already knew deer.

For Morrison, however, flowers were the essential articulation of a Yoeme theory of ritual, one that made Catholicism understandable and desirable. A yearly spectator at the Easter ceremonies in Guadalupe, Arizona, Dr. Morrison arrived at his interpretations as a result of close ethnographic attention and perceptual abilities, the importance of which he passed on to his students, including Shorter. As a person who lived happiest on a mountain, communing with trees and flowers, Morrison related with plants. Flowers, in the many ways they bloom in Yoeme culture, showed Morrison that Yoeme people have been prioritizing core values since before contact with the Europeans. He argued that the flower embodied "all the ways in which the Yaqui work toward fulfilling their responsibilities in the overall, cosmic scheme of things" (Morrison 1992:209). His essay accentuated that Yoeme ritual, like life, depends on sacrifice, gift, presence, work, and gratitude, all notions embodied by flowers, their pollinators, and their patrons. Around that same time, Larry Evers and Felipe Molina had completed *Yaqui Deer Songs/Maso Bwikam* (1987). Their research brought together oral history and research surrounding deer songs and *aniam*. They drew on the work of Guadalupetuka'u, and of course on Molina's own experience as a deer singer. In the early 1990s, the insights of these scholars preceded the wave of Indigenous studies theory that later brought wider attention to Indigenous agency across multiple contact zones.

We felt compelled to join this volume to contribute a Yoeme perspective to flower world studies since the flower world is so central to Yoeme culture. But we also want to accentuate the real and present nature of the *sea ania*. The flower world is not simply metaphorical or symbolic. We have both seen the *sea ania* and stood within that realm. As a deer singer, Molina personally brings the *sea ania* into Yoeme social spaces. Yoemem across history and in multiple communities agree that the *sea ania* is not confined to a primordial or visionary state. For example, Muriel Painter specifically asked many Yoemem whether the *sea ania* is a "mythical world," and different residents near Tucson insisted that "it is real" and "it is the living beautiful part of our present world" (Painter 1986:18–19). Refugio Savala, a Yoeme writer and poet, also told of the *sea ania*'s actuality: "Tucson was pretty on my side of town. The irrigation canal from Silver Lake Dam went through, so the *seya aniya* was lively and lovely, and there was a willow tree grove across from our house" (Savala and Sands 1980:27). Ways of speaking, of course, are ways of knowing.

Aniam are both physical and immaterial realms. They cannot be reduced to the dichotomy of "real" or "not real"; they are complexly intertwined topographic dimensions leading to richly symbolic and actual association. As not only physical spaces, *aniam* help Yoemem share their identity wherever Yoeme song and dance come to life. In a very unique example of multidimensionality, the *aniam* show how the geographical and the metaphysical can be understood as both unitary and multiple. The *huya ania* is the wilderness world as well as the range of beings in that world, the realm of possibility for their encounters and power sharing. The *sea ania* is the wilderness world in bloom and the world of the deer brought to life in the here and now anywhere a deer ceremony begins. Since the deer songs and deer dance come from the *sea ania*, that dimension manifests itself in the ritual space, providing ceremonial participants an opportunity to gain insights, knowledge, and health from this respected world. These dimensions with physical references provide Yoeme communities with a strategy for identity maintenance even in the face of diaspora, land loss, and changes in modes of sustenance. Being able to materialize the core dimension of their identity through performance, Yoeme are able to endure any hardship, including colonialism and its forced movements, as long as they continue to share the flower.

NOTES

1. As readers may note in the songs below, Yoeme words have extra letters when in song form. This "song language" enables singers to accentuate one word over various rhythms and to provide layered meanings to songs. Flowers are omnipresent in deer songs, and they have been recorded with many slightly different spellings: *sea, seya, seeya, sewa, seywaa,* and so forth.

2. *Yoem Bwiara* map created courtesy of Dr. Larry Evers and Felipe S. Molina based on their work in *Yaqui Deer Songs/Maso Bwikam* (1987) and "The Holy Dividing Line" (1992) as well as Edward Spicer's *The Yaquis: A Cultural History* (1980).

3. When added to the end of a proper name, the suffix "-*tuka'u*" indicates that the person has passed.

4. According to some of Painter's collaborators, the entire world of the *surem* is known as the *yo ania* (Painter 1986:9–10).

5. In using "re-member," I aim to draw attention to the bodily, and not simply cognitive, production of memories (Connerton 1989; Fentress and Wickham 1992; Lipsitz 1990).

6. A. Irving Hallowell (1975:142–47) offered a useful guide for ethnographic interpretations to be grounded in the language (grammars, vocabularies), the ways of speaking (language content, metaphors, self-interpretations), and behavior (actions).

7. A few of these songs ended up being included in the Larry Evers, ed., *The South Corner of Time* (1980), presented here with an updated translation.

8. Presented here with an updated translation.

9. Shorter (2009:225–28) explains how Christian Catholicism shaped how two recognized non-Yoeme ethnographers of Yoeme culture chose to interpret and verbalize those interpretations in overtly hierarchical ways.

REFERENCES

Connerton, Paul. 1989. *How Societies Remember*. New York: Cambridge University Press.

Evers, Larry, ed. 1980. *The South Corner of Time: Hopi, Navajo, Papago, and Yaqui Tribal Literature*. Tucson: University of Arizona Press.

Evers, Larry, and Felipe S. Molina. 1987. *Yaqui Deer Songs/Maso Bwikam*. Tucson: Sun Tracks and University of Arizona Press.

Evers, Larry, and Felipe S. Molina. 1992. "The Holy Dividing Line: Inscription and Resistance in Yaqui Culture." *Journal of the Southwest* 34(1):3–46.

Fentress, James, and Chris Wickham. 1992. *Social Memory*. Cambridge, Mass.: Blackwell.

Hallowell, A. Irving. 1975. "Ojibwa Ontology, Behavior, and Worldview." In *Teachings from the American Earth: Indian Religion and Philosophy*, edited by Dennis Tedlock and Barbara Tedlock, 141–74. New York: Liveright.

Lipsitz, George. 1990. *Time Passages: Collective Memory and American Popular Culture*. Minneapolis: University of Minnesota Press.

Molina, Felipe S., and David Delgado Shorter. 2015. "Geographies: Yoeme." In *The World of Indigenous North America*, edited by Robert Warrior, 105–22. New York: Routledge.

Morrison, Kenneth M. 1992. "Sharing the Flower: A Non-Supernaturalistic Theory of Grace." *Religion* 22:207–19.

Painter, Muriel Thayer. 1986. *With Good Heart: Yaqui Beliefs and Ceremonies in Pascua Village*. Tucson: University of Arizona Press.

Savala, Refugio, and Kathleen Mullen Sands. 1980. *Autobiography of a Yaqui Poet*. Tucson: University of Arizona Press.

Shorter, David. 2005. "Yoeme (Yaqui) Ritual." In *The Encyclopedia of Religion and Nature*, edited by Bron Taylor, 1780–82. Bristol: Thoemmes Continuum.

Shorter, David Delgado. 2009. *We Will Dance Our Truth: Yaqui History in Yoeme Performances*. Lincoln: University of Nebraska Press.

Shorter, David Delgado. 2016. "Spirituality." In *The Oxford Handbook of American Indian History*, edited by Fredrick Hoxie, 487–505. London: Oxford University Press.

Spicer, Edward H. 1980. *The Yaquis: A Cultural History*. Tucson: University of Arizona Press.

4

Flower World Concepts in Hopi Katsina Song Texts

Dorothy K. Washburn

Cosmological ideas such as Jane Hill's flower world exist within a culture imbedded in many verbal and visual formats. Such Indigenous materials speak directly about the principles and practices that shape and sustain a culture. The papers in this volume describe many manifestations of this concept held by Uto-Aztecan-speaking peoples of Mesoamerica and the American Southwest. Dating as early as the Classic and continuing into the present in Mesoamerican sites and among contemporary peoples, these expressions have been inscribed in glyphs and imagery on stelae, staircases, lintels, palace walls, and ceramics (see Washburn 2012). Among the Nahuatl-speaking Aztecs—as well as the Maya, Mixtecs, and Zapotecs of Oaxaca and the Tarascans and Otomis of Central Mexico (Leon-Portilla 1969)—exists a rich body of myths, ritual hymns, poetry, discourse, drama, and legends. In the American Southwest, many have described flowery imagery and its import (Hays-Gilpin and Hill 1999; Hays-Gilpin 2006; Hays-Gilpin and Schaafsma 2010; Jones and Drover 2018).

In this chapter I will explore how concepts of the flower world are embodied in ritual song texts. Songs are windows into the ways Indigenous peoples conceive of their place and role in the natural world during their lives as well as in the afterworld. In this context, song is a particularly apt medium for transmitting flowery concepts. Burkhart has observed that the Nahuatl see "the flowery world [as] a place filled with song; song calls the world into being" (Burkhart 1992:90). The life-giving forces of the universe—embodied in iridescent feathers of birds, colorful flowers, and glittering raindrops—have their voice in these flowery expressions of a paradisiacal world. Gossen, Knab, and Heyden remark on how the power of ritual song as a medium for communication between pre-Columbian peoples and their deities pervaded the cultures of Central Mexico as well as those among the Maya (Gossen 1986; Heyden 1986; Knab 1986). As Gossen (1986:7) notes,

Beautifully executed speech and song are the only substances, with the possible exception of blood, that the human body can produce which are accessible to, and worthy before, divine beings. The Aztec theory of language, song, and poetics was expressed in the metaphor of plants and flowers. Flowers are the most beautiful, perfect achievement of plants, and also their medium for continuity through seed production. So too are song and poetry the most beautiful realization of the human spirit, making this essence worthy before the deities. If divine beings are pleased, human life is allowed to continue.

Louise Burkhart (1992) argued that Christianity was readily accepted in the Americas after Cortés's conquest precisely because the Christian concept of heaven corresponded to the flowery world of the gods of the Classic and Postclassic (Córdova, this volume). Here I explore how a particular southwestern vision of the flower world concept characterizes the world of the Hopi, a northern Uto-Aztecan people living in northeastern Arizona (Map 2).[1] In particular I will explore how flower world ideas are manifest in katsina songs of the Hopi.

THE FLOWER WORLD IN HOPI KATSINA SONG

Sung by spiritual ancestors of the Hopi during the growing season, the katsinas' songs both encourage and admonish Hopis to follow a suite of traditional practices that will ensure continuity of life. While encouraging Hopis with imagery of beautiful butterflies and colorful birds that bespeak a life of happiness and fulfillment, they preface this future life with a focus on the hard realities of the daily work of raising food and family as well as performing a full schedule of ritual reciprocities and family obligations. In this way, the flower world of the Hopi differs from expressions of a paradisiacal flower afterworld among many Mesoamerican peoples.

Nevertheless, there are distinct threads in concept and practice that unite the flowery worlds of Mesoamerican peoples with those of the American Southwest. For example, even today, descendants of these pre-Columbian cultures practice rituals that display the same ideas about the beauty of renewed life that comes with rain. And many of these ideas and practices are expressed in song. For example, young Maya boys in the village of Yaxuna stand at the corners of a temporary arbor built for the Ch'a-Chak rainmaking ritual making the croaking sounds of happy frogs listening to the sounds of rain as men water small corn plants at the four corners of the arbor (Freidel et al. 1993:Figure 1:11). A *Koyemsi* (Mudhead) katsina song (no. 117) similarly celebrates the toad's cries as they emerge from the earth after a rain. Metaphors for the rebirth of life, the Hopis see the toads' cries, like those of the Maya frogs, as representing the peoples' happiness at the coming of the rains that will water their planted fields:

> Throughout the midst of the planted fields when puddles form,
> The toads will be dancing as they make their cries.
> Waaq, waaq, they will say.

I first address how Hopis reference their flowery world. In my interactions with them, it is notable that nowhere have Hopis explicitly, either in discussions with me or in katsina song texts, used the term "flower world" or "flowery world." Further, Hopi katsina song does not celebrate the idea that Hopis at death will go to a flowery paradise, such as that conceived by Aztecs, for example. Rather, for Hopis, the concept of a flower world refers to the perfection of their lives in their utopian past which they must constantly strive to achieve in their present lives. Katsina songs are focused on encouraging Hopis to live by the moral imperatives of this past perfected paradise, when everyone worked together harmoniously and lived a life of mutual caring and respect. Phillip Tuwaletstiwa (personal communication, 2018) captures this sense in his characterization of the flower world as "a state of mind," stating, "The Flower World is a metaphoric place where moisture is ever present, where the earth is lush and verdant—a place of frogs, dragonflies, butterflies, birds, and, of course, flowers. Such a physical place has never and never will exist on Hopi. Hopi land is and always will be a desert. Nonetheless, in the internalized flower world where goodness is ever present, dreams can sprout, grow, and emerge. It is a place where men's and women's spiritual lives can become manifest. It is a metaphor for the creative and collective unconscious."

RECIPROCITY AND MORAL IMPERATIVES
IN HOPI LIFE

Katsinas, spiritual ancestors, remind Hopis in their songs sung at dance performances during the growing season of this past utopian state of beauty and plenty. With their advice and encouragement—and sometimes pointed admonishments for errant behavior—they help Hopis to strive to live the perfect life of the past in the present. This hoped-for life is one of happiness, health, and freedom from want into old age. The essence of this perfect life is embodied in creative song word metaphors that celebrate the renewal of life as it is embodied in the beauty of flowers and other colorful, vibrant, living beings—flitting butterflies, fields of vigorously growing plants, and the happy cries of all creatures that live by water—collectively referenced as *pavopkomat*.

This idea is exemplified in a song of the *Qaötotimuy* (Corn Boy katsinas, no. 142), who remind Hopis of this past perfect life and how beautiful it was, likening it to a "land brightened with flowers." They are reminding the Hopis that when they live a life of "caring of one another," *naavaastoti*, both plants and their children will thrive. This perfect life is imaged as *sìitàlpuva*, "along a land brightened with flowers," using flowers as a way to connote that life has a vital radiance akin to the luminous beauty of flowers.

> Remember how it was long ago.
> Remember how it used to become bright with flowers along the land,
> And how these, the water creatures, used to go along there chasing one
> another with happy hearts.
> Become caring of one another,
> My mothers and fathers.
> When you begin living with the will to live the beautiful life here,
> [We] will come as rain from the different directions around.
> You will look in awe along a land brightened with flowers.

However, in order to attain this perfect life, one must live according to a communally shared set of values and practices: caring for one another, selflessly sharing, working hard, and sacrificing one's goals for the welfare of the community. This hard life was preordained at their emergence into this the Fourth World when *Màasaw*, guardian of the earth, offered them a life of raising the short, plain ear of corn by hand with a planting stick. The sustaining importance of raising corn is embedded in one Hopi's comment that planting corn is one's destiny. "This is where we start life . . . you plant one kernel of corn and it's going to produce more kernels . . . from only one kernel your life is forever" (Eric Polingyouma, personal communication 1994).

Emory Sekaquaptewa (personal communication 2002) characterized these life-promoting practices, *natwani*, necessary to live this life of hard work, personal suffering, and selfless communal living as moral imperatives. Whether it be hoeing corn or sex for procreation, all of these personal and collective practices are work that contributes to the rejuvenation and continuation of life. Every Hopi must accept his or her burden of obligations and responsibilities to kin and clan through birth and to religious societies by virtue of their initiated membership for the welfare and continuity of the community.

Katsinas, as perfected beings, have the countenance of the perfect life to which everyone aspires. Their vocal beauty in performance as well as the beauty of their dress—replete with imagery of flowers, corn, rain, clouds, and other symbols of life—lifts the spirits of the people and gives them hope as they navigate the daily trials of living. Katsina songs construct a hoped-for world in which flowers and pollinators are the representative "seeds" of new life. A song of the *Korowista* katsinas (no. 10) describes the new generations of animate beings who reappear each spring season as having the countenance (*pitsangwa*) of life. As butterflies and yellow jackets move from flower to flower covering themselves with pollen, they are "adorning their faces," that is, giving themselves the countenance of life:

> The yellow butterflies will be chasing one another about colorfully as they
> go along adorning their faces with the pollen of the corn blossom maidens.

Katsina songs focus on the beauty and vitality of life's renewal. This process is often likened to a growing corn plant (Black 1984). Eric Polingyouma (personal communication, 1994) describes this process: "There are many phases in life. I was conceived and planted, now I germinate and [in] so many days I pop up and pretty soon I'm a little child."

Immature corn in the husk, *timoki*, is described as "child bundles." Young corn plants with developing cobs on the stalks are conceived of as "corn maidens," *paavönmamant*, being likened to young girls who are maturing in their capacity to reproduce. *Sa'lako* maidens (no. 38) describe how mature corn, in turn, is like a mother that nurtures the people from birth to old age:

> The perfect ear of glossy-kernelled corn is my mother.
> They are nurturing us like children here.

Living the Hopi way by the moral imperatives proscribed by the katsinas leads to the perpetuation of new life. This new life is constantly being imaged in song with reminders of the reciprocity between the katsinas' gift of rain and the flowering of the planted fields and the singing of happiness of all beings. *Angaktsinas* (Long-Haired katsinas, no. 25) describe the beauty in the flowering of the corn in the fields and how this will ensure food for the Hopis:

> When it rains beautifully during the summer for you,
> it restores your beauty.
> Just think, at last the tassels of your corn plants are quite visible,
> Just think, their "tendrils" are cascading down along them.
> Along them their corn silk is cascading down.
> I want it this way for you.
> This is what you are praying for,
> my fathers.
> How delightful, delightful, delightful.
> Just think, at last your children will be eating.
> Just think, at last they will get full.
> Just think, at last all of you will be eating.

In order to emphasize the continuity of thought and ritual among Uto-Aztecans throughout Mesoamerica and the American Southwest that encapsulates these concepts of the flower world, I refer briefly to the songs of the Cora, a maize-raising people of northwest Mexico. In the song "The Growing of the Corn" (Preuss n.d.:130), they similarly describe the process of maize growth as beautiful.[2]

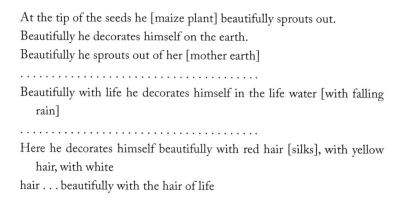

At the tip of the seeds he [maize plant] beautifully sprouts out.
Beautifully he decorates himself on the earth.
Beautifully he sprouts out of her [mother earth]
. . . .
Beautifully with life he decorates himself in the life water [with falling
     rain]
. . . .
Here he decorates himself beautifully with red hair [silks], with yellow
     hair, with white
hair . . . beautifully with the hair of life

But this perfect life is aspirational. It is achieved only by living a life of reciprocated ritual activities between a people and their ancestral deities. This relationship is described in this volume by Felipe Molina and David Delgado Shorter for the Yoeme, who depend on reciprocities between respectful humans and compassionate deer (Morrison 1992:211; Shorter 2009). Just as the Yoeme ask permission of deer to hunt them, so, too, do Hopis ask permission to hunt, but only for food. This reciprocity between people and the natural world is illustrated in an image painted on a Hopi yellowware bowl (#75493) currently in the collections of the Field Museum of Natural History, Chicago. A man is asking permission to hunt the deer as indicated by his proffering a gourd of sanctified water, and in return the animal is shown being pierced by his arrow (Color Plate 6).

For Hopis, achieving the perfect life entails reciprocities between adherence to the moral imperatives of right living and, in return, receiving the gift of life-giving rain from the katsinas. But in daily living, Hopis often fail to live selflessly and communally, and so the katsinas come to reenergize their efforts through songs that pointedly voice the reciprocity between the kind of behavior by the people that will sustain the life of the community and the benevolence of the katsinas who reward these life practices with their life-renewing rains. In their songs, the katsinas describe how they listen to the Hopis' prayers, observe their efforts to live according to the moral imperatives, and in return promise to reward them with the resources to live a life of freedom from want, pain, and suffering and full of happiness and well-being into old age. In return for a life of caring and sharing and hard work, the katsinas promise to water their planted fields with the nurturing powers of their rain. An

Angaktsina (Long-Haired katsina, no. 1) song describes this reciprocity between living right and their arrival at a Hopi village clothed in rain—a reference to their coming as clouds and then descending as rain on the peoples' planted fields:

> We are coming to you as rain, coming this way.
> Along your planted fields, we will make the clouds come all day long.
> We want it to be this way here . . .
> We wonder if your life is in accord with Hopi teachings here.
> Perhaps you are living here in accord with Hopi teachings,
> If it is that way, then we clouds, with happy hearts, after clothing ourselves,
> Start out coming from there on a journey as rain.

Similarly, the Cora direct prayers to their ancestors, the rain clouds, at ceremonies called *mitotes* that are performed at the three critical stages in the growth and maturation of corn (Coyle 2001). On the last day masked dancers called *Urracas* appear as representations of the clouds wearing an eight-pointed star crown of paper flowers and magpie feathers. Hanging from a veil in front of the dancer's face are strings of colored glass beads that mask the human identity of the dancer, transforming him into a representative of the deceased countenanced with falling rain. The beauty of dancers moving with their crowns of colored beads in front and long colored ribbons in back recalls the dress of the Hopi katsinas—both are adorned with the beauty of the rain that brings life to all living things. A Cora song, "The Arrival of the Rain Gods" (Preuss n.d.:158) celebrates the beauty of the clouds, thunder, and rain:

> Our mother [earth] decorates herself.
> She decorates herself beautifully with life water, with dew, with clouds.
> The Boy Hatsikan [morning star] decorates himself beautifully with his
>   feathers,
> With his crown [feather headdress], with his paint [color],
> With his thoughts and words [songs] . . .
> Already they [clouds] prepare themselves up in the East . . .
> Beautifully white are the clouds . . .
> Beautifully they come down,
> Beautifully in threads [beaded veil] they wind themselves downwards.

Importantly, the katsinas will only come if Hopis prepare for the ceremonials and pray with pure hearts free of animosity toward others and selfish desires for themselves. A song of the *Hehey'a* katsinas (no. 78) reminds Hopis that only their most heartfelt prayers and properly prepared prayer feathers will be reciprocated with the beauty of flowering plants on the land that results from their gift of rain:

O, my fathers, [Hopis]
After you sit down here as (ritual) leaders,
And after you smoke the pipe with untroubled minds,
And after you clothe your prayer feathers with markings,
You pray for an all-day rain.
By means of that,
From the different directions around,
While going along with lightning flashing and going along thundering,
The rain will make it glisten with puddles of water throughout the planted
    fields.

This reciprocity between sincere prayerful ritual and katsina rain is invoked pictorially in a fifteenth-century kiva mural from Awat'ovi (Smith 1952:Figure 80b) in which particulate matter, metaphorically both rain drops and corn meal, is falling into bowls held by two figures who are breathing in the goodness of this nourishing food. The words of a twentieth-century *Hewto* katsina song (no. 138) recorded by Emory Sekaquaptewa precisely describe this scene, indicating that oral tradition is extremely effective in preserving and passing along over generations song texts that speak to the beauty of a flowery world vitalized by rain. Ideas about the corn lifeway have continued over centuries (Mathiowetz, this volume):

For their part,
for their part,
along the cloud dwelling places,
the cumulus cloud maidens,
have prepared their rainwater as cornmeal on a tray coming from there,
and along here, they will make it rain on those plants of yours.
Like this,
You are praying for it to be like this.

Katsina songs clearly invoke the beauty of flowers as symbols of the perfected harmonious world of the past. But further, by evoking them, the songs are pointed reminders that if certain traditional behaviors and work are not followed, then the flowery beauty of life's renewal will not happen. A number of katsina songs describe the kinds of behaviors that are necessary to ensure the continuity of life in the community. For example, *Sivu'ikwiwtaqa*, below the Pot Carrier katsina (no. 147), sings about how his katsina sisters are demonstrating how to toast corn. This is a reminder to young Hopi girls that they need to learn about their traditional roles, one of which is preparing corn meal that will be used in daily foods as well as ritual offerings. In this song, the katsinas dance as they show the Hopi girls how to grind—a way of saying that grinding, like dancing, is beautiful because it is one of the activities that they must perform daily after they get married to ensure that life goes on. In the last line the repeated process of pulling the corn meal up with one's hand on the metate and then pushing it down as it is ground with the mano is described with the verb *haahannaya*, "be moving things down." This allusion to the *repeated* motions using the imperfective verb form ("be moving") that is involved in grinding corn is a metaphor that also references how the lives of Hopi women should be lived—they should be constantly in motion, caring for others:

> While the Pot Carrier Katsina is seemingly a useless one,
> These little sisters of his are using the load on his back, the toasting pot,
> to toast cornmeal.
> And while they are showing the girls how to do it,
> They are dancing along here.
> That's why they,
> when they learn,
> When they go to begin their weddings,
> They happily push and push down along here while they grind flour.

Similarly, *Angaktsinas* (Long-Haired katsinas, no. 61) advise Hopi girls that when they visit friends in other homes they should not simply gossip but make themselves useful. In this way their helping rejuvenates life. The girls are metaphorically referred to as "butterfly maidens of various colors" to emphasize their beauty as potential mothers and providers:

Listen this way,

When you learn our song,

These butterfly maidens of various colors, should, using it (singing it) grind corn.

It seems clear that a life is lived in many ways like this.

If a girl enters a house not of a relative,

She goes to the grinding bin and grinds and grinds corn . . .

Life is being rejuvenated over there

In houses belonging to other people.

Nukushehey'a katsinas (no. 93) pointedly remind single women of their role and obligations to the continuing vitality of the community. They remind them that even plain-looking men will be good providers. Girls should marry and perform the duties of a wife and mother and in so doing contribute to the rejuvenation of life:

Why do you women sitting in corners remain attracted to living single?

It would be good to consider the plain looking man

who spends his days working in his field.

Look at him . . .

To one side and the other of his dirty hands,

the loads of watermelons and loads of muskmelons are known community wide.

In other songs, the katsinas admonish Hopis about lapses in their work ethic. The importance of work is clearly emphasized in this volume by Alan Sandstrom as he describes the prodigious amount of work preparing for a ceremonial undertaken by Nahua people in the southern Huasteca of Mexico. In the following song (no. 103), *Tsa'kwayna* katsinas imply that the Hopis are not taking care of their fields by describing their eroded fields as being "marked." By citing lapses in the hard work of raising corn that have led to the deterioration of the land, the katsinas are also metaphorically alluding to other kinds of moral decay in the community.

I am Tsa'kwayna.

I am walking around here feeling dejected.

I am asking our fathers to go there.
I am looking around in your fields.
Your lands are marked

In another song (no. 102), these same katsinas accuse Hopis of only
pretending to live the Hopi way but still expecting reciprocities from the
katsinas. Here, having a Hopi identity (*hopimatsiwta*) does not refer to
one's ethnic identity but to being a participating member of the Hopi
community where everyone performs their obligations and responsibilities according to Hopi principles and practices. The katsinas accuse
Hopis of not following traditional practices such as performing the hard
work of grinding, wearing traditional hairstyles that signal one's life stage,
and running to greet the sun. These activities are symbolic of the humble
practices of living and prayerful activities that have for so long insured
the survival of Hopi communities.

My fathers,
You here have forgotten the recollections and advice from long ago.
Here you come to me (katsinas) as though you have been initiated as
    Hopis.
Here you appear to me as though you have a Hopi identity
. . . .
O you, my fathers,
When your heartfelt wishes and your words unite together,
We will make it rain in the cornfields and in the bean fields
. . . .
At Mùnqapi, a girl doesn't know the *naasomi* hairdo
You'll recall also early in the morning,
When she used to be grinding cornmeal into flour,
And would be caught up in singing,
It sounded beautiful
. . . .
At Mùnqapi, the young men don't know the hairknot
You'll recall also early in the morning
When they used to get up to run somewhere (to greet the sun) and pray,
And would start clanking their bells throughout,
It sounded beautiful.

At the last dance of the katsina year, a song of the *Angaktsinas* (Long-haired katsinas, no. 126) describes the appearance of new brides dressed in robes embroidered with symbols of life. By appearing at this time before the katsinas, women who have become brides during the past year become sanctified and fully fledged into their new stage of motherhood. As potential mothers of the next generation, they represent the future regeneration of life. The brides are metaphorically referenced as white cloud maidens because, like clouds with rain, they have the potential power to nurture new life. The beauty referenced here is not the physical appearance of the women, but rather the beauty of their role in perpetuating life:

> Let's be thankful.
> It has become the time that you set.
> That's why the white cloud maidens from around here,
> After having adorned themselves with their corn and with their rain lines,
> Have begun their journey to us from around here.
> That's why, when you, for your part,
> Provide us with your heartfelt prayers
> As the perfection of sincerity that we are due,
> And we, for our part, come with the message,
> You will look in awe
> Along a land brightened with flowers.

CONCLUSION

The use of analyst-created terms to describe ineffable aspects of the worlds of Indigenous peoples is fraught with difficulty. At the very least, we need to understand when our terms are research-oriented labels for what we perceive as constellations of ideas or things and when our terms are attempts to represent ideas, sensibilities, and processes embedded in the experiential world of Indigenous peoples who reference and orient themselves in relation to the powers and processes of the natural world (Toelken 1976). Jane Hill (1992) observed something that she called the "Flower World" in the collective profusion of flowery references in words and imagery among Uto-Aztecan and other Mesoamerican and southwestern peoples. While Mesoamerican peoples, beginning even in the Formative period, certainly referenced flowers in their songs and images of flowers appeared everywhere in their material world (Taube 2004), we do not know whether they conceptualized these flowers as making up a cosmological entity they might have called their "Flower World."

Nowhere do Hopis, in their katsina songs, use the term *flower world*. Yet these songs describe a very real perfected world of the past that was referenced as flowery and beautiful. This world is the measure by which Hopis should act and live in the present. In order to reach this life of fulfillment and happiness, Hopis must live according to a suite of work practices that sustains everyone in the community. Katsinas, their ancestral spiritual selves, perform at the mesa-top villages yearly during the growing season to encourage Hopis to follow this life of selfless work. In return the katsinas reciprocate with their natural forces of clouds, thunder, lightning, and rain. This reciprocity is the structural pivot between the Hopis' lives in the present world and their hoped-for life in the other, perfected world. This latter world is visualized in song texts by the vibrant beauty of flowers, birds, and butterflies that encapsulate the life for which they so fervently strive. By working hard to bring forth flowering fields in the present, Hopis bring forth the fruits of these flowers—the renewal of life in the future.

ACKNOWLEDGMENTS

This paper is based on a decade of study with Emory Sekaquaptewa of Hopi song, mural depictions, and ceramic design. I owe an immeasurable debt of gratitude to Emory and to Eric Polingyouma and Phillip Tuwaletstiwa, who have shared their knowledge of Hopi life with me. I especially thank Ken Hill who worked with Emory and me to produce the compilation, *Hopi Katsina Songs* (Sekaquaptewa et al. 2015).

NOTES

1. The katsina songs excerpted here are referenced by the katsina singing the song and by their number in *Hopi Katsina Songs* (Sekaquaptewa et al. 2015). This volume contains full transcriptions, translations, and accompanying explanatory text for 150 katsina song texts collected by ethnographers, archaeologists, and musicologists since the turn of the twentieth century. The orthography follows that given in the Hopi Dictionary Project (1998).

2. See Washburn and Fast (2018) for a more detailed comparative study of Hopi and Cora songs.

REFERENCES

Black, Mary E. 1984. "Maidens and Mothers: Analysis of Hopi Corn Metaphors." *Ethnology* 23:279–88.

Burkhart, Louise M. 1992. "Flowery Heaven: The Aesthetic of Paradise in Nahuatl Devotional Literature." *RES: Anthropology and Aesthetics* 21:88–109.

Coyle, Philip E. 2001. *Náyari History, Politics, and Violence: From Flowers to Ash*. Tucson, University of Arizona Press.

Freidel, David, Linda Schele, and Joy Parker. 1993. *Maya Cosmos: Three Thousand Years on the Shaman's Path*. New York: William Morrow.

Gossen, Gary H. 1986. "Mesoamerican Ideas as a Foundation for Regional Synthesis." In *Symbol and Meaning Beyond the Closed Community: Essays in Mesoamerican Ideas*, edited by Gary H. Gossen, 1–8. Studies on Culture and Society, vol. 1. Albany: Institute for Mesoamerican Studies, State University of New York Press.

Hays-Gilpin, Kelley, ed. 2006. *Murals and Metaphors*. Vol. 1, no. 3 of *Plateau: The Land and People of the Colorado Plateau*. Flagstaff: Museum of Northern Arizona.

Hays-Gilpin, Kelley, and Jane H. Hill. 1999. "The Flower World in Material Culture: An Iconographic Complex in the Southwest and Mesoamerica." *Journal of Anthropological Research* 55(1):1–37.

Hays-Gilpin, Kelley, and Polly Schaafsma, eds. 2010. *Painting the Cosmos: Metaphor and Worldview in Images from the Southwest Pueblos and Mexico*. Museum of Northern Arizona Bulletin 67. Flagstaff: Museum of Northern Arizona.

Heyden, Doris. 1986. "Metaphors, Nahualtocaitl, and other 'Disguised' Terms Among the Aztecs." In *Symbol and Meaning Beyond the Closed Community: Essays in Mesoamerican Ideas*, edited by Gary H. Gossen, 35–43. Studies on Culture and Society, vol. 1. Albany: Institute for Mesoamerican Studies, State University of New York Press.

Hill, Jane H. 1992. "The Flower World of Old Uto-Aztecan." *Journal of Anthropological Research* 48(2):117–44.

Hopi Dictionary Project. 1998. *Hopi Dictionary: Hopìikwa Lavàytutuveni; A Hopi-English Dictionary of the Third Mesa Dialect*. Tucson: University of Arizona Press.

Jones, Bernard M., Jr., and Christopher E. Drover. 2018. "Visual Prayer and Breath Bodies: Flower World Metaphor in Pueblo III and IV Rock Art." In *Rock Art Papers*, vol. 19, edited by Ken Hodges and Anne McConnell, 153–67. San Diego, Calif.: San Diego Rock Art Association.

Knab, T. J. 1986. "Metaphor, Concepts, and Coherence in Aztec." In *Symbol and Meaning Beyond the Closed Community: Essays in Mesoamerican Ideas*, edited by Gary H. Gossen, 45–55. Studies on Culture and Society, vol. 1. Albany: Institute for Mesoamerican Studies, State University of New York Press.

León-Portilla, Miguel. 1969. *Pre-Columbian Literatures of Mexico*. Norman: University of Oklahoma Press.

Morrison, Kenneth M. 1992. "Sharing the Flower: A Non-Supernaturalistic Theory of Grace." *Religion* 22:207–19.

Preuss, Konrad. N.d. *Die Nayarit Expedition*. Translated by Angela Schiller. NAA MS 7530, Washington, D.C.: National Anthropological Archives, Smithsonian Institution

Sekaquaptewa, Emory, Kenneth C. Hill, and Dorothy K. Washburn. 2015. *Hopi Katsina Songs*. Lincoln: University of Nebraska Press.

Shorter, David Delgado. 2009. *We Will Dance Our Truth: Yaqui History in Yoeme Performances*. Lincoln: University of Nebraska Press.

Smith, Watson. 1952. *Kiva Mural Decorations at Awatovi and Kawaika-a*. Papers of the Peabody Museum of American Archaeology and Ethnology, vol. 37. Cambridge, Mass.: Harvard University, Peabody Museum.

Taube, Karl A. 2004. "Flower Mountain: Concepts of Life, Beauty, and Paradise Among the Classic Maya." *RES: Anthropology and Aesthetics* 45:69–98.

Toelken, Barre. 1976. "Seeing with a Native Eye: How Many Sheep Will It Hold?" In *Seeing with a Native Eye: Essays on Native American Religion*, edited by Walter Holden Capps, 9–24. New York: Harper and Row.

Washburn, Dorothy K. 2012. "Shared Image Metaphors of the Corn Lifeway in Mesoamerica and the American Southwest." *Journal of Anthropological Research* 68:473–502.

Washburn, Dorothy K., and Sophia Fast. 2018. "Ritual Songs of the Cora of West Mexico and the Hopi of the American Southwest: Shared Ideas Related to Maize Agriculture." *Journal of the Southwest* 60(1):73–113.

PART II

HISTORICAL FLOWER WORLDS

5

The Goddess in the Garden

An Exploration of Gender in the Flower Worlds of the
Pacific Coast of Guatemala

Oswaldo Chinchilla Mazariegos

In her pathbreaking study of the Uto-Aztecan Flower World, Jane Hill
addressed the gender connotations of flowers in southwestern and Mesoamerican cultures. While flowers were often related to femininity—as in
the use of flower names for women—they were also regarded as androg-
ynous or predominantly male. They were associated with fecundity and
agriculture but also with emphatically male activities such as hunting. In
Nahuatl poetry, flowers served as metaphors for the short and glorious
life of warriors (Hill 1992:132–34). Hill (1992:122) concluded that "flowers can stand for female beauty and fecundity, but the flower symbol
is even more frequently associated with male strength and spirituality."
Later studies have tended to reaffirm the masculine connotations of the
Mesoamerican flower worlds. Karl Taube's (2004:81) iconographic inquiries focused on representations of flowering mountains that he regarded as "the dwelling place of the ancestors and the means by which
they and the celestial gods ascend to the sky." He recognized deceased
royal women portrayed as lunar goddesses on flowering mountains, as in
El Chicozapote Lintel 2, but did not delve extensively into the presence
of women in those mythical realms (Taube 2004:81–82).

Whereas Hill acknowledged the chromatic and flowery qualities of
various mythical places in Nahua religion, such as Tlalocan and Tamoanchan, Taube's interpretations stressed the correspondences of Flower
Mountain with the path of the sun and the solar paradise as an afterlife
destiny for the souls of kings and warriors (Taube 2004:86–88; 2006:153).
Both wrote the terms *Flower World* and *Flower Mountain* with initial
capitals, suggesting that they named specific places (Hill 1992; Taube
2004). Nevertheless, Hill (1992:128) noted that people tended to split the
flower world and the closely associated spirit land into several distinct
places with their own unique properties. The landscape and associations

of Mesoamerican flower worlds varied considerably within and across different communities, and the beliefs likely shifted through time. The variations are significant to understand the nature of these places and the character of their inhabitants.

I use the plural *flower worlds* to designate a variety of portentous places that share the chromatic qualities that Hill identified in Uto-Aztecan songs. The question is whether we can recognize such diversity in ancient Mesoamerican art and writing. In this chapter, I discuss flowering places that are not primarily associated with the sun and the male qualities of warriors but instead are linked to women, female deities, sexuality, and fertility. In the first section, I examine the feminine connotations of flowers and the association of flowering places with goddesses in early colonial Nahua and Maya sources. I compare them with modern ethnographic data extending to western and northern Mexico. The next section is an overview of previous studies about flower world beliefs and representations in the Pacific coast of Guatemala. In subsequent sections I examine flowering places portrayed on Early Classic Teotihuacan-style ceramic objects from that region and probe their feminine connotations.

FLOWERING PLACES AND MESOAMERICAN GODDESSES

For his interpretation of flowering mountains in Lowland Maya and Teotihuacan art, Taube drew important clues from Louise Burkhart's studies of colonial Nahua devotional literature. Burkhart identified reminiscences of the flowering places of pre-Columbian Nahua religion in texts that described the Christian Garden of Eden and the heavens for the new converts (Burkhart 1992:89). Taube highlighted passages from Bernardino de Sahagún's (1993 [1583]) *Psalmodia Christiana* that relate flowering mountains with dawn and describe flowers as the *tonalli*—a Nahua term that can refer to warmth, sunshine, and the soul—of Christ, who is often assimilated with the sun in colonial and modern Mesoamerica (Taube 2004:87–88, 2006:158). These passages reinforced the association of Maya flower mountains with the sun and maize gods, which made them comparable to Tonatiuh Ilhuicac, the solar heaven of the sixteenth-century Nahua.

The solar aspects that Taube noticed in Maya flower mountains correspond only partially with the paradisiacal gardens of the early colonial Nahua. Burkhart showed that Nahua devotional literature contained more garden-related references to the Virgin than to any other Christian character (Burkhart 1992:100). The metaphors derived from European sources compared the Virgin and other female saints with flowers, connoting their virginity, purity, and beauty. But the meanings shifted considerably in Nahuatl texts: "the language of flowers spoke much more persuasively of fertility and sensuality than of maidenly innocence. Although Nahuas were made well aware of Mary's sexually abstinent lifestyle, flower terminology tied her to the flowery world rather than to any cult of virginity."

The flowering places of Nahua accounts were distinctly associated with particular deities. Tlaloc, the god of earth and rainstorms, presided over Tlalocan, a lush place of abundant water and vegetation where the drowned, those who were hit by lightning, and those who suffered certain skin diseases went. Tonatiuh Ilhuicac was the realm of the sun god, a desertic place of cactuses, magueys, and mesquites where the sun ascended in glory at dawn greeted by the warriors who died in battles or who were captured and sacrificed (Sahagún 1950–1982:Book 3:49). But the souls of dead warriors were also believed to reside in a very different place called Tamoanchan, where they transformed into butterflies and birds of bright plumage. Tamoanchan was a portentous place where a flowering tree grew amid an abundant landscape of groves and streams. Nahuatl songs evoked it as a place of mist where beautiful birds perched on the branches of the tree while blossoms swirled down like rain (López Austin 1997:84–91; Ragot 2000:156). The gods resided there in the beginning until one of them—a goddess—cut a flower or a branch, or ate a fruit from the tree, causing it to break.

The Tamoanchan goddess was variously identified as Ixnextli, Xochiquetzal, Tlazolteotl Ixcuina, Itzpapalotl, or Cihuacoatl (Graulich 1997:55). All belong in H. B. Nicholson's (1971:420–22) "Teteoinnan complex," comprising mother goddesses who were broadly related to the earth, fertility, sexuality, and childbirth. According to a narrative recorded by Diego Muñoz Camargo (Acuña 1984:202–3), Tamoanchan was the residence of Xochiquetzal, a beautiful goddess who lived secluded in that bountiful place guarded from pretenders, until Tezcatlipoca stole her. For

Michel Graulich (1997:52–59) and Alfredo López Austin (1997:86–91),
the abduction of Xochiquetzal was akin to the cutting of fruits, branches,
or flowers that caused the tree to break in other versions of the myth.
They interpreted these acts as transgressions with marked sexual overtones.[1] While Muñoz Camargo identified Tezcatlipoca as the god who
abducted Xochiquetzal, several sources link her with a god named Piltzinteuctli. In the "Song of Xochiquetzal," Piltzinteuctli weeps for the
goddess (Seler 1990–1998:3:264). Some narratives assert that the couple
fathered Xochipilli or Centeotl. Yet another version makes Piltzinteuctli
the first man and the one who married a woman created from the hair of
Xochiquetzal (Tena 2002:31, 153, 155).

Flowers are frequently associated with femininity and sexuality in
sixteenth-century Nahua sources (Dupey García 2013; Sigal 2011) and
in contemporary beliefs from western and northern Mexico. "Taking
flowers" is a sexual metaphor in a Cora account recorded by Konrad
Preuss at the turn of the twentieth century. The older brother Sautari
(the evening star) admonished his younger brother Hatsikan (the morning star) not to cut the flowers he would find along the way that would
take them through the cardinal directions. Sautari resisted the entreaties
of the earth and moon goddess to cut the flowers. Hatsikan initially
resisted, but when he reached the west, a girl seduced him and "took all
his flowers." He slept with her and was defeated (Neurath and Gutiérrez
2003:310–12). Preuss also recorded Cora songs in which the earth goddess
took the cicada's flower ornaments and put them inside her gourd—
likely alluding to her womb—to fertilize the world. The Cora regard
cicadas as harbingers of rain and fertility, whose singing announces the
rainy season (Aedo 2003:175; Alcocer 2003:183; Taube, this volume).

Huichol, Mexicanero, and Yoeme versions of the birth of Christ describe how the Virgin took a flower and put it in her belly, her blouse, or
between her breasts, thus becoming pregnant (Aedo 2003:179; Jáuregui
and Neurath 1998:356; Medina Miranda 2015:55; Shorter 2003:199). In
these episodes, flowers seem to play the role of male agents that inseminated the Virgin just as the flowers of the cicada inseminated the
earth goddess in the Cora account. They evoke the Tamoanchan narrative and, more broadly, a recurrent theme in Mesoamerican myths about
the portentous seduction and impregnation of a tightly guarded maiden
(Chinchilla Mazariegos 2010). Commenting on the Huichol and Cora

accounts, Ángel Aedo noted that flowers primarily convey the joy of life, rain, and blossoming vegetation, but at the same time they evoke the perils of falling in the trap of sexual desire, a moral failure that generally leads to defeat and death in Mesoamerican narratives (Aedo 2003:175).

Flowers evoke femininity and sexual desire in colonial Yucatec sources. Knowlton (2010:78) noted that the word *nicte*, or "flower," was also glossed in the *Motul Dictionary* as "dishonesty, vice of the flesh, and mischief of women." *Nicteil than*, literally "flowery words," refers to "dishonest and lascivious words"; *nicteil winik* is a "woman who is bad with her body", and *nicteil kay* are "dishonest songs and [songs of] love, and to sing them" (Ciudad Real 2001:435). Elsewhere, Knowlton discussed an incantation from the *Ritual of the Bacabs* against the "wind of the flowering tree seizure," which was interpreted as "a chaotic or mad lust, an association between flowering trees and sexual desire" (Knowlton 2016:325). A variant of the name of Piltzinteuctli—Xochiquetzal's partner in some Nahua sources—appears in the Katun 11 Ajaw myths of the *Books of Chilam Balam*, which describe the descent of several gods to a place of sprouting flowers. The flowers have names that begin with the *ix* prefix, denoting their feminine gender. After listing numerous flowers, the text of the *Chumayel* focuses on one of them, named Ix Ha U Lah Nicte, and recounts how the god Bolon Ti Ku "caused his sin to enter her" (Knowlton 2010:79). In this context, "sin" (*keban*) refers to sexual intercourse. In the next passage, the god Pizlim Tec—likely a Mayanized version of Piltzinteuctli—descended and, taking the appearance of a hummingbird, sucked the nectar from another flower, the Bolon Yal Nicte.[2] Sexual connotations are explicit in the phrase that follows: "so Ix Ho Yal Nicte took a husband" (Knowlton 2010:79). Eric Thompson (1970:313) linked this passage with modern Q'eqchi' and Mopan accounts in which the sun transformed into a hummingbird to approach the moon, an attractive maiden who had rejected his initial advances. This passage reappears in numerous iterations across Mesoamerica and relates to the Tamoanchan myths. The parallel explains the adaptation of the name of Piltzinteuctli in the Maya texts to designate the suitor who succeeded in his amorous approaches. The basal frieze of the Lower Temple of the Jaguars at Chichén Itzá features representations of the portent, with hummingbirds biting the breast of women who emerge from large open flowers (Chinchilla Mazariegos 2010:52).

Knowlton (2010:80) compared the landscape of sprouting flowers of the *Books of Chilam Balam* with the flower worlds described by Hill (1992) and Taube (2004). But the landscape that he discussed is far removed from the path of the sun and the solar heaven. Instead, this is a place of feminine flowers that entice descending gods to copulate. In Mesoamerican myths, sexual intercourse does not lead to dawn and glory. Its immediate outcome is generally about downfall and decay even though it may be ultimately conducive to fertility and the reproduction of life. While the *Books of Chilam Balam* did not describe the defeat or death of Pizlim Tec, the sequel to his sexual union with the flowers was a time dominated by debauchery and decay, not unlike the rupture of the tree and the expulsion of the gods from Tamoanchan in Nahua accounts. Dawn occurred only after a deluge that finished that wicked age (Roys 1967:105–7).

The Nahua Tamoanchan was not unrelated to the sun and, in fact, the sunrise was sometimes deemed to take place in Tamoanchan. In the "Song of Atamalcualiztli," the arrival of the goddess Tlazolteotl and the birth of the maize god Centeotl in Tamoanchan prelude the rise of the sun: "Now will the sun rise, now will the day dawn, let all the various firebirds sip nectar where flowers stand erect" (Sahagún 1950–1982:Book 3:238). The abduction of Xochiquetzal from Tamoanchan (or other misdeeds that brought about the rupture of the marvelous tree) triggered a succession of creative events that culminated with the discovery of maize, the rising of the sun, and the advent of people. Yet Tamoanchan differed in significant ways from the solar heaven. Like the flowering place of the *Books of Chilam Balam*, this was a place of femininity. Goddesses resided there, although other gods were also present or arrived in the role of suitors. Rather than the glorious advent of the sun or its transit through the heavens, the dominant themes associated with Tamoanchan involved femininity, sexuality, fertility, and procreation. The following paragraphs explore similar themes represented in Early Classic ceramics from the Pacific coast of Guatemala.

FLOWER WORLDS ALONG THE PACIFIC COAST

Examples from the Pacific coast were relevant for Taube's inquiries about flower world representations in Maya and Teotihuacan art (Taube 2004, 2005, 2006). Flower world iconography first appeared in cities that participated in the Southern City-State Culture of the Late and Terminal Preclassic (Love 2016). Hallmarks of these cities were rich sculptural arrays that exalted rulership and its religious validation, incorporating precocious use of calendrics and inscriptions. The coastal cities were hubs for extensive networks of interaction with strong ties to the Gulf Coast, the Guatemala and Chiapas highlands, and the Maya Lowlands (Chinchilla Mazariegos 2020).

Taube (2004:82) identified personified flowering mountains on either side of the basal level of Tak'alik Ab'aj Stela 4 (Figure 5.1) with wide-open mouths like caves that contain a pool of water. From this pool rises an undulating serpent carrying solar symbols in its coils—centipede heads and a solar disk. A human-faced character emerges from the serpent's maw. The stela has definite solar connotations, yet it seems to represent two distinct places: an earthly, aquatic location below and a heavenly location above, with the ascending serpent thrusting out of the former to reach the latter. The flowering mountains belong in the lower, earthly, and aquatic level, but the water that they contain provides a substrate for the ascent of the sun, evoking solar metaphors related to childbirth and the human life cycle.

The Preclassic iconographic conventions of Stela 4 fell into disuse during the Early Classic period when coastal artists adopted the Teotihuacan artistic language, merging it inextricably with local motifs (Berlo 1984; Chinchilla Mazariegos 2008). They reinterpreted flower world beliefs from Preclassic times and adapted them to express the religious beliefs of the Teotihuacanos, particularly in newly dominant cities located in the coastal plain of Escuintla (Bove and Medrano Busto 2003). Building on previous work by Laurette Séjourné (1961) and Janet Berlo (1984), Taube (2005) linked representations of butterflies, flowers, shells, jewels, and quetzal birds in Escuintla ceramic censers with sixteenth-century Nahua beliefs about the transformation of the souls of dead warriors and their afterlife destiny in solar heaven. In tandem, he examined vessels from Teotihuacan that show scenes of blowgun hunters in mountainous places where cacao trees grow. Birds that include long-tailed quetzals are sucking the flowers or perching on the trees, and the hunters are sometimes shooting at them. In an earlier study, Mary Gaines (1980) recognized that these vessels evoked the tropical lowland regions of southern Mesoamerica, and she suggested that they depicted a landscape of abundance related to the

Figure 5.1 Tak'alik Ab'aj Stela 4. Photo by Oswaldo Chinchilla Mazariegos/Proyecto Nacional Tak'alik Ab'aj, Ministerio de Cultura y Deportes, Guatemala.

afterlife. Taube agreed and related the blowgun hunting scenes to the eastern solar paradise: "As with later Aztec belief, the Teotihuacan solar paradise was to the east, the place of the rising sun and the source of such riches as quetzal plumes, jade and cacao" (Taube 2005:38).

There is no doubt that these vessels portray tropical lowland landscapes that were located to the east from the perspective of Teotihuacan, and the representations of cacao and quetzals point to places in Guatemala. But it appears that the Teotihuacanos had in mind places that were closer to Tamoanchan or Tlalocan than to the solar heaven of the sixteenth-century Nahua. Sahagún's informants referred to *ichan Tonatiuh ilhuicac*, "the home of the sun, in heaven," as a semidesertic place that had little resemblance to the cacao lands of the coastal lowlands or to the high-altitude cloud forest habitats of quetzals. This was "a place like a desert . . . and where the war dead were, there were the magueys, the tziuactli plants [a cactaceae], the mezquite groves" (Sahagún 1950–1982:Book 3:49). The description resembles the semiarid valleys of central and northern Mexico rather than the verdant, water-rich landscapes of the Pacific coast. The Nahua house of the sun was not a place of water; abundant rain and mist belonged in other places of beauty and abundance that were also conceived as afterlife destinies, namely Tlalocan and Tamoanchan (López Austin 1997; Ragot 2000).

The following sections focus on Early Classic Teotihuacan-style objects from the coastal plain of Escuintla, but it is relevant to note that flower world religious beliefs endured in this region through the Late Classic period and later. Flower world representations abound in the sculptural corpus of Cotzumalhuapa, the great city of the Late Classic period in the Escuintla piedmont (Chinchilla Mazariegos 2013, 2015). In these carvings, groups of ritual performers invoke the flower world through dancing and singing while presenting offerings that include headdresses, game animals, and human victims. Their songs take the shape of flowering vines that grow to extraordinary size and complexity. Male and female deities or ancestors sprout like blossoms among mazes of vines that produce many kinds of fruits, flowers, and precious objects. In previous work, I compared these carvings with flower world beliefs that persist in the traditional religion of Santiago Atitlán, a modern Tz'utujil community that straddles the coastal piedmont and the adjacent highlands (Carlsen and Prechtel 1991; Christenson 2001). From Late Preclassic sculptures to modern Atiteco religion, flower world beliefs are surprisingly resilient in the Pacific coast despite marked shifts in the region's demographic and cultural configuration.

THE GODDESS IN THE GARDEN

Cylinder tripod vases with molded designs were distinctive products of Early Classic Escuintla potters. The molded panels of a unique example

Figure 5.2 Drawing of molded design on cylinder tripod vase (after photos by Nicholas Hellmuth, Dumbarton Oaks photo archives). Drawing by Oswaldo Chinchilla Mazariegos.

(Figure 5.2) show characters reclining on their right side within a cross-sectioned shallow basin with everted rim. The shallow basin is a frequent motif in Escuintla censers, where it is sometimes filled with banded or undulating designs that represent water or other liquids. It frequently occupies the basal portion of designs or glyphic collocations that Taube (2000b:9) interpreted as place names in the Teotihuacan writing system. In this case, the basin is adorned with earspools, possible bivalve shells, and snail shells.

The reclining character wears a large headdress with jewels and feathers, a nosepiece, earspools, bracelets, and anklets. The collar conceals the upper body, while the legs are covered with a knee-length banded skirt. The character's pose, with the left leg and the right arm raised, is unusual. Most interesting is the cacao plant that seems to grow from the character's back (although it may also be growing from behind) with several pods hanging from the trunk and branches. Three birds are perched on the tree and on the character's headdress. This is indeed a lush place of abundance, wealth, and beauty, but who is this character? Is it a human being or a deity? Is it a male or female?

While some Teotihuacan deities have nonhuman features, others take human appearance and their gender is hard to establish. Naked or bare-breasted women are nearly absent at Teotihuacan. Most often, the only keys to feminine gender come from garments such as *huipils* and skirts (De Lucia 2008:20–21). For the character in this cylinder tripod, the garments provide inconclusive indications of gender. The posture does not necessarily denote femininity, since there are reclining ceramic effigies that appear to be male at Teotihuacan (Séjourné 1966, Plate 44). A better indication may come from the cacao tree, because cacao is often associated with female characters in the Pacific coast (Chinchilla Mazariegos 2016).

A TEOTIHUACAN MAIZE GODDESS?

Full-figure characters are unusual but not absent in Teotihuacan-style censer lids from Escuintla. One extraordinary example is a lid that shows a seated character wearing a skirt and a pointed blouse (Figure 5.3). The garments suggest that this is a female. Full-figure male characters in Early Classic Escuintla wear loincloths, sometimes combined with short pieces of cloth covering their bottom. They may wear short capes but no blouses. Female characters normally wear skirts with or without blouses. In Postclassic Mesoamerica, the pointed blouse known as *quechquemitl* was primarily a female garment (Anawalt 1981:211–12).

The seated female can be recognized as a maize goddess or a woman impersonating a maize goddess. A large maize ear crowns her headdress and there are numerous maize ear *adornos* on the lid. The headdress consists of a large diadem formed by six oval elements that may correspond to mirrors or large flowers, and the projecting head of a butterfly-raptor—an avian creature that combines the eyes and beak of a raptorial bird with the proboscis and antennae of a butterfly. This composite creature reappears in other censer lids from Escuintla (Chinchilla Mazariegos 2016).

Like the reclining female in the cylinder tripod vase, this lady sits on a water-filled basin—the liquid indicated by diagonal lines and bivalve shells. In both hands she holds objects that contain water scrolls crowned with tufts of feathers and maize cobs. The water scrolls have coastal precedents in the Late Preclassic Stela 23 from Izapa, and there

Figure 5.3 Ceramic censer from the Pacific coast of Guatemala. Banco Industrial, Guatemala City. Photo by Mauricio Acevedo.

are identical scrolls in the hands of the deity of the Tepantitla murals at Teotihuacan—generally identified as a goddess—who has abundant drops of liquid falling down from her hands (Paulinyi 2006). Torrents of liquid pour down from the lady's hands in the Escuintla censer carrying precious objects that include snail shells, bivalve shells, and objects that appear to be composite jewels or bells. This is likely a maize goddess, who is also portrayed as a bringer of water and precious objects. There is a probable counterpart in the bell-shaped censer lid in Figure 5.4.[3] While there are no clues about gender, the character portrayed in that lid has flowers and maize ears in the headdress, and there are more flowers and shells—including *Spondylus*—in the lower part of the lid.

Figure 5.4 Ceramic censer lid from the Pacific coast of Guatemala. Drawing by Oswaldo Chinchilla Mazariegos.

In a recent review, Matthew Robb (2018) highlighted the paucity of representations of maize deities at Teotihuacan. Zoltán Paulinyi (2013) presented arguments for the identification of a maize goddess, although his examples had no explicit maize imagery. Taube (2017) identified a young maize god at Teotihuacan whose elongated head with a tuft of hair—reminiscent of the shape of a maize cob—parallels the physical aspect of the Maya maize god and may derive from that model. There are no clues about the relationship of this young god with the maize goddess portrayed on the coastal censers, who may be a local adaptation of a little-known Teotihuacan goddess or a coastal deity presented in Teotihuacan garb. The multiplicity of maize deities is not surprising. The sixteenth-century Nahua maize god Centeotl—sometimes regarded as female—coexisted with Chicomecoatl, a goddess of maize and all kinds of food, and with Xilonen, the goddess of tender corn (Nicholson 1971:417).

OTHER CENSERS WITH WATER, MOUNTAIN, AND FLOWER ADORNOS

Recognition of a maize goddess raises questions about the gender of other characters portrayed in the Escuintla censers. Noting the militaristic themes found in many censers, Berlo (1984:1:94–106) and Taube (2000a:308–9) interpreted them as representations of warriors' mortuary bundles with the implicit understanding that they correspond to males. The fact is that only the head and hands are generally visible, leaving open the possibility that some censers represent females. Berlo explored links with sixteenth-century Nahua goddesses such as Xochiquetzal and Itzpapalotl, focusing on their warlike aspects.

The censer in Color Plate 7 shows only the bust and hands, and no distinctive female garments are visible. Nevertheless, it has important parallels with the maize goddess censer (Figure 5.3). The character has streams of liquid and precious objects pouring down from the hands, and there is a large basin with wavy water and shellfish at the forefront. There are no maize cobs but the *adornos* make reference to earth and rain themes (Figure 5.5). They consist of triple mountains and composite *adornos* showing storm gods superimposed on inverted "reptile eye" glyphs.[4] In parallel with examples from Teotihuacan (Caso 1966:253), the storm gods hold undulating lightning bolt symbols and emerge from scroll-bordered clouds containing groups of shells, which double as their pectorals. The triple-dart *adornos* in the corners of the headdress suggest martial connotations, perhaps related to the warlike attributes of the storm god (Nielsen and Helmke 2018; Pasztory 1974). If this censer represents a mortuary bundle, the storm god *adornos* suggest that it belonged to someone who was destined for a place that was akin to the sixteenth-century Nahua Tlalocan.

Censers from Escuintla were sometimes shaped as models of temples (Chinchilla Mazariegos 2019). In one example the shrine is covered with *adornos* that include temples, trapeze-and-ray signs, and flowers of various kinds (Figure 5.6). The occupant of this shrine has no distinctive

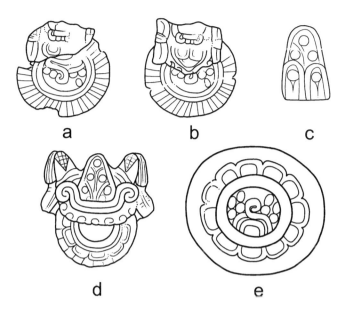

Figure 5.5 Adornos from ceramic censers in Figure 5.6 and Color Plate 7.
(a) and (b) Storm gods superimposed on inverted Reptile Eye signs.
(c) Triple mountains. (d) Shallow basin containing triple mountain and
maize cobs, superimposed on a flower. (e) Flower with reptile eye sign in
the center. Drawings by Oswaldo Chinchilla Mazariegos.

gender traits, but the *adornos* suggest associations with water, fertility, and
flowering places. Most interesting are a series of composite *adornos* that
feature a mountain flanked by two maize ears within a shallow bowl, all
placed over a circular flower. The compound seems to evoke the widespread Mesoamerican concept of a mountain of sustenance conflated
with a flower that evokes the chromatic qualities of flower worlds. The
bowl may evoke the watery aspect that is commonly associated with the
mountain of sustenance. Unlike previous examples, this censer has no
water basin in the forefront, but the large shells in the same position may
have aquatic connotations.

   The occupant of this temple censer has obsidian-inlaid eyes. In Mesoamerican art, the eyes are important markers of the qualities of individuals and deities, and the choice of materials to render them was not ar-
bitrary. Comparing the symbolic meanings of obsidian and chert, Taube
noted that obsidian is mostly associated with the night, darkness, and

Figure 5.6 Ceramic censer from the Pacific coast of Guatemala representing a temple model with an obsidian-eyed character inside. Banco Industrial collection, Guatemala City. Photo by Mauricio Acevedo.

the west (Agurcia Fasquelle et al. 2016:12–15). The eyes of this character are indicators of nocturnal rather than solar and diurnal qualities. Those qualities contrast with the character's yellow hair, which is suggestive of solar connotations (Taube 2005:39). Nevertheless, the dominant symbolism of this censer relates to earthly themes that include water, mountains, and sustenance.

Figure 5.7 Ceramic censer from the Los Chatos sector of Montana, Escuintla. Museo Nacional de Arqueología y Etnología, Guatemala, Photo ID# 2499. Photo © 2009 GalasdeGuatemala.com/Maynor Marino Mijangos.

The eye inlays are relevant for the censer found in the Los Chatos sector of Montana, Escuintla—the lone example of this genre that has been documented in an archaeological context (Figure 5.7; Bove and Medrano Busto 2003; Medrano 1994). The inlays are mica, a material that had nocturnal and lunar connotations for the sixteenth-century Nahua who called it *metzcuitlatl*, "excrement of the moon" (Sahagún 1950–1982:Book

II:235; Ximénez 1888:302). As in the previous example, the probable nocturnal qualities of the eyes contrast with the character's yellow hair. The
gushes of liquid and precious objects flowing from the hands evoke the
maize goddess censer (Figure 5.3). In the chest there is a large flower
with a reptile eye glyph in the center, and the headdress has birds that
Taube (2005) identified as quetzals. He suggested that the Teotihuacanos
associated quetzals with the eastern solar paradise, but the ancient people
of Escuintla were likely aware that quetzals inhabit cloud forests at high
elevations. These are moist habitats characterized by high biomass and
persistent cloud cover reducing the amount of sunlight that penetrates
the forest canopy. While the Teotihuacanos may have ignored this, the
quetzal habitats resemble the misty ambience of Tamoanchan, the realm
of the goddess Xochiquetzal rather than the sunny, bright landscape of
the sixteenth-century Nahua Ichan Tonatiuh Ilhuicac.

CONCLUSION

The common elements of the objects described in previous sections include motifs related to water, sustenance, and femininity. In addition,
they share a surprising paucity of martial imagery. While not entirely
absent, butterfly attributes are limited, as are weapons such as shields and
darts that are commonplace in other Escuintla censers (Berlo 1984:I:94–
96). The distinctions are not clear cut, and there are censers that combine
martial imagery with motifs related to water and sustenance (Hellmuth
1975:44–45). But at best, warlike allusions are oblique in the objects described in this chapter, which seem to concentrate on themes of water and maize, flowers, and precious shells, all related to abundance and
wealth. Establishing the gender of the characters is impossible in the
majority of censers, but the comparison with female characters such as
the maize goddess (Figure 5.3) opens the possibility that other censers
may also portray women or goddesses.

Feminine imagery is not rare in the Pacific Coast. Other censer lids
from this area show large effigies of bare-breasted women or goddesses
holding bowls, cacao pods, birds, or butterflies in their hands. The attire and other attributes of these females depart markedly from Teotihuacan models, suggesting that they portray coastal goddesses (Berlo

1984:1:108–10; Chinchilla Mazariegos 2016; Hellmuth 1975, back cover). Their provenance and dating are uncertain, but they overlap functionally with Teotihuacan-style censers and may be partly contemporary.

As Gaines and Taube pointed out, representations of blowgun hunters in flowering places of cacao and quetzal birds on ceramic vessels evoked the lush landscapes of the Pacific coast of Guatemala, as conceived from the perspective of artists at Teotihuacan. But rather than the Nahua solar paradise, these places had more in common with the misty ambience of Tamoanchan or the water-rich realm of Tlalocan. The feminine connotations that are apparent in ceramic objects from Escuintla narrow down the possible Nahua comparisons to places that are akin to Tamoanchan. The presence of goddesses or their impersonators in association with flowers and flowering places is consistent with widespread Mesoamerican beliefs about mythical places of beauty related to fertility, sexuality, femininity, and reproduction. Those places bear a relationship of contrast and complementarity with flowering realms related to the solar afterlife of warriors.

To conclude, I return to the cylinder tripod showing a reclining lady surrounded by birds, whose body seems to generate cacao (Figure 5.2). It appears that she is not just a female deity in a flowering place but also that she embodies that sumptuous landscape perhaps related to an idealized version of the Pacific Coast itself. This is a flower world of abundance, wealth, and beauty, a place of water, lush vegetation, and femininity, closer to Tamoanchan or Tlalocan than to the Ichan Tonatiuh Ilhuicac of the sixteenth-century Nahua.

ACKNOWLEDGMENTS

Karl Taube's inspiring 2004 article and his input during a 2006 meeting at the Museo Popol Vuh spiked my interest in flower world iconography. I thank the museum and Yale University for their institutional support and the collaboration of Coralia de Rodríguez that allowed me to photograph the Banco Industrial censers. My special thanks to Andrew Turner and Michael Mathiowetz. This chapter benefitted from conversations with Andrew through several years and from an intense week of discussion gently hosted by Christine Szuter at the Amerind.

NOTES

1. A recent critique raised important questions about Graulich's and López Austin's interpretations (Oudijk 2020) but ignored the prevalence and importance of sexual misdeeds in cosmogonic narratives across Mesoamerica, which are often conveyed metaphorically, as in the Tamoanchan myths (Chinchilla Mazariegos 2010; 2017:83–103; 2018).

2. Knowlton (2010:79) translated *Yax bak dzunun ix v uayinah* as "and First Scattering Hummingbird dreamed." However, *uayinah* can also be translated as "tomar figura fantástica de otro," "transfigurarse o tomar figura por hechicería" (Ciudad Real 2001:569; Pío Pérez 1877:375). I follow Roys's (1967:105) translation, "he took the figure of a humming-bird with green plumage on its breast."

3. Auctioned in 2014. https://www.invaluable.com/auction-lot/superb-complete -mayan-incensario-101g-c-b3ad5a5bcc, accessed December 13, 2019.

4. The inverted position of the reptile eye glyphs is unusual. The question of whether these composite *adornos* resulted from modern intervention by restorers who put together pieces that were found separate from each other cannot be securely addressed without a detailed examination of the original, but I am confident that they were part of the original composition. Unlike many examples in public and private collections, the censers in the Banco Industrial collection (Figures 5.3, 5.6 and Color Plate 7) show minimal intervention by modern restorers limited to joining fragments without infilling of breaks and missing sections, overpainting, or other modifications. Unlike many censers from Teotihuacan, those from Escuintla were not disassembled before deposition, and the *adornos* are normally found attached to their intended position in the censers.

REFERENCES

Acuña, René, ed. 1984. *Relaciones geográficas del siglo XVI: Tlaxcala*. Vol. 1. Mexico City: Universidad Nacional Autónoma de México.

Aedo, Ángel. 2003. "Flores de lujuria e influjos siniestros: Fuentes nocturnas del simbolismo huichol del cuerpo humano." *Anales de Antropología* 37:173–204.

Agurcia Fasquelle, Ricardo, Payson Sheets, and Karl Taube. 2016. *Protecting Sacred Space: Rosalila's Eccentric Chert Cache at Copan and Eccentrics Among the Classic Maya*. San Francisco: Precolumbia Mesoweb Press.

Alcocer, Paulina. 2003. "El mitote parental de la chicharra (metineita tsikiri) en Chuísete'e." In *Flechadores de estrellas: Nuevas aportaciones a la etnología de coras y huicholes*, edited by Jesús Jáuregui and Johannes Neurath, 181–206. Mexico City: Instituto Nacional de Antropología e Historia and Universidad de Guadalajara.

Anawalt, Patricia. 1981. *Indian Clothing Before Cortés: Mesoamerican Costumes from the Codices*. Norman: University of Oklahoma Press.

Berlo, Janet C. 1984. *Teotihuacan Art Abroad: A Study of Metropolitan Style and Provincial Transformation in Incensario Workshops.* 2 vols. British Archaeological Reports International Series, vol. 199. Oxford: British Archaeological Reports.

Bove, Frederick J., and Sonia Medrano Busto. 2003. "Teotihuacan, Militarism, and Pacific Guatemala." In *The Maya and Teotihuacan: Reinterpreting Early Classic Interaction*, edited by Geoffrey Braswell, 45–79. Austin: University of Texas Press.

Burkhart, Louise M. 1992. "The Aesthetic of Paradise in Nahuatl Devotional Literature." *RES: Anthropology and Aesthetics* 21:88–109.

Carlsen, Robert S., and Martin Prechtel. 1991. "The Flowering of the Dead: An Interpretation of Highland Maya Culture." *Man* 26:23–42.

Caso, Alfonso. 1966. "Dioses y signos teotihuacanos." In *Teotihuacán: Onceava Mesa Redonda*, 249–75. Mexico City: Sociedad Mexicana de Antropología.

Chinchilla Mazariegos, Oswaldo. 2008. "Los estilos artísticos del período clásico en la costa sur de Guatemala: ¿Reflejos de identidad etnica?" In *El territorio maya: Memoria de la V Mesa Redonda de Palenque*, edited by Rodrigo Liendo Stuardo, 455–74. Mexico City: Instituto Nacional de Antropología e Historia.

Chinchilla Mazariegos, Oswaldo. 2010. "Of Birds and Insects: The Hummingbird Myth in Ancient Mesoamerica." *Ancient Mesoamerica* 21:45–61.

Chinchilla Mazariegos, Oswaldo. 2013. "The Flower World of Cotzumalhuapa." In *The Maya in a Mesoamerican Context: Comparative Approaches to Maya Studies; Proceedings of the 16th European Maya Conference, Copenhagen, December 5–10, 2011*, edited by Jesper Nielsen and Christopher Helmke, 79–92. Acta Mesoamericana, vol. 26. Markt Schwaben: Anton Saurwein.

Chinchilla Mazariegos, Oswaldo. 2015. "Sounds in Stone: Song, Music, and Dance on Bilbao Monument 21, Cotzumalhuapa." *PARI Journal* 16(1):1–12.

Chinchilla Mazariegos, Oswaldo. 2016. "Human Sacrifice and Divine Nourishment in Mesoamerica: The Iconography of Cacao on the Pacific Coast of Guatemala." *Ancient Mesoamerica* 27:361–75.

Chinchilla Mazariegos, Oswaldo. 2017. *Art and Myth of the Ancient Maya.* New Haven, CT: Yale University Press.

Chinchilla Mazariegos, Oswaldo. 2018. "Imágenes sexuales en el Popol Vuh." *Anales de Antropología* 52:153–164.

Chinchilla Mazariegos, Oswaldo. 2019. "Temples to the Great Bird: Architecture, Mythology, and Ritual in Teotihuacan-Style Censers from Escuintla, Guatemala." *RES: Anthropology and Aesthetics* 71/72:78–96.

Chinchilla Mazariegos, Oswaldo. 2020. "The Southern Cities: Urban Archaeology in Pacific Guatemala and Eastern Soconusco, Mexico." *Journal of Archaeological Research.* https://doi.org/10.1007/s10814-020-09145-x.

Christenson, Allen J. 2001. *Art and Society in a Highland Maya Community: The Altarpiece of Santiago Atitlán.* Austin: University of Texas Press.

Ciudad Real, Antonio de. 2001. *Calepino Maya de Motul*, edited by René Acuña. Mexico City: Plaza y Valdés.

De Lucia, Kristin. 2008. "Looking Beyond Gender Hierarchy: Rethinking Gender at Teotihuacan, Mexico." In *Gender, Households, and Society: Unraveling the Threads of the Past and the Present*, edited by Elizabeth M. Brumfiel and Cynthia Robin, 17–36. Archeological Papers of the American Anthropological Association 18. Malden, Mass.: Blackwell.

Dupey García, Élodie. 2013. "De pieles hediondas y perfumes florales: La reactualización del mito de creación de las flores en las fiestas de las veintenas de los antiguos nahuas." *Estudios de Cultura Maya* 45:7–36.

Gaines, Mary E. 1980. "A Pre-Columbian Ceremonial Vase from Teotihuacan." *Bulletin of the Museum of Fine Arts, Houston*, n.s., 8(2):3–13.

Graulich, Michel. 1997. *Myths of Ancient Mexico*. Translated by Bernard Ortiz de Montellano and Thelma Ortiz de Montellano. Norman: University of Oklahoma Press.

Hellmuth, Nicholas M. 1975. *The Escuintla Hoards: Teotihuacan Art in Guatemala*. St. Louis, Mo.: Foundation for Latin American Anthropological Research.

Hill, Jane H. 1992. "The Flower World of Old Uto-Aztecan." *Journal of Anthropological Research* 48(2):117–44.

Jáuregui, Jesús, and Johannes Neurath, eds. 1998. *Fiesta, literatura y magia en el Nayarit: Ensayos sobre coras, huicholes y mexicaneros de Konrad Theodor Preuss*. Mexico City: Instituto Nacional Indigenista.

Knowlton, Timothy W. 2010. *Maya Creation Myths: Words and Worlds of the Chilam Balam*. Niwot: University Press of Colorado.

Knowlton, Timothy W. 2016. "Filth and Healing in Yucatan: Interpreting Ix Hun Ahau, a Maya Goddess." *Ancient Mesoamerica* 27:319–32.

López Austin, Alfredo. 1997. *Tamoanchan and Tlalocan: Places of Mist*. Translated by Bernard R. Ortiz de Montellano and Thelma Ortiz de Montellano. Niwot: University of Colorado Press.

Love, Michael W. 2016. "Early States in the Southern Maya Region." In *The Origins of Maya States*, edited by Loa Traxler and Robert J. Sharer, 271–327. Philadelphia: University of Pennsylvania Museum of Archaeology and Anthropology.

Medina Miranda, Héctor M. 2015. "Nuestra madre la joven águila Wexika: La imagen de la Virgen de Guadalupe en la mitología wixarika." *Revista Euroamericana de Antropología* 0:49–58.

Medrano, Sonia. 1994. "Un incensario estilo Teotihuacano de Escuintla." In *VII Simposio de Investigaciones Arqueológicas en Guatemala, 1993*, edited by Juan Pedro Laporte and Héctor Escobedo, 107–17. Guatemala City: Museo Nacional de Arqueología y Etnología.

Neurath, Johannes, and Arturo Gutiérrez. 2003. "Mitología y literatura del Gran Nayar (coras y huicholes)." In *Flechadores de estrellas: Nuevas aportaciones a la etnología de coras y huicholes*, edited by Jesús Jáuregui and Johannes Neurath,

289–337. Mexico City: Instituto Nacional de Antropología e Historia and Universidad de Guadalajara.

Nicholson, Henry B. 1971. "Religion in Prehispanic Central Mexico." In *Handbook of Middle American Indians*, vol. 10, *Archaeology of Northern Mesoamerica*, pt. 1, edited by Gordon F. Ekholm and Ignacio Bernal, 395–446. Austin: University of Texas Press.

Nielsen, Jesper, and Christophe Helmke. 2018. "The Storm God: Lord of Rain and Ravage." In *Teotihuacan: City of Water, City of Fire*, edited by Matthew H. Robb, 138–43. San Francisco: Fine Arts Museum of San Francisco-De Young; Los Angeles: University of California Press.

Oudijk, Michel R. 2020. "The Making of an Academic Myth." In *Indigenous Graphic Communication Systems*, edited by Katarzyna Mikulska and Jerome A. Offner, 340–75. Niwot: University Press of Colorado.

Pasztory, Esther. 1974. *The Iconography of the Teotihuacan Tlaloc*. Studies in Pre-Columbian Art and Archaeology 15. Washington, D.C.: Dumbarton Oaks.

Paulinyi, Zoltán. 2006. "The 'Great Goddess' of Teotihuacan: Fiction or Reality?" *Ancient Mesoamerica* 17:1–15.

Paulinyi, Zoltán. 2013. "The Maize Goddess in the Teotihuacan Pantheon." *Mexicon* 35:86–90.

Pío Pérez, Juan. 1877. *Diccionario de la lengua Maya*. Mérida: Imprenta de Juan F. Molina Solís.

Ragot, Nathalie. 2000. *Les au-delàs Aztèques*. British Archaeological Reports International Series, vol. 881. Oxford: British Archaeological Reports.

Robb, Matthew H. 2018. "The Maize God." In *Teotihuacan: City of Water, City of Fire*, edited by Matthew H. Robb, 150–53. San Francisco: Fine Arts Museum of San Francisco-De Young; Los Angeles: University of California Press.

Roys, Ralph. 1967. *The Book of Chilam Balam of Chumayel*. 2nd ed. Norman: University of Oklahoma Press.

Sahagún, Bernardino de. 1950–1982. *Florentine Codex: General History of the Things of New Spain*. 12 vols. Translated by Arthur J. O. Anderson and Charles Dibble. Santa Fe, N.Mex.: School of American Research; Salt Lake City: University of Utah Press.

Sahagún, Bernardino de. 1993 [1583]. *Bernardino de Sahagún's Psalmodia Christiana (Christian Psalmody)*. Translated by Arthur J. O. Anderson. Salt Lake City: University of Utah Press.

Séjourné, Laurette. 1961. "El culto a Xochipilli y los braseros teotihuacanos." *El México Antiguo* 9:111–24.

Séjourné, Laurette. 1966. *Arqueología de Teotihuacán: La cerámica*. Mexico City: Instituto Nacional de Antropología e Historia.

Seler, Eduard. 1990–1998. *Collected Works in Mesoamerican Linguistics and Archaeology*. 6 vols. Edited by Frank E. Comparato. Culver City, Calif.: Labyrinthos.

Shorter, David. 2003. "Binary Thinking and the Study of Yoeme Indian Lutu'uria/Truth." *Anthropological Forum* 13:195–203.

Sigal, Peter. 2011. *The Flower and the Scorpion: Sexuality and Ritual in Early Nahua Culture*. Durham, N.C.: Duke University Press.

Taube, Karl A. 2000a. "The Turquoise Hearth: Fire, Self-Sacrifice, and the Central Mexican Cult of War." In *Mesoamerica's Classic Heritage: From Teotihuacan to the Aztecs*, edited by Davíd Carrasco, Lindsay Jones, and Scott Sessions, 269–340. Boulder: University Press of Colorado.

Taube, Karl A. 2000b. *The Writing System of Ancient Teotihuacan*. Barnardsville, N.C.: Center for Ancient American Studies.

Taube, Karl A. 2004. "Flower Mountain: Concepts of Life, Beauty, and Paradise Among the Classic Maya." *RES: Anthropology and Aesthetics* 45:69–98.

Taube, Karl A. 2005. "Representaciones del paraíso en el arte cerámico del Clásico Temprano de Escuintla, Guatemala." In *Iconografía y escritura teotihuacana en la Costa Sur de Guatemala y Chiapas*, edited by Oswaldo Chinchilla Mazariegos and Bárbara Arroyo, 35–54. U Tz'ib, Serie Reportes, vol. 1, no. 5. Guatemala City: Asociación Tikal.

Taube, Karl A. 2006. "Climbing Flower Mountain: Concepts of Resurrection and the Afterlife at Teotihuacan." In *Arqueología e historia del centro de México: Homenaje a Eduardo Matos Moctezuma*, edited by Leonardo López Luján, Davíd Carrasco, and Lourdes Cué, 153–70. Mexico City: Instituto Nacional de Antropología e Historia.

Taube, Karl A. 2017. "Aquellos del este: Representaciones de dioses y hombres mayas en la pintura realistas de Tetitla, Teotihuacan." In *Las pinturas realistas de Tetitla, Teotihuacan: Estudios a través de la obra de Agustín Villagra Caleti*, edited by Leticia Staines Cicero and Christophe Helmke, 71–99. Mexico City: Universidad Nacional Autónoma de México, Instituto de Investigaciones Estéticas.

Tena, Rafael, ed. 2002. *Mitos e historias de los antiguos Nahuas*. Mexico City: Consejo Nacional para la Cultura y las Artes.

Thompson, J. Eric S. 1970. *Maya History and Religion*. Norman: University of Oklahoma Press.

Ximénez, Francisco. 1888. *Cuatro libros de la naturaleza y virtudes de las plantas y animales, de uso medicinal en la Nueva España*, edited by Antonio Peñafiel. Mexico City: Oficina Tipográfica de la Secretaría de Fomento.

6

The Flowery Mountains of Copan
Pollen Remains from Maya Temples and Tombs

Cameron L. McNeil

The pre-Columbian city of Copan is found on the southeastern periphery of the Maya area in Honduras (Map 1). The Maya dynasty at this site began in the early fifth century A.D. At the heart of the urban center lies the Acropolis, a human-produced hill constructed over a four-hundred-year span as elite structures were built and then canceled and built over. Tunnels dug into the Acropolis revealed early temples, elite compounds, and royal tombs. Pollen analysis of samples taken from the floors of the interred structures suggests that flowers and flowering plants were used by the Classic period Maya to actualize paradisiacal places of creation, fecundity, and power imbued with the perfume of blossoms. The Copan Maya were selective in the plants used within temples, possibly more so than tombs, choosing to include species or genera embodying aspects of their worldview and the ritual practices that reproduced it. While some contexts contain a large diversity of genera, there are at least four specific botanical species found in ritual contexts over a two-hundred-year span. Three of these flowers are yellow, but the fourth is predominantly white and fragrant and embodies the Maya concept of the breath soul, which Taube (2004) associates with Flower Mountain. One of the yellow flowers comes from a plant used to produce an alcoholic beverage whose inebriating effects may have played a role in ritual communications. The white and yellow flowers with their verdant greenery would have been framed against the deep red and bright white of the structure walls (McNeil 2006, 2012).

The ritual use of flowers is found in many parts of the world as are concepts of a paradise filled with flowering plants (Goody 1993). The concepts of the Flower World in Mesoamerica and in the southwestern United States are connected by the shared traditions found in their versions of a flowery paradise (Hays-Gilpin and Hill 1999; Hill 1992;

Taube 2004). Taube (2004:69) defines the unique aspects of Mesoamerica's Flower World as "a floral mountain that served both as an abode for gods and ancestors and as a means of ascent into the paradisal realm of the sun. The floral paradise closely related to the concept of the breath soul, a vitalizing force frequently symbolized by flowers." The soul was particularly symbolized by fragrant flowers, and their scent was interpreted as a product of respiration.

Flowers are an important part of modern Maya rituals, but until research at Copan found pollen residues of ritual plants in temples and tombs (McNeil 2006), knowledge of specific species favored by the ancient Maya was the subject of conjecture. Most studies of flowers important to the pre-Columbian and early-contact Maya have focused solely on the analysis of iconography, hieroglyphic inscriptions, and the rare colonial written accounts. The Maya value for the fragrance of flowers is illustrated in pre-Columbian iconography by the depiction of scent lines on blooms indicating that they give off a pleasing smell (e.g., on the North Wall of the San Bartolo murals, where the flowers are also yellow and white) (Color Plate 1; Saturno et al. 2005) and in images that show elites with bouquets held up to their noses (as can be found in the Kerr Maya Vase Database on K1599). Still, when considering ancient ritual spaces, scholars often conceive of them as smoky and heavy with the smell of copal and other burned materials without considering the pleasurable perfume of blossoms and vegetation that would have also have been present.

This chapter will review the context of the areas sampled at Copan for pollen and then explore the methodology used to procure materials from the Classic-period floors of the Acropolis. Following this, the four botanical species that have been identified from multiple ritual spaces at Copan will then be discussed individually. These are not the only species found on the Copan structure floors; some pollen grains remain unidentified and some contexts require more analysis.

AN ANCESTRAL MOUNTAIN: ROSALILA AND THE EARLIEST ROYAL TOMBS

Within their pre-Columbian centers, the Maya created idealized natural landscapes with mountains embodied in the pyramidal structures capped by temples and primordial seas in their plazas (Stuart 1997; Vogt

1981). These locations, like some natural mountains, were places particularly conceived to communicate with ancestors and gods (Schele and Mathews 1998; Vogt 1981).

At Copan, the Late Classic–constructed mountains hide the remains of at least one hundred structures beneath them. The Copan Maya, like many of the Classic-period Maya of other polities, constructed new buildings over earlier ones, sometimes preserving much of the preceding ones but more often saving only platforms or platforms and lower wall sections. The Late Classic Temple 16 marks the heart of the polity. This structure in its last manifestation bore the Teotihuacan-associated goggle-eyed motif of Tlaloc, which by that time was also used as a referent to the first Maya ruler of the site, K'inich Yax K'uk' Mo'. Deep below Temple 16—inside a structure called Hunal—lies a royal tomb purported to belong to this ruler (Burial 95–2) (Sharer 2004; Sharer et al. 1999) who died in A.D. 437. Just above this is found a second, more elaborate tomb in the Margarita Structure (Burial 93–2), which holds a royal lady. Her tomb has a lower chamber (Chamber 1) holding her body and an upper chamber for offerings (Chamber 2). On the outer walls of the Margarita Structure, a stucco façade survives that bears the name of K'inich Yax K'uk' Mo' (Sharer et al. 1999). Both the Hunal Tomb chamber and the lower chamber of the Margarita Tomb flooded, likely repeatedly, dislodging offerings and filling the floors with sediment and debris. The contents of Chamber 2 of the Margarita Tomb were much better preserved. A *petate* (a twill woven mat) rested on its surface, and layers of finely woven mineralized textiles were recovered above it. There is evidence that the Margarita Tomb was reentered on multiple occasions, including bowls placed to the side and nested in one another when new offerings were brought in. Well-preserved food residues such as dark layers of cacao in vessels, small riverine fish mixed with cacao, and shrimp shells survived (McNeil 2006). The surface was covered with decayed organic material at least some of which was the remains of flowers.

K'inich Yax K'uk' Mo' is the most revered ancestor in Copan's history. Altar Q relates that he arrived in Copan in A.D. 427 after receiving the emblems of office elsewhere, probably at the center of Teotihuacan (Stuart 2007), the Place of the Cattails (Stuart 2000). He is referred to as a "Three Hills Water" (Caracol in Belize) lord on Stela 63, and isotopic analysis of his bones also demonstrates that he did not come from Copan

(Price et al. 2010), whereas, the middle-aged lady in the Margarita tomb was locally raised (Buikstra et al. 2004; Price et al. 2010). After their death, these two individuals then became the ancestral mother and father of the Copan polity.

Over the tombs of Hunal and Margarita rests the carefully preserved Rosalila Temple (Agurcia Fasquelle and Fash 2005). A hieroglyphic step on the stairs of Rosalila has a date that corresponds with A.D. 571 (Agurcia Fasquelle 1997), and little more than one hundred years later the structure is believed to have been buried and built over. This temple was constructed above the tombs to draw on the power of the first royal couple of Copan. On Rosalila's façade, *witz* designs mark it as a sacred mountain (Agurcia Fasquelle 1997), and iconography recalls K'inich Yax K'uk' Mo'. Unlike most structures within the Acropolis, which were partially disassembled upon burial, the Rosalila Temple was buried intact and with great care (Agurcia Fasquelle 2004). Its floors were carefully packed with sediments, and the rooms were filled to the top.

The two contexts with the best-preserved pollen signatures within the Acropolis are Chamber 2 of the Margarita Tomb and the South Room of the Rosalila Temple. The Central Room of Rosalila was largely cleared during excavation and could not be sampled. Its West Room had a large doorway that opened to the West Plaza, and pollen may have been blown away by the wind or swept away by those charged with keeping the temple clean. The East Room also contained pollen, but not in the same quantity as the South Room. Within some sections of Rosalila's interior, *petate* fragments were found, indicating that mats were left in place as the building was filled. The pollen from flowers adorning the structure may have filtered through the floor mats and been protected beneath them much in the way that dirt and dust filters through and is preserved under household rugs.

METHODOLOGY

In 1999, at the suggestion of Robert J. Sharer I began sampling floors for pollen residues within the Acropolis tunnels. These samples were taken from the excavations of three projects: the Early Copan Acropolis Program (ECAP) of the University of Pennsylvania Museum of Archaeology and Anthropology, directed by Sharer; the excavations of the Asociación Copán, directed by Ricardo Agurcia; and Harvard University's excavations, directed by William L. Fash. The abovementioned projects in the 1980s and 1990s constructed an elaborate network of tunnels allowing access to many of the Early Classic structures that had been interred inside the Acropolis.

The tunnels offered an excellent environment for pollen sampling. In most cases, the majority of the floors were still covered. Small sections of the floor were freshly excavated, often consisting of an area less than 15 cm × 15 cm. Samples were taken of the fill, the surface of the floor, and the floor itself to ascertain whether the pollen could have been introduced into the structure when the rooms were sealed or whether it was a product of the production process of the stucco that covered most of the interior rooms.

Forty structures inside the Acropolis were sampled. When possible, at least three samples were taken from each room of the structure. Floors that contained the best pollen were sampled more thoroughly in later years. In addition, the pollen of a sediment core extracted from the Petapilla Pond, 6 km from the Acropolis, was analyzed to provide information concerning the ambient pollen during the Classic Period (McNeil 2006; McNeil et al. 2010). Overall, most samples processed were not informative. In some cases, the walls of the buildings had been destroyed, and the floors may have been subjected to various weathering processes before being buried.

POLLEN IN THE RITUAL CONTEXTS OF THE ACROPOLIS

In order to produce viable seeds, pollen must reach the often-sticky stigma of the flower, where it is then conducted down to the ovules at its base. Some pollen is dependent on the wind (anemophilous) to move from the stamens to the stigma, and such species tend to produce copious amounts of pollen to insure fertilization. Other flower species are pollinated by insects or animals (zoophilous), and these plants produce less pollen. Zoophilous pollen grains in ritual contexts are less likely to be the product of wind-borne contamination. Certain anemophilous pollen grains, because of their size or complexity, are also unlikely to travel far from their dispersal point. Anemophilous grains that are known to travel far distances on the wind are not discussed here because of the difficulty of determining whether their presence in the Copan structures are a product of intentional human actions.

FOUR FLOWERING PLANTS AND THEIR POSSIBLE ASSOCIATIONS: MAIZE, CATTAILS, COYOL, AND *ESQUISÚCHIL*

The four flowers represented by pollen repeatedly in Copan ritual spaces were maize, cattails, *coyol*, and *esquisúchil*. In the case of maize and cattails, their abundant flowery yellow pollen can be more visible than the petals of their male flowers. Coyol has pale yellow flowers. *Esquisúchil*, which is known by multiple names in Mesoamerica, is a white fragrant flower. Each of these species will be discussed below.

ZEA MAYS (MAIZE)

Maize pollen is anemophilous, although it is a large grain and rarely travels far from its stalk (Figure 6.1; Treu and Emberlin 2000). Maize pollen was identified on the floors of the Rosalila Temple, the Margarita Tomb, Ruler Twelve's tomb, as well as on the floors of four additional structures: Perico, Juilin, Motmot, and Clavel. In some of these contexts, maize pollen could be present because of contamination, but the relative amounts in the Margarita Tomb's Upper Offering Platform and in Room Two of Rosalila suggest that in these two contexts, pollen or flowering stalks were brought into the ritual spaces.

Figure 6.1 Maize stalks with yellow pollen. Photo by Cameron L. McNeil.

For the Maya and Mesoamericans in general, maize was the principal food. This fact is demonstrated in their art and myths (Taube 1985, 2000), including images of their rul-

Figure 6.2 Uaxaklajuun Ub'aah K'awiil, Copan's thirteenth ruler, in the guise of the Maize God, Temple 22. Late Classic period, Copan, Honduras. Courtesy of the Instituto Hondureño de Antropología e Historia. Drawing by Elvin Arias.

ers as the Maize God (Figure 6.2). Carlsen and Prechtel (1991:27) write that "Flowering Mountain Earth is a place at the world's center whose primary manifestation is a maize plant or tree." The Maya may have decorated the interiors of their temples with flowering maize stalks to recreate or recall this place in the same way that stone sculptures such as Palenque's World Tree of the Temple of the Foliated Cross do (Carlsen and Prechtel 1991; Taube 1985).

TYPHA (CATTAIL)

Typha pollen was identified inside the Rosalila Temple and in the Margarita Tomb's Chamber 2 as well as on the floor of the Aguila Structure (Figure 6.3a). Evidence from the pre-Columbian period to the present supports a tradition whereby the Maya, Toltecs, and Mexica recalled the Place of the Cattails or the Place of the Reeds, a location of origins (Akkeren 2000; Heyden 1983; Schele and Kappelman 2001; Schele and Mathews 1998; Stuart 2000). As discussed earlier, K'inich Yax K'uk' Mo' likely received his rulership from Teotihuacan. This center may not have been the first Place of the Cattails, but probably was the central one during the Early Classic period (Stuart 2007).

Images of cities and ritual spaces designated by cattails are common in Postclassic documents from highland Mexico (Color Plate 8; Figure 6.3b), and references to the Place of the Cattails continue to be found among the Maya (Akkeren 2000; Tedlock 1994). Tedlock (1994) proposed that for the Quiche Maya, Copan was this place of origin. In Santiago Atitlán, the Tz'utujil Maya place cattail leaves around the

A   **B**

Figure 6.3 (a) Cattail stalk laden with pollen. Photo by Cameron L. McNeil. (b) Platform with a cattail plant at the top of its steps acts as part of the place sign for San Miguel Tulancingo (Smith 1973:256). From the *Lienzo of Tlapiltepec*. Drawing by Cameron L. McNeil (after Smith 1973:Figure 66).

entrances to their *cofradia* houses and the altars within them, designating these ritual spaces as the navel of the world (McNeil 2006:Figure 9.7).

Cattails and maize may have been used in the form of flowering stalks within these ritual spaces. They would have formed a powerful ritual pair: one representing water, the wild, and fertility; the other sustenance, domestication, and fertility. Their leafy stalks and pollen-laden flowers would have been decorative and demonstrative within the ritual spaces of the Acropolis.

The use of pollen from these species has also been found in the south-western United States in multiple contexts (Elmore 1943; Gish 1991; Williams-Dean and Bryant 1975). For example, Gish (1991) identified layers of *Typha* and *Zea mays* pollen around a stone proto-Navajoan effigy offered in a ceremonial floor.

ACROCOMIA ACULEATA (COYOL)

Pollen from *Acrocomia aculeata* (the coyol-palm tree) was also found on floors of the Rosalila Temple, and fragments of grains were recovered from the Margarita Tomb and the Papagayo Structure. Coyol-palm flowers are pale yellow. Scariot et al. (1991:20) describe the flower as having a "fruity-putrescent" aroma, although a modern Copaneco related that the smell was appealing. The inflorescence of this palm is packed with hundreds of flowers and can be as long as a meter (Figure 6.4; Breedlove and Laughlin 1993:192). In Mesoamerica the spathes of these trees are

Figure 6.4 Coyol inflorescence on a tree in Copan. Photo by Elisandro Garza.

still used for ritual adornments. Sandstrom (this volume) notes that the fronds of the coyol tree play an important role in the Nahua rituals of the Amatlán community.

At Copan, archaeological evidence supports the economic importance of this tree to the community (Lentz 1990; McNeil 2006). Many parts of the coyol palm are edible: the inflorescence can be consumed when it is immature; both the mesocarp and the pit of the nut are eaten; oil can be extracted from inside the endocarp; the heart of the tree can be consumed (McNeil 2012). Coyol oil would have been particularly important for cooking and food preparation in the pre-Columbian period as animal fats and some vegetable shortenings used by modern Maya would not have been available. Lentz (1990) has suggested that this species was introduced to Copan by the Maya since the plant's endocarps are first found in middens following the Acbi-Bijac transition (ca. A.D. 400), around the time that K'inich Yax K'uk' Mo' arrived. The analysis of the sediments from the Petapilla Pond found that the pollen of *A. aculeata* first appeared approximately 23 cm before ash from the eruption of the Ilopango volcano (McNeil et al. 2010), which is now believed to have occurred around A.D. 539/540 (Dull et al. 2019). Curiously, the signature of the pollen of this tree ceases abruptly with the rapid regrowth of the forests, which signal the demographic drop found at the end of the Classic period (McNeil 2006; McNeil et al. 2010), and coyol is completely absent from later sediment layers.

Coyol was undoubtedly also valued because its sap can be fermented to produce an alcoholic beverage, one that was still commonly consumed in Copan until about 30 years ago (McNeil 2006). The production of wine from coyol sap was once widespread in Central America (Freytag 1953). Various artistic renderings on pre-Columbian Maya vases suggest that people of this culture used alcoholic drinks and enemas (which may have contained alcohol-laced contents) in ritual performance (Houston et al. 2006:117).

BOURRERIA HUANITA (*IK'AL TE* OR *ESQUISÚCHIL*)

The fourth flower found in both Chamber 2 of the Margarita Tomb and in the South Room of the Rosalila Temple as well as on two other structure floors is a member of the *Bourreria* genus (most likely *Bourreria huanita*)

Figure 6.5 (a) *Boureria huanita* blossoms. Photo by Cameron L. McNeil. (b) Illustration of *Bourreria huanita* from the *Badianus Manuscript*, a sixteenth-century codex. Drawing by Cameron L. McNeil.

(Figure 6.5a; McNeil 2006, 2012). The Nahua name for this flower is *esquisúchil*. Maya names documented for *Bourreria huanita* are *ter-ech-mach* and *ik'al te* (Balick et al. 2000; Breedlove and Laughlin 1993). The use of *B. huanita* by people of highland Mexico in the colonial and early contact period is well documented (Figure 6.5b; Bierhorst 1985; Sahagún 1950–1982).

Current evidence indicates that *Bourreria* is the most important ritual flower of the Maya to have been forgotten or lost in the time since the conquest. Its lovely, sweet-smelling, yellow-centered white flowers would have imbued the buildings with a powerful paradisiacal fragrance. Only a handful of blossoms will fill a room with their scent in the evening, when the flowers smell the strongest.

Bourreria is not wind-pollinated, and it is therefore unlikely that its pollen reached the interiors of the Rosalila Temple and the Margarita Tomb accidentally. Trees of this genus no longer grow in the Copan Valley, and there are only two known *Bourreria huanita* trees in all of Honduras (Nelson 2008). *Bourreria huanita*, *B. oxyphylla*, and *B. pulchra* are the only species with a history of ritual, medicinal, or ornamental use in Mesoamerica, and of these species, *B. huanita* is most commonly cited as a valued plant. The flowers of these plants are similar, and it may be that populations used their local species of *Bourreria*. The pollen found on the floors could be *B. huanita* or *B. oxyphylla*, but only *B. huanita* has been known to grow locally (in the Ch'orti Maya lands just across the border in Guatemala).

Bourreria huanita trees can live for hundreds of years. The rare surviving trees are often very old, such as one that is found outside the Cathedral of San Miguel de Tegucigalpa, Honduras (McNeil 2006) and another—planted in 1657—that was in Antigua, Guatemala, outside of the Ermita del Santo Calvario church (Torres 2006), until it fell in 2020. Many of the surviving trees are found adjacent to colonial churches, which may point to a pre-Columbian practice of placing them outside of temples. These trees bear small white flowers and are intensely fragrant. The tree has the ability to produce flowers during any time of the year, but most commonly it blooms during the rainy season.

Most of what is known about the pre-Columbian and contact-period use of *Bourreria* comes from documents written about the cultures of Mexico. The white fragrant flowers of this tree were associated with the dead and used by the Mexica of highland Mexico as offerings in temples, in sacred gardens, as medicine, in cacao beverages, and as garlands to adorn individuals for sacred rites (Sahagún 1950–1982). There is a widely told legend that a war was waged over the acquisition of these trees between the Mexica and the Mixtec. Emmart (1940:275) writes that *B. huanita* was "one of the most frequently used and best known of the Aztec [Mexica] plant remedies," although she does not provide enough information regarding its uses. Hernández (2000 [1651]) recorded that the flowers "are very beautiful and coveted by all—are very fragrant and really could be used for ornaments in the Garden of our Lord," and also that they were sometimes called "*teoyzquixochitl* (sacred *izquitl* flower)" (Emmart 1940:276). In the *Florentine Codex*, Sahagún (1950–1982:Book 11:202) writes of the tree, "It is of pleasing odor, fragrant, aromatic; its odor is dense, strong, harsh. Its fragrance is like that of the *tlacopatli*; it penetrates one's nose. It stands blooming, rustling, spreading its branches. It is raining, scattering, showering, showering down [its blossoms]. Producing perfume which, as it lies, spreads over the whole land—spreads billowing, spreads swirling." The name of the flower in Nahua and Spanish translates to "popcorn flower." It likely was given this name because the flowers have the appearance of popped corn, although some colonial Spanish chroniclers relate that it bears this name because the seeds pop like those of maize.

The important pre-Columbian and modern pilgrimage site of Esquipulas in Guatemala is said to translate to "place where the isquitzuchil are abundant" (Arriola 1941), referring specifically to these trees and their blossoms. Today in Esquipulas there is only one surviving tree in the backyard of a private family home.

Connections Between the Dead, Souls, and Bourreria

When one investigates the recorded information—both pre-Columbian and modern—concerning *Bourreria*, there is a pattern of associations between this genus, the soul, and the dead. White flowers in general have been associated with the soul in some areas of Mesoamerica (Pohl 1994). At Copan, at least one temple placed over a tomb bears iconography suggesting that it exudes a white flowery breath, the breath soul, of the deceased ancestor (Plank 2003:128). Houston and Taube (2000:273) write that the breath soul can be depicted as a white flower or by the wind sign *ik'*. One of the Maya names for the *Bourreria huanita* tree is Ik'al, which may reflect these older connections between the wind, fragrant white flowers, and death.

In diverse areas of Mesoamerica, *Bourreria*, or close relatives, were also associated with the dead. Referencing research by John Monaghan, Pohl (1994:124) has written that in the modern Mixtec community of Nuyoo, white flowers represent the soul of deceased individuals, and Pohl proposes that these are probably jasmine flowers (members of the *Bourreria* genus). Smith identified these flowers by their Mixtec name, *yuhu*, which can mean "tomb" (Pohl 1994). Among the Zapotec, these same flowers are called *guie' xhuuba'*, which translates to "flowers of the tomb." Atran (1993:652) records that the Itzaj of Peten, Guatemala, placed the leaves of *Bourreria oxyphylla* "beneath the corpse to absorb 'the heat of the dead' so [the] spirit will not haunt the home."

In addition, there may have been connections between dead warriors and *Bourreria* flowers among the Mexica. In the poetic song 87 of the *Cantares mexicanos*, recorded by a Jesuit priest after the conquest, the author sings, "Our poor soldier men are where these popcorn flowers lie. And there I'll go dear mama. I'll carry off my flowers" (Bierhorst 1985:407). The famed Mexica sculpture of Xochipilli in the Museo Nacional de Antropología in Mexico City may bear *Bourreria* blossoms on its base, although these features were previously mistaken for mushrooms (Wasson 1973). Butterflies, a symbol for the soul of dead warriors, hover around these flowers (Figures 6.6, 7.1e).

Medicinal Plant with Wound-Healing Properties

Bourreria is also tied to blood in many of its medicinal uses, and the plant may have been used to heal the wounds of autosacrifice. Charles Wisdom (n.d.), the early twentieth-century ethnographer of the Maya, wrote in his ethnobotany of the Ch'orti' that Maya women consumed a "tea of *Bourreria* [*huanita*] flowers, mixed with powdered kaolin" to reduce excessive menstrual flow. *Bourreria* species, as well as some species in the genus of its close cousin, *Cordia*, are used to heal wounds in Mesoamerica and the Caribbean. Kremer and Flores (1996) described the practice of the Yucatec Maya of cutting strips of *B. pulchra* bark and placing them over accidental cuts for healing, and they hypothesized that the pre-Columbian Maya would have done the same.

Figure 6.6 Statue of Xochipilli, Tlalmanalco, Museo Nacional de Antropología, Mexico City. Drawing by Mauricio Díaz García.

CONCLUSION

In the Rosalila Temple the Maya created a Flower Mountain with blossoms full of meaning. The structure breathed with the fragrance of white *Bourreria* flowers, possibly channeling the breath soul of the deceased ancestral parents of the polity, or perhaps ushering them on to their flowery paradise. The cattails would likely have designated the structure as a watery area of fecundity and power and—along with maize, the food of

Mesoamericans—formed an important ritual pairing that is also found in the southwestern United States. Long spathes of coyol flowers probably hung within these spaces as spathes of palms often do on modern Maya ritually adorned altars (McNeil 2012). The plants used within the Rosalila Temple reflected a practice over one hundred years old that is first found in Chamber 2 of the Margarita Tomb.

Chamber 2 has a larger diversity of pollen types than is found in the Rosalila Temple, and many await identification. In this area flower offerings may have been replenished on multiple occasions as new vessels of comestibles were brought in with fresh flowers joining fresh foods. Not only the flowers and their fragrances but also their essence may have been perceived as an important offering to deified ancestors (Dupey García 2013).

The analysis of sediment samples from ritual contexts in the Acropolis of Copan, Honduras, provides added depth to our knowledge of pre-Columbian Maya flower use that previously was based solely on hieroglyphic decipherment and early colonial accounts. Various scholars have written about the flowers probably used by the Maya in the pre-Columbian period, but no one has analyzed the microbotanical remains from temple and tomb floors to determine exactly what flowers actually had a role in rituals. This is unfortunate; archaeologists have swept away a wealth of information on ancient plant use as they uncovered the stone, stucco, and dirt of ritual spaces. The analysis of pollen from the Acropolis brings to light some of the lost fragrances of ancient ritual and provides a more complicated scentscape for these areas that undoubtedly combined the dense smoke of pine with the crisp smell of pine needles as well as pungent copal, with heavily fragrant flowers such as *Bourreria* and with the sweetly sour odor of the verdant cattail, maize stalks, and coyol spathes. This olfactory information augments visual conceptions of the use of interior temple spaces painted bright white and deep red but often empty of artifacts on their surface. One can now imagine the interiors accented with white and yellow inflorescences and green leaves.

ACKNOWLEDGMENTS

I would like to thank Michael Mathiowetz and Andrew Turner for inviting me to participate in this volume and the Amerind Foundation for hosting the conference. I appreciate the support of the Instituto

Hondureño de Antropología e Historia. This work was conducted at the suggestion of Robert J. Sharer, who directed the Early Copan Acropolis Program. Ricardo Agurcia Fasquelle and William L. Fash generously allowed me to sample floors from their excavations. This research was funded by a Fulbright Fellowship from 2000–2001 and a Foundation for the Advancement of Mesoamerican Studies. Inc. grant in 2002. This chapter benefitted from suggestions by all of the wonderful participants at the Amerind conference as well as from John Byram, Mauricio Díaz García, Edy Barrios, and C. Steven LaRue. Lastly, the analysis presented in this chapter could not have been accomplished without the generous mentorship of palynologists Lida Pigott Burney and David Burney.

REFERENCES

Agurcia Fasquelle, Ricardo. 1997. "Rosalila, an Early Classic Maya Cosmogram from Copan." *Symbols* (Spring):32–36.

Agurcia Fasquelle, Ricardo. 2004. "Rosalila, Temple of the Sun-King." In *Understanding Early Classic Copan*, edited by Ellen E. Bell, Marcello A. Canuto and Robert J. Sharer, 101–111. Philadelphia: University of Pennsylvania Museum of Archaeology and Anthropology,

Agurcia Fasquelle, Ricardo, and Barbara W. Fash. 2005. "The Evolution of Structure 10L-16, Heart of the Copan Acropolis." In *Copán: The History of an Ancient Maya Kingdom*, edited by E. Wyllys Andrews and William L. Fash, 201–37. Santa Fe, N.Mex.: School of American Research Press.

Akkeren, Ruud van. 2000. *Place of the Lord's Daughter: Rab'inal, Its history and Dance-Drama*. Leiden: Research School CNWS, School of Asian, African, and Amerindian Studies.

Arriola, Jorge Luis. 1941. *El libro de las geonimias de Guatemala*. Guatemala City: Seminario de Integración Social Guatemalteca.

Atran, Scott. 1993. "Itza Maya Tropical Agro-Forestry." *Current Anthropology* 34(5):633–700.

Balick, Michael J., Michael H. Nee, and Daniel E. Atha. 2000. *Checklist of the Vascular Plants of Belize*. Memoirs of the New York Botanical Garden Press, vol. 85. Bronx: New York Botanical Garden Press.

Bierhorst, John. 1985. *Cantares mexicanos: Songs of the Aztecs*. Stanford, Calif.: Stanford University Press.

Breedlove, Dennis E., and Robert M. Laughlin. 1993. *The Flowering of Man: A Tzotzil Botany of Zinacantán*. Smithsonian Contributions to Anthropology 35, 2 vols. Washington, D.C.: Smithsonian Institution Press.

Buikstra, Jane, T. Douglas Price, Lori E. Wright, and James H. Burton. 2004. "Tombs from the Copan Acropolis: A Life History Approach." In *Under-*

standing Early Classic Copan, edited by Ellen E. Bell, Marcello Canuto, and Robert Sharer, 191–212. Philadelphia: University of Pennsylvania Museum of Archaeology and Anthropology.

Carlsen, Robert S., and Martin Prechtel. 1991. "The Flowering of the Dead: An Interpretation of Highland Maya Culture." *Man* 26(1):23–42.

Dull, Robert A., John R. Southon, Steffen Kutterolf, Kevin J. Anchukaitis, Armin Freundt, David B. Wahl, Payson Sheets, Paul Amaroli, Walter Hernandez, Michael C. Wiemann, and Clive Oppenheimer. 2019. "Radiocarbon and Geologic Evidence Reveal Ilopango Volcano as Source of the Colossal 'Mystery' Eruption of 539/540 CE." *Quaternary Science Reviews* 222:1–17.

Dupey García, Élodie. 2013. "De pieles hediondas y perfumes florales: La reactualización del mito de creación de las flores en las fiestas de las veintenas de los antiguos nahuas." *Estudios de cultura Náhuatl* 45:7–36.

Elmore, Francis H. 1943. *Ethnobotany of the Navajo*. University of New Mexico Bulletin Monograph Series, vol. 1, no. 7. Albuquerque: University of New Mexico Press.

Emmart, Emily W. 1940. *The Badianus Manuscript: An Aztec Herbal of 1552*, with a foreword by Henry E. Sigerist. Baltimore: Johns Hopkins Press.

Freytag, George F. 1953. "The Coyol Palm as a Beverage Tree." *Missouri Botanical Garden Bulletin* 41(3):47–49.

Gish, Jennifer W. 1991. "Appendix B: Pollen Results from Three Sites Near Navajo Reservoir, Northwestern New Mexico." In *The Effigy Site: Archaeological Investigations at LA 78784, a Navajo Ceremonial Site near Smith Pass, Rio Arriba County, New Mexico*, edited by S. Wilcox and B. P. Johnson, 1–13. Bloomfield, N.M.: Salmon Ruin Museum.

Goody, Jack. 1993. *The Culture of Flowers*. Cambridge: Cambridge University Press.

Hays-Gilpin, Kelley, and Jane H. Hill. 1999. "The Flower World in Material Culture: An Iconographic Complex in the Southwest and Mesoamerica." *Journal of Anthropological Research* 55(1):1–37.

Hernández, Francisco. 2000 [1651]. *The Mexican Treasury: The Writings of Dr. Francisco Hernández*, edited by Simon Varey and translated by Rafael Chabran, Cynthia L. Chamberlin, and Simon Varey. Stanford, Calif.: Stanford University Press.

Heyden, Doris. 1983. "Reeds and Rushes: From Survival to Sovereigns." In *Flora and Fauna Imagery in Precolumbian Cultures: Iconography and Function*, edited by Jeanette F. Peterson, 93–112. British Archaeological Reports International Series, vol. 171. Oxford: British Archaeological Reports.

Hill, Jane H. 1992. "The Flower World of Old Uto-Aztecan." *Journal of Anthropological Research* 48(2):117–44.

Houston, Stephen, David Stuart, and Karl Taube. 2006. *Memory of Bones: Body, Being, and Experience Among the Classic Maya*. Austin: University of Texas Press.

Houston, Stephen, and Karl Taube. 2000. "An Archaeology of the Senses: Perception and Cultural Expression in Ancient Mesoamerica." *Cambridge Archaeological Journal* 10(2):261–94.

Kremer, Jürgen, and Fausto Uc Flores. 1996. "Ritual Suicide of Maya Rulers." In *Eighth Palenque Round Table, 1993*, edited by Martha J. Macri and Jan McHargue, 79–91. San Francisco: Pre-Columbian Art Research Institute.

Lentz, David L. 1990. "*Acrocomia Mexicana*: Palm of the Ancient Mesoamericans." *Journal of Ethnobiology* 10(2):183–94.

McNeil, Cameron L. 2006. "Maya Interactions with the Natural World: Landscape Transformation and Ritual Plant Use at Copan, Honduras." Unpublished Ph.D. dissertation, Department of Anthropology, Graduate Center, City University of New York.

McNeil, Cameron L. 2012. "Recovering the Color of Ancient Maya Floral Offerings at Copan, Honduras," in "Color in American Prehistory," edited by Alexandre Tokovinine and Cameron McNeil, special section, *RES: Journal of Anthropology and Aesthetics* 61/62:301–14.

McNeil, Cameron L., David A. Burney, and Lida Pigott-Burney. 2010. "Evidence Disputing Deforestation as the Cause for the Collapse of the Ancient Maya Polity of Copan, Honduras." *Proceedings of the National Academy of Sciences* 107(3):1017–22.

Nelson, Cirilo. 2008. *Catalogo de las plantas vasculares de Honduras, espermatofitas*. Tegucigalpa: Secretaría de Recursos Naturales y Ambiente.

Plank, Shannon E. 2003. "Monumental Maya Dwellings in the Hieroglyphic and Archaeological Records: A Cognitive-Anthropological Approach to Classic Maya Architecture." Unpublished Ph.D. dissertation, Department of Anthropology, Boston University.

Pohl, John M. D. 1994. *The Politics of Symbolism in the Mixtec Codices*. Nashville, Tenn.: Vanderbilt University.

Price, T. Douglas., James H. Burton, Robert J. Sharer, Jane E. Buikstra, Lori E. Wright, Loa P. Traxler, and Katherine A. Miller. 2010. "Kings and Commoners at Copan: Isotopic Evidence for Origins and Movement in the Classic Maya Period." *Journal of Anthropological Archaeology* 29(1):15–32.

Sahagún, Fray Bernardino. 1950–1982. *Florentine Codex: General History of the Things of New Spain*. 12 vols. Translated by Arthur J. O. Anderson and Charles Dibble. Santa Fe, N. Mex: School of American Research; Salt Lake City: University of Utah Press.

Saturno, William A., Karl A. Taube, and David Stuart. 2005. *The Murals of San Bartolo, El Petén, Guatemala Part 1: The North Wall*. Ancient America 7. Barnardsville, N.C.: Center for Ancient American Studies.

Scariot, Aldicir O., Eduardo Lleras, and John D. Hay. 1991. "Reproductive Biology of the Palm *Acrocomia aculeata* in Central Brazil." *Biotropica* 23: 12–22.

Schele, Linda, and Julia Guernsey Kappelman. 2001. "What the Heck's Coatépec? The Formative Roots of Enduring Mythology." In *Landscape and Power in Ancient Mesoamerica*, edited by Rex Koontz, Kathryn Reese-Taylor, and Annabeth Headrick, 29–53. Boulder, Colo.: Westview Press.

Schele, Linda, and Peter Mathews. 1998. *The Code of Kings*. New York: Scribner.

Sharer, Robert J. 2004. "External Interaction at Early Classic Copan." In *Understanding Early Classic Copan*, edited by Ellen E. Bell, Marcello A. Canuto, and Robert J. Sharer, 297–318. Philadelphia: University of Pennsylvania Museum of Archaeology and Anthropology.

Sharer, Robert J., Loa P. Traxler, David W. Sedat, Ellen E. Bell, Marcello A. Canuto, and Christopher Powell. 1999. "Early Classic Architecture Beneath the Copan Acropolis: A Research Update." *Ancient Mesoamerica* 10(1):3–23.

Smith, Mary E. 1973. *Picture Writing from Ancient Southern Mexico: Mixtec Place Signs and Maps*. Norman: University of Oklahoma Press.

Stuart, David. 1997. "The Hills Are Alive: Sacred Mountains in the Maya Cosmos." *Symbols* (Spring):13–17.

Stuart, David. 2000. "'The Arrival of Strangers': Teotihuacan and Tollan in Classic Maya History." In *Mesoamerica's Classic Heritage: From Teotihuacan to the Aztecs*, edited by David Carrasco, Lindsay Jones, and Scott Sessions, 465–513. Boulder: University of Colorado Press.

Stuart, David. 2007. "The Origin of Copan's Founder." *Maya Decipherment: Ideas on Ancient Maya Writing and Iconography*, January 25. https://maya decipherment.com/2007/06/25/the-origin-of-copans-founder.

Taube, Karl A. 1985. "The Classic Maya Maize God: A Reappraisal." In *Fifth Palenque Round Table, 1983*, edited by Virginia M. Fields, 171–82. San Francisco: Pre-Columbian Art Research Institute.

Taube, Karl A. 2000. "Lightning Celts and Corn Fetishes: The Formative Olmec and the Development of Maize Symbolism in Mesoamerica and the American Southwest." In *Olmec Art and Archaeology in Mesoamerica*, edited by John M. Clark and Mary Pye, 297–337. Washington, D.C.: National Gallery of Art.

Taube, Karl A. 2004. "Flower Mountain: Concepts of Life, Beauty, and Paradise Among the Classic Maya." *RES: Anthropology and Aesthetics* 45:69–98.

Tedlock, Dennis. 1994. *Breath on the Mirror: Mythic Voices, and Visions, of the Living Maya*. Albuquerque: University of New Mexico Press.

Torres, Miguel F. 2006. "El esquisúchil o árbol del Santo Hermano Pedro en el jardín de El Calvario patrimonio cultural de Guatemala, capítulo V." In *El tesoro del calvario patrimonio de la antigua Guatemala*, edited by M. F. Torres. Guatemala: Fundación G & T Continental.

Treu, Rob, and Jean Emberlin. 2000. *Pollen Dispersal in the Crops Maize (Zea mays), Oil Seed Rape (Brassica napus ssp. oleifera), Potatoes (Solanum tuberosum), Sugar Beet (Beta vulgaris ssp. vulgaris) and Wheat (Triticum aestivum).*

A report for the Soil Association from the National Pollen Research Unit. Worcester: University College.

Vogt, Evon Z. 1981. "Some Aspects of the Sacred Geography of Highland Chiapas." In *Mesoamerican Sites and World Views*, edited by Elizabeth P. Benson, 119–38. Washington, D.C.: Dumbarton Oaks.

Wasson, R. Gordon. 1973. "The Role of 'Flowers' in Nahuatl Culture: A Suggested Interpretation." *Botanical Museum Leaflets* (Harvard University) 23(8):305–24.

Williams-Dean, Glenna, and Vaughn M. Bryant Jr. 1975. "Pollen Analysis of Human Coprolites from Antelope House." *Kiva* 41(1):97–111.

Wisdom, Charles. N.d. Unpublished manuscript. National Anthropological Archives Manuscript 4826, 774–1006. Washington, D.C.: Smithsonian Institution.

7

Beauty in Troubled Times

The Flower World in Epiclassic Central Mexico, A.D. 600–900

Andrew D. Turner

In marked contrast to the flower worlds of the Classic Maya, the flower world traditions of Teotihuacan (100 B.C.–A.D. 600) and the Mexica (A.D. 1325–1521) promoted state-sponsored militarism through ideologies of self-sacrifice and the apotheosis of deceased warriors as nectar-drinking birds and butterflies. Despite their apparent similarities, little is known of how and in what form these beliefs persisted in Central Mexico during the centuries that separated these two traditions. The collapse of Teotihuacan led to drastic and long-term economic, political, and demographic changes that restructured societies locally and affected the whole of Mesoamerica during the Epiclassic period (A.D. 600–900) in Central Mexico. Although much of the focus on the Epiclassic has been on the social upheaval and political reorganization brought about by Teotihuacan's collapse, it was probably during this time that the flower world became thoroughly intermeshed with politics, the economy, and militarism in Central Mexico.

The Central Mexican Epiclassic period is generally characterized by rampant interpolity conflict, far-ranging economic activity, and the advent of new art styles (Diehl and Berlo 1989:3; Hirth 1989:69; Webb 1978). Polities including Cacaxtla, Teotenango, and Xochicalco (Map 1) quickly rose to prominence in Central Mexico in the wake of Teotihuacan's collapse. These centers were rapidly built on hilltops that were fortified with defensive features such as terraces, moats, and ramparts (e.g., Armillas 1946; Hirth 1995:239), suggesting fierce and violent rivalry. Increased competition among states for exotic luxury items may have fueled cross-polity conflict during the Epiclassic (Webb 1978), a development that was arguably paralleled in the Maya Lowlands through a shift toward an increasingly commercialized economy from the tribute-based economies of the Early Classic (McAnany 2010). Monumental artwork at Epiclassic sites is often described as "eclectic," with scholars pointing to "influences" from the Gulf Coast, Oaxaca, Teotihuacan, and the Maya Lowlands (e.g., Kubler 1980), although this broad characterization may mask deliberate ideological underpinnings behind such works (Stone 1989; Turner 2016).

While studies of Epiclassic Central Mexico have tended to focus on warfare, economy, and artwork, the role of religion has received relatively little attention. Studies by López Austin and López Luján (2000) and Ringle et al. (1998) provide productive frameworks for understanding how religion worked in tandem with royal legitimization and network building, the exchange of prestige goods, and the development of "cosmopolitan" art styles, but they do not consider the role that preexisting beliefs and ideologies pertaining to flower worlds played in shaping these interactions. This chapter argues that Epiclassic polities such as Cacaxtla, Teotenango, and Xochicalco elaborated and reconfigured Teotihuacan flower world themes in more broadly legible art styles through small-scale artwork and monumental public architectural programs, modifying their relationship to state ideology, their associated imagery, and the contexts in which they appear in response to new cross-regional patterns of interaction and changes in social structure and religious practice. As a result, these manifestations of the flower world not only served as a basis for the apparent continuities among later Central Mexican Flower World traditions but also contributed to the social developments that characterize the Epiclassic period as a whole.

BIRDS AND BUTTERFLIES OF FLOWER WORLD

Artwork from Teotihuacan and ethnohistoric sources pertaining to the Mexica portray radiant butterflies and colorful birds as manifestations of the souls of deceased warriors who dwell in a floral paradise. Teotihuacan artists evoked the flower world through figurines and theater-style censers portraying deceased warriors and other beings (introduction and Chinchilla Mazariegos, this volume) and painted scenes of paradise and the butterflies and colorful birds that populate it. These representations influenced later forms, but significant stylistic transformations took place in Central Mexico during the Epiclassic period. Teotihuacan butterflies usually have large eyes with goggles and feathered antennae, and a prominent curling proboscis that may emerge from the top of the head (Figures 7.1a–7.1d). Butterfly wings may be naturalistic, trilobed, or geometricized (Figure 7.1d) in the form of butterfly nose ornaments. In the art of the Late Postclassic International Style (A.D. 1200–1521), the antennae tend to be reduced, the snouts and lower lips curl, and both forms emulate a proboscis (Figures 7.1e–7.1g). Teotihuacan quetzals are distinguishable by their long, green tails and exaggerated crests, but they also sport nonnaturalistic features, including hooked raptorial beaks, a band that runs the length of the wing and spirals as it meets the body, and often a feature at the base of the tail that resembles a conch shell in cross section (Figure 7.2a). These features remain consistent in Epiclassic representations and persist during the Postclassic (Figure 7.2b–7.2d).

Butterflies and birds are sometimes conflated on painted tripod vessels and theater-style censers from Teotihuacan (Figure 7.2e; Headrick 2003:153–55; Paulinyi 2014), and such composite creatures also appear in later traditions. A prominent Epiclassic example appears on the Trapezoidal Stone from Teotenango (Figure 7.2f). A large butterfly on one of the monument's faces has a segmented body, large forelimbs, and spots on its wings, but it has an avian beak, a crest on top of its head that may be that of a quetzal, and it wears a necklace. The butterfly on the Trapezoidal Stone anticipates Early Postclassic representations of supernatural butterflies identified by Taube (2020) as the souls of deceased warriors. Epiclassic butterflies may also appear with hooked beaks (Figure 7.2g), conflating butterfly and quetzal and prefiguring the curled snouts and lower lips of Late Postclassic butterflies.

SHIFTING CONTEXTS

Teotihuacan's pervasive influence did not disappear after the city's collapse. The production of censers similar to those from Teotihuacan continued in some regions that had been in Teotihuacan's immediate sphere of influence but with stylistic differences that reflect shifting patterns of interaction. While based in Teotihuacan symbolism, a censer lid from Xico, located in the Basin of Mexico (Figure 7.3a; Map 1), deviates from Teotihuacan's more schematic and stylized theater-style censers by showing a more naturalistic figure flanked by hand-built blossoms. The censer is liberally decorated with Maya Blue, a pigment that does not appear in

Figure 7.1. Representations of butterflies from Teotihuacan and Late Postclassic Central Mexico. (a) Detail of Teotihuacan-style carved tripod vessel (after Séjourné 1966:Figure 39). (b) Detail of Teotihuacan-style stuccoed tripod vessel in the Los Angeles County Museum of Art. (c) Detail of Teotihuacan-style carved vessel (after Seler 1990–1998:6, Figure 167). (d) Detail of Teotihuacan-style stuccoed vessel (after Séjourné 1966:Figure 93). (e) Detail of stone sculpture from Tlalmanalco, Estado de México, in the Museo Nacional de Antropología. (f) Detail of *Codex Borgia*, page 18 (after Franco 1959:Plate 10.7). (g) Detail of petroglyph, Cuahilama, Mexico City. (h) Detail of Mexica relief showing Itzpapalotl ("obsidian butterfly") (after Franco 1959:Plate 19.7). Drawings by Andrew D. Turner.

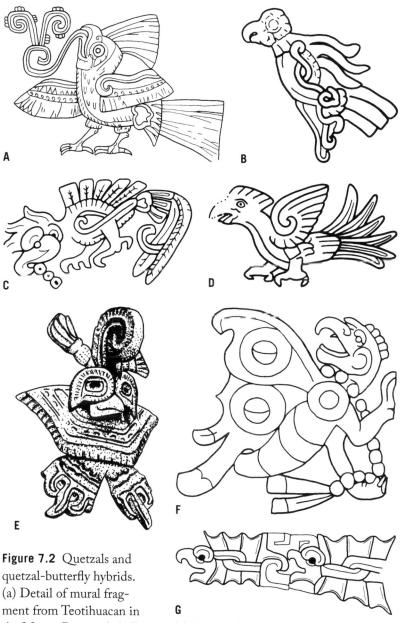

Figure 7.2 Quetzals and quetzal-butterfly hybrids.
(a) Detail of mural fragment from Teotihuacan in the Museo Beatriz de la Fuente. (b) Detail of censer lid from Xico (see Figure 7.3a). (c) Detail of ball court ring from Xochicalco (see Figure 7.6f). (d) Detail of stone box from Chalco, Estado de México, in the Museo Nacional de Antropología. (e) Detail of censer lid from Teotihuacan in the Museo Nacional de Antropología. (f) Detail of Trapezoidal Stone from Teotenango. (g) Detail of Gulf Coast *palma* in the St. Louis Art Museum. Drawings by Andrew D. Turner.

Teotihuacan material culture and comes from specific sources in Yucatán. Aside from being a valuable import from the distant Maya Lowlands, Maya Blue evokes shimmering quetzal plumes and jade in Epiclassic artwork. The paired blossoms and quetzals (Figures 7.2b, 7.3a) on either side, which probably denoted the floral paradise in Teotihuacan and Early Classic Maya traditions (Taube 2005:38), retain the flattened, stylized appearance of Teotihuacan appliqués.

Censers deposited at Ojo de Agua, a spring near Teotenango, recall those from Teotihuacan but may reflect conceptions of the soul of the deceased that are more similar to those from the Maya Lowlands. Two maskettes from Ojo de Agua censers (Figures 7.3b, 7.3c) represent figures with heavy eyelids, suggesting death, while the large four-petaled flowers in front of the nose and mouth denote the floral breath soul. A pair of censer fragments in the form of the heads of monstrous fanged butterflies with crenellated wings—evoking fanged butterflies from Teotihuacan (Figure 7.1c)—exhale floral breath blossoms (Figure 7.3d). Flowers commonly appear in front of the nose or mouth of figures in Classic Maya art, and a common Maya euphemism for death proclaims the end of the "white flower breath" of the deceased (Houston et al. 2006:143; McNeil, this volume). The Ojo de Agua censers probably predate the Epiclassic but reflect changing patterns of representation that were already in place in some regions before Teotihuacan's collapse. The masklike faces in earlier censers from Teotihuacan and Escuintla do not emit floral breath, but rather tend to wear nose ornaments shaped like stylized butterflies (Figure I.2c). Placed over the nose and mouth, these ornaments may also represent the breath soul, and they seem to belong to the same conceptual domain as breath blossoms, but these distinct nose ornaments seldom appear after the collapse of Teotihuacan.

Three similar Epiclassic urns from Cacaxtla that likely represent the apotheosis of deceased warriors in a floral paradise are deeply rooted in prior Teotihuacan symbolism but present imagery in novel manners and contexts. One of the urns (Color Plate 9), now housed in the Museo Regional de Tlaxcala, was found in 1985 on Cacaxtla's acropolis and may have been part of a dedication for an expansion of the Great Plaza (Delgadillo Torres 2007:475–76). Unanalyzed ashes found in the urn were presumably cremated human remains. A large, central figure dressed as a butterfly with antennae, a curled snout and small bat-like wings projects

Figure 7.3 Epiclassic censers and censer fragments. (a) Censer lid from Xico in the Museo Rufino Tamayo. Drawing by Andrew D. Turner. (b) Censer fragment with closed eyes and floral breath from Ojo de Agua, no. 1AMA00035487. (c) Censer fragment with closed eyes and breath blossom from Ojo de Agua, nos. 1AMA00035568 & 1AMA00035571. (d) Censer fragments in the form of fanged butterflies with breath blossoms from Ojo de Agua, nos. 1AMA00035461, 1AMA00035462, and 1AMA00036391 (lote de dos piezas). Photos by Andrew D. Turner, courtesy of Museo Municipal Techialoyan Tepemaxalco, San Antonio la Isla, Estado de México, and Proyecto Arqueológico del Valle de Toluca.

from the surface of the urn. The figure's facial painting is shaped like a stylized butterfly, recalling Teotihuacan nose ornaments. Two smaller figures wearing only loincloths and necklaces flank the butterfly figure while holding conch-shell trumpets. The plants that sprout on either side of the central figure appear to produce cacao pods, and the scene is framed by perforated Maya Blue "jade" disks (Contreras Martínez 2007:538).

The modeled scene on the urn is remarkably similar to earlier imagery on a Teotihuacan-style mirror back, now in the Cleveland Museum of Art (Figure 7.4e). On the mirror back, a central figure with a butterfly nose ornament and a butterfly headdress consisting of a curling proboscis, wings, and antennae is flanked by two smaller figures who sing as the butterfly figure seems to rise out of a shell-filled ocean, perhaps the eastern sea at dawn. This image recalls the "Tlalocan" mural from the Tepantitla apartment compound in Teotihuacan (Figure 7.5a; Young-Sánchez 1990:331–32), which itself is set in a floral paradise. Two intertwining and flowering branches surrounded by singing quetzals sprout from the central figure on the Tepantitla mural and contain spiders on one side and butterflies on the other, an arrangement that seems to prefigure the gendered insect and arachnid souls of later Central Mexican traditions with the presumably masculine butterflies representing deceased warriors and the weaving spiders representing the female inhabitants of the flower world (Headrick 2003:164–67).

All three urns from Cacaxtla appear to portray the same pair of flanking figures. I have argued elsewhere (Turner 2016) that the flanking figure with a central crest and side tassel on its head is an Epiclassic predecessor of Xochipilli (also known as Seven Flower), a deity of music, dance, fertility, and the newly arisen eastern sun (Aguilera 2004; Miller and Taube 1993:190; Nicholson 1971b:417–18; Pohl, this volume). Xochipilli may also personify the idealized human soul, closely aligned with the floral paradise and afterlife (Séjourné 1976 [1956]:146–47; Taube 2005:35). The right figure on an urn from Cacaxtla (Figure 7.4f) and the being on the right of the Cleveland mirror back bear Xochipilli's central crest and the rosettes that appear on either side of the head. The other figure on the Cacaxtla urns (Figure 7.4a) is arguably a maize deity. The bearded figure on the mirror back resembles Early Classic maize deities from Isthmian and Petén Maya traditions (Figures 7.4b, 7.4c; see Taube 1996), whereas examples from Cacaxtla, with forelocks of hair and shaved crowns, are closer in appearance to maize deities from Teotihuacan (Figure 7.4d; see Taube 2017). As beings of agricultural abundance, beauty, and regeneration, Mesoamerican maize deities are strongly associated with flower worlds (Taube 2004:79–81). Furthermore, the Late Postclassic maize deity Centeotl shares several characteristics with Xochipilli (Nicholson 1971b:417; Sandstrom, this volume).

The lid of the urn (Color Plate 9) is decorated with flower blossom appliqués as well as a larger four-petaled flower on top. These blossoms—along with circular jades and cacao plants—evoke the flower world as

Figure 7.4 Maize God and Xochipilli imagery. (a) Detail of urn from Cacaxtla showing probable Maize God. (b) Isthmian Maize God (after Taube 1996:Figure 18h). (c) Early Classic Maya Maize God (after Taube 1996:Figure 20i). (d) Teotihuacan-style maize deity (after Taube 2017:Figure 2). (e) Teotihuacan-style mirror back in the Cleveland Museum of Art. (f) Detail of urn from Cacaxtla showing probable Xochipilli. (g) Head of Late Postclassic Xochipilli. Yale University Art Gallery. Drawings by Andrew D. Turner.

a radiant solar paradise and place of the dawning sun with a central butterfly being that emerges through a jewel-lined portal as a pair of deities announce its journey. The similarities between the urn and the Teotihuacan-style mirror back exemplify not only the remarkable continuity of Teotihuacan Flower World themes after the city's decline but also the translation of themes into more visually legible art styles that were not tied directly to Teotihuacan state ideology.

In addition to the Cacaxtla urns (Color Plate 9), Cleveland mirror back (Figure 7.4e), and the Tepantitla mural (Figure 7.5a), the general pattern of two figures flanking a central being or tree occurs with surprising frequency in Mesoamerican art. A well-known codex-style painted scene on the interior of a Late Classic Maya plate portrays the Maize God growing from a cracked turtle carapace while he is flanked on either side by Hero Twins who appear to pour liquid and adorn him with ornaments (Figure 7.5b). The Tablet of the Cross at Palenque portrays the ruler Kan B'ahlam as both a youth and as an adult presenting offerings on either side of a tree decorated with mirrors and jade. Palenque's Tablet of the Foliated Cross mimics this arrangement with the same characters flanking a jewel-bedecked tree that sprouts anthropomorphic maize cobs (Stuart 2006:116, 140). Both scenes are set against an otherworldly backdrop of floating jewels. On page 53 of the Late Postclassic Central Mexican *Codex Borgia* (Figure 7.5c), deities on either side of a maize-sprouting tree fertilize it with penile blood. In the tree birth scene set at Apoala, Oaxaca, on page 37 of the roughly contemporaneous Mixtec *Codex Vienna*, two figures carve the surface of an anthropomorphic tree as important lineage founders emerge from a cleft in its branches. The probable spindle whorls and darts that appear on either side of the tree's trunk seem to parallel the connotations of weaving and warfare presented by the spiders and butterflies in the branches of the much earlier tree in the Tepantitla mural at Teotihuacan (Figure 7.5a). These scenes appear in different contexts from grave goods to ritual spaces to sacred books. What links them thematically is that ancestors, the deceased, agricultural abundance, flowers, and jewels—themes central to Mesoamerican Flower Worlds—are invoked or activated through giving offerings, singing and playing music, and artistic embellishment. These examples recall the flowering trees of paradise in oral traditions (Chinchilla Mazariegos and Sandstrom, this volume) and demonstrate how broader flower world

Figure 7.5 (a) Detail of "Tlalocan" mural from Tepantitla, Teotihuacan. After painting by Agustín Villagra Caleti. (b) Detail of Late Classic Maya Codex-style plate (after Robicsek and Hales 1981:91). (c) Detail of *Codex Borgia*, page 53. Drawings by Andrew D. Turner.

beliefs and conventions could serve as a basis for the elaboration of local mythologies and power structures.

FLOWER WORLD AND THE MESOAMERICAN BALL GAME

A fragmentary urn similar to those from Cacaxtla was left as an offering in the Cámara de las Ofrendas, the antechamber of Structure A at Xochicalco. Although only the face and limbs of the frontal figure remain, a small curling tongue or proboscis on the headdress (Figure 7.6a), ornaments painted in Maya Blue, and a circular shield indicate that this figure represents a butterfly-costumed warrior. This vessel was found along with stone ball game paraphernalia consisting of two undecorated yokes and a tenoned head that likely was an *hacha* (see Sáenz 1962:21). This offering links Flower World ceremonialism to the Mesoamerican ball game, which had its greatest proliferation in the form of ballcourts and paraphernalia in Epiclassic Central Mexico and the broader Mesoamerican Late Classic period.

Stone ball game paraphernalia was widely distributed throughout Late Classic Mesoamerica and occasionally served as a vehicle for flower world imagery. Although it remains unresolved whether or not they were worn, U-shaped stone yokes resemble belts worn by ballplayers in representations. While most stone yokes are either plain or carved in the form of a toad, one example takes the form of a squatting human figure dressed as a butterfly (Figure 7.6c). *Hachas*, stones typically carved as human heads, appear to have been worn on a player's belt. An *hacha* from Xochicalco (Figure 7.6b) represents the head of a butterfly with reduced antennae and both an upturned curling snout and a spiraled proboscis. Elongated Gulf Coast *palmas*, objects worn similarly to *hachas*, also occasionally appear decorated with butterflies (Figure 7.2g).

Although representations of ballplayers are scarce in Epiclassic Central Mexico, figures wearing ball game paraphernalia perform ceremonies invoking flower worlds in contemporaneous monuments from other parts of Mesoamerica. On Monuments 1–8 from Bilbao, Cotzumalhuapa, figures wearing yokes dance, sing, and perform sacrifices while solar deities, ancestors, and other beings descend from the sky amid showers of jewels and flowering vegetation (Chinchilla Mazariegos 2013:84–86). Similarly,

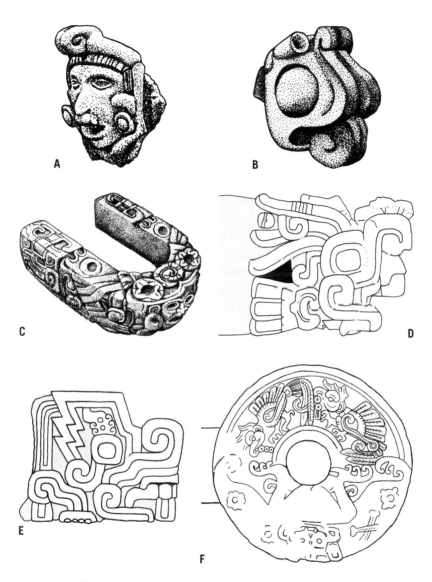

Figure 7.6 Flower world imagery associated with the ball game. (a) Figure in butterfly costume from Cámara de las Ofrendas, Xochicalco. (b) *Hacha* in the form of a butterfly head from Xochicalco. (c) Yoke with butterfly figure from Cuicatlán, Oaxaca (after Covarrubias 1957:Figure 79). (d) Eastern ballcourt marker from Plazuelas. (e) Western ballcourt marker from Plazuelas. (f) Ring from the East Ballcourt of Xochicalco. Drawings by Andrew D. Turner.

on a relief-carved scene from the South Ballcourt of El Tajín, figures wearing yokes and *palmas* sacrifice another player as a skeletal being descends to receive the offering (Koontz 2009:50). Finally, reliefs from the Great Ballcourt of Chichén Itzá portray flowering vines sprouting from the necks of decapitated ballplayers wearing yokes and *palmas*, presenting the invocation of flower world as the outcome of ball game sacrifice.

Flower world imagery appears on monumental ballcourt markers at the northwest margin of Late Classic Mesoamerica at the site of Plazuelas in the Bajío region of Guanajuato (Map 1). The eastern ballcourt marker of the roughly north–south oriented ballcourt represents a monstrous butterfly identifiable by its prominent curled snout and recurved lower lip (Figure 7.6d). Other butterfly features on the marker include a diminutive trilobed wing, a large circular eye, and a long, feathery antenna. Its long, curved fangs may derive from Teotihuacan butterflies (Figure 7.1c). The sculpture was paired with a western ballcourt marker, carved as a catlike beast with a curled snout, fanged maw, smoke or flame emanating from a ringed eye, and stylized feline paw (Figure 7.6e). This being is identifiable as an Epiclassic manifestation of the Teotihuacan War Serpent (Taube 2012:120). As beings of fire and warfare, the War Serpent and its Late Postclassic counterpart, the Xiuhcoatl, are inherently related to Central Mexican flower worlds. Aside from displaying butterfly attributes, both entities are likened to fiery caterpillars (Darlington 1931; Taube 2000, 2012; Turner 2017). Considered as a caterpillar-butterfly pair, the ballcourt markers from Plazuelas embody the fiery metamorphosis of the deceased into butterfly souls, which is at the core of flower world ideology in Central Mexico.

A ring from the East Ballcourt of Xochicalco appears to denote the vertical partitioning of the cosmos into celestial and underworld realms represented by opposed creatures (Figure 7.6f). The upper portion of the ring portrays a pair of quetzals, which, as Taube (2018:276) has suggested, may denote the floral celestial realm in the art of Teotihuacan and other traditions. The paired quetzals and jewels on the ring are juxtaposed with the earth's dark interior, represented by a monstrous bat carved on the lower portion. While this would appear to be a case of opposites, the quetzals and bats may represent complementary diurnal and nocturnal beings of flower world. Bats, many of which are pollinators, are conceptually related to hummingbirds in Maya folklore (Benson 1988:112) and are referred to as "black butterflies" in Oaxaca and other parts of Mexico (Parsons 1936:318). The Late Postclassic Central Mexican deity Itzpapalotl ("obsidian butterfly") is a being of the eastern paradise realm of Tamoanchan (Miller and Taube 1993:100). Although in one Mexica example she appears as a butterfly with obsidian knives on her wings in a style that recalls fanged butterflies of Teotihuacan (Figure 7.1h), she is usually portrayed as a beast that combines butterfly and bat attributes. In their discussion of flower world imagery in the ancient American Southwest, Hays-Gilpin and Hill (1999:5–7) note that bats are among the creatures that appear with floral symbols on their wings. A Mimbres example that they provide bears a striking resemblance to the bat on the Xochicalco ballcourt ring. Bats also figure prominently in mythology related to flower worlds. The gloss of page 62 (recto) of the *Codex Magliubechiano* discusses a bat that brought a piece of Xochiquetzal's flesh to the Underworld, which brought forth aromatic flowers (Benson 1988:110; Boone 1983:206). This tale may relate to page 44 of the *Codex Borgia*, in which a multicolored flowering tree grows from the abdomen of a prone goddess, possibly Xochiquetzal, within a four-sided enclosure lined with flowers and jewels reminiscent of a paradise garden (Chinchilla Mazariegos, Sandstrom, this volume). A bat-costumed figure holding an excised heart descends into the enclosure in a shower of blood, flowers, and jewels.

A large *hacha*-shaped ballcourt marker in the form of the head of a macaw (Figure 7.7a), found in Xochicalco's South Ballcourt (López Luján 1995:55), further links the ball game to Epiclassic flower world symbolism. The ballcourt marker recalls vertically tenoned macaw ballcourt markers within Copan's ballcourt (Figure 7.7b; Noguera 1945:134) as well as a supernatural macaw rendered in stucco near the court (Figure 7.7c). Although Copan is unique among Maya sites in specifically associating macaw imagery with ballcourts, some non-Maya sites along the southern Pacific coast that show marked Teotihuacan influence, including Kaminaljuyú, Guatemala, and Cerro Bernal, Chiapas, do prominently feature macaw imagery (García-Des Lauriers 2005:4; Paulinyi 2014:42). Taube (2005) links the Copan stucco macaw, which has several smaller macaw heads on its wings, to similar beings at El Tajín and Teotihuacan. In addition to the sun, the Teotihuacan entity may be related to Xochipilli, who can appear dressed as a macaw in Late Postclassic imagery

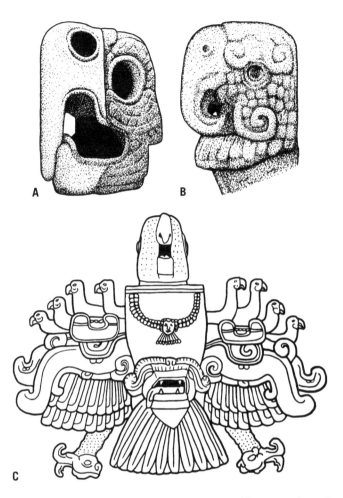

Figure 7.7 Macaws in association with ballcourts. (a) *Hacha*-shaped sculpture from Xochicalco in the Museo Nacional de Antropología. (b) Ballcourt marker from Copan. (c) Reconstructed stucco sculpture from Copan. Drawings by Andrew D. Turner.

(Aguilera 2004; Séjourné 1976 [1956]:162; Taube 2005). Furthermore, the Late Postclassic Xochipilli was a patron of the ball game (Mathiowetz 2011:493–96; Seler 1990–1998:3:282). These shared associations suggest that the proliferation of ballcourts, stone ball game paraphernalia, and Xochipilli veneration may be linked through Epiclassic flower world ceremonialism.

FLOWER WORLD AND THE BUILT ENVIRONMENT

With the notable exception of the Temple of Quetzalcoatl, which Taube (2004:88–90; 2006) argues was an artificial Flower Mountain in the heart of the city, Teotihuacan Flower World imagery is confined to smaller-scale objects and private spaces. This pattern changes in Epiclassic Central Mexico when flower world themes appear more frequently on public monuments. This trend is most apparent at Xochicalco, where a series of features appear to transform the acropolis into a permanent manifestation of flower world. In this regard, it may not be coincidental that Xochicalco ("Flower House Place") may have been considered the legendary Tamoanchan among later traditions (León Portilla 1995:46–51; Nicholson 1971a:105–7; Piña Chán 1989).

In 1993 and 1994, excavators unearthed fragments of a relief sculpture, or sculptures, in the form of a butterfly (Figure 7.8a; Garza Tarazona and Mayer Guala 2005:379). One slab represents a partial butterfly wing decorated with large spots, which is attached to a segmented portion of a thorax or abdomen. Another slab, which is carved with a segmented abdomen and two visible limbs, appears to have been placed on the corner of a building or as part of a door jamb. Part of a zoomorphic face, showing an open maw and the lower rim of a large, circular eye, was presumably found with the wing and abdomen fragments. Although it is unclear which building or buildings the slabs adorned, they constitute one of the largest and most prominent butterfly representations in Mesoamerican art.

The Pyramid of the Plumed Serpents, one of Xochicalco's most prominent monuments, symbolically evokes Teotihuacan's Temple of Quetzalcoatl (Turner 2016:129), an anthropogenic Flower Mountain (Taube 2004:88; 2006). On the lower register of the Pyramid of the Plumed Serpents, lords—or perhaps deceased ancestors—sit among the undulating bodies of the feathered serpents. Although only traces of red-painted stucco are plainly visible on the building's façade, Adela Breton noted that the figures were once brightly painted with other colors, including blue, green, yellow, white, and black (Baquedano 2010; Breton 1906).

Many studies have commented on the Maya-like postures of the seated figures on the Pyramid of the Plumed Serpents and their resemblance to Maya lords that appear on widely circulating Nebaj-style jade plaques.

Figure 7.8 Butterfly imagery from Xochicalco. (a) Blocks from the acropolis (after Garza Tarazona and Mayer Guala 2005:Photo 53). (b) Detail of Pyramid of the Plumed Serpents showing seated figure with butterfly breath or speech scroll. (c–d) Butterflies from plaques from the Animal Ramp. Drawings by Andrew D. Turner.

Despite much scholarly attention devoted to these figures, their distinct butterfly-shaped speech or breath scrolls that bear trilobed wings, curling proboscises, and paired antennae have hitherto escaped modern attention (Figure 7.8b). Although the seated figures have been commonly linked to the anthropomorphic Quetzalcoatl of later Central Mexican traditions because of their association with feathered serpents, they seem to have more in common with anonymous deceased Teotihuacan warriors with butterfly breath souls. Like Teotihuacan warriors that appear as enthroned mortuary bundle figurines or theater-style censers, these figures also appear to wear War Serpent headdresses with antennae and large fanged maws; otherwise they are seldom seen in profile at Xochicalco but are shown frontally on the Xochicalco stela triad (see Sáenz 1961). Furthermore, the seated Maya lords on the jade plaques that these figures emulate often appear deceased and have closed eyes or are seated within the mouths of caves. As deceased nobles were manifest as jewels according to one telling (Mendieta 1980:97), the figures on jade plaques may physically embody deceased royal ancestors rather than simply representing them. As such, the figures on the Pyramid of the Plumed Serpents may be conjured ancestors carried on the backs of feathered serpents. Widely regarded as manifestations of wind, feathered serpents serve as the "flowery road" on which the sun and other celestial beings travel (e.g., Hill 1992:125; Saturno et al. 2005:25; Taube 2010:175–76). The brightly colored building thus appears to present the arrival of apotheosized ancestors from a solar paradise.

Xochicalco's Animal Ramp, a sloping feature on the eastern edge of the acropolis near the East Ballcourt, was paved with nearly four hundred stone plaques with incised images of animals. Forty of the 286 stones analyzed by Corona (2014) represent butterflies, often with curling snouts and antennae and crenellated wings (Figures 7.8c–7.8d). Many of the creatures represented on the ramp—including quetzals and other types of birds—and feathered serpents are animals associated with flower worlds. The east–west oriented Animal Ramp may have been an earthly reflection of the diurnal path of the sun and a "flowery road" decorated with birds, butterflies, and other beings that accompany the sun on its journey. Xochicalco's acropolis may have been constructed and envisioned as a point of access to the flower world, with features such as the floodable East Ballcourt (Taube 2018:275–76), the Animal Ramp that guides the sun and its retinue as it emerges from the eastern sea, and the summit of the acropolis, which is decorated with large, sculpted butterflies and seated figures singing or exhaling butterfly scrolls. The fortified hilltop acropolis of Xochicalco was not only defensible but also appears to have been conceived as a human-built manifestation of the solar paradise.

CONCLUSION

One of the most salient aspects of the Teotihuacan Flower World, later adopted by the Mexica, was its distinct relationship to warfare and self-sacrifice. The artwork of Teotihuacan celebrates warriors who died in service to the state by emphasizing their apotheosis as nectar-drinking birds and butterflies. The anonymity of these beings stands in contrast to the apotheosized rulers and elite ancestors of Classic Maya flower worlds. Among the living, this particular aspect of Teotihuacan religious ideology was reinforced through sensory experience and ritual actions such as singing and giving offerings of fragrant incense. Small-scale objects and murals in restricted settings that evoke the flower world suggest that such actions were most often private, rather than collective and public, perhaps prioritizing personal sensory experience and the obligations of the individual to the state.

Teotihuacan remained a source of legitimacy for elites across Mesoamerica long after its collapse (e.g., Stone 1989; Taube 2000). This is especially true for Epiclassic polities of Central Mexico, where elites adopted and perpetuated certain aspects of Teotihuacan Flower World ideology while discarding or expanding others. As at Teotihuacan, Epiclassic flower worlds were populated by warrior souls that took the form of birds and butterflies but with martial overtones that were unmoored from ideology specific to the Teotihuacan state. New fields of expression, such as ball game architecture and paraphernalia, became major vehicles for flower world imagery, and monumental structures (and perhaps their hilltop locations) were permanent manifestations of Flower Mountains in urban environments, a pattern that continued in Central Mexico at cities such as Cholula and Tenochtitlan (Pohl, González López and Vázquez Vallín, this volume).

The collapse of Teotihuacan permitted new patterns of interaction and the rise of polities in areas that had been politically marginal. For elites at Cacaxtla, Teotenango, and Xochicalco, flower world was a source of legitimacy. The importance of colorful feathers, incense, and jewels in public display and spectacle promoted exchange of goods among multicultural networks of elites. New art styles drew on themes in Teotihuacan artwork but incorporated foreign elements that proclaimed direct ties to the regions from which such goods originate, especially the Maya region, and cross-regional exchange probably contributed to the development of "international" styles that made use of shared artistic conventions. At the same time, flower world ideology fueled interpolity conflict by promoting militarism through competition over access to wealth and the glorification of the deceased who fell in battle. The distinct ways in which flower world ceremonialism articulated with warfare, economy, and politics thus contributed to and responded to the sociopolitical changes that characterize the Epiclassic period as a whole and link the flower worlds of Teotihuacan to later Central Mexican traditions.

REFERENCES

Aguilera, Carmen. 2004. "Xochipilli dios solar." *Estudios de Cultura Náhuatl* 35:69–74.

Armillas, Pedro. 1946. "Los olmeca-xicalanca y los sitios arqueológicos del suroeste de Tlaxcala." *Revista Mexicana de Estudios Antropológicos* 8:137–45.

Baquedano, Elizabeth. 2010. "Xochicalco y Adela Breton." *Arqueología Mexicana* 17(101):68–71.

Benson, Elizabeth P. 1988. "The Maya and the Bat." *Latin American Indian Literatures Journal* 4(2):99–124.

Boone, Elizabeth Hill. 1983. *The Codex Magliabechiano*. Berkeley: University of California Press.

Breton, Adela. 1906. "Some Notes on Xochicalco." In *Transactions of the Department of Archaeology, Free Museum of Science and Art*, vol. 2, pt. 1, 51–67. Philadelphia: Department of Archaeology, University of Pennsylvania.

Chinchilla Mazariegos, Oswaldo. 2013. "The Flower World of Cotzumalhuapa." In *The Maya in a Mesoamerican Context: Comparative Approaches to Maya Studies; Proceedings of the 16th European Maya Conference, Copenhagen, December 5–10, 2011*, edited by Jesper Nielsen and Christophe Helmke, 79–92. Acta Mesoamericana, vol. 26. Markt Schwaben: Anton Saurwein.

Contreras Martínez, José Eduardo. 2007. "Representaciones del cacao en la zona arqueológica de Cacaxtla, Tlax." In *Memorias del Primer Coloquio Internacional Cacaxtla a sus treinta años de investigación*, 530–43. Tlaxcala: Centro Instituto Nacional de Antropología e Historia, Tlaxcala.

Corona-M., Eduardo. 2014. "Relieves con motivos zoomorfos en Xochicalco, Morelos." *Revista Archaeobios* 8(1):17–25.

Covarrubias, Miguel. 1957. *Indian Art of Mexico and Central America*. New York: Alfred A. Knopf.

Darlington, H. S. 1931. "The 'Fire-Snakes' of the Aztec Calendar Stone." *Anthropos* 26(5/6):637–46.

Delgadillo Torres, Rosalba. 2007. "Las urnas policromadas de Cacaxtla, Tlax. (Estudio preliminar)." In *Memorias del Primer Coloquio Internacional Cacaxtla a sus treinta años de investigación*, 466–91. Tlaxcala: Centro Instituto Nacional de Antropología e Historia, Tlaxcala.

Diehl, Richard A., and Janet C. Berlo. 1989. Introduction to *Mesoamerica After the Decline of Teotihuacan: AD 700–900*, edited by Janet C. Berlo and Richard A. Diehl, 1–6 Washington, D.C.: Dumbarton Oaks Research Library and Collection.

Franco, José Luis. 1959. "Representaciones de la mariposa en Mesoamérica." In *El México Antiguo*, 9:195–244. Mexico City: Sociedad Alemana Mexicanista.

García-Des Lauriers, Claudia. 2005. "La iconografía y simbolismo de la escultura de Cerro Bernal, Chiapas." In *Iconografía y escritura teotihuacana en costa sur de Guatemala y Chiapas*, edited by Oswaldo Chinchilla Mazariegos and Bárbara Arroyo, 1–16. Utz ib Series Reports, vol. 1, no. 5. Guatemala City: Asociación Tikal.

Garza Tarazona, Silvia, and Pablo Mayer Guala. 2005. "Arquitectura: Materiales y sistemas constructivos en Xochicalco." In *IV Coloquio Pedro Bosch Gimpera: El occidente y centro de México*, edited by Ernesto Vargas Pacheco, 349–83. Mexico City: Instituto de Investigaciones Antropológicas, Universidad Nacional Autónoma de México.

Hays-Gilpin, Kelley, and Jane H. Hill. 1999. "The Flower World in Material Culture: An Iconographic Complex in the Southwest and Mesoamerica." *Journal of Anthropological Research* 55(1):1–37.

Headrick, Annabeth. 2003. "Butterfly War at Teotihuacan." In *Ancient Mesoamerican Warfare*, edited by M. Kathryn Brown and Travis W. Stanton, 149–70. Walnut Creek, Calif.: AltaMira Press.

Hill, Jane H. 1992. "The Flower World of Old Uto-Aztecan." *Journal of Anthropological Research* 48(2):117–44.

Hirth, Kenneth G. 1989. "Militarism and Social Organization at Xochicalco, Morelos." In *Mesoamerica After the Decline of Teotihuacan: AD 700–900*, edited by Janet C. Berlo and Richard A. Diehl, 69–81. Washington, D.C.: Dumbarton Oaks Research Library and Collection.

Hirth, Kenneth G. 1995. "Urbanism, Militarism, and Architectural Design: An Analysis of Epiclassic Sociopolitical Structure at Xochicalco." *Ancient Mesoamerica* 6:237–50.

Houston, Stephen D., David Stuart, and Karl A. Taube. 2006. *The Memory of Bones: Body, Being, and Experience Among the Classic Maya.* Austin: University of Texas Press.

Koontz, Rex. 2009. *Lightning Gods and Feathered Serpents: The Public Sculpture of El Tajín.* Austin: University of Texas Press.

Kubler, George. 1980. "Eclecticism at Cacaxtla." In *Third Palenque Round Table, 1978*, pt. 2, edited by Merle Greene Robertson, 163–72. Austin: University of Texas Press.

León Portilla, Miguel. 1995. "Xochicalco en la historia." In *La Acrópolis de Xochicalco*, 35–87. Mexico City: Instituto de Cultura de Morelos.

López Austin, Alfredo, and Leonardo López Luján. 2000. "The Myth and Reality of Zuyuá: The Feathered Serpent and Mesoamerican Transformations from the Classic to the Postclassic." In *Mesoamerica's Classic Heritage: From Teotihuacan to the Aztecs*, edited by Davíd Carrasco, Lindsay Jones, and Scott Sessions, 21–84. Boulder: University of Colorado Press.

López Luján, Leonardo. 1995. "Xochicalco: El lugar de la casa de las flores." In *Xochicalco y Tula*, 15–141. Milan: Editoriale Jaca Book.

Mathiowetz, Michael D. 2011. "The Diurnal Path of the Sun: Ideology and Interregional Interaction in Ancient Northwest Mesoamerica and the American Southwest." Unpublished Ph.D. dissertation, Department of Anthropology, University of California, Riverside.

McAnany, Patricia A. 2010. *Ancestral Maya Economies in Archaeological Perspective*. New York: Cambridge University Press.

Mendieta, Gerónimo de. 1980. *Historia eclesiástica indiana*. Mexico City: Porrúa.

Miller, Mary, and Karl Taube. 1993. *The Gods and Symbols of Ancient Mexico and the Maya*. London: Thames and Hudson.

Nicholson, Henry B. 1971a. "Major Sculpture in Pre-Hispanic Central Mexico." In *Handbook of Middle American Indians*, vol. 10, *Archaeology of Northern Mesoamerica*, pt. 1, edited by Gordon F. Ekholm and Ignacio Bernal, 92–134. Austin: University of Texas Press.

Nicholson, Henry B. 1971b. "Religion in Prehispanic Central Mexico." In *Handbook of Middle American Indians*, vol. 10, *Archaeology of Northern Mesoamerica*, pt. 1, edited by Gordon F. Ekholm and Ignacio Bernal, 395–446. Austin: University of Texas Press.

Noguera, Eduardo. 1945. "Exploraciones en Xochicalco." *Cuadernos Americanos* 19:119–57.

Parsons, Elsie Clews. 1936. *Mitla: Town of Souls*. Chicago: University of Chicago Press.

Paulinyi, Zoltán. 2014. "The Butterfly Bird God and His Myth at Teotihuacan." *Ancient Mesoamerica* 25:29–48.

Piña Chán, Román. 1989. *Xochicalco: El mitico Tamoanchan*. Serie Arqueología. Mexico City: Instituto Nacional de Antropología e Historia.

Ringle, William M., Tomás Gallareta Negrón, and George J. Bey III. 1998. "The Return of Quetzalcoatl." *Ancient Mesoamerica* 9(2):183–232.

Robicsek, Francis, and Donald M. Hales. 1981. *The Maya Book of the Dead: The Ceramic Codex*. Charlottesville: University of Virginia Art Museum.

Sáenz, César A. 1961. "Tres estelas en Xochicalco." *Revista Mexicana de Estudios Antropológicos* 17:39–65.

Sáenz, César A. 1962. *Xochicalco Temporada 1960*. Informes 11. Mexico City: Instituto Nacional de Antropología e Historia.

Saturno, William A., Karl A. Taube, and David Stuart. 2005. *The Murals of San Bartolo, El Petén, Guatemala Part 1: The North Wall*. Ancient America 7. Barnardsville, N.C.: Center for Ancient American Studies.

Séjourné, Laurette. 1966. *Arqueología de Teotihuacan: La cerámica*. Mexico City: Fondo de la Cultura Económica.

Séjourné, Laurette. 1976 [1956]. *Burning Water: Thought and Religion in Ancient Mexico*. Berkeley, Calif.: Shambhala.

Seler, Eduard. 1990–1998. *Collected Works in Mesoamerican Linguistics and Archae-ology*, 6 vols. Edited by Frank E. Comparato. Culver City, Calif.: Labyrinthos.

Stone, Andrea. 1989. "Disconnection, Foreign Insignia, and Political Expansion: Teotihuacan and the Warrior Stelae of Piedras Negras." In *Mesoamerica After the Decline of Teotihuacan: AD 700–900*, edited by Janet C. Berlo and Rich-ard A. Diehl, 153–72. Washington, D.C.: Dumbarton Oaks Research Library and Collection.

Stuart, David. 2006. "The Palenque Mythology: Inscriptions from the Cross Group at Palenque." In *Sourcebook for the 30th Maya Meetings, March 14–19, 2006*, 86–194. Austin: Department of Art and Art History, University of Texas.

Taube, Karl A. 1996. "The Olmec Maize God: The Face of Corn in Formative Mesoamerica." *RES: Anthropology and Aesthetics* 29/30:39–81.

Taube, Karl A. 2000. "The Turquoise Hearth: Fire, Self-Sacrifice, and the Cen-tral Mexican Cult of War." In *Mesoamerica's Classic Heritage: From Teotihua-can to the Aztecs*, edited by Davíd Carrasco, Lindsay Jones, and Scott Sessions, 269–340. Boulder: University of Colorado Press.

Taube, Karl A. 2004. "Flower Mountain: Concepts of Life, Beauty, and Paradise Among the Classic Maya." *RES: Anthropology and Aesthetics* 45:69–98.

Taube, Karl A. 2005. "Representaciones del paraíso en el arte cerámico del Clásico Temprano de Escuintla, Guatemala." In *Iconografía y escritura teoti-huacana en la Costa Sur de Guatemala y Chiapas*, edited by Oswaldo Chinchilla Mazariegos and Bárbara Arroyo, 35–54. U Tz'ib, Serie Reportes, vol. 1, no. 5. Guatemala City: Asociación Tikal.

Taube, Karl A. 2006. "Climbing Flower Mountain: Concepts of Resurrection and the Afterlife at Teotihuacan." In *Arqueología e historia del Centro de Mex-ico: Homenaje a Eduardo Matos Moctezuma*, edited by Leonardo López Lujan, Davíd Carrasco, and Lourdes Cué, 153–70. Mexico City: Instituto Nacional de Antropología e Historia.

Taube, Karl A. 2010. "At Dawn's Edge: Tulúm, Santa Rita, and Floral Symbolism in the International Style of Late Postclassic Mesoamerica." In *Astronomers, Scribes, and Priests: Intellectual Interchange Between the Northern Maya Low-lands and Highland Mexico in the Late Postclassic Period*, edited by Gabrielle Vail and Christine Hernández, 145–91. Washington, D.C.: Dumbarton Oaks Research Library and Collection.

Taube, Karl A. 2012. "The Symbolism of Turquoise in Ancient Mesoamerica." In *Turquoise in Mexico and North America: Science, Conservation, Culture and Collection*, edited by J. C. H. King, Max Carocci, Carolyn Cartwright, Colin McEwan and Rebecca Stacy, 115–32. London: Archetype and the British Museum.

Taube, Karl A. 2017. "Aquellos del este: Representaciones de dioses y hombres mayas en las *pinturas realistas* de Tetitla, Teotihuacan." In *Las pinturas realistas de Tetitla, Teotihuacán: Estudios a través de la obra de Agustín Villagra Caleti*, edited by Leticia Staines Cicero and Christophe Helmke, 71–99. Mexico City: Universidad Nacional Autónoma de México, Instituto de Investigaciones Estéticas.

Taube, Karl A. 2018. "The Ballgame, Boxing and Ritual Blood Sport in Ancient Mesoamerica." In *Ritual, Play and Belief in Evolution and Early Human Societies*, edited by Colin Renfrew, Iain Morley, and Michael Boyd, 264–301. Cambridge: Cambridge University Press.

Taube, Karl A. 2020. "In Search of Paradise: Religion and Cultural Exchange in Early Postclassic Mesoamerica." In *A Forest of History: The Maya After the Emergence of Divine Kingship*, edited by Travis W. Stanton and M. Kathryn Brown, 154–86. Boulder, University Press of Colorado.

Turner, Andrew D. 2016. "Cultures at the Crossroads: Art, Religion, and Interregional Interaction in Central Mexico, AD 600–900." Unpublished Ph.D. dissertation, Department of Anthropology, University of California, Riverside.

Turner, Andrew D. 2017. "Ixtapan del Oro Monument 1 and the Transition from War Serpent to Xiuhcoatl in Late Classic Mesoamerica." *Mexicon* 39(3):55–64.

Webb, Malcolm C. 1978. "The Significance of the 'Epiclassic' Period in Mesoamerican Prehistory." In *Cultural Continuity in Mesoamerica*, edited by David L. Browman, 155–78. The Hague: Mouton.

Young-Sánchez, Margaret. 1990. "Veneration of the Dead: Religious Ritual on a Pre-Columbian Mirror-Back." *Bulletin of the Cleveland Museum of Art* 77(9):326–51.

8

Life in Bloom

The Casas Grandes Flower World and Its Antecedents in Northwest Mesoamerica, Northern Mexico, and the American Southwest

Michael D. Mathiowetz

One key issue in the study of flower worlds is determining the chronology, the nature of local and regional manifestations, and the history of its transmission from Mesoamerica to the southwestern United States (Maps 1, 2). The expression of flower worlds is well documented in the ethnology of north and west Mexican Indigenous groups, including the Huichol (Wixárika), Cora (Náyari), Tarahumara (Rarámuri), Yaqui (Yoeme), and others (Hill 1992; Molina and Shorter, Neurath, this volume). However, the chronology of flower worlds in far western Mesoamerica and northwest Mexico during the pre-Hispanic era has been less well defined due to lack of study and partly because Jane Hill's historical-linguistic approach was unable to assign a date to flower worlds for the American Southwest (Hays-Gilpin and Hill 2000:413). In the absence of visual or material evidence, scholars proposed that flower world may have simply "always" existed in the Southwest in oral canons or performance but rarely in material expression (Hays-Gilpin et al. 2010:122; Weiner 2015:223–24). The most secure means to determine the presence or absence of flower world tenets in the archaeology is the identification of affiliated material culture, symbolism, and oral histories—a point where collaboration with Indigenous groups is key. Questions of chronology and the dissemination of flower worlds require the examination of the pre-Hispanic manifestations in the regions between the Southwest and Mesoamerica proper.

The primary aim of this essay is to provide context and definition to current understandings of the Casas Grandes culture in northwest Mexico by situating its flower world expression among broader historical dynamics of northwest Mesoamerica and the American Southwest. First, I examine the earliest expressions of key flower world tenets in far west Mexico among the Aztatlán culture after A.D. 850/900 as detailed in recent literature. Next, I define two main stages of flower world expressions in the American Southwest and northwest Mexico in relation to increasing engagement with the Aztatlán culture and the differential adaptation of flower world among the Chaco Canyon and Mimbres cultures between A.D. 850/900 and 1150. I focus on the distribution of scarlet macaws, copper, cacao, and the presence of floral, maize, and breath/cloud symbolism, all of which are commonly associated with flower world in Mesoamerica. Here I characterize sociopolitical organization and ritual economies of the Chaco and Mimbres regions as they relate to cultural developments along the Pacific coast of west Mexico. I then turn to the demographic changes that followed the dissolution of these systems and the subsequent southward shift in socioreligious power to the Chihuahuan desert in northern Mexico around A.D. 1200.

Finally, I then focus on the second stage of flower world expressions in the Casas Grandes Flower World as it relates to the Aztatlán region while noting similarities and differences with the earlier Chaco and Mimbres Flower Worlds. I conclude by characterizing the Casas Grandes Flower World as the culmination of historical processes of increasing engagement between southwestern and northern Mexican societies with Aztatlán populations, particularly the coastal core zone of Nayarit and southern Sinaloa, where flower world was first and most intensively expressed in far west Mexico. The flower worlds model may be the most suitable approach for characterizing the nature of pre-Hispanic Mesoamerican and southwestern United States interaction and the social, political, religious/ritual, and economic changes that are linked to its adoption and adaptation.

FLOWER WORLDS IN NORTHWEST MEXICO AND THE AMERICAN SOUTHWEST: INSIGHTS ON MESOAMERICA AND SOUTHWEST CONNECTIONS

Assessments on the distributional, contextual, and chronological data on pre-Hispanic flower world imagery have found striking temporal and geographical limitations with the first firmly dated flower world–related objects found among the Chaco Canyon and Mimbres cultures (roughly between A.D. 1000 and 1150) of broader northwestern New Mexico and the Mogollon region of southern New Mexico, respectively (Hays-Gilpin and Hill 1999:Appendixes A–E; 2000:413, Table 1). Flower depictions in the American Southwest before A.D. 1000, however, are considered to be either "rare" or "possible flowers" or as isolated elements that almost never appear with other flower world symbols on the same object. These characterizations indicate that evidence for flower world before this time is equivocal (introduction, this volume).

Many of the characteristics identified by Karl Taube (2000, 2001, 2010) as constituting flower world in Mesoamerica—such as solar, feathered/horned serpent, or maize deities; ancestral cloud and breath imagery; cacao; Flower Road (the path of the sun) and Flower Mountain (the eastern mountain from where the sun arises)—do not occur in the Southwest until after A.D. 900–1000. Given that maize agriculture was transmitted from Mesoamerica into northern Mexico (ca. 3000/2500 B.C.) and the American Southwest (ca. 2000 B.C.), an unresolved question is, Why does flower world ritualism not appear until thousands of years later in limited examples of southwestern material culture by A.D. 900/1000–1150? A clue to this answer involves the identification of flower worlds in the intervening regions among the Aztatlán culture of far west Mexico and the Casas Grandes culture of Chihuahua, Mexico.

A SYNOPSIS OF THE AZTATLÁN FLOWER WORLD

Flower world has not yet been identified in the material culture of west Mexico before the Postclassic period, including the Shaft Tomb era and the Epiclassic-period centers of La Quemada and Alta Vista, which is curious considering the evidence of flower world in Epiclassic highland Mexico (Turner, this volume). Beekman (2003) proposed flower world associations for circular Late Formative to Classic Teuchitlán architecture of highland Jalisco as a possible plan-view maize cob or flower. This identification is complicated by the lack of explicit floral or solar imagery identified on any Teuchitlán material culture and increasing evidence that maize *mitote* ritualism dates to the Postclassic period. The depiction of Flower World first occurs most clearly in material remains of the Aztatlán culture (Mathiowetz 2011, 2018a, 2018b, 2019a, 2019b, 2020, 2021; Mathiowetz et al. 2015), particularly along the Pacific-coastal core zone extending from Mazatlán, Sinaloa, southward to Banderas Bay, Jalisco. While chronology building remains a critical task in Aztatlán studies, a general conclusion is that naturalistic imagery of flower world is largely absent in the geometric symbolism of pre-Aztatlán ceramics until A.D. 850/900 and became increasingly apparent in coincidence with connections to Toltec and then Nahua-Mixteca societies of highland and southern Mexico.

Flower world symbolism and ritualism in the Aztatlán core zone accompanied dramatic transformations in macroregional social dynamics, architecture, site layout, demography, art, and political and economic organization, including the concentration of political power among elites in paramount centers apparently situated within individual provinces. Powerful elite lineages headed by *caciques* or *cacicas* appear to have resided in paramount Aztatlán centers at the center of a web of interconnected smaller sites. These changes involved the adoption of Xochipilli (Piltzintli) solar ritualism and symbolism from highland central and southern Mexico (Figures 8.1a, 8.1b; Mathiowetz 2011). As the god of flowers, dawn, fertility, love, music, dance, art, life, and maize, Xochipilli was a major flower world deity in Postclassic (and historic) Mesoamerica and far west Mexico (Pohl, Sandstrom, and Turner, this volume) and served as the prototype for the Casas Grandes and Puebloan Sun Youth (Mathiowetz 2011, 2018a, 2018b). Xochipilli worship in west Mexico was accompanied by new Venus (Mathiowetz et. al. 2015), feathered serpent (Quetzalcoatl), Tlaloc, and Xipe Totec symbolism, which were key components of a new form of maize agricultural, cloud, and rain ritualism linked to the development of *mitote* ritualism in far west Mexico (Figures 8.1c–8.1f; Mathiowetz 2011, 2019b, 2021). The practice of public *mitote* ceremonialism and ritual obligations that integrated large and smaller sites coincided with the appearance of copper bells (crotals) and ornaments during the Aztatlán era, which evoked the sounds and colors of flower world (Hosler 1994) in their use by participants during *mitote* rites.

Cacao use by Aztatlán elites was linked to feasting and flower world, and its consumption became prominent in the core zone after A.D. 850/900 near the pre-Hispanic cacao cultivation zone that ranged from central coastal Nayarit to Banderas Bay, Jalisco (Mathiowetz 2011, 2019b). The new development of intensive cotton and weaving industries in the coastal core zone further linked together ideologies of cloud making, ancestral rain, and the road of the sun. The practice of weaving by Aztatlán individuals was a form of labor that from their perspective probably created and brought the flower world into presence, much like for Huichol women who weave today (Mathiowetz 2011, 2020). Flower symbolism on Aztatlán ceramics occurs most explicitly in the coastal core zone. For example,

Xochipillâ.

A

E

B

C

D

F

G

H

Figure 8.1 The Aztatlán Flower World. (a) Detail of toponym for Juchipila (Zacatecas) depicting solar deity Xochipilli holding marigold flowers (*Lienzo de Tlaxcala*, Page 58). (b) Highland Mexican-style solar disk with A-shaped solar rays. Santiago Engraved, Amapa, Nayarit (after Meighan 1976:Plate 162). (c) Skeletal Venus war god. Cerritos Polychrome, Museo Regional de Nayarit (from photo by author). (d) Feathered serpent. Ixcuintla Polychrome, Amapa, Nayarit (after Bell 1960:Figure 27). (e) Copper bell with face of rain god Tlaloc, Amapa, Nayarit (Meighan 1976:Plate 108a). Reproduced with permission from the UCLA Fowler Museum. (f) Male smoking a pipe with raindrops above pipe bowl. Iguanas Polychrome (after Von Winning 1977:Figure 2). (g) *En face* blossom with probable ancestor in center. Ixcuintla Polychrome, Amapa, Nayarit (after Meighan 1976:Plate 148a). (h) Butterfly head. Ixcuintla Polychrome, Amapa, Nayarit (after Bell 1960:Figure 25). Drawings by Michael D. Mathiowetz.

one *en face* flower design contains a probable ancestor who resided in the blossom interior as aroma (Figure 8.1g) while Central Mexican-style butterfly heads complemented the presence of flower world symbolism (Figure 8.1h; see Figure 7.1f). A common design on bowl and jar forms is the incised or modeled "lobed" motif that encircles the entire exterior surface, thereby signifying the vessel as an open "blossom." This same floral design on pipes indicates that smoking signified cloud making (and floral aroma) to create the ancestral rain clouds (Mathiowetz 2011:557–66). Aspects of Aztatlán Flower World cosmology appear to be related to the post-A.D. 850/900 expression of the Chaco and Mimbres Flower Worlds, and it was an increasing engagement with the Aztatlán region and their powerful elites that probably led to the desire by southwestern societies to obtain flower world–related items from west Mexico and more distant locales in Mesoamerica.

A SYNOPSIS OF FLOWER WORLDS IN THE AMERICAN SOUTHWEST BEFORE A.D. 1150

Ritual commodities from Mesoamerica—including scarlet macaws, copper, and cacao (Crown and Hurst 2009; Vargas 1995; Watson et al. 2015)—were imported as part of flower world–related ritual economies relatively late in southwestern history and long after the beginning of maize agriculture. Copper and cacao were imported from west Mexico (Hosler 1994; Mathiowetz 2019b; Vargas 1995), and it is reasonable to presume that scarlet macaw acquisition strategies followed a Pacific-coastal route through west Mexico to Oaxaca rather than via a Gulf Coast route (but see Gilman et al. 2014). Given the evidence for increasing Pacific-coastal connections after A.D. 850/900 (Pohl and Mathiowetz, forthcoming), it is critical to consider the chronology and spatial distribution of flower world expressions in ritual and symbolism among southwestern cultures.

CHACO CANYON, MIMBRES, AND HOHOKAM FLOWER WORLDS

An assessment of the pre-A.D. 1300 visual and material expressions of key flower world elements in the Chaco, Mimbres, Hohokam, and

Kayenta cultures may help to characterize the nature of this cosmology before Paquimé and the Pueblo IV period.

Scarlet Macaws

Osteological evidence in the Southwest includes rare isolated bones of two scarlet macaws in Arizona at the Hohokam site of Snaketown dating around A.D. 600–700 (Crown 2016:337). The low number and dispersed contexts indicate that acquisition patterns were infrequent and not part of systematized exchange networks (Vokes and Gregory 2007:329). The earliest imported scarlet macaws at Ancestral Pueblo sites date to A.D. 900–975 at Pueblo Bonito in Chaco Canyon (George et al. 2018). In the Mimbres region, macaw skeletons and depictions date between A.D. 1000 and 1150 (Figure 8.2a; Crown 2016:337; Schwartz 2020; Watson et al. 2015). While Gilman and colleagues (2014) consider Mimbres scarlet macaws to be associated with Maya *Popol Vuh* ritualism derived from the Gulf Coast, the appearance of solar-related scarlet macaws in this region in my estimation may be an antecedent to the later use of scarlet macaws in Flower World-related Sun Youth ritualism in the Casas Grandes region that derives from the Aztatlán coastal core zone (Mathiowetz 2011, 2019a, 2019b, 2020, 2021).

Breath, Wind, and Cloud Symbolism

In Mesoamerica, the feathered serpent Quetzalcoatl is affiliated with wind as a conduit for rain. The earliest depictions of related horned/feathered serpents in the Southwest occur on Classic Mimbres bowls (MimPIDD #1604, 1650, 3874, 4010, 8082, 8628, 9303) and more commonly in Casas Grandes, Jornada Mogollon, and Rio Grande-region visual culture after A.D. 1200 (Figure 8.2b; Schaafsma 2001:142; Taube 2001). Mimbres horned serpents include full-figure depictions and human males with a horned serpent headdress. The conception of clouds as breath and feathers—a theme of Pueblo IV katsina ritualism—first occurs in Mimbres art where animals depicted with terraced clouds and breath feathers form part of a wind and rain ritualism linked to flower world (Figure 8.2c; Taube 2001:116). Depictions of pipe-smoking males may relate to cloud making (Figure 8.2d).

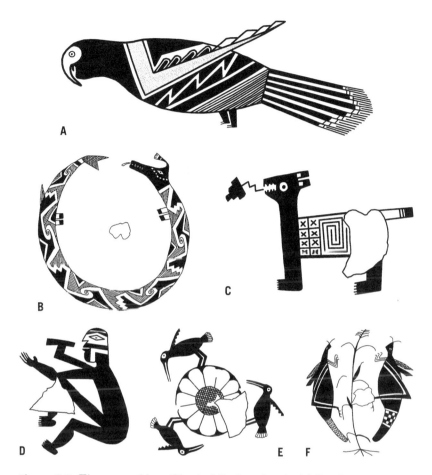

Figure 8.2 Flower world on Classic Mimbres bowls. (a) Scarlet macaw (after MimPIDD #3528). (b) Horned serpent (after MimPIDD #3874) (drawing by Will Russell). (c) Breath cloud (after MimPIDD #5044). (d) Male smoking pipe for possible cloud making, Eby site (MimPIDD #7865). (e) Flower flanked by birds, Galaz site (after MimPIDD #2815). (f) Maize plant flanked by grasshoppers (after MimPIDD #4533). Drawings by Michael D. Mathiowetz.

Flower Symbolism

Flower world symbolism before A.D. 1300 is "weak to nonexistent" in the American Southwest except for Chaco Canyon and Mimbres visual culture dating no earlier than A.D. 1000 (Hays-Gilpin and Hill 1999:5).

Plant and flower symbolism appear late in the pre-Hispanic Southwest (Hays-Gilpin and Hegmon 2005). Chaco Canyon flower symbolism is limited to one cache of painted wooden objects in the form of flowers and birds in Room 93 at Chetro Ketl, a Chacoan great house, dating to A.D. 1052–1120 (Figure I.3b; Hays-Gilpin and Hill 1999:9). Together with the copper bells and cacao from west Mexico and imported scarlet macaws, this cache constitutes the best evidence for flowers (and flower world) in Chacoan material culture (Weiner 2015).

Flowers, birds, butterflies, and macaws on Mimbres ceramics occur largely as isolated motifs rarely in association with one another (Hays-Gilpin and Hill 1999:5–7, Figure 2). Plant depictions are few in number, nonspecific as to species, and often are simple bushes or flowers with elongated buds, radial petals, or both (Hays-Gilpin and Hegmon 2005:92). Mimbres vessels contain single radial figures probably representing flowers in the interior of Mimbres bowls (Hays-Gilpin and Hill 2000:415; Taube 2010:Figure 5.29d). A handful of naturalistic depictions include insects or birds encircling flowers (Figure 8.2e; e.g., MimPIDD #2815, 5506, 8673). Portrait-style dragonflies, macaws, butterflies, and other scenes reveal a more developed flower world pictorial tradition than Chaco's visual program.

Flower world in Hohokam material culture generally does not appear until after A.D. 1300 (Hays-Gilpin and Hill 1999:4) save for pockets of earlier examples in petroglyphs near Tucson after A.D. 950 (Hernbrode and Boyle 2017). The most "unequivocal" early Hohokam flower designs occur on one Gila Butte Red-on-Buff bowl recovered from the Hardy Site near Tucson, Arizona (Figure I.3a; Hays-Gilpin and Hill 2000:Figure 19.1b). Initially dated to A.D. 500 (Hays-Gilpin and Hill 2000), this ceramic type was redated to A.D. 750–850 (Jim Heidke and Henry Wallace, personal communication 2017), the latter date in this range corresponding with the earliest evidence of flower world in the Aztatlán region.

Maize Symbolism

There are no clear depictions of maize plants or cobs in Chaco Canyon art, but maize plant/cob icons in Classic Mimbres ceramics occur on at least eight bowls. These include a grid garden with maize plants as well as maize stalks depicted in proximity to or eaten by a crane, a canine, a gopher, a rabbit, or grasshoppers (Figure 8.2f). Portraiture of icons in the bowl interiors tend to highlight the animals as the main focus, not the corn

(Hays-Gilpin and Hegmon 2005:90). One maize plant appears to emerge from a cloud terrace—the only explicit example of a link between corn and rain (see MimPIDD #3875, 4533, 5006, 7364, 7933, 8148, 8769, 8799).

Copper Bells

Copper bells (crotals) from west Mexico were imported into the Southwest probably as part of a burgeoning interest in the sensory qualities linking their sounds and iridescent colors to flower world (Hosler 1994; Vargas 1995). West Mexican bells in the Southwest correlate with two temporal periods, Phase I (A.D. 800–1250) and Phase II (post-A.D. 1250) (Vokes and Gregory 2007:322–27). Phase I bells cluster at Chaco Canyon, Mimbres, Hohokam, and Flagstaff-area sites, while the largest cluster in Phase II is Paquimé and the Casas Grandes region and Mogollon, Hohokam, and Salado sites (Vokes and Gregory 2007). A refined chronology of bells may clarify temporal discrepancies (such as early dates for Phase I bells), but the general trend is that bells occur along with more developed expressions of flower world.

Cacao

By A.D. 900–1000, cacao was imported to Chaco Canyon (Crown and Hurst 2009) in the context of flower world–style ritualism (Mathiowetz 2011, 2019b; Weiner 2015). Cacao seeds, including the inspiration for Mesoamerican-style cylinder jars at Chaco, probably derive from the Pacific coast of Nayarit or southern Sinaloa (Mathiowetz 2011, 2019b). Some contend that cacao was present at southwestern sites by A.D. 750 (Washburn et al. 2011, 2013), a time that would predate the Aztatlán tradition and its flower world ceremonialism. Further research is needed on cacao use in the American Southwest, northern Mexico, and west Mexico for a more refined chronology.

FLOWER WORLD AND SOUTHWESTERN SOCIAL DYNAMICS BEFORE A.D. 1150: A SUMMARY

While the evidence of flower world at Chacoan sites corresponds with an era of pronounced social hierarchies and complexity, the Classic Mimbres Flower World coincided with architectural and social changes in which there is little evidence of hierarchies (see Gilman et al. 2014). Mimbres socioreligious changes have been attributed by some to a *Popol Vuh* and Hero Twins–related cosmology from the Gulf Coast Huastec region (Gilman et al. 2014); however, the importation of key ritual objects from west Mexico points toward an Aztatlán Flower World influence. Genetic analyses indicate the presence of an immigrant west Mexican woman (closely related to Huichol and Cora) living at the NAN Ranch site around A.D. 940–1010 (Snow et al. 2011), just as the Mimbres Flower World took form. This indicates that Aztatlán Flower World ideologies brought by immigrants may have shaped Mimbres cosmology and social organization. No genetic evidence yet exists for Aztatlán people at Chaco, which may account for differences in the Chacoan and Mimbres Flower World manifestations.

Mimbres Flower World is characterized by the first limited illustrations of key flower world concepts that are typical in Mesoamerica, such as horned/feathered serpents, maize, katsina-like breath and clouds, and emergence symbolism (Taube, this volume). The interrelated cloud, rain, maize, sun, and horned/feathered serpent themes that are typical of flower world are largely absent in Southwest visual culture before A.D. 1000. Not until the post-A.D. 1300 florescence of flower world images are intertwined conceptual metaphors most fully expressed (see Hays-Gilpin and Hill 1999, 2000; Hays-Gilpin et al. 2010; Hill 1992; Mathiowetz 2011, 2018a, 2018b, 2021; Sekaquaptewa and Washburn 2004; Taube 2000, 2001, 2010). The best evidence for flower world following Mimbres and Chaco expressions are isolated cave caches of wooden flowers and birds in Late Pueblo III–period Kayenta sites dating between A.D. 1200 and 1300 at Sunflower Cave (northern Arizona), Bonita Creek Cave (southern Arizona), and Montezuma Creek (southern Utah) (Hays-Gilpin and Hill 2000)—which coincides with the rise of the Casas Grandes culture and Paquimé (Figures I.3c–I.3d). A key question remains: How does Casas Grandes (A.D. 1200–1450) cosmology relate to the end of the Chaco and Mimbres Flower Worlds by A.D. 1150 and the Pueblo IV–period flower world expressed after A.D. 1300?

CASAS GRANDES CULTURE AND COSMOLOGY (A.D. 1200–1450)

The nature of the Casas Grandes culture's religion/ritual, social organization, and origin has been at the forefront of debate since the 1958–1961 excavations led by Charles Di Peso and Eduardo Contreras revealed diverse cultural roots. For many decades, Mesoamerican religion, deities, and related ritual practices were the primary bases for characterizing Casas Grandes socioreligious and political organization (Di Peso 1974; Di Peso et al. 1974). Others have since proposed models focused on the ingestion of hallucinogens and shamanic-style vision quests (VanPool and VanPool 2007), while scholars versed in Mesoamerican cosmology have focused on the rain, wind, and breath aspects of Casas Grandes cosmology that have limited Mimbres antecedents but ultimate origins in Mesoamerica (Schaafsma 2001; Taube 2001). Only in the last decade has flower world been invoked as a central organizing principle of Casas Grandes society (Mathiowetz 2011).

IDENTIFYING THE CASAS GRANDES FLOWER WORLD

An assessment of the solar, rain, maize, and floral components of Casas Grandes cosmology in relation to Mesoamerican and southwestern flower worlds can shed light on the expression and ritual practice of the Casas Grandes Flower World.

Casas Grandes Solar Ceremonialism

Among the most compelling figures in post–A.D. 1250 Casas Grandes ceramic art are human males with a scarlet macaw head or headdress, sometimes depicted alongside or astride the horned/feathered serpent (Figure 8.3a; Color Plate 10). While VanPool and VanPool (2007) consider this figure to be an intoxicated shaman in the midst of ecstatic transformation, it probably instead represents the ethnographically known Puebloan solar deity generally known as Sun Youth, who shares a remarkable correspondence in character attributes with the Mesoamerican solar deity Xochipilli (Mathiowetz 2011, 2018a, 2018b, 2019a, 2019b, 2021). Both wear scarlet macaw headdresses as the young god of dawn and are the patrons of flowers, music, dance, sexuality, life, butterflies, and the soul— including links to the maize agricultural cycle and the returning corn maidens. Around A.D. 1275, aviculture programs at Paquimé in northern Mexico were dedicated to breeding macaws; the remains of around 322 scarlet macaws and 100 macaws of undetermined species have been recovered (Crown 2016:337; Di Peso et al. 1974; Schwartz 2020). This breeding program probably related to Sun Youth ritualism that was disseminated northward during the Pueblo IV period, where macaw feathers would be integral to Puebloan katsina regalia and the Sun Youth dance standard (Mathiowetz 2011, 2018b, 2021).

The Sun Youth is recognized today by thirteen of the nineteen Pueblos of New Mexico, the Hopi of Arizona, and most probably other New Mexico pueblos where ethnographic information is sparse. Parallels between these solar deities may relate to his acquisition by Puebloan people from the Aztatlán region via Paquimé, perhaps by the late 1200s to early 1300s, as evidenced in oral traditions, migration histories, and the archaeological record (Mathiowetz 2011, 2018a, 2018b, 2021). Solar and rain symbolism on Chihuahuan polychromes was probably integrated into a program of seasonal maize-agricultural ceremonialism, which may have been scheduled by "sun priests" through solar observation and disseminated to hinterland communities via a network of hilltop *atalaya* signaling systems centered at the nearby Cerro Moctezuma, the highest peak in the Casas Grandes Valley (Mathiowetz 2011, 2019a, 2021).

Casas Grandes Rain Ceremonialism

The feathered serpent Quetzalcoatl is generally accepted as an analogue for the horned/feathered serpent in Casas Grandes and southwestern cosmology in relation to water, wind, and breath (Figure 8.3a; Di Peso 1974; Mathiowetz 2011; Schaafsma 2001; Taube 2001). Rain ritualism may be affiliated with the Mesoamerican deity Tlaloc (Schaafsma 1999; Schaafsma and Taube 2006; Taube 2001), and one west Mexican copper bell in the form of Tlaloc was found at Paquimé (Figure 8.3b; see Di Peso et al. 1974:7:526). Carved stone cylindrical sculptures in the form of human heads with terraced cloud headdresses were recovered at Paquimé and nearby sites (Figure 8.3c; Di Peso et al. 1974:7:293–97). The elite burials in Unit 4 (where cloud-terraced sculptures were found) located directly north of Reservoir I indicates a constructed ritual landscape that included "the high status dead as powerful rainmakers" (Schaafsma and Taube 2006:247). Their return as rain to Casas Grandes communities was probably integral to the germination and maturation of crops and the creation of a flowering landscape. Human effigy vessels with pipes

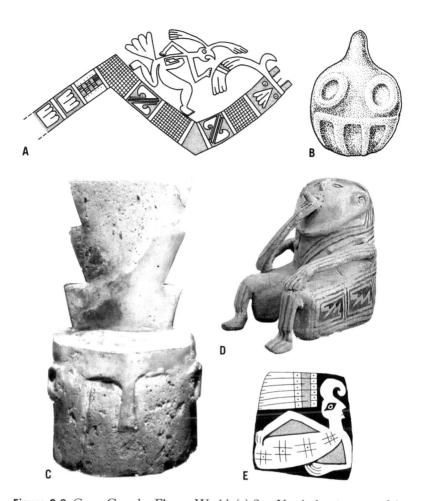

Figure 8.3 Casas Grandes Flower World. (a) Sun Youth dancing out of the underworld atop body of horned/feathered serpent, Ramos Polychrome, Dallas Museum of Art, Catalog number 1980.15-v04 (after photos by John M. D. Pohl). (b) Rain deity Tlaloc portrayed on copper bell from Paquimé. Digital image of line art drawing originally published in Di Peso 1974:2:565, Figure 350–2. Courtesy of the Amerind Foundation, Inc., Dragoon, Arizona. Alice Wesche, artist. (c) Stone sculpture of probable ancestor with cloud terrace headdress. Digital image of Amerind negative number CG/356L-2. Originally published in Di Peso 1974:2:557, Figure 341–2. Courtesy of the Amerind Foundation, Inc., Dragoon, Arizona. (d) Smoker effigy vessel. Digital image of Amerind object catalog number 4879. Courtesy of the Amerind Foundation, Inc., Dragoon, Arizona. (e) Anthropomorphic sprouting maize seed. Detail of Ramos Polychrome after catalog number 1986.18.1.1, Museum of Peoples and Cultures, Brigham Young University (after photo courtesy of Scott Ure). Drawings by Michael D. Mathiowetz.

(sometimes depicted with emergent breath feathers) conflate breath and clouds of smoke as rain (Figure 8.3d; Mathiowetz 2011:741–53).

This Tlaloc-related ancestral rain ceremonialism at Paquimé points to the presence of Casas Grandes directional cloud or rain chiefs, which are a key tenet in Puebloan and Mesoamerican rain ceremonialism (see Schaafsma and Taube 2006). For Keresans, the Sun Youth awakens the directional clouds (Boas 1928:76–77), and similar water-bringing directional clouds or rain chiefs may have been manifested in performances atop the four circular dance platforms at the terminal points of the Mound of the Cross—a solstice and equinoctial observatory probably dedicated to the annual solar (Sun Youth) and maize-agricultural cycle (Mathiowetz 2011:507; 2021). Mimbres and Casas Grandes wind, rain, and cloud symbolism probably inspired later katsina rain ritualism (Schaafsma 1999; Schaafsma and Taube 2006).

Casas Grandes Maize Ceremonialism

The highland Mexican maize god Centeotl (the alter ego of Xochipilli) is often portrayed with maize foliation sprouting from the head (Taube 1992:41–50). Related maize ritualism at Paquimé may have accompanied the acquisition of Xochipilli worship from west Mexico. Ethnological data indicate that the Mesoamerican solar deity Xochipilli (as Centeotl) and his analogues (the Casas Grandes and Puebloan Sun Youth) are manifested as the maize plant itself. On two Ramos Polychromes, a human figure bears a prominent curling element emerging from the head (Figure 8.3e). As a central figure in the shamanism model, this being was characterized as a transforming shaman who grew a horn during hallucinations after consuming intoxicating tobacco or datura (VanPool and VanPool 2007). However, this "horned" being instead may be an anthropomorphized sprouting seed. The body of this figure is marked by "pound signs" with a central dot, which may relate to the "dot-in-a-square" motif representing corn or the living germ of the kernel (see Webster et al. 2006). The placement of this dotted corn marking on the Sun Youth's body in other examples indicates that the Casas Grandes solar deity probably was a powerful force in overlapping conceptual metaphors linking the growth of maize and the "sprouting" of human life (Mathiowetz 2021). Although rarely portrayed on Chihuahuan polychromes, the "sprouting seed" icon occurs on ceramics that encode an elite ideology, which indicates that this being occupies a key role in the regional solar and rain ritualism expressed in the intertwined Sun Youth and feathered/horned serpent symbolism. The "sprouting seed" icon may be the maize aspect of the Casas Grandes Sun Youth.

Flower Symbolism on Chihuahuan Polychromes

Given that a well-developed solar, rain, and maize ceremonialism expressed on Ramos Polychromes by A.D. 1280–1300 probably influenced the Pueblo IV–period expression of flower world, representations of flowers should occur on Casas Grandes material culture. Fifteenth-century murals at Awat'ovi and Kawàyka'a on the Hopi mesas contain geometric flowers with various rayed, crossed, quartered, or central dot designs (Hays-Gilpin and Hegmon 2005:97–98; Smith 1952:227, Figures 18jj–18qq), and geometric flowers occur in Pottery Mound murals and various ceramics (Figures 8.4a–8.4e; see Crown 1994:158, Figures 5.11, 5.40, 9.28). Similar circular designs occur in Classic Mimbres ceramics (MimPIDD #706, 1496, 2201, 4284, 4488, 4884), which may have inspired Casas Grandes floral forms.

Naturalistic plant imagery on Casas Grandes ceramics is largely absent, and depictions of flowers are geometric. Examples of "unequivocal" flowers include "rayed circles" with a central dot and peripheral tick marks (Hays-Gilpin and Hill 2000:418). A variety of these circular designs appear on Chihuahuan polychromes and bichromes. Following Smith's (1952:227, Figures 18jj–18qq) identification of geometric flowers at Awat'ovi, I proposed that "rayed circles" on Casas Grandes ceramics are geometric flowers (Figures 8.4e, 8.5a; Mathiowetz 2011:288–312). Many examples have black- or red-colored central dots (Di Peso et al. 1974:6:236, 269, 274–276; Townsend 2005:154, 171, Plates 92a, 109).

None of these circular flowers are depicted on Viejo-period ceramics (see Di Peso et al. 1974:6:21–76), which indicates that the ideology that these floral designs represent was probably absent during the Viejo period. Aside from Ramos Polychrome and Ramos Black-on-White (Di Peso et al. 1974:6:262, 266, 267, 272–276; Powell 2006:Plate 5), these circular floral-medallion forms occur on types including Babicora Polychrome (Powell 2006:Plate 9), Escondida Polychrome (Di Peso et al. 1974:6:231,

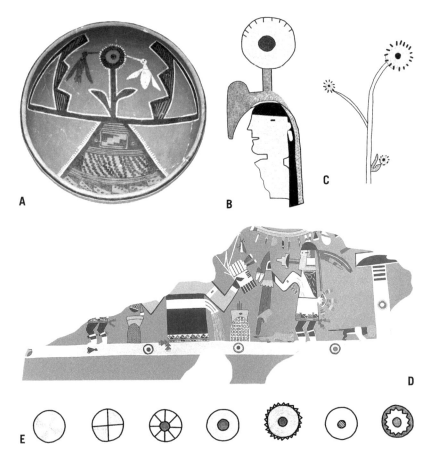

Figure 8.4 Geometric flowers in Pueblo IV art. (a) Ancestral Pueblo, 1300–1400. Fourmile Polychrome bowl: flower and hummingbirds. Ceramic and paints, 4½ × 10 × 10 in. (11.43 × 25.4 × 25.4 cm). Catalog number 1988.100.FA, Dallas Museum of Art, Foundation for the Arts Collection, anonymous gift. Photo by Brad Flowers. (b) Detail of sunflower from Kiva 2, Layer 1, north wall, Pottery Mound, New Mexico (after Hibben 1975:Figure 14). (c) Detail of sunflowers in Kiva 1, Layer 1, north wall, Pottery Mound, New Mexico (after Hibben 1975:Figure 8). (d) Flowers in baseband. Reproduction of Awat'ovi Room 788, east wall, layer 1, Arizona (Museum of Northern Arizona, Catalog number NA820.R788.5a and B/23099D). (e) Schematic depiction of various geometric flowers depicted in basebands in Awat'ovi kiva murals (after Smith 1952:Figures 18kk–18qq). Drawings by Michael D. Mathiowetz.

Figure 8.5 Probable circular geometric flowers on Chihuahuan polychromes and bichromes. (a) Examples of schematic forms of geometric flowers on Casas Grandes ceramics (drawing by Michael D. Mathiowetz). (b) Ramos Polychrome. Digital image of Amerind object catalog number 6281. Courtesy of the Amerind Foundation, Inc., Dragoon, Arizona. (c) Ramos Black-on-White. Digital image of Amerind object catalog number 3394. Courtesy of the Amerind Foundation, Inc., Dragoon, Arizona. (d) Villa Ahumada Polychrome, Catalog number 59.9.220. Courtesy of the El Paso Museum of Archaeology Collection. (e) Escondida Polychrome. Courtesy of the El Paso Archaeological Society, Naylor Collection. (f) Ramos Polychrome. Digital image of Amerind object catalog number 9404. Courtesy of the Amerind Foundation, Inc., Dragoon, Arizona. (g) Madera Black-on-Red. Catalog number 65.24.72a. The Alves Collection. Courtesy of the Maxwell Museum of Anthropology, University of New Mexico.

236, 241, 242; Townsend 2005:Plate 123), Huerigos Polychrome (Di Peso et al. 1974:6:247), Villa Ahumada Polychrome (Di Peso et al. 1974:6:316), and Madera Black-on-Red (Figures 8.5b–8.5g), although less frequently. This indicates that elements of flower world symbolism were present on non-Ramos ceramic types produced in zones of manufacture across the Casas Grandes polity.

The numerous variations of the "rayed circle" floral icons on Chihuahuan polychromes occur within the context of an apparently institutionalized and hierarchical flower world political-ritual program that was centered on the paramount site in the Casas Grandes macroregional polity. Here, a redundant symbolic repertoire was dedicated to the Sun Youth and feathered/horned serpent deities along with ancestral cloud and sprouting maize seeds that together form an integrated ritual program. On Ramos Polychrome, floral medallions occur with scarlet macaws, horned/feathered serpents, on human faces or bodies, and beside (or on) various birds and other animals or reptiles (e.g., Di Peso et al. 1974:6:266, 269, 270, 274, 276, 284; Powell 2006:Plates 10, 25; Townsend 2005:Plates 28a–30, 39, 88, 92b, 108, 111, 113b), which indicates that this integrated symbol set comprised a constellation of related ideas. The Mimbres and Casas Grandes Flower World similarities do not necessarily indicate a linear evolution but instead may represent an initial influx of ideas that relates to an increasing Mimbres awareness of the Aztatlán Flower World ideology followed by a newly elaborated variation to an extraordinary degree at Paquimé.

CONCLUSION: THE ORIGIN AND NATURE OF THE CASAS GRANDES FLOWER WORLD

Maize agriculture arrived into northern Mexico and the American Southwest from Mesoamerica over four millennia ago. While key aspects of Puebloan Flower World ceremonialism centered on rain and maize have deep roots in Mesoamerica dating to the Formative Olmec (Taube 2000, 2001), it has been less clear when and how these ideas arrived in the southwest and northern Mexico. Flower world visual expressions, however, first appear clearly by A.D. 900–1000 in Chacoan and Mimbres material culture, respectively, intensifying elsewhere after A.D. 1200/1300. Two phases of flower world appear to correlate with increasing degrees of engagement with Aztatlán Flower World ritualism. Phase I dates between A.D. 850/900 and 1150 and includes the Mimbres and Chaco Canyon cultures. Phase II dates after A.D. 1200/1300 and primarily includes the Casas Grandes and Pueblo IV worlds with somewhat spare expressions in parts of the Kayenta and Hohokam regions. While interpretations of Casas Grandes social and political organization remain debatable, it is evident that Paquimé was a major proponent of a heightened form of flower world ceremonialism, significant aspects of which remain vibrant in contemporary Puebloan ritual and worldview.

Striking correlations exist between late pre-Hispanic and contemporary flower world–oriented maize-agricultural *mitote* cycles in the Gran Nayar and the flower world–related maize ceremonialism of Pueblo IV–period and contemporary Pueblos (Mathiowetz 2011, 2018a, 2018b, 2019a, 2019b, 2020, 2021; Mathiowetz et al. 2015; Washburn and Fast 2018). With the development of the Aztatlán Flower World after A.D. 850/900, those distant relations began to materialize in the Chaco, Mimbres, Casas Grandes, and Pueblo IV Flower Worlds.

A basic outline of Medio-period Casas Grandes cosmology and ritualism includes a central concern with the paramount reverence for the daily and annual passage of the sun (i.e., Sun Youth) across the sky. The proposed institutional office of paramount Sun Priest at Paquimé appears to be the precursor to similar Puebloan caciques and sun watchers who today observe the sun at horizon points for timing agricultural planting, harvesting, and ceremonial cycles. With the warmth of the sun, the waters of the underworld (as ancestors) rose into the atmosphere through the process of convection. Encouragement for the return of the rain-filled clouds formed part of reciprocal relations between Casas Grandes people and their deceased ancestors that minimally involved (1) private smoking rituals by initiated males for cloud and rain making, and (2) public rituals of feasting and *tesgüino* consumption (King et al. 2017) which fueled community dances by shell- and copper-jewelry-laden participants who incorporated solar-related scarlet macaw feathers into their regalia. Musical instruments including copper bells, shell trumpets, ceramic hand drums, musical rasps, shell tinklers, and bone whistles probably produced a cacophony of sound amid spectacular colorful performances (Figures 8.6a–8.6e; see Di Peso 1974:2:582–85).

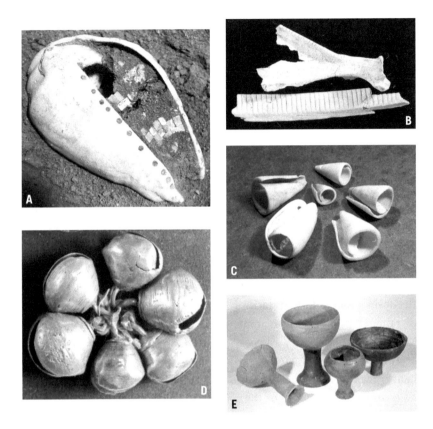

Figure 8.6 The sounds of flower world at Paquimé. (a) Shell trumpet. Digital image of Amerind negative number CG/595F-29. Originally published in Di Peso 1974:2:579, Figure 366–2. Courtesy of the Amerind Foundation, Inc., Dragoon, Arizona. Russell Rosene, photographer. (b) Notched bone musical rasp set. Digital image of Amerind negative number CG/571L-22. Originally published in Di Peso 1974:2:551, Figure 331–2. Courtesy of the Amerind Foundation, Inc., Dragoon, Arizona. (c) Shell tinklers. Digital image of Amerind negative number CG/556L-14. Originally published in Di Peso 1974:2:492, Figure 244–2, left side. Courtesy of the Amerind Foundation, Inc., Dragoon, Arizona. (d) Copper crotals (bells). Digital image of Amerind negative number CG/381L-2. Originally published in Di Peso 1974:2:493, Figure 245–2. Courtesy of the Amerind Foundation, Inc., Dragoon, Arizona. (e) Ceramic hand drums. Digital image of Amerind negative number CG/576L-9. Originally published in Di Peso 1974:2:584, Figure 373–2. Courtesy of the Amerind Foundation, Inc., Dragoon, Arizona.

Like Puebloan katsinam, Casas Grandes ancestral cloud and rain spirits surely were attracted by the beauty of these colorful entreaties in vibrant public ceremonialism and were then conveyed back to Casas Grandes communities by the wind- and rain-bringing horned/feathered serpent. With the increasing heat of day and the arrival of the ancestral rains, the Chihuahuan desert landscape was probably transformed into an iridescent and bountiful lived experience akin to what Hopi describe as *siitálpuva*, variously translated as "along (or throughout) the flowery land," "along the fields in bloom," and "the land brightened with flowers" (Hays-Gilpin et al. 2010:122; Washburn, this volume). The sun and rains nourished the maize plants, portrayed on ceramics as anthropomorphized sprouting maize seeds. Circular floral blossoms on various Chihuahuan polychromes embodied this flowery world of beauty and abundance and stability in the midst of a chaotic, unstable world (Sandstrom, this volume). Much like in other parts of Mesoamerica and the Southwest, the Casas Grandes Flower World was probably conceived as an idealized and perfect state of being. The political and ritual center at Paquimé and related sites in the macroregion far beyond the Casas Grandes core zone together appear to have formed an integrated network of participants in this ritual program (to varying degrees). For example, Ramos Polychrome vessels were manufactured at multiple locales in the Casas Grandes region and widely traded (Britton 2018), which indicates willful participation in the flower world cosmology encoded in the symbolism of these elite ceramics.

The highly elaborated Casas Grandes Flower World ritual program focused on the Sun Youth deity parallels key elements of the flower world then flourishing in the Aztatlán coastal core zone, including the ball game (Mathiowetz 2011:479–525), that were not adopted in the Chacoan and Mimbres regions. Despite speculation that Viejo-period cosmology evolved into Medio-period ritualism, the flower world described herein did not have Viejo-period antecedents and instead appears to have been introduced from west Mexico during the Medio period as a well-formed political-ritual system. Medio-period Paquimé may have been an "international" center for the Sun Youth–oriented flower world that was adapted by Pueblo IV people in New Mexico and Arizona who sought scarlet macaw feathers and bells for flower world ritualism via direct acquisition or other social networks and strategic alliances. The moral and ethical tenets inherent in this realm of beauty, life, balance, and abundance that is linked to the sun, ancestral rain, and maize in Casas Grandes ritualism remain a living legacy among Puebloan people today.

ACKNOWLEDGMENTS

Special thanks to Emma Britton and Thatcher Rogers for Chihuahuan polychrome type identifications and to Will Russell for patiently working with us to create the volume's maps.

REFERENCES

Beekman, Christopher S. 2003. "Fruitful Symmetry: Corn and Cosmology in the Public Architecture of Late Formative and Early Classic Jalisco." *Mesoamerican Voices* 1:5–22.

Bell, Betty B. 1960. "Analysis of Ceramic Style: A West Mexican Collection." Unpublished Ph.D. dissertation, Department of Anthropology, University of California, Los Angeles.

Boas, Franz. 1928. *Keresan Texts.* Publications of the American Ethnological Society, vol. 8, pt. 1. New York: American Ethnological Society.

Britton, Emma L. 2018. "The Mineralogical and Chemical Variability of Casas Grandes Polychromes Throughout the International Four Corners." Unpublished Ph.D. dissertation, Department of Anthropology, University of California, Santa Cruz.

Crown, Patricia L. 1994. *Ceramics and Ideology: Salado Polychrome Pottery.* Albuquerque: University of New Mexico Press.

Crown, Patricia L. 2016. "Just Macaws: A Review for the U.S. Southwest/Mexican Northwest." *Kiva* 82(4):331–63.

Crown, Patricia L., and W. Jeffrey Hurst. 2009. "Evidence of Cacao Use in the Prehispanic American Southwest." *Proceedings of the National Academy of Sciences* 106:2110–13.

Di Peso, Charles C. 1974. *Casas Grandes: A Fallen Trading Center of the Gran Chichimeca.* 3 vols. Flagstaff, Ariz.: Northland Press.

Di Peso, Charles C., John B. Rinaldo, and Gloria J. Fenner. 1974. *Casas Grandes: A Fallen Trading Center of the Gran Chichimeca.* 5 vols. Flagstaff, Ariz.: Northland Press.

George, Richard J., Stephen Plog, Adam S. Watson, Kari L. Schmidt, Brendan J. Culleton, Thomas K. Harper, Patricia A. Gilman, Steven A. LeBlanc, George Amato, Peter Whiteley, Logan Kistler, and Douglas J. Kennett. 2018. "Archaeogenomic Evidence from the Southwestern US Points to a Pre-Hispanic Scarlet Macaw Breeding Colony." *Proceedings of the National Academy of Sciences* 115(35):8740–45.

Gilman, Patricia A., Marc Thompson, and Kristina C. Wyckoff. 2014. "Ritual Change and the Distant: Mesoamerican Iconography, Scarlet Macaws, and Great Kivas in the Mimbres Region of Southwestern New Mexico." *American Antiquity* 79(1):90–107.

Hays-Gilpin, Kelley, and Michelle Hegmon. 2005. "The Art of Ethnobotany: Depictions of Maize and Other Plants in the Prehispanic Southwest." In *Engaged Anthropology: Research Essays on North American Archaeology, Ethnobotany, and Museology; Papers in Honor of Richard I. Ford*, edited by Michelle Hegmon and B. Sunday Eiselt, 89–113. Anthropological Papers 94. Ann Arbor: Museum of Anthropology, University of Michigan.

Hays-Gilpin, Kelley, and Jane H. Hill. 1999. "The Flower World in Material Culture: An Iconographic Complex in the Southwest and Mesoamerica." *Journal of Anthropological Research* 55(1):1–37.

Hays-Gilpin, Kelley, and Jane H. Hill. 2000. "The Flower World in Prehistoric Southwest Material Culture." In *The Archaeology of Regional Interaction: Religion, Warfare, and Exchange Across the American Southwest and Beyond; Proceedings of the 1996 Southwest Symposium,* edited by Michelle Hegmon, 411–28. Boulder: University Press of Colorado.

Hays-Gilpin, Kelley, Elizabeth Newsome, and Emory Sekaquaptewa. 2010. "*Siitálpuva,* 'Through the Land Brightened with Flowers': Ecology and Cosmology in Mural and Pottery Painting, Hopi and Beyond." In *Painting the Cosmos: Metaphor and Worldview in Images from the Southwest Pueblos and Mexico*, edited by Kelley Hays-Gilpin and Polly Schaafsma, 121–38. Museum of Northern Arizona Bulletin 67. Flagstaff: Museum of Northern Arizona.

Hernbrode, Janine, and Peter Boyle. 2017. "Broad Distribution of Flower World Imagery in Hohokam Petroglyphs." In *American Indian Rock Art*, vol. 43, edited by Ken Hedges and Mark Calamia, 75–83. San Jose, Calif.: American Rock Art Research Association.

Hibben, Frank C. 1975. *Kiva Art of the Anasazi at Pottery Mound.* Las Vegas, Nev.: KC Publications.

Hill, Jane H. 1992. "The Flower World of Old Uto-Aztecan." *Journal of Anthropological Research* 48(2):117–44.

Hosler, Dorothy. 1994. *The Sounds and Colors of Power: The Sacred Metallurgical Technology of Ancient West Mexico.* Cambridge, Mass.: MIT Press.

King, Daniel J., Michael T. Searcy, Chad L. Yost, and Kyle Waller. 2017. "Corn, Beer, and Marine Resources at Casas Grandes, Mexico: An Analysis of Prehistoric Diets Using Microfossils Recovered from Dental Calculus." *Journal of Archaeological Science: Reports* 16:365–79.

Mathiowetz, Michael D. 2011. "The Diurnal Path of the Sun: Ideology and Interregional Interaction in Ancient Northwest Mesoamerica and the American Southwest." Unpublished Ph.D. dissertation, Department of Anthropology, University of California, Riverside.

Mathiowetz, Michael D. 2018a. "From this Day Forward I Am Your Way of Life: The *Capitan* Icon on Rio Grande Glaze Wares in the Southwestern United States (AD 1300–1700)." *Journal of the Southwest* 60(3):699–752.

Mathiowetz, Michael D. 2018b. "The Sun Youth of the Casas Grandes Culture (A. D. 1200–1450)." *Kiva* 84(3):367–90.

Mathiowetz, Michael D. 2019a. "El hijo de Dios que está en el Sol: Autoridad política y personificación del Dios Sol en el antiguo Noroccidente de México." In *Aztatlán: Interacción y cambio social en el Occidente de México ca. 850–1350 d.C.*, edited by Laura Solar Valverde and Ben A. Nelson, 287–312. Zamora: El Colegio de Michoacán.

Mathiowetz, Michael D. 2019b. "A History of Cacao in West Mexico: Implications for Mesoamerica and U.S. Southwest Connections." *Journal of Archaeological Research* 27(3):287–333.

Mathiowetz, Michael. 2020. "Weaving Our Life: The Economy and Ideology of Cotton in Postclassic West Mexico." In *Ancient West Mexicos: Time, Space, and Diversity*, edited by Joshua D. Englehardt, Verenice Heredia Espinoza, and Christopher S. Beekman, 302–48. Gainesville: University Press of Florida.

Mathiowetz, Michael D. 2021. "The Dance of the Sprouting Corn: Casas Grandes Maize Ceremonialism and the Transformation of the Puebloan World." In *Borderlands Histories: Ethnographic Observations and Archaeological Interpretations*, edited by John Carpenter and Matthew Pailes. Salt Lake City: University of Utah Press.

Mathiowetz, Michael, Polly Schaafsma, Jeremy Coltman, and Karl Taube. 2015. "The Darts of Dawn: The Tlahuizcalpantecuhtli Venus Complex in the Iconography of Mesoamerica and the American Southwest." *Journal of the Southwest* 57(1):1–102.

Meighan, Clement W., ed. 1976. *The Archaeology of Amapa, Nayarit*. Monumenta Archaeologica, vol. 2. Los Angeles: Institute of Archaeology, University of California.

Pohl, John M. D., and Michael D. Mathiowetz. Forthcoming. "Our Mother the Sea: The Pacific Coastal Exchange Network of Late Postclassic Mexico." In *Waves of Influence: Pacific Maritime Networks Connecting Mexico, Central America, and Northwestern South America*, edited by Christopher S. Beekman and Colin McEwan. Washington D.C.: Dumbarton Oaks.

Powell, Melissa S., ed. 2006. *Secrets of Casas Grandes: Precolumbian Art and Archaeology of Northern Mexico*. Santa Fe: Museum of New Mexico Press.

Schaafsma, Polly. 1999. "Tlalocs, Kachinas, Sacred Bundles, and Related Symbolism in the Southwest and Mesoamerica." In *The Casas Grandes World*, edited by Curtis F. Schaafsma and Carroll L. Riley, 164–92. Salt Lake City: University of Utah Press.

Schaafsma, Polly. 2001. "Quetzalcoatl and the Horned and Feathered Serpent of the Southwest." In *The Road to Aztlan: Art from a Mythic Homeland*, edited by Virginia M. Fields and Victor Zamudio-Taylor, 138–49. Los Angeles: Los Angeles County Museum of Art.

Schaafsma, Polly, and Karl A. Taube. 2006. "Bringing the Rain: An Ideology of Rain Making in the Pueblo Southwest and Mesoamerica." In *A Pre-Columbian World*, edited by Jeffrey Quilter and Mary Miller, 231–85. Washington, D.C.: Dumbarton Oaks Research Library and Collection, Harvard University Press.

Schwartz, Christopher W. 2020. "Scarlet Macaws, Long-Distance Exchange, and Placemaking in the U.S. Southwest and Mexican Northwest." Unpublished Ph.D. dissertation, School of Human Evolution and Social Change, Arizona State University.

Sekaquaptewa, Emory, and Dorothy Washburn. 2004. "They Go Along Singing: Reconstructing the Hopi Past from Ritual Metaphors in Song and Dance." *American Antiquity* 69(3):457–86.

Smith, Watson. 1952. *Kiva Mural Decorations at Awatovi and Kawaika-a with a Survey of Other Wall Paintings in the Pueblo Southwest*. Papers of the Peabody Museum of Archaeology and Ethnology 37. Cambridge, Mass.: Harvard University Press.

Snow, Meradeth, Harry Shafer, and David G. Smith. 2011. "The Relationship of the Mimbres to Other Southwestern and Mexican Populations." *Journal of Archaeological Science* 38:3122–33.

Taube, Karl A. 1992. *The Major Gods of Ancient Yucatan*. Studies in Precolumbian Art and Archaeology 32. Washington, D.C.: Dumbarton Oaks.

Taube, Karl A. 2000. "Lightning Celts and Corn Fetishes: The Formative Olmec and the Development of Maize Symbolism in Mesoamerica and the American Southwest." In *Olmec Art and Archaeology in Mesoamerica*, edited by John E. Clark and Mary E. Pye, 297–337. New Haven, Conn.: Yale University Press.

Taube, Karl A. 2001. "The Breath of Life: The Symbolism of Wind in Mesoamerica and the American Southwest." In *The Road to Aztlan: Art from a Mythic Homeland*, edited by Virginia M. Fields and Victor Zamudio-Taylor, 102–23. Los Angeles: Los Angeles County Museum of Art.

Taube, Karl A. 2010. "At Dawn's Edge: Tulúm, Santa Rita, and Floral Symbolism in the International Style of Late Postclassic Mesoamerica." In *Astronomers, Scribes, and Priests: Intellectual Interchange Between the Northern Maya Lowlands and Highland Mexico in the Late Postclassic Period*, edited by Gabrielle Vail and Christine Hernández, 145–91. Washington, D.C.: Dumbarton Oaks Research Library and Collection.

Townsend, Richard F., ed. 2005. *Casas Grandes and the Ceramic Art of the Ancient Southwest*. New Haven, Conn.: Yale University Press.

VanPool, Christine S., and Todd L. VanPool. 2007. *Signs of the Casas Grandes Shamans*. Salt Lake City: University of Utah Press.

Vargas, Victoria. 1995. *Copper Bell Trade Patterns in the Prehispanic U.S. South-west and Northwest Mexico.* Arizona State Museum Archaeological Series 187. Tucson: Arizona State Museum.

Vokes, Arthur W., and David A. Gregory. 2007. "Exchange Networks for Exotic Goods in the Southwest and Zuni's Place in Them." In *Zuni Origins: Toward a New Synthesis of Southwestern Archaeology,* edited by David A. Gregory and David R. Wilcox, 318–60. Tucson: University of Arizona Press.

Von Winning, Hasso. 1977. "Rituals Depicted on Polychrome Ceramics from Nayarit." In *Pre-Columbian Art History: Selected Readings,* edited by Alana Cordy-Collins and Jean Stern, 121–34. Palo Alto, Calif.: Peek Publications.

Washburn, Dorothy K., and Sophia Fast. 2018. "Ritual Songs of the Cora of West Mexico and the Hopi of the American Southwest: Shared Ideas Related to Maize Agriculture." *Journal of the Southwest* 60(1):74–114.

Washburn, Dorothy K., William N. Washburn, and Petia A. Shipkova. 2011. "The Prehistoric Drug Trade: Widespread Consumption of Cacao in Ancestral Pueblo and Hohokam Communities in the American Southwest." *Journal of Archaeological Science* 38:1634–40.

Washburn, Dorothy K., William N. Washburn, and Petia A. Shipkova. 2013. "Cacao Consumption During the 8th Century at Alkali Ridge, Southeastern Utah." *Journal of Archaeological Science* 40:2007–13.

Watson, Adam, Stephen Plog, Brendan J. Culleton, Patricia A. Gilman, Steven A. LeBlanc, Peter M. Whiteley, Santiago Claramunt, and Douglas J. Kennett. 2015. "Early Procurement of Scarlet Macaws and the Emergence of Social Complexity in Chaco Canyon, NM." *Proceedings of the National Academy of Sciences* 112:8238–43.

Webster, Laurie D., Kelley A. Hays-Gilpin, and Polly Schaafsma. 2006. "A New Look at Tie-Dye and the Dot-in-a-Square Motif in the Prehispanic Southwest." *Kiva* 71(3):317–48.

Weiner, Robert S. 2015. "A Sensory Approach to Exotica, Ritual Practice, and Cosmology at Chaco Canyon." *Kiva* 81:220–46.

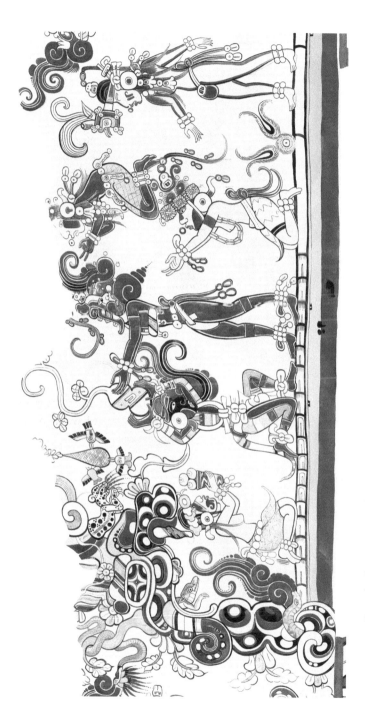

Color Plate 1 Detail of reconstructed mural depicting emergence from Flower Mountain. San Bartolo, Guatemala, Structure 1, Pinturas Sub-1, North Wall. San Bartolo Mural. Illustration by Heather Hurst © 2004.

Color Plate 2 Mural depicting anthropomorphized butterflies or insects carrying or alighting on sunflower stalks. Pottery Mound Kiva 1, Layer 1, North Wall (Hibben 1975:Figure 8). KC Publications.

Color Plate 3 Nahua altars model the layered cosmos with the arch, platform surface, and area underneath corresponding to the sky, the earth's surface, and the interior earth. Ritual participants decorate the altar to reproduce the flower world where spirit entities receive offerings of food and drink. The ritual specialist, at right, chants, imploring the spirit entities to partake of the feast laid out before him. Photo by Alan Sandstrom.

Color Plate 4 *Peyotera* Lupita Robles. Keuruwit+a, Jalisco. Photo by Anahí Luna, 2012.

Color Plate 5 Having been tricked by the wilderness world into driving in circles, the elders in the truck—Fernando Romero and Angel "Eligio" Romero—noted to Felipe Molina and David Shorter that at least "the *sea ania* showed up for us." Photo by David Shorter, 1995.

Color Plate 6 Illustration of Sikyatki Polychrome bowl depicting the reciprocity between people and their natural world. Illustration by Will Russell after Field Museum of Natural History, negative no. A114268_14D, catalog no. 75493. Photo by John Weinstein.

Color Plate 7 Ceramic censer lid from the Pacific coast of Guatemala. Banco Industrial, Guatemala City. Photo by Mauricio Acevedo.

Color Plate 8 Cattails mark a place of ritual importance where the ball game occurs. *Historia Tolteca-Chichimeca*. Bibliothèque Nationale de France.

Color Plate 9 Urn from Cacaxtla with a central figure in a butterfly costume flanked by two smaller figures (possibly a maize deity and ancestral Xochipilli) emerging with cacao through a jewel-lined portal. Blossoms adorn the lid of the vessel. A.D. 600–900. Museo Regional de Tlaxcala. Photo by Andrew D. Turner. Reproducción Autorizada por el Instituto Nacional de Antropología e Historia.

Color Plate 10 Macaw-headed Casas Grandes Sun Youth positioned atop the body of the horned/plumed serpent. Mogollon, Casas Grandes, 1060–1340 (A.D. 1200–1450). Ramos Polychrome jar with parrot man motif. Ceramic, slips, and paint. Overall: 15.24 × 18.893 × 18.893 cm. Diameter (at lip): 11.43 cm. Dallas Museum of Art, General Acquisitions Fund. Catalog no. 1980 15-v04.

Color Plate 11 Scene of human with massive hunchback supporting bowl and gourd water ladle or canteen flanked by four cicada nymphs and four mature winged cicada. Mimbres Black-on-White bowl. Illustration by Will Russell after the de Young Museum, Fine Arts Museums of San Francisco, Catalog no. 2013.76.79.

Color Plate 12 Tecama-phase (A.D. 1150–1350) Cholula Polychrome plate with an image of the Classic Maya God M as a ritual singer-clown. Private Collection.

Color Plate 13 Stone relief from Templo Mayor portraying butterfly soul. Note the round mirror on the back and the triangular turquoise jewel ear ornament. Illustration by Mauricio Díaz García (after Barrera Rodríguez et al. 2012:22).

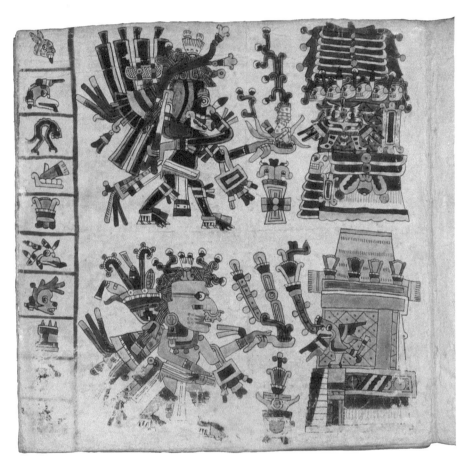

Color Plate 14 *Codex Cospi*, page 13. Biblioteca Universitaria di Bologna.

Color Plate 15 Miguel Cabrera. *Virgin of Guadalupe with Apparitions and a View of Her Sanctuary.* 1760. Oil on canvas. Museo Nacional de la Básilica de Santa María de Guadalupe, Mexico City. D.R. © Archivo del Museo de la Básilica de Guadalupe.

Color Plate 16 *Pottery Mound: Germination.* Lomawywesa (Michael Kabotie) and Choosiwukioma (Delbridge Honanie). 2002. Acrylic on canvas, 4.6 × 1.8 m. Museum of Northern Arizona, Catalog numbers C2417A–C. Photo by Gene Balzer. Composite image Robert Mark, Rupestrian CyberServices.

9

At the Reed of Life

The Cicada and the Emergence in the Ancient and
Contemporary American Southwest

Karl A. Taube

Jane Hill (1992) provided a broad perspective on concepts of flower world
among Uto-Aztecan peoples, including its importance in traditional
songs and its relation to chromatism through bright feathers, jewels,
drops of dew, and flowers. Subsequent research has explored portrayals of
flower world among ancient Puebloan cultures of the American Southwest, including scenes on ceramics and mural paintings (Hays-Gilpin
and Hill 1999; Hays-Gilpin et al. 2010; Mathiowetz 2011; Taube 2010).
In addition to flower world, I (Taube 2004) have called attention to the
widespread concept of Flower Mountain among the ancient Maya and
Teotihuacan cultures as well as among Puebloan peoples of the American Southwest, a paradise realm of the ancestors and a mythical place
of emergence from the underworld. Dating to the first century B.C., the
North Wall mural at San Bartolo in Guatemala graphically portrays the
Maya maize god and humans emerging with maize and a water gourd
on the back of a serpent from this flowering hill (Color Plate 1; Saturno
et al. 2005). In addition, the early colonial *Historia Tolteca-Chichimeca*
from Central Mexico has two graphic scenes of humans emerging from
Chicomoztoc, the seven caves of origin within a mountain covered with
flowering cacti (Kirchhoff et al. 1989). For the Hopi, there is Sitsom'o, or
"Flower Mound," a hill inhabited by Muy'ingwa, the being of maize and
germination and a place closely related to the reed of emergence.

In ancient highland Mexico and among Puebloan peoples of the
American Southwest, although not for the ancient Maya, insects are very
much part of the flower world as pollinators, especially butterflies, and
as colorful and frequent visitors to blossoms. However, in the American
Southwest there is another insect very much connected to the flower
world: the cicada, a creature closely related to the warm, summer season
of growth and blossoming, the playing of floral flutes, Sitsom'o, and the

emergence. Dating to roughly the eleventh century A.D., a Mimbres bowl from southern New Mexico graphically portrays the origin story of the emergence and features a human figure riding a flying insect before some sort of vertical pole with a spider near the top (Map 2; Figure 9.1a). Because of the prominent spider, Richard Townsend (2005:45) states that "part of an emergence myth may be depicted in a scene featuring a black widow spider-grandmother on a pole, confronting one of the Hero Twins riding a large mosquito." Although Spider Woman occurs widely in emergence stories of the American Southwest, the cicada is even more closely identified with the emergence.

THE CICADA AND ITS REPRESENTATION

In many Southwest studies, the cicada is erroneously referred to as a "locust." True locusts are actually grasshoppers occurring in destructive swarms and entirely distinct from cicadas in terms of appearance and behavior. Early ethnographers may have preferred the term *locust* for its "biblical cachet," but such wording masks the remarkable behavior and life cycle of cicadas, which as nymphs in the warm summer months burrow out of the earth, climb up plant stalks and trees, and make buzzing "music" to attract mates (Snodgrass 1921:408). In a discussion of "locusts" (cicadas) in the American Southwest, Barbara Moulard (1981:130) notes, "the locust's life cycle involves a vertical orientation, beginning in the below, penetrating the surface, climbing upward, and finally, flying into the above. Its actual transformation to a flying insect can be observed over an hour-long period." As creatures that climb *en masse* out of the earth, cicadas are an excellent metaphor for the mythic act of human emergence. As will be noted, the cicada features prominently in Navajo as well as Puebloan emergence mythology. In a Navajo text recorded by Edward Sapir in 1929, "the people of the lower world are the locusts of this one" (Sapir 1942:n22). In this perspective, cicadas annually emerge as newly risen, living ancestors from a previous world. Along with climbing out from the earth, they are day creatures of sunlight and warmth that react quickly to changes in temperature and even cloud shadows in terms of their shrill trilling (Myers 1929:205). The Hopi artist Fred Kabotie (1982:40) described the relation of cicadas to the sun and heat: "In the early part of the summer when the Sun Father is roasting the land, the

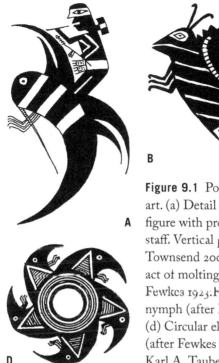

Figure 9.1 Portrayals of cicadas in Mimbres art. (a) Detail of flying cicada carrying human figure with probable flute and feathered dance staff. Vertical pole and spider not shown (after Townsend 2005:49). (b) Probable cicada in act of molting from nymph exoskeleton (after Fewkes 1923:Figure 101). (c) Possible cicada nymph (after Brody and Swentzell 1996:114). (d) Circular element with five cicada nymphs (after Fewkes 1923:Figure 119). Drawings by Karl A. Taube.

locusts [cicadas] make their presence known by the shrill sounds that they produce." In this study, I highlight aspects of cicada behavior that relate to emergence mythology: its ability to dig out of the earth, climb flowering stalks, and then sound music.

As with Townsend (2005:45), I believe that the Mimbres scene concerns the emergence with the presence of Spider Woman, although I consider the flying figure to be a cicada and not a mosquito (Taube 2010:113). Its legs are turned upward toward the thorax region in "praying mantis" fashion, the common pose of cicadas while grasping stalks and branches. Along with having similar legs held upward near the thoracic region, another likely Mimbres cicada has a bifurcated element at the end of its abdomen, a trait also found with cicadas (Figure 9.1b). In addition, there are Mimbres depictions of insects with a comma-shaped, rotund body and a narrow and pointed face, probably a cicada nymph before gaining the capacity for flight (Figures 9.1c, 9.1d, 9.7b). For one Mimbres bowl five of these creatures rim a central circle. This scene may portray cicadas emerging from a central hole.

One of the most striking traits of cicada behavior is their propensity to climb stalks and trees immediately after emerging from the earth. One Mimbres bowl portrays two virtually identical scenes of men collecting insects from a tree or bush and impaling them on a stick (Figure 9.2a). According to Fred Kabotie (1982:39), the creatures are cicadas, which Hopis ate as food until recent times: "In the picture [Mimbres bowl] the four men are busily engaged in picking locusts [cicadas] off the shrubs. They are carefully picking them off the branches and stringing them up by piercing sticks through their bodies, as was also done during my grandmother's day." Ekkehart Malotki (2000:63–64) also discusses the Hopi use of cicadas as sustenance and even provides a traditional Hopi recipe. The cicadas being harvested are virtually identical to the bugs

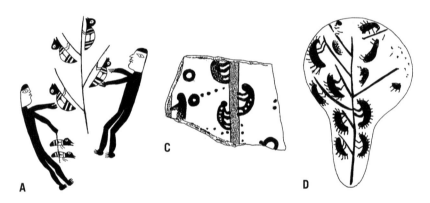

Figure 9.2 Cicadas in Mimbres and Pueblo IV ceramic art. (a) Detail of Mimbres vessel portraying harvesting of cicada nymphs (after Brody et al. 1983:Figure 101). (b) Line of cicada nymphs, detail of Mimbres bowl (after Brody et al. 1983:Color plate 30). (c) Jeddito Black-on-Yellow potsherd from Awat'ovi portraying cicada-like figures climbing stalks. Peabody Museum of American Archaeology and Ethnology, Harvard University, Catalog number 38-120-10/13681. (d) Pueblo IV–period Zuni ladle showing probable cicadas on plant stem (after Smith et al. 1966:Figure 80f). Drawings by Karl A. Taube.

appearing on another Mimbres bowl, where they are oriented in a single line between two large frontal-facing human heads (Figure 9.2b). It is possible that the pair refer to the Hero Twins of the Zuni and Hopi or perhaps the two sisters in Keresan Puebloan emergence stories.

As has been mentioned, cicadas quickly climb foliage upon emerging from the earth, and the cicada harvest scenes on the Mimbres bowl graphically portray this natural behavior. Portrayals of climbing cicadas continue in later Pueblo IV ceramics and kiva murals. A Hopi sherd from Awat'ovi features diminutive creatures climbing stalks or branches, and although having the curving hunchback found in Mimbres portrayals of cicadas, they are more anthropomorphic, with four limbs and partly defined heads (Figure 9.2c). A ceramic ladle from the Pueblo IV Zuni site of Hawikku depicts a forked branch quite like the Mimbres collecting scenes laden with cicadas having curving backs and a pair of upper limbs grasping the branches (Figure 9.2d). The curious, spiky back elements suggest the exoskeleton "husks" left behind by the mature, flying cicadas.

A Pueblo IV Hopi Sikyatki Polychrome bowl portrays a probable cicada flying before a flowering plant, probably a sunflower (Figure 9.3a). Rather than rendering the wings in solid colors, the Hopi artist may have been trying to allude to the transparent, membranous wings of the cicada. This is certainly the case with a Pueblo IV mural at Pottery Mound, which features a series of anthropomorphic insects grasping or climbing flowering stalks of what again may be sunflowers (Figure 9.3b). According to the excavator Frank Hibben (1975:115), these insect beings "may be cicadas or grasshoppers." The cicada identification is surely correct, and along with the membranous, veinlike wings, their limbs are oriented much the same as the Mimbres scene of cicada harvesting and the Hawikku ladle. In addition, the end of the abdomen has the same aforementioned protruding elements naturally found with cicadas (Figure 9.1b). These membranous wings also appear on a probable cicada from a Sikyatki Polychrome bowl (Figure 9.3d). A roughly contemporaneous mural from Awat'ovi portrays a diminutive cicada (or butterfly) grasping a stalk, and although much of the plant is missing, a flower can be discerned at the upper edge (Figure 9.3c). The cicada appears to be piercing the stalk with his proboscis, a natural feeding behavior of cicadas, which suck the sap from stalks in sharp contrast to butterflies, which consume the nectar

A   B   C

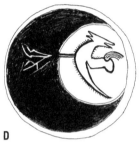

D

Figure 9.3 Probable portrayals of cicadas in Pueblo IV art. (a) Cicada before probable sunflower plant. Detail of Sikyatki Polychrome vessel, Peabody Museum of American Archaeology and Ethnology, Harvard University. (b) Anthropomorphic male cicada grasping probable sunflower plant. Detail of mural, Pottery Mound, New Mexico (after Hibben 1975:Figure 8). (c) Cicada sucking flowering stem. Detail of Awat'ovi mural (after Smith 1952:Figure 81b). (d) Sikyatki Polychrome bowl possibly portraying Cicada and Badger at hole of emergence (after Fewkes 1898:Plate 130d). Drawings by Karl A. Taube.

of flowers. The wing form of this cicada is virtually identical to that appearing on the bowl from nearby Sikyatki (Figure 9.3a).

CICADA AND HIS FLUTE

Along with the cited examples on painted ceramics and kiva murals, the most common pre-Hispanic depictions of cicadas appear as hunchback flute players. Although many have identified this being as analogous to the Hopi Kokopelli, the Hopi Kokopelli is based squarely on the robber fly (*Asilidae*) and not the cicada (Hays-Gilpin 2019; Malotki 2000). In terms of this study, I will refer to the humpbacked being in ancient Puebloan art as well as contemporary southwestern belief as Cicada. As in the case of the cicada nymphs appearing on the two Mimbres bowls, the bodies of many Cicada figures resemble a D in outline, with the curving portion corresponding to the back. According to Parsons (1939:192), this ancient being is a "locust," or in other words, Cicada: "That 'humpbacked flute player' so intriguing to the archaeologist in the Southwest is Locust." Similarly, entomologist John Capinera (1995:84) noted that in the Navajo emergence narrative, "cicadas, not locusts or grasshoppers, played the essential role in the creation myth." In the most comprehensive study devoted to Kokopelli to date, Ekkehart Malotki (2000:137) notes that according to Hopi consultants, the flute-playing figure in rock art is the cicada, or *maahu*. Clearly enough, Cicada's flute relates not only to the music created by the cicada but also to its stiff proboscis, which resembles a flute. In addition, the thorax of nymph and adult cicadas has a pronounced hump. In many petroglyphs, Cicada appears with antennae and a back protuberance suggestive of wings, and although this flute-playing being can range between being highly anthropomorphic to strongly insectile, its underlying meaning is clearly Cicada (Figures 9.4a, 9.4c, 9.4d, 9.6d).

For the Hopi, Cicada is closely identified with flutes and serves as the patron of the Flute Societies, whose summer ceremonies alternate every other year with the Snake Dance (Malotki 2000:67). The relation of this being to flutes, summer heat, and growth is profound in Hopi thought: "The cicada roams the corn plants playing his flute. It goes around encouraging them, for it owns the heat" (Malotki 2000:66). In the Puebloan Southwest, flutes are widely identified with fertility and abundance, as for the Zuni Payatamu, a being also present among other Puebloan peoples (Mathiowetz 2011:71–80). Parsons (in Stephen 1936:153n1) provides the following account for the Hopi form of Payatamu: "In the early world T'aiowa [Taawa] or Paiyatemu, the Sun Youth, played his flute as the young men sang and the Corn Maidens ground. The songs were for the return of warmth and vegetation."

CICADA AND EMERGENCE NARRATIVES IN THE AMERICAN SOUTHWEST

As with Spider Woman, Cicada plays a prominent role in emergence narratives of the American Southwest, including for the Navajo. Although not Puebloan, of all the Southern Athapaskans, the Navajo share the most cultural traits with Puebloan peoples, and this includes similarities

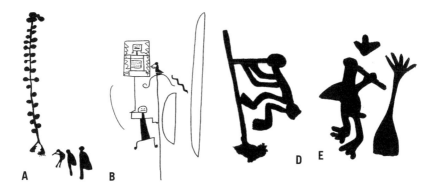

Figure 9.4 Southwest petroglyphs of flute players before plants and other vertical elements. (a) Cicada flute player and two others figure before tree with foliation or flowers (after Malotki 2000:Plate 32). (b) Human figure playing flute next to pole topped by Cicada flute player; note bows and possible lightning near pole (after Malotki 2000:Figure 11m). (c) Arrow point aimed at Cicada lying on his back while playing his flute (after Malotki 2000:Figure 11g, Plate 12). (d) Flute player ascending vertical pole. Petroglyph near Holbrook, Arizona (after Malotki 2000:Plate 29). (e) Cicada before possible Hopi-style flute standard. V-Bar-V petroglyph site, Beaver Creek, Arizona (after photo by author). Drawings by Karl A. Taube.

in emergence narratives. According to Navajo emergence accounts, people climb to the surface through a hollow reed with Cicada, who tunnels a hole upward to the surface of the earth. Another expert at burrowing holes, Badger digs around the pit to make it larger. In one account recorded by Father Berard Haile, Badger first attempts to dig the passage, but it is Cicada that is finally successful: "boring through the hard ground he made his way up until he reached the other side, just as he does today" (Haile 1981:118). Challenged by the "White Nostrils" water beings of the four directions, Locust bravely pierces his own body with arrows: "In this manner the Locust won the country for the people by excelling these four monsters in power" (Haile 1981:119). In other Navajo accounts, Cicada faces a challenge by water birds that he draw arrows through his body, which he effortlessly performs to attain dominion over the earth's surface

(Oakes and Campbell 1943:21–23; Stephen 1930; Zolbrod 1984:77–78). In addition, a pre-Hispanic Puebloan petroglyph near Chinle, Arizona, portrays an arrow point aimed at Cicada lying on his back with his flute, probably referring to the challenge he faced in Puebloan and Navajo emergence accounts (Figure 9.4c).

Although many studies discuss Cicada in terms of the Navajo emergence (e.g., Capinera 1995), there has been little academic interest linking Navajo creation narratives to those of the Pueblos in large part because of differences in historic origins, language, and culture. Nonetheless, Navajo versions are clearly related in many respects. Malotki (2000:73) notes that for the Hopi alone, "The fact that the cicada is part of several emergence and origin myths is a good indicator not only of its over-all significance in Hopi cosmology, but probably also that the insect has been deeply entrenched in Hopi oral traditions for a long time." Cicada's role in emergence narratives is present in Puebloan accounts from Zuni, Acoma, Zia, and Santa Ana as well as among the Navajo and Hopi.

Dating to 1883 but not published until forty years later, Cushing's (1923:164–67) account of the Hopi emergence for Oraibi is at this point the earliest published account I know for the Hopi, and it describes Cicada and Spider Woman at the reed of emergence with Cicada again facing the challenge of being pierced by arrows and reviving. In a Walpi account recorded by Alexander Stephen (1929:5–6), after Spider Woman plants the reed of emergence, both Badger and Cicada ascend to the surface, with Badger widening the *sipapu* hole. Cicada sounds his flute, and his music attracts the wrath of the four directional Cloud Chiefs who pierce him with their "arrows," surely their lightning. Much like the Father Berard Haile account for the Navajo, by being framed by the clouds of the four color directions of the horizontal plane, Cicada at the *sipapu* constitutes the sacred axis mundi, or world center. The piercing of Cicada in Navajo and Hopi emergence accounts may well relate to a natural trait of insects well known to entomologists. As noted by Capinera (1995:84), "Insects, including cicadas, are surprisingly difficult to kill by impaling," recalling the aforementioned Mimbres scenes of people gathering cicada nymphs by impaling them on sticks for ready carrying (Figure 9.2a). It could well be that this curious power ascribed to cicadas among the Hopi and Navajo derives from the mundane process of impaling them while collecting them as food.

Cicada is also mentioned in a Zuni emergence narrative in which he travels through various underworlds but cannot reach the earth's surface (Bunzel 1932:588–89). However, narratives of the Keresan-speaking pueblos of Zia, Acoma, and Santa Ana all describe Cicada at the emergence climbing out of the *sipapu*. In a Zia account, Spider fashions the reed of emergence and instructs Cicada to create the *sipapu*: "You know best how to pass through the earth, go and make a door for us" (Stevenson 1894:36–37). Badger then widens the hole for the first people to emerge. In another Zia version, Badger digs out the emergence hole, which is then smoothed by Cicada (White 1962:117). Acoma and Santa Ana accounts also mention the roles of Badger and Cicada in creating and finishing the *sipapu* (Stirling 1942:2; White 1942:89–91).

Recall that in one Hopi account from Walpi, Cicada plays his flute atop the reed of emergence upon climbing to the earth surface. Music makes the reed or tree of emergence grow in many accounts. For Zia, "They sang songs to make it grow faster" (White 1962:116; for Hopi, see Voth 1905:10). In addition, as in the case of the flute played by the Zuni Payatamu, the reed flute also causes growth and abundance and is associated with the warm summer months. Barton Wright (1979:82) notes the close relation between Hopi flutes to the summer and cicadas: "It is considered as an instrument of summer time and portends flowers and growing things with the cicadas singing in their fields." In Navajo thought, the hollow reed of emergence can be a flute, as can be seen in a Navajo emergence account recorded in 1885 by Alexander M. Stephen (1930:101), which describes a pair of youths with two magic flutes, one of reed and the other from a sunflower stalk: "One had a piece of hollow reed with four holes in its side, the other a sunflower stem with four holes in its stem (i.e. flutes). . . . These flutes had four holes. The first hole was for Black Wind, second for Yellow, third for Blue, and fourth [for] White, and these winds guarded the holes in the flute." Although two stalks are mentioned, it is the reed flute that carries humans to the face of the earth.

According to Navajo singer Jeff King (Oakes and Campbell 1943:23), the emergence reed contained a cotton string, and in another Navajo account, a downy feather was placed at its end (Zolbrod 1984:75). The two distinct and separate Navajo accounts describing a downy feather at the upper end of the reed or a cotton string inside recall Hopi sacred flutes, which have a cotton string tipped with a downy feather to indicate breath

emerging from the floral bell end. The Hopi refer to this feather cord as
len hikswi, or "flute breath" (Wright 1979:82). In a Hopi painting pertaining to the summer Flute Ceremony, Fred Kabotie (1977:116) portrays the
flute with a floral bell form at the distal end containing a cord ending
with a downy feather as its breath. This flute is played before a living stalk
of corn, clearly indicating the growth of the plant by the flute's power.
Although I am not aware of a contemporary Puebloan account explicitly
describing the emergence reed as a flute, given the prominence of the
flute-playing Cicada and the flute's ontology as a hollow reed, the reed
of origin probably bears a fundamental connection to flutes in Puebloan
thought. As I have noted, "The reed of emergence is a great flute and its
music is the breath wind of the ancestors" (Taube 2001:121).

To return to the Mimbres bowl scene featuring Spider Woman and a
man riding a flying cicada, all of these figures face the vertical pole that I
(Taube 2010) identify as the reed of emergence (Figure 9.1a). In addition,
the long element grasped near the mouth of the flying male is probably
a flute or whistle. An elaborate petroglyph from New Mexico portrays a
human figure playing a flute with a vertical line connecting to a complex
rectangular image, perhaps in some way alluding to the music emanating
from the flute (Figure 9.4b). An adjacent vertical pole is topped by a cicada also playing a flute, surely a version of the Hopi emergence account
of Cicada first playing his flute on the earth's surface at the *sipapu*. The
scene also has two prominent bows along with the possible remains of
a third. For the largest bow, an undulating element extends from what
would be the central, arrow region directly to the flute-playing cicada. In
historic Hopi iconography, this serpentine form is a basic lightning symbol and often appears emanating from clouds (Stephen 1936:Figures 118,
126, 144–46; Plates 5, 6, 7). This rock art scene may portray a mythic
episode comparable in complexity to the Mimbres bowl depiction of
the emergence reed with Spider and Cicada. The petroglyph panel may
depict another flute-playing individual before the emergence reed but in
this case with the newly emerged cicada playing his music while facing
lightning arrows shot by the bows of the cloud chiefs.

Other petroglyphs of Cicada playing before vertical elements include
one near Bluff, Utah, where he and two other individuals face a tall,
ladderlike plant, probably a floral branch of a foliated tree of emergence
(Figure 9.4a). Another petroglyph portrays a flute player who not only

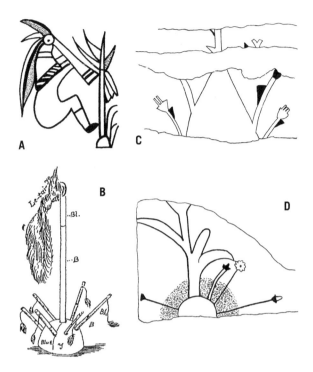

Figure 9.5 Reed of emergence and Flower Mound in ancient and historic
Hopi art. (a) Cicada flute player before flute standard. Painted sandstone tile, Walpi (after Stephen 1936:Plate 22). (b) Hopi flute standard
with Flower Mound as support. Walpi (from Stephen 1936:Figure 427).
(c) Pueblo IV portrayal of Sitsom'o. Awat'ovi (after Smith 1952:Figure 58a).
(d) Sitsom'o with central reed element as maize stalk. Awat'ovi (after
Smith 1952:Figure 69d). Drawings by Karl A. Taube.

faces a vertical pole but is actually *climbing* it, suggesting again the reed
of emergence (Figure 9.4d). A petroglyph from the V-Bar-V petroglyph
site south of Flagstaff, Arizona, portrays a winged cicada blowing his
flute before a plantlike form with a pronounced broad base resembling
the basal portion of the aforementioned tall plant (Figure 9.4a, 9.4e).
This petroglyph is especially similar to the standards appearing in the
summer Hopi Flute Ceremony, including images of Cicada playing his
instrument before one (Figures 9.5a, 9.5b).

CICADA AND SUSTENANCE IN EMERGENCE NARRATIVES

An early Hopi historic-period bowl from Mishongnovi portrays Cicada playing his flute before the reed of emergence, which not only recalls the Mimbres bowl and ancient petroglyphs but also the Hopi Summer Flute Ceremony (Figure 9.6a), which according to Armin Geertz (1987:10) concerns the birth of the sun and the emergence episode: "The creation of the sun and the primordial drama of the emergence are reenacted." In his detailed account of the Flute Ceremony held at Walpi in early August of 1892, Alexander Stephen describes the setting of four painted sandstone tiles of the directional Cloud Chiefs of the horizontal plane around the Flute Standard, that is, the same standard associated with the tiles portraying Cicada blowing his flute (Stephen 1936:798–99). It will be recalled that in one Hopi account, when Cicada first emerged from the reed blowing his flute, he was attacked by the Cloud Chiefs, who shot him with their lightning arrows. It is noteworthy that this early account was recorded from the very same community of Walpi. Thus, the setting of these tiles around the standard replicates the convergence of the Cloud Chiefs around Cicada playing his flute at the reed of emergence. Clearly enough, the reed is the Flute Ceremony standard placed atop the rounded dome of Sitsom'o, Flower Mound. This basal support of the vertical standard, Sitsom'o, is the central nadir of the underworld inhabited by Muy'ingwa, the Hopi being of maize, germination, and growth.

Pueblo IV–period Hopi murals from Awat'ovi portray ancient examples of Flower Mound (Figure 9.5c, 9.5d; Smith 1952:230–31). Although the upper portions are missing, one clearly has a growing corn stalk instead of the reed pole known for the Flute Ceremony standard (Figure 9.5d). In terms of the emergence, there is a clear overlap between reeds and the maize plant in ancient Puebloan iconography. A Pueblo IV Jeddito Black-on-Yellow bowl depicts a segmented reed with one side marked with a pair of feathers and the other maize leaves (Figure 9.6b). According to Emory Sekaquaptewa and Dorothy Washburn (2010:159), this reed may represent the "path of emergence." Its uppermost end is notched, indicating an arrow shaft, an item fashioned from reeds. Images very similar to the Jeddito reed also appear in Pueblo IV petroglyphs,

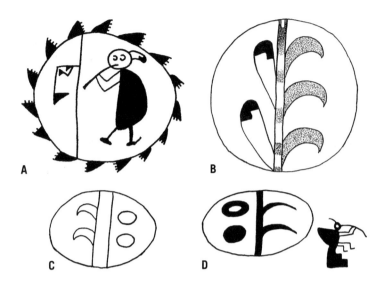

Figure 9.6 Vertical reeds and maize stalks in ancient ceramics and petroglyphs of the American Southwest. (a) Early historic bowl of cicada playing flute before probable reed of emergence. From a Hopi vessel excavated
at Mishongnovi (after Taube 2010:Figure 5.27b). (b) Jeddito Black-on-
Yellow bowl portraying probable reed of emergence merged with corn stalk
(after Sekaquaptewa and Washburn 2010:Figure 7.17). (c) Petroglyph of
probable conflation of reed and stalk of corn. Galisteo region, New Mexico
(after Schaafsma 1980:Figure 200). (d) Cicada on stairway next to reed and
corn stalk. Petroglyph near Albuquerque (after Schaafsma 1975:Figure 137).
Drawings by Karl A. Taube.

including one near Galisteo, New Mexico, which depicts a reed/corn
stalk with one side marked with maize leaves (Figure 9.6c). A virtually
identical example appears on a petroglyph from the Albuquerque area
(Figure 9.6d). However, in this case it is with a flute player sounding his
flute, much as in accounts of the emergence. He sits atop a set of steps,
possibly to denote his upward ascent.

    Along with the clinging spider, the reed on the Mimbres emergence
bowl also has a curious rhomboid at the top marked with squares containing single dots, a motif used to represent kernels in Pueblo IV and
contemporary Hopi portrayals of ears of corn. Given the fact that the reed
of emergence symbolically overlaps with a maize stalk, it is conceivable

that the rhomboid element denotes a corn ear atop the central axis of the reed. In addition, maize is a dominant theme in emergence narratives and in Hopi accounts. Màasaw, the god of death and fire, greeted the Hopi upon emergence with a gourd canteen for water and the varied types and colors of maize. The Hopi wisely chose the short but hardy blue corn (Malotki and Lomatuway'ma 1987; Wall and Masayesva 2004:435–36, 440). For Keresan-speaking peoples, the earth goddess Iariko, who assists in the migration, is also described as the spirit of corn (Tyler 1964:121–24). Among the Navajo, First Man and First Woman, who led the people out of the underworld, were made from two perfect ears of corn (Zolbrod 1984:50–51). For ancient Mesoamerica, some of the most detailed scenes of the emergence occur in the *Historia Tolteca-Chichimeca*, which portrays humans in the seven-lobed emergence cave of Chicomoztoc. An accompanying text states that upon their emergence, the first people ate corn to make them mature human beings (Kirchhoff et al. 1989:169). As has been noted, the earliest known portrayal of the emergence in the New World occurs on the North Wall mural at San Bartolo, Guatemala, with the central figure being the maize god relaying maize tamales and a water gourd out of Flower Mountain, the mountain cave of origin (Color Plate 1; Saturno et al. 2005).

An elaborately painted Mimbres bowl portrays a long oval form covered with the dot-in-a-square motif, and given the shape, this probably is an ear of corn (Figure 9.7a). A black hole containing a curious human figure with a prominent hunchback transects the cob center, probably a human form of Cicada emerging from the *sipapu*. With his arms raised in "praying mantis" fashion, he appears to be digging or climbing out of the hole. The pit is flanked by two mammals, and given their short ears, thick bodies and banded stubby tails, these creatures are probably badgers featured so prominently in emergence accounts in the Southwest. Their rear legs remain *inside* the hole, suggesting that like the central hunchback, they are exiting the *sipapu*. Their umbilical cords connecting to the *sipapu* also suggest the themes of birth and emergence. In contrast to the Mimbres bowl portraying the emergence reed in profile, this scene provides a "bird's-eye" view of this event from above. Another Mimbres vessel portrays what appears to be four comma-shaped cicada nymphs on one side and four mature winged cicadas on the other (Figure 9.7b, Color Plate 11). A male with a massive hunchback occupies the center,

A   **B**

Figure 9.7 Mimbres scenes of hunchbacks probably pertaining to emergence mythology. (a) Mimbres portrayal of hunchback apparently in hole of emergence flanked by maize and a pair of badgers (after Brody 1991:Figure 161). (b) Scene of human with massive hunchback supporting bowl and gourd water ladle or canteen flanked by four cicada nymphs and four mature winged cicada (after Catalog no. 2013.76.79, de Young Museum, Fine Arts Museums of San Francisco). (c) Human hunchback carrying woman with basket on back (after Brody et al. 1983:Figure 64). Drawings by Karl A. Taube.

C

with his back bearing a complex spiral—a basic sign of the emergence in the Southwest. His back supports a bowl and gourd ladle or canteen, recalling the accounts mentioning food and water to sustain humans upon emerging into the present world. He holds a vertical element, and on close inspection, a notch can be seen at the upper end, indicating a reed arrow shaft, as has been noted for the Jeddito bowl's reed (Figure 9.6a).

The Mimbres emergence bowl depicts Spider Woman, Cicada, the human musician, and the pole of emergence topped with a probable maize cob. There is, however, one other item: the large basket at the base. In Mimbres art, these are carrying baskets, that is, items used in traveling rather than simply storage, and many images in Mimbres art depict individuals carrying game, firewood, and even macaws in them. For the Mimbres emergence scene, this basket is probably to carry items up to the surface of the earth. According to one Acoma

Figure 9.8 Ancestral Pueblo effigy vessel of Cicada playing flute with pair human figures on shoulders (after Lambert 1967:Figures 1, 2). Drawing by Karl A. Taube.

account, baskets containing all things needed for life were brought up at the emergence (Stirling 1942:1–2). Another Mimbres bowl depicts a hunchbacked man supporting on his back or shoulders a woman with a carrying basket, quite possibly carrying humankind out of the netherworld (Figure 9.7c). In this regard, this scene recalls a remarkable Pueblo II effigy vessel of a flute player with a cicada body and a pair of human figures painted on both its shoulders (Figure 9.8). Human figures are notably rare in Ancestral Puebloan pottery apart from Mimbres, and this example may be a unique portrayal of Cicada carrying the first couple out of the earth at the emergence, a scene that may have taken place at Flower Mound.

CONCLUSION

As with ancient Mesoamerica, the narrative of emergence is of great antiquity in the American Southwest and can be documented in Mimbres ceramics by at least as early as A.D. 1130. This origin story is squarely related to the flower world in terms of the concept of a floral hill or mountain and Cicada, a being directly pertaining to music, the emergence, and the summer season of warmth and growth. Indeed, the reed of emergence was clearly related to the concept of cicadas climbing flowering branches as they emerge from the earth to molt and procreate.

In the American Southwest, the reed of emergence thematically overlaps with flutes and arrow shafts, both created from reeds, but also with a stalk of corn that appears growing from Flower Mound in Hopi Pueblo IV kiva murals. Along with Spider Woman, Cicada is a major being in ancient and contemporary versions of the emergence among both the Navajo and Puebloan peoples and appears in ancient petroglyphs as a flute player. Flute-player figures can have insect traits such as antennae and wings, or at times they are wholly anthropomorphic hunchbacks. Because of the general scholarly disconnect between Cicada and the emergence episode in Puebloan research, there has been little or no systematic study of ancient Cicada images in relation to the emergence, both in terms of forms of his flute as well as associated elements, including vertical poles or trees, darts or arrows, and aquatic birds. Given the ubiquity of this being in the Southwest, this promises to be a fertile field indeed.

ACKNOWLEDGMENTS

I am indebted to Oswaldo Chinchilla Mazariegos, Kelley Hays-Gilpin, Bryan Just, and Michael Mathiowetz for their comments and suggestions during the course of preparing this chapter. In addition, I wish to thank the Amerind Foundation for hosting the Flower World symposium in September 2019 as well as all the participants who contributed to such a lively and fruitful discussion.

REFERENCES

Brody, J. J. 1991. *Anasazi and Pueblo Painting*. Albuquerque: University of New Mexico Press.

Brody, J. J., Catherine J. Scott and Steven A. LeBlanc. 1983. *Mimbres Pottery: Ancient Art of the American Southwest*. New York: Hudson Hills Press.

Brody, J. J., and Rina Swentzell. 1996. *To Touch the Past: The Painted Pottery of the Mimbres People*. Minneapolis, Minn.: Frederick R. Weisman Art Museum.

Bunzel, Ruth L. 1932. "Zuni Origin Myths." In *Forty-Seventh Annual Report of the Bureau of American Ethnology, 1929–1930*, 545–609. Washington, D.C.: Smithsonian Institution.

Capinera, John L. 1995. "Humpbacked Flute Player and Other Entomomorphs from the American Southwest." *American Entomologist* 41(2):83–88.

Cushing, Frank Hamilton. 1923. "Origin Myth from Oraibi." *Journal of American Folklore* 36:163–70.

Fewkes, Jesse W. 1898. Archaeological Expedition to Arizona in 1895. *Seventeenth Annual Report of the Bureau of American Ethnology, 1895–1896*, 519–752. Washington, D.C.: Smithsonian Institution Press.

Fewkes, Jesse W. 1923. *Designs on Prehistoric Pottery from the Mimbres Valley, New Mexico.* Smithsonian Miscellaneous Collections, vol. 74, no. 6. Washington, D.C.: Smithsonian Institution.

Geertz, Armin W. 1987. *Hopi Indian Altar Iconography.* Iconography of Religions, sec. 10, no. 5. Leiden: E. J. Brill.

Haile, Father Berard. 1981. *The Upward Moving and Emergence Way: The Gishin Biye' Version.* Lincoln: University of Nebraska Press.

Hays-Gilpin, Kelley. 2019. "Kokopelli and the Fluteplayer: A Case of Mistaken Identity." In *Rock Art: A Vision of a Vanishing Cultural Landscape*, edited by Jonathan Bailey, 76–83. Denver, Colo.: Johnson Books.

Hays-Gilpin, Kelley, and Jane H. Hill. 1999. "The Flower World in Material Culture: An Iconographic Complex in the Southwest and Mesoamerica." *Journal of Anthropological Research* 35(1):1–37.

Hays-Gilpin, Kelley, Elizabeth Newsome, and Emory Sekaquaptewa. 2010. "*Sìitalpuva*, 'Through the Land Brightened with Flowers': Ecology and Cosmology in Mural and Pottery Painting, Hopi and Beyond." In *Painting the Cosmos: Metaphor and Worldview in Images from the Southwest Pueblos and Mexico*, edited by Kelley Hays-Gilpin and Polly Schaafsma, 121–38. Museum of Northern Arizona Bulletin 67. Flagstaff: Museum of Northern Arizona.

Hibben, Frank C. 1975. *Kiva Art of the Anasazi at Pottery Mound.* Las Vegas, Nev.: KC Publications.

Hill, Jane H. 1992. "The Flower World of Old Uto-Aztecan." *Journal of Anthropological Research* 48(2):117–44.

Kabotie, Fred. 1977. *Fred Kabotie: Hopi Indian Artist.* Flagstaff: Museum of Northern Arizona.

Kabotie, Fred. 1982. *Designs from the Ancient Mimbreños with a Hopi Interpretation.* San Francisco, Calif.: Grayborn Press.

Kirchoff, Paul, Lina Odena Güemes, and Luis Reyes García. 1989. *Historia Tolteca-Chichimeca.* Mexico City: Fondo de Cultura Económica.

Lambert, Marjorie. 1967. "A Kokopelli Effigy Pitcher from Northwestern New Mexico." *American Antiquity* 32(3):298–400.

Malotki, Ekkehart. 2000. *Kokopelli, the Making of an Icon.* Lincoln: University of Nebraska Press.

Malotki, Ekkehart, and Michael Lomatuway'ma. 1987. *Maasaw: Profile of a Hopi God.* Lincoln: University of Nebraska Press.

Mathiowetz, Michael D. 2011. "The Diurnal Path of the Sun: Ideology and Interregional Interaction in Ancient Northwest Mesoamerica and the American Southwest." Unpublished Ph.D. dissertation, Department of Anthropology, University of California, Riverside.

Moulard, Barbara L. 1981. *Within the Underworld Sky: Mimbres Ceramic Art in Context*. Pasadena, Calif.: Twelvetrees Press.

Myers, J. G. 1929. *Insect Singers: A Natural History of the Cicadas*. London: George Routledge and Sons.

Oakes, Maud, and Joseph Campbell. 1943. *Where the Two Came for Their Father: A Navajo War Ceremonial Given by Jeff King*. Princeton, N.J.: Princeton University Press.

Parsons, Elsie Clews. 1939. *Pueblo Indian Religion*. 2 vols. Chicago: University of Chicago Press.

Sapir, Edward. 1942. *Navajo Texts*. Iowa City: Linguistic Society of America, University of Iowa.

Saturno, William, Karl Taube, and David Stuart. 2005. *The Murals of San Bartolo, El Peten, Guatemala, Part 1: The North Wall*. Ancient America 7. Barnardsville, N.C.: Center for Ancient American Studies.

Schaafsma, Polly. 1975. *Rock Art in New Mexico*. Albuquerque: University Press of New Mexico.

Schaafsma, Polly. 1980. *Indian Rock Art of the Southwest*. Albuquerque: University of New Mexico Press.

Sekaquaptewa, Emory, and Dorothy Washburn. 2010. "Living in Metaphor: Hopi Traditions in Song and Image." In *Painting the Cosmos: Metaphor and Worldview in Images from the Southwest Pueblos and Mexico*, edited by Kelley Hays-Gilpin and Polly Schaafsma, 139–77. Museum of Northern Arizona Bulletin 67. Flagstaff: Museum of Northern Arizona.

Smith, Watson. 1952. *Kiva Mural Decorations at Awatovi and Kawaika-a with a Survey of Other Wall Paintings in the Pueblo Southwest*. Papers of the Peabody Museum of Archaeology and Ethnology, no. 37. Cambridge, Mass.: Harvard University Press.

Smith, Watson, Richard B. Woodbury, and Nathalie F. S. Woodbury. 1966. *The Excavation of Hawikuh by Frederick Webb Hodge: Report of the Hendricks-Hodge Expedition, 1917–1923*. Contributions from the Museum of the American Indian, Heye Foundation, vol. 20. New York: Museum of the American Indian, New York.

Snodgrass, R. E. 1921. The Seventeen-Year Locust. *Reports of the Smithsonian Institution of Washington 1919*, 381–409. Washington, D.C.: Smithsonian Institution Press.

Stephen, Alexander M. 1929. "Hopi Tales." *Journal of American Folklore* 42:1–72.

Stephen, Alexander M. 1930. "Navajo Origin Legend." *Journal of American Folklore* 43:88–104.

Stephen Alexander M. 1936. *Hopi Journal of Alexander M. Stephen*, edited by Elsie C. Parsons. Columbia University Contributions to Anthropology 23. New York: Columbia University Press.

Stevenson, Matilda C. 1894. "The Sia." *Eleventh Annual Report of the Bureau of American Ethnology to the Secretary of the Smithsonian Institution, 1889–1890*, 3–157. Washington, D.C.: Smithsonian Institution.

Stirling, Matthew W. 1942. *Origin Myths of the Acoma and Other Records*. Bureau of American Ethnology Bulletin 135. Washington, D.C.: Smithsonian Institution.

Taube, Karl A. 2001. "The Breath of Life: The Symbolism of Wind in Mesoamerica and the American Southwest." In *The Road to Aztlan: Art From a Mythic Homeland*, edited by Virginia M. Fields and Victor Zamudio-Taylor, 102–23. Los Angeles, Calif.: Los Angeles County Museum of Art.

Taube, Karl A. 2004. "Flower Mountain: Concepts of Life, Beauty, and Paradise Among the Classic Maya." *RES: Anthropology and Aesthetics* 45:69–98.

Taube, Karl A. 2010. "Gateways to Another World: The Symbolism of Flowers in Mesoamerica and the American Southwest." In *Painting the Cosmos: Metaphor and Worldview in Images from the Southwest Pueblos and Mexico*, edited by Kelley Hays-Gilpin and Polly Schaafsma, 73–120. Museum of Northern Arizona Bulletin 67. Flagstaff: Museum of Northern Arizona.

Townsend, Richard F. 2005. "Casas Grandes in the Art of the Ancient Southwest." In *Casas Grandes and the Ceramic Art of the Ancient Southwest*, edited by Richard E. Townsend, 14–65. Chicago: Art Institute of Chicago.

Tyler, Hamilton A. 1964. *Pueblo Gods and Myths*. Norman: University of Oklahoma Press.

Voth, H. R. 1905. *Traditions of the Hopi*. Field Columbian Museum Publication 96, Anthropological Series 8. Chicago: Field Columbian Museum.

Wall, Dennis, and Virgil Masayesva. 2004. "People of the Corn: Teachings in Hopi Traditional Agriculture, Spirituality, and Sustainability." *American Indian Quarterly* 28(3):435–53.

White, Leslie A. 1942. *The Pueblo of Santa Ana, New Mexico*. Memoirs of the American Anthropological Association 60. Menasha, Wis.: American Anthropological Association.

White, Leslie A. 1962. *The Pueblo of Sia, New Mexico*. Bureau of American Ethnology Bulletin 184. Washington, D.C.: Smithsonian Institution.

Wright, Barton. 1979. *Hopi Material Culture: Artifacts Gathered by H.R. Voth in the Fred Harvey Collection*. Flagstaff, Ariz.: Northland Press.

Zolbrod, Paul G. 1984. *Diné bahané: The Navajo Creation Story*. Albuquerque: University of New Mexico Press.

10

The Flower World of Cholula

John M. D. Pohl

Many ancient civilizations have maintained cults to deities that epit-
omized the ideals of the ranking elite and reflected the behavior that
distinguished them as a privileged class. In Late Postclassic Mexico,
the cult of Xochipilli had an extraordinarily broad appeal in this regard. Xochipilli was venerated as the patron of royal palaces, artists, and
craftspeople throughout highland Mexico, but his cult embodied the
ideology of elite gift giving and reciprocity that was the focus of Postclassic southern Mexican alliance networks in particular (Map 1; Pohl
1994, 2003b, 2003d; Turner 2016:75–80). His name is derived from the
Nahuatl *xochitl*, meaning "flower," and *pilli*, meaning hereditary "noble,"
but Xochipilli bore a number of titles, and some seem to identify avatars
of the god worshipped with their own cults. Piltzintecuhtli or *piltzintli*
means simply "prince," but *tecuhtli* indicates that the deity was regarded
as a "lineage head." Xochipilli was also known by the calendrical name
Chicomexochitl (meaning Seven Flower, the patron of royal marriages
and sexual procreation) and as Seven Flower–Tonacatecuhtli, Lord of
our Sustenance. He was even regarded as the father of the gods who
presided over the thirteenth or highest heaven, a paradise-like garden
world where only the royal born were admitted after death (Figure 10.1a).

Xochipilli was the patron of feasting rituals during which intoxicants
were consumed by those who believed that they could actually conjure the
place of afterlife to discuss matters of utmost importance—such as marriages, inheritance, land distribution, and even the curing of diseases—
with their deceased ancestors. Nahua festivals held in his honor were
celebrated by lords and ladies with bacchanal-like banquets during which
participants lavished gifts of woven garments, feathers, and jewels on
one another. The Nahuas believed that Xochipilli was equated with Maquilxochitl, or Lord Five Flower—one of the five Maquiltonaleque, or

Figure 10.1 (a) Xochipilli represented as his avatar Seven Flower, or Tonacatecuhtli, Lord of our Sustenance in *Codex Vaticanus A*, IV. (*Códice Vaticanus A* 1996). (b) Xochiquetzal, consort of Xochipilli, weaving with a backstrap loom in the *Primeros Memoriales*, 254r (Sahagún 1993). The tree bears seven flowers and signifies the celestial paradise garden of the gods at Tamoanchan. Tamoanchan was a Maya name meaning "Place of Mist" but also "Place of the Moan Bird-Snake." It was equated with the watery paradise of Tlalocan (López Austin 1997; Taube 1992:81–88). Illustrations by John M. D. Pohl.

patrons, of courtly diviners (Pohl 2007b). Maquilxochitl was regarded as the patron of dance, song, ritual clowning, and feats of acrobatics. He was especially venerated by *patolli* players, which suggests a close association between gambling and divination in the Nahua mind. The attributes of both Maquilxochitl and Xochipilli are also shared with Ixtlilton, the patron of singers, artists, buffoons, and scribes (Pohl 2003b:202 and n3, 2007b; Rojas Martínez Gracida 2008). There is also a close association between Xochipilli and Centeotl, or One Flower, the Nahua maize god. Not only were both deities regularly depicted with maize plant iconography but they also could be portrayed in nearly identical ritual dress. Xochipilli's consort was Xochiquetzal (Figure 10.1b).

CHOLULA AND THE ORIGINS OF THE XOCHIPILLI CULT

Maize symbolism connects Xochipilli to the Maya Young Lord–Maize God, a creation hero that appears from the ninth century B.C. Olmec through the Preclassic period to become the alter ego of Late Classic Maya kings like Pakal of Palenque (Coe 1982; Taube 1985, 1989a, 2004). Stratigraphic excavations at Cholula have produced a ceramic-based developmental sequence for the Late Postclassic International Style together with its associated iconographic system that clearly connects it to Classic Maya antecedents. The synthesis of highland and lowland Mexican influences at Cholula is reflected in the master plan of the ancient city's ceremonial center dominated by its Great Pyramid. The foundation of this edifice, one of the largest artificial constructions in the world, dates to the first century B.C. at a time when Cholula was drawing populations in from communities throughout the Valley of Puebla (Plunket Nagoda and Uruñuela Ladrón de Guevara 2018).

Between the Late Preclassic and the Classic, the pyramid was enlarged through four successive building stages, ultimately reaching a height of twenty-five meters. However, sometime around the eighth century A.D., the city suffered a cataclysmic disaster when the Popocatepetl volcano erupted and covered much of Cholula with ash and other debris. The urban population was forced to abandon the city. Some returned to their original communities, while others moved north out of the fallout zone to establish a new ceremonial center at Cacaxtla (Plunket Nagoda and Uruñuela Ladrón de Guevara 2018:167–80). Here they were joined by the Olmeca-Xicalanca population that migrated into the Puebla Valley from Tabasco, an area that had been incorporated into the political sphere of influence of the Maya city states of the upper Usumacinta River (Turner 2016:210–31). The influence of the Olmeca-Xicalanca is dramatically displayed in Cacaxtla's Classic Maya-style frescoes, while the cult of Flower Mountain was celebrated with the construction of a temple platform on the adjoining hill of Xochitecatl where a cult to a Late Classic antecedent to Xochiquetzal flourished (Spranz 1973a, 1982).

When Cholula's population returned, construction of the Great Pyramid was resumed between A.D. 800 and 1000. What was left of the earlier ruin was intentionally buried under a shell of adobe brick to transform the exterior into what seems to have been a metaphorical mountain (Figure 10.2a, 10.2b). Olmeca-Xicalanca rulers constructed a palace complex on one of the upper terraces, while the lower acropolis of staircases and plazas was erected as a symbolic artifice to frame the naturalistic setting. The investment in Classic Maya ritualism inherited from Cacaxtla and Xochitecatl was then manifested through the reintroduction of the Classic Maya polychrome tradition. That tradition ingeniously drew Cholula's constituent noble families into feasting systems of elite reciprocity and mutual obligations of support through royal intermarriage just as it had among the lowland Maya centuries earlier.

An early Cholula Aquiahuac–phase polychrome plate dating to between A.D. 950 and 1150 depicts an anthropomorphic sorcerer's hand marked with the hieroglyphic name for the Young Lord–Maya Maize God (Figure 10.3a; Pohl and Coltman 2020). The overall composition of the face in profile featured in the center of the plate with the radiating bands of color surrounding it invoked the appearance of the Classic Young Lord–Maize God depicted on plates originating in the Central Petén a century and a half earlier, while the human hand attribute is associated with the Akan complex of Classic Maya *wahy* beings. Cholula plates of this kind therefore represent a conflation of attributes between the spirit entities that were closely associated in Classic Maya art.

By the Tecama phase between A.D. 1150 and 1350, we see a standardization of both flower world and sorcery themes in Cholula ceramics (Figure 10.3b). A predominant twelfth-century Cholula image appearing on polychrome plates and *cajetes* is remarkably standardized. In most portrayals, it represents a male with a bulbous forehead and a "mohawk"-style hair crest, but in others his face resembles more of a spider monkey with ribbonlike designs curving up over the lips and around the eyes. An elaborate song scroll emerges from the personage's mouth. In some cases the being is painted entirely black and sports paint around the mouth and eye that I originally proposed was diagnostic of both the Maya God M or the Nahua god Ixtlilton, patron of scribes, diviners, healers, and *octli* drinkers (Pohl 2003b: 202n3; Rojas Martínez Gracida 2008; Spranz 1973b:339; Taube 1992). Other details link these two conceptions, including buffoon-like attributes with distended lips, oddly shaped heads, and either phallic or pug-shaped noses (see Taube 1989b for discussion of Maya buffoons and clowns). A star symbolized as an eye appearing

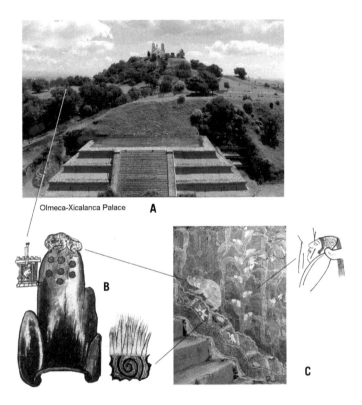

Olmeca-Xicalanca Palace **A**

B

C

Figure 10.2 (a) The Great Pyramid at Cholula surmounted by the Church of the Virgen de los Remedios. The staircase is ornamented with the *mat* motif emblematic of Maya rulership. It served as the principal approach to the landscape paradise of Tamoanchan and the ruins of an Olmeca-Xicalanca palace located on the lower northeastern platform. (b) The Great Pyramid named as Seven Flower Mountain in the *Historia Tolteca-Chichimeca* with the effigy toad crouched at the summit. This effigy may still exist as a monumental head with toad-like features displayed in the Patio of the Altars (Kirchhoff et al. 1976; McCafferty 2001:301). The pyramid was said to be planted with maize and inhabited by wild creatures (Motolonia 1950:88–89). Ritual maize fields are still planted around the ruins of the palace today. (c) The Olmeca-Xicalanca portrayal of Tamoanchan as a mountain slope on which a crop of personified Maya Young Lord–Maize God plants flourishes and through which the toad crawls at Cacaxtla. The merchant God L appears at this paradise at Cacaxtla. It seems that his cult was replaced by that of God M at Cholula (Taube 1992:90). The epigraphic, art historical, and archaeological evidence together indicates that a Late Classic cult of Tamoanchan at Cacaxtla-Xochitecatl was transferred to the Great Pyramid at Early Postclassic Cholula. Illustrations by John M. D. Pohl.

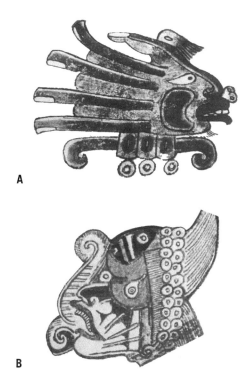

Figure 10.3 (a) Aquiahuac-phase plate depicting a conflation of the Classic Maya nominal glyph for the Young Lord–Maize God with the human hand associated with Akan, Maya god of intoxication, disease, and curing (Murck 1968; Taube 1985:174, Figure 3d). (b) Tecama-phase plate depicting Akan as a singer and ritual buffoon. The yellow band across the face and the white hand over the mouth anticipates the attributes of Maquilxochitl in Late Postclassic iconography (López Alonso et al. 2002). Illustrations by John M. D. Pohl.

overhead accompanies both gods as well. Face paint is frequently marked or labeled as ash in codices, and the two gods clearly share attributes with the "ash-mouths," a common name for the buffoons and clowns of the Zuni, Hopi, and Rio Grande Pueblo peoples (Figures 10.4a, 10.4b; Color Plate 12; Wright 1994).

We shouldn't be too surprised to see the Cholula Tecama–phase deity's attributes, such as the white hand over the mouth and the yellow band across the face, anticipate the iconography of the Maquiltonaleque as well. Like Xochipilli, the Cholula deity's relationship to both Ixtlilton and

A

B

Figure 10.4 (a) Tecama-phase plate with an image of the Classic Maya God M as a ritual singer-clown (private collection). (b) The Classic Maya God M as a merchant-emissary (Coe 1978:64–69; Taube 1992:88–92). Illustrations by John M. D. Pohl.

the Maquiltonaleque has a Classic Maya antecedent in a patron god of alcoholic drink known as Akan (Figures 10.5a–10.5b; Grube 2004). Buffoonish with a bloated face and body, we know that one of Akan's avatars named Mok Chih translates as "Knot Mouth" after an element of ritual dress with which he is associated (Grube 2004:67). Four Maquiltonaleque including Maquilxochitl appear in *Codex Vaticanus B* wearing knots over their mouths that substitute for the human hand in the same configuration as the Maya *wahy* being (*Codex Vaticanus B* 3773 1972) (Figures 10.5c–10.5d). Mok Chih was regarded as a god of sickness and appears on Maya vases cradling an *octli* olla surrounded by insects, a Classic Maya allusion to a story that anticipates that of the Maquiltonaleque, the Cihuatateo, and the creation of disease as a penitential punishment inflicted on humankind by the gods for transgressions against the social and natural environment and portrayed in *Codex Borgia* (see Pohl 2007b:29–31).

THE FLOWER MOUNTAIN OF CHOLULA

The roots of the Late Postclassic International Style lie in the ritual form of feasting behavior practiced at Cholula and originally associated with the Classic Maya Young Lord–Maize God cult together with a sorcery theme associated with Akan and other related *wahy* beings. However, it is

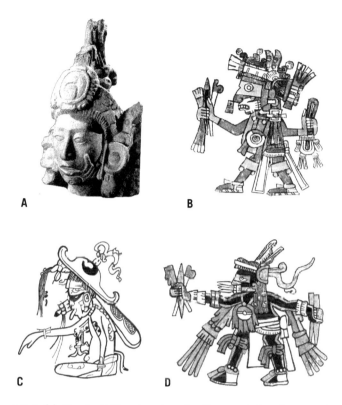

Figure 10.5 (a) Head of Akan bearing the diagnostic hand across the mouth. The sculpture was probably displayed together with portraits of the Maize God found at Copan Temple 22. (b) Maquilxochitl appears with the diagnostic yellow band across the eyes and white hand across the mouth as one of the five Maquiltonaleque in *Codex Borgia*, page 48 (*Códice Borgia* 1992). (c) The Maya god of disease, gluttony, and intoxication Mok Chih, or "Knot Mouth," appears as a buffoonish character on a Maya vase, K2286. (d) Maquilxochitl appears as "Knot Mouth" in *Vaticanus B* 79. (*Codex Vaticanus B* 3773 1972). Illustrations by John M. D. Pohl.

only after A.D. 1300 that we start to see the full expression of the Nahua-Mixteca style together with a complete iconographic system, at which time it is deployed by over fifteen different language groups extending throughout southern Mexico (Lind 1994:81). By the Late Postclassic Martír Phase, people, places, and things appear in Cholula's polychrome ceramic tradition in much the same way as they appear in the *Borgia* group of divinatory codices and the Mixtec group of historical codices. The iconography associated with Xochipilli is pervasive, as is the closely associated cult of the Maquiltonaleque, while other imagery symbolizes the adoption of the cults of deities from Early Postclassic Toltec proto-types, including the culture hero Quetzalcoatl, his father Mixcoatl, and his legendary nemesis Tezcatlipoca (Cobean et al. 2012:202–3).

According to Indigenous histories, Olmeca-Xicalanca hegemony over Cholula was compromised by Nahua-speaking peoples calling them-selves Tolteca-Chichimeca who migrated into the region after the leg-endary fall of their own capital of Tula. The Tolteca-Chichimeca claimed to have been led to Cholula by the divine guidance of their man-god Quetzalcoatl. They settled to the north of Great Pyramid, but it was not long before they attacked their Olmeca-Xicalanca hosts, destroyed their shrines, and dedicated their own temple to Quetzalcoatl at their new ceremonial center, even going so far as to declare Cholula their new Tollan. The subsequent division of the city between the two fac-tions, Tolteca-Chichimeca and Olmeca-Xicalanca, persisted throughout the Postclassic and Colonial periods and has even been proposed as the source of municipal rivalry between San Pedro and San Andrés Cholula that continues up through the present day (Knab and Pohl 2019; Mc-Cafferty 2000:356–57).

The *Historia Tolteca-Chichimeca* graphically demonstrates how the two factions integrated their respective cults during the Late Postclassic. The temple of Quetzalcoatl together with shrines dedicated to other Nahua deities were constructed on what is today Cholula's Main Plaza. By some accounts, the temple was said to have been even larger than the Templo Mayor of Tenochtitlan. The foundation of Cholula's authority was a re-ligious ceremony dedicated to Quetzalcoatl in which an aspirant prince was elected a *tecuhtli*, or lineage head, and was thereby granted—through Quetzalcoatl's divine authority—the rulership of a royal estate or *teccalli*. The appeal of the cult of Quetzalcoatl and the *tecuhtli* ceremony was that it transcended all local religious customs and bound ethnically diverse peoples together into similar social and political units, thereby facilitating elite alliance and economic exchange throughout the Central and South-ern Mexican Highlands (Pohl 2003a).

Far less attention has been paid to the Great Pyramid at this time, as archaeologists have tended to treat it as a vestigial ruin with little or no direct connection to the active social, political, and economic life of the city during the Late Postclassic. However, the *Historia Tolteca-Chichimeca* suggests that the structure continued to play a significant part in the ritual life of the city just as it does today. The excavation of Late Postclassic altars and other ritual architectural features surrounding the base of the pyramid confirm this (Plunket Nagoda and Uruñuela Ladrón de Guevara 2018:226–33). Although it appears as part of Cholula's central ceremonial precinct, it is clear that in contrast to the surrounding built environment, the structure was maintained in its natural state as an artificial mountain surmounted by a monument depicting a toad in reference to the pyramid's Postclassic Nahua name as Tlachiualtepetl, or "Hill Made by Hand," but also "Hill of the Effigy" (Plunkett Nagoda and Uruñuela Ladrón de Guevara 2018:67–70; Pohl 1998:163). According to legend, the Olmeca-Xicalanca had built the structure so high that they offended a god who then cast a giant stone in the shape of a toad down onto the construction during a thunderstorm as a warning to the builders not to raise the platform any higher. The association of the toad with the thunderstorm suggests that the offended god was Tlaloc, the patron of a watery afterworld called Tlalocan, but this paradise was also known as a place where Xochipilli presided:

> I give commands
> As the giver of things in Tlalocan
> As given things in Tlalocan
> I give commands
>
> Song of Xochipilli, Sahagún (1950–1982:Book 2:231)

Just as significant as the effigy are the flowers, tule plants, and a tree surrounding the hill, which suggests that the pyramid was maintained as a gardened environment throughout the Postclassic. It might be compared to the royal pleasure gardens of Texcotzinco and Chapultepec, documented for the Aztec emperors of the Valley of Mexico (Evans 2000, 2007). But while these served as exclusive retreats and pleasure houses, Cholula's Great Pyramid appears to have functioned as a devotional center that served not only Cholula's population of over thirty thousand people but many of the communities of southern Puebla. The fact that the place sign for the Great Pyramid is qualified by seven large red flowers invokes the calendrical date of Seven Flower for the celebration of the ritualism that was practiced there as well as the founding date of Cholula according to *Mapa de Cuauhtinchan no. 2*. Seven Flower was the name of Xochipilli-Tonacatecuhtli, Lord of our Sustenance (McCafferty 1996:14; Pohl 1994). The deity appears in *Codex Ríos* dressed in the array of Xochipilli while seated on a mat of maize plants as the god of the thirteenth or highest level of the heavens. As father of the gods, he presided over a celestial garden paradise called Tamoanchan together with his wife, Xochiquetzal-Tonacacihua, a goddess of courtly charm, grace, beauty, and human creativity (Figure 10.6a; López Austin 1997:51–122; McCafferty and McCafferty 1999). Here they lived in eternal bliss among groves of trees, aromatic flowers, springs, and rivers (Muñoz Camargo 1984:202–3).

Buffoons, jesters, dwarfs, and hunchbacks were appointed to serve as the realm's administrators and emissaries. They also entertained the gods playing music, singing, and dancing while Xochiquetzal spun and wove all manner of wondrous textiles and garments (Figures 10.6b, 10.6c). We have seen that the predominant iconographic theme expressed through polychrome feasting vessels during the early Postclassic at Cholula featured these legendary buffoons and singers. They would have served as spiritual intermediaries between Cholula's human celebrants within the city's noble residences and the worship of Tonacatecuhtli and Tonacacihuatl at the Great Pyramid representing Tamoanchan, the royal paradise and home of the gods. Given that the Olmeca-Xicalanca had been so highly influenced by Classic Maya ritualism, it should come as no surprise that the name Tamoanchan is in fact a Maya-language term meaning "Place of the Mist" (López Austin 1997).

By the Late Postclassic, Xochipilli was being celebrated during two important feasts. One was called Tecuilhuitontli, or the "small feast day of the lords," when the nobility issued invitations to each other to participate in bacchanal-like feasts during which they exchanged gifts of woven garments and jewels (Durán 1971:434–35). The celebration featured processions in which a great image of Xochipilli was displayed on a palanquin festooned with maize plants. The second feast was called Xochilhuitl, or "feast of flowers," and was celebrated on the day Seven Flower (Boone 1983:200). At this time, the painters and the weavers made offerings—the men to the god Xochipilli and the women to the

Figure 10.6 (a) The goddess Xochiquetzal. (b) Her emissary Ixtlilton, patron of singers, clowns, and scribes in *Codex Borgia* (*Códice Borgia* 1992). (c) Hunchback buffoon serving as an emissary to Lord Eight Deer in *Codex Colombino* 11 (*Códice Colombino* 2005). Illustrations by John M. D. Pohl.

goddess Xochiquetzal—so that they would be blessed in their efforts to excel at art and craft production (Sahagún 1950–1982:Book 2:35–36, 4:7). Aztec penitents seeking divine protection against disease specifically invoked Seven Flower–Xochipilli and Xochiquetzal and confessed their sins to them as well at this time (Durán 1971:238–47; Sahagún 1950–1982:Book 1:31, 2:35–36, 4:7). According to Durán (1971:245), priests dictated that the celebrants "should wash and purify themselves warning that those who did not would suffer ills and contagious diseases. It was thought that these ills appeared because of sin and that the gods sent them as vengeance." In accordance with the number of sins that the person had committed, he or she was required to pass an equal number of sticks through his tongue. The priests collected the sticks and burned them. The participants were then made to feel as though they had been cleansed and pardoned for their transgressions. In traditional Indigenous ideology, sin is punished by the gods with disease, and the contemporary use of bundled sticks in curing ceremonies has been well documented throughout southern Mexico (Pohl 1996:7–8).

We know that syncretic creation stories were subsequently deployed to integrate the cults of the Nahua hero Quetzalcoatl and the Olmeca-Xicalanca-inspired deity Tonacatecuhtli-Xochipilli at Cholula during the Late Postclassic. Following the creation of the sun, the gods lamented that there was no one to worship or perform penances to them. Quetzalcoatl took it on himself to travel into the underworld of Mictlan, the land of the dead, where he called on Mictlantecuhtli to give him the precious bones of the ancestors. Mictlantecuhtli acquiesced at first but later attempted to entrap the hero. Quetzalcoatl persevered and returned to Tamoanchan, where the goddess Cihuacoatl ground the bones up to make a meal from which to form the first human beings. Quetzalcoatl then shed his fertilizing blood over the mixture and brought the people to life. Before long the gods realized that their people needed sustenance, and so Quetzalcoatl went on a quest to find Tonacatepetl, the Mountain of Sustenance. Transforming himself into an ant so that he could enter the mountain, Quetzalcoatl removed the maize stored therein and returned with it to Tamoanchan for the gods to distribute it to the people.

The origin of Cholula's Tamoanchan cult was rooted in the reverence for actual geographical features associated with Popocatepetl that continue to the present day. Archaeological excavations indicate that the origins of Cholula lie in the formative remains of communities located at the base of Popocatepetl. When the ceremonial center was established, the pyramid was raised to transfer the mountain cult associated with the great volcano to the city center itself (Plunket Nagoda and Uruñuela Ladrón de Guevara 2018:167–69). Tamoanchan was the name of a sacred site located between Popocatepetl and Iztac Cihuatl, while Tlalocan is recognized as a location at the adjacent volcano of Mount Tlaloc by Nahua diviners throughout the region today (López Austin 1997:62, 83). Nahua diviners continue to conduct pilgrimages to these sites to petition for rain and productive maize crops as well as healing, and there is remarkable consistency between this ritualism and that maintained by the Nahuas of the Sierra de Puebla to the north. For example, the Nahua people of Amatlán, a pseudonymous village in the southern Huasteca, recount a creation legend associated with a local summit named Postectli or Broken Mountain (Sandstrom, this volume).

In comparing the Postectli Mountain and the Tamoanchan creation stories, the similarities in narrative together with the relative attributes of the principal deities are unmistakable and are directly comparable to the continuation of ritual practices at the Great Pyramid of Cholula today. Far from representing some reduced or vestigial practice of the past, the Postectli cult is representative of such practices among the Nahuas that extends back to preconquest times: "The principal aim in praying and pleading, was not to honor the hill itself. Nor should it be considered that the hills were held to be gods or worshipped as such. The aim was another: to pray from that high place to the Almighty, the Lord of Created Things, the Lord by Whom They Lived" (Durán 1971:259). These honorific titles of "creator" and "sustenance" were specifically associated with Tonacatecuhtli (McCafferty 2001:301–4). Today the church of the Virgen de los Remedios surmounts the summit of the Great Pyramid. The cult is a manifestation of the Virgin Mary developed by the Trinitarian Order in Spain. The saint's devotion became tied to the Reconquista under Castile's King Enrique IV (1425–1474) and was later favored by Cortés as a devotional image during the conquest. Each year more than one hundred fifty thousand people continue to journey to Cholula to celebrate the feast of the Virgin de los Remedios on September 8 and to attend the richest Indigenous market in Central Mexico. Farmers travel by foot, muleback, truck, bus, and train from Tlaxcala, Veracruz, Hidalgo, Morelos, Mexico, Guerrero, and Oaxaca to pay reverence to the shrine that sits atop Tlachiualtepetl.

The market itself is a vision of traditional Indigenous prosperity, and after nearly a week of citywide celebrations, thousands of participants in the festivities gather at the summit of Cholula's Great Pyramid to celebrate a feast sponsored by the mayordomo. The mayordomo's feast takes weeks to prepare and draws on vast amounts of capital that the mayordomo had amassed in the years before his election. The finale is a massive display where a fifteen-foot-tall image of the mayordomo, festooned with whirling fireworks, spins and spits dangerously. The climax comes when a panel mounted on the chest of the effigy suddenly explodes and showers a rain of fruits and candies to the cheers of the thousands in attendance. The mayordomo then officially concludes the weeklong celebration and descends from the mountain to leave the sponsorship of the following year's feast to the incoming year's mayordomo (Knab 2012; Knab and Pohl 2019).

Elsewhere I have demonstrated a remarkable continuity in ritualism between the cult of Quetzalcoatl and the present-day cults of San Gabriel and San Miguel at Cholula (Knab and Pohl 2019; Pohl and Lyons 2016:13–14). The fact that Xochipilli and Xochiquetzal were so closely associated with the diagnosis and curing of disease suggests an equal concern on the part of the Franciscans and the Cholulteca with preserving the essential aspects of both the belief system and the ritualism associated with Tamoanchan at Tlachihualtepetl and the cult of the Virgen de los Remedios. We know that the construction of the adobe pyramid was sponsored by a residential Olmeca-Xicalanca elite who designed it to represent a landscape garden that was framed by ritual courts and staircases surrounding its base around which stelae and altars were erected to celebrate the cult of their gods. Early imagery preserved on polychrome plates suggests that feasting ritualism of the community was rooted in cults associated with the Classic Maya Young Lord–Maize God and Akan, the patron of disease, healing, and divination. Avatars with which these gods were associated emphasized their aspects as musicians, singers, buffoons, and entertainers as well as courtly emissaries, ambassadors, and merchants. This clearly favored a theme in their feasts that predominated through the Early Postclassic to anticipate the attributes of the Late Postclassic cults of Tonacatecuhtli-Xochipilli, his consort Tonacacihuatl-Xochiquetzal, and the Maquiltonal Maquilxochitl that subsequently emerge along with the development of Late Postclassic International Style and symbol set at Cholula.

Both historical sources and archaeological findings confirm that by 1150, a significant population of Tolteca-Chichimeca entered the Puebla Valley—by some accounts at the invitation of the Olmeca-Xicalanca—and established themselves to the north of the Great Pyramid. Here they erected a temple to their god Quetzalcoatl and introduced the ritualism associated with the Toltec title of *tecuhtli*, or lineage head, perhaps as complementary to the role of the *pilli*, or prince, whose authority was rooted in conceptions of divinely inherited kingship of the Classic Maya tradition subsequently embodied in the cult of Xochipilli. Regardless, it is clear that the complementary roles of these two deities, representing a solar complex on the one hand and a plumed serpent complex on the other, have their roots in Cholula and from there were conveyed into the belief systems of the eastern Nahuas, Mixtecs, and Zapotecs together with those that they dominated throughout southern Mexico.

CONCLUSION

Aztec-centric studies have tended to view the cult of Xochipilli as relatively superfluous when compared with the imperialist cults of ominous or even frightening deities like Huitzilopochtli, Xipe Totec, Tlazolteotl, Tezcatlipoca, Quetzalcoatl, and Tonatiuh, who presided over cosmic creation, fate, warfare, human sacrifice, and agriculture (Nicholson 1971). However, when viewed from the perspective of its origins in the Classic Maya Young Lord–Maize God and Akan complexes, it takes on an entirely different dimension as being essential to the palace-based behavior that characterized southern Mexico during the Late Postclassic. The royal marriages over which Xochipilli-Tonacatecuhtli and Xochiquetzal-Citlalicue presided both perpetuated control over territory by the ruling families of individual kingdoms and linked them together into larger political constellations. This was the time when palaces as great houses dominated elite social life across the Plain of Puebla through southern Mexico. They were ideally suited to proliferation of an unequalled level of craft production as well as the private feasting and drinking parties that were such an integral part of alliance formation. The value of wealth acquired from distant lands was amplified through artistic transformation, and there is considerable evidence that the elite themselves served as the principal artists, scribes, craft producers, and merchants.

Royal feasts were the primary means by which ruling nobles bound their constituents into systems of mutual reciprocity and promoted their eligibility as potential alliance partners through lavish outlays of gifts crafted by court artisans. The profound relationship between material acquisition, craft, and exchange networks became the basis of what evolved into a Late Postclassic economy in which the greater a royal house's ability to acquire exotic materials and to craft them into exquisite jewels, textiles, and feather work, the better marriages it could negotiate. The better marriages it could negotiate, the higher the rank a royal house could achieve within an emerging confederacy and in turn the better access it would have to more exotic materials, merchants, and craftspeople (Pohl 2003c). This package of traits is embodied in the cult of Xochipilli and is the legacy and becomes the basis for *In Tlilli—In Tlapalli*, or what should more correctly be translated as the "Black and the Colored," as the origin of the Late Postclassic International Style and symbol set manifested not just in the codices—far more than simply a writing system—but in the associated instruments of polychrome ceramic, fresco, bone, wood, and shell with which the codices were deployed as a total communication system (Domenici, this volume; Pohl 2007a, 2007b). The Olmeca-Xicalanca were fully aware of what writing really was through their association with the Classic Maya. Consequently, it appears that true writing was intentionally rejected at Cholula, while the imagery associated with Classic Maya vase painting and a form of sorcery was used for the foundation of a communication system that relied as much on performative ritual as on reading a text.

The fact that the musician-jester aspect of the emergent Xochipilli and Maquiltonaleque complexes was adopted as a fundamental symbol of the twelfth-century feast at Cholula should come as no surprise considering how fundamental this performer's behavior was to American Indian ritualism in general. Ixtlilton, the buffoon aspect of Xochipilli, used soot, ash, and clay for facial decoration—the antithesis of proper face paint used by deity impersonators. Clowns have been enigmatic in ritual studies. From the Maya Blackman and Monkey impersonators of highland Chiapas to the Zuni Newekwe, their behavior is regarded as the antithesis of a culture's most esteemed values, with its outrageous parodies combined with public displays of gluttony, alcoholic overindulgence, sexual intercourse, exposure of social transgressions among community members, and the consumption of garbage or excrement among other forms of foul conduct. Clowning is integrally woven into the fabric of dance and performance as the essential part of the American Indian ritual humor that juxtaposes the profoundly reverent with the outrageously absurd, thereby creating an atmosphere of the unworldly, even surreal, that characterizes feasts, dances, and ritual performances of the most sacred nature. The clowns themselves may rank among the most highly regarded community leaders. Finally, we see in the pairing of the cults of Xochipilli and Quetzalcoatl at Cholula during the Postclassic the basis for conveying a system of remarkably flexible social, political, religious, and economic forms into southern Mesoamerica, west Mexico, northern Mexico, and the greater American Southwest that transcend cultural differences and yet can be configured within each culture's own value system (Mathiowetz 2011, 2018, 2019).

REFERENCES

Boone, Elizabeth. 1983. *The Codex Magliabechiano and the Lost Prototype of the Magliabechiano Group.* 2 vols. Berkeley: University of California Press.

Cobean, Robert H., Elizabeth Jiménez García, and Alba Guadalupe Mastache. 2012. *Tula.* Mexico City: Fondo de Cultura Económica and El Colegio de México.

Códice Borgia. 1992. Mexico City: Fondo de Cultura Económica.

Códice Colombino. 2005. Colecciones de la Biblioteca Nacional de Antropología e Historia, Serie Códices de México 2. Mexico: CONACULTA-INAH.

Códice Vaticanus A. 1996. Mexico City: Fondo de Cultura Económica.

Codex Vaticanus B 3773. 1972. Rome, Biblioteca Apostolica Vaticana; Graz: Akademische Druck- u. Verlagsanstalt (ADEVA).

Coe, Michael D. 1978. *Lords of the Underworld: Masterpieces of Classic Maya Ceramics.* Princeton, N.J.: Princeton University Press.

Coe, Michael D. 1982. *Old Gods and Young Lords: The Pearlman Collection of Maya Ceramics.* Utica, N.Y.: Brodock Press.

Durán, Diego. 1971. *Book of the Gods and Rites and the Ancient Calendar.* Translated and edited by Fernando Horcasitas and Doris Heyden. Norman: University of Oklahoma Press.

Evans, Susan Toby. 2000. "Aztec Royal Pleasure Parks: Conspicuous Consumption and Elite Status Rivalry." *Studies in the History of Gardens and Designed Landscapes* 20(3):206–28.

Evans, Susan Toby. 2007. "Precious Beauty: The Aesthetic and Economic Value of Aztec Gardens." In *Botanical Progress, Horticultural Innovation and Cultural Change,* edited by Michel Conan and W. John Kress, 81–101. Washington D.C.: Dumbarton Oaks.

Grube, Nikolai. 2004. "Akan: The God of Drinking, Disease, and Death." In *Continuity and Change: Maya Religious Practices in Temporal Perspective,* edited by Daniel Graña Behrens, Nikolai Grube, Christian M. Prager, Frauke Sachse, Stefanie Teufel, and Elisabeth Wagner, 59–76. Markt Schwaben: Anton Saurwein.

Kirchhoff, Paul, Lina Odena Güemes, and Luis Reyes García. 1976. *Historia Tolteca-Chichimeca.* Mexico City: Instituto Nacional de Antropología e Historia.

Knab, Timothy J. 2012. "Bells, Bombs, Music, and Madness: *Mayordomías* and Social Cohesion in Cholula." In *Children of the Plumed Serpent: The Legacy*

of Quetzalcoatl in Ancient Mexico, edited by Virginia M. Fields, 134–46. Los
Angeles: Los Angeles County Museum of Art.

Knab, Timothy J., and John M. D. Pohl. 2019. "Round and Round We Go:
Cholula, Rotating Power Structures, Social Stability and Trade in Mesoamerica." In *Interregional Interaction in Ancient Mesoamerica*, edited by Joshua D.
Englehardt and Michael D. Carrasco, 292–312. Louisville: University Press
of Colorado.

Lind, Michael D. 1994. "Cholula and Mixteca Polychromes: Two Mixteca-Puebla
Regional Sub-styles." In *Mixteca-Puebla: Discoveries and Research in Meso-
american Art and Archaeology*, edited by H. B. Nicholson and Eloise Quiñones
Keber, 79–100. Culver City, Calif.: Labyrinthos.

López Alonso, Sergio, Zaíd Lagunas Rodríguez, and Carlos Serrano Sánchez.
2002. *Costumbres funerarias y sacrificio humano en Cholula prehispánica*. Mexico City: Instituto de Investigaciones Antropológicas, Universidad Nacional
Autónoma de México.

López Austin, Alfredo. 1997. *Tamoanchan, Tlalocan: Places of Mist*. Boulder: University Press of Colorado.

Mathiowetz, Michael D. 2011. "The Diurnal Path of the Sun: Ideology and Inter-
regional Interaction in Ancient Northwest Mesoamerica and the American
Southwest." Unpublished Ph.D. dissertation, Department of Anthropology,
University of California, Riverside.

Mathiowetz, Michael D. 2018. "The Sun Youth of the Casas Grandes Culture,
Chihuahua, Mexico (AD 1200–1450)." *Kiva* 84(3):367–90.

Mathiowetz, Michael D. 2019. "A History of Cacao in West Mexico: Implications for Mesoamerica and U.S. Southwest Connections." *Journal of Archaeological Research* 27(3):287–333.

McCafferty, Geoffrey G. 1996. "Reinterpreting the Great Pyramid of Cholula,
Mexico." *Ancient Mesoamerica* 7:1–17.

McCafferty, Geoffrey G. 2000. "The Cholula Massacre: Factional Histories and
Archaeology of the Spanish Conquest." In *The Entangled Past: Integrating
History and Archaeology*, edited by Matthew Boyd, John C. Erwin, and Mitch
Hendrickson, 347–59. Proceedings of the 30th Annual Chacmool Conference.
Calgary, Alberta: University of Calgary.

McCafferty, Geoffrey G. 2001. "Mountain of Heaven, Mountain of Earth: The
Great Pyramid of Cholula as Sacred Landscape." In *Landscape and Power
in Ancient Mesoamerica*, edited by Rex Koontz, Kathryn Reese-Taylor, and
Annabeth Headrick, 279–316. Boulder, Colo.: Westview Press.

McCafferty, Geoffrey G., and Sharisse D. McCafferty. 1999. "The Metamorphosis of Xochiquetzal: A Window on Womanhood in Pre- and Post-Conquest
Mexico." In *Manifesting Power: Gender and the Interpretation of Power in Archaeology*, edited by Tracy L. Sweely, 103–25. London: Routledge Press.

Motolinía, Toribio de. 1950. *Motolinía's History of the Indians of New Spain*. Translated and edited by Elizabeth Andros Foster. Berkeley, Calif.: Cortes Society.

Muñoz Camargo, Diego. 1984. *Descripción de la Ciudad y Provincia de Tlaxcala*. Edited by René Acuña. Mexico City: Instituto de Investigaciones Antropológicas, Universidad Nacional Autónoma de México.

Murck, Alfreda J. 1968. "Acquisitions 1967." *Record of the Art Museum, Princeton University* 27(1):35–41.

Nicholson, Henry B. 1971. "Religion in Prehispanic Central Mexico." In *Handbook of Middle American Indians*, vol. 10, *Archaeology of Northern Mesoamerica*, pt. 1, edited by Gordon F. Ekholm and Ignacio Bernal, 395–446. Austin: University of Texas Press.

Plunket Nagoda, Patricia, and Gabriela Uruñuela Ladrón de Guevara. 2018. *Cholula*. Mexico City: Fondo de Cultura Económica and El Colegio de México.

Pohl, John M. D. 1994. "Weaving and Gift Exchange in the Mixtec Codices." In *Cloth and Curing: Continuity and Change in Oaxaca*, edited by Grace Johnson and Douglas Sharon, 3–13. San Diego Museum of Man Papers 32. San Diego, Calif.: San Diego Museum of Man.

Pohl, John M. D. 1996. "The Identification of the Xipe Bundle—Red and White Bundle Place Sign in the Mixtec Codices." *Journal of Latin American Lore* 19:3–29.

Pohl, John M. D. 1998. *Exploring Mesoamerica*. Oxford: Oxford University Press.

Pohl, John M. D. 2003a. "Creation Stories, Hero Cults, and Alliance Building: Postclassic Confederacies of Central and Southern Mexico from A.D. 1150–1458." In *The Postclassic Mesoamerican World*, edited by Michael E. Smith and Frances F. Berdan, 61–66. Salt Lake City: University of Utah Press.

Pohl, John M. D. 2003b. "Ritual and Iconographic Variability in Mixteca Puebla Polychrome Pottery." In *The Postclassic Mesoamerican World*, edited by Michael E. Smith and Frances F. Berdan, 201–6. Salt Lake City: University of Utah Press.

Pohl, John M. D. 2003c. "Ritual Ideology and Commerce in the Southern Mexican Highlands." In *The Postclassic Mesoamerican World*, edited by Michael E. Smith and Frances F. Berdan, 172–77. Salt Lake City: University of Utah Press.

Pohl, John M. D. 2003d. "Royal Marriage and Confederacy Building Among the Eastern Nahuas, Mixtecs, and Zapotecs." In *The Postclassic Mesoamerican World*, edited by Michael E. Smith and Frances F. Berdan, 243–48. Salt Lake City: University of Utah Press.

Pohl John M. D. 2007a. *Narrative Mixtec Ceramics of Ancient Mexico*. Cuadernos 10. Princeton, N.J.: Princeton University Program in Latin American Studies.

Pohl, John M. D. 2007b. *Sorcerers of the Fifth Heaven: Nahua Art and Ritual of Ancient Southern Mexico*. Cuadernos 9. Princeton, N.J.: Princeton University Program in Latin American Studies.

Pohl, John M. D., and Jeremy Coltman. 2020. Sorcery and Witchcraft in the Mesoamerican World: An Introduction. In *Sorcery in Mesoamerica*, edited by Jeremy Coltman and John M. D. Pohl, 3–54. Boulder: University Press of Colorado.

Pohl, John M. D., and Claire L. Lyons. 2016. Introduction. In *Altera Roma: Art and Empire from Mérida to Mexico*, edited by John M. D. Pohl and Claire L. Lyons, 1–20. Los Angeles: Cotsen Institute of Archaeology Press, University of California, Los Angeles.

Rojas Martínez Gracida, Araceli. 2008. "Los entretenedores en los polícromos del tipo Albina de Cholula: Una propuesta iconográfica." *Arqueología* 39:77–92.

Sahagún, Bernardino de. 1950–1982. *Florentine Codex: General History of the Things of New Spain*, 12 vols. Translated by Arthur J. O. Anderson and Charles E. Dibble. Santa Fe, N. Mex.: School for American Research; Salt Lake City: University of Utah Press.

Sahagún, Bernardino de. 1993. *Primeros Memoriales*. Norman: University of Oklahoma Press.

Spranz, Bodo. 1973a. "Late Classic Figurines from Tlaxcala, Mexico and Their Possible Relation to the Codex Borgia Group." In *Mesoamerican Writing Systems*, edited by Elizabeth P. Benson, 217–26. Washington, D.C.: Dumbarton Oaks.

Spranz, Bodo. 1973b. *Los dioses en los codices mexicanos del Grupo Borgia*. Mexico City: Fondo de Cultura Económica.

Spranz, Bodo. 1982. "Archaeology and Art of Mexican Picture Writing." In *The Art and Iconography of Late Post-Classic Central Mexico*, edited by Elizabeth Hill Boone, 159–74. Washington, D.C.: Dumbarton Oaks.

Taube, Karl A. 1985. "The Classic Maya Maize God: A Reappraisal." In *Fifth Palenque Round Table, 1983*, edited by Merle Greene Robertson, 171–81. San Francisco: Pre-Columbian Art Research Institute.

Taube, Karl A. 1989a. "The Maya Maize God and the Mythic Origins of Dance." In *The Maya and Their Sacred Narratives: Text and Context in Sacred Maya Mythologies*, edited by Genevieve Le Fort, Raphaël Gardiol, Sebastian Matteo, and Christophe Helmke, 41–52. Proceedings of the 12th European Maya Conference, Geneva, Switzerland. Markt Schwaben: Anton Saurwein.

Taube, Karl A. 1989b. "Ritual Humor in Classic Maya Religion." In *Word and Image in Mayan Culture*, edited by William A. Hanks and Donald S. Rice, 351–82. Salt Lake City: University of Utah Press.

Taube, Karl A. 1992. *The Major Gods of Ancient Yucatan*. Washington D.C.: Dumbarton Oaks.

Taube, Karl A. 2004. "Flower Mountain: Concepts of Life, Beauty, and Paradise Among the Classic Maya." *RES: Anthropology and Aesthetics* 45:69–98.

Turner, Andrew D. 2016. "Cultures at the Crossroads: Art, Religion, and Interregional Interaction in Central Mexico, AD 600–900." Unpublished Ph.D. dissertation, Department of Anthropology, University of California, Riverside.

Wright, Barton. 1994. *Clowns of the Hopi, Tradition Keepers and Delight Makers*. Flagstaff, Ariz.: Northland.

11

The Flower World in Tenochtitlan
Sacrifice, War, and Imperialistic Agendas

Ángel González López and Lorena Vázquez Vallín

Ethnohistorical accounts reveal that the flower worlds of the Late Post-classic period in Mesoamerica correlate with sets of shared beliefs of the floral paradise identified in the work of Jane Hill (1992) and Karl Taube (2000, 2001, 2005, 2006). This chapter expands on this research by combining the study of material culture, the analysis of historical texts, and iconographic analyses of stone sculpture from Tenochtitlan, the Mexica (Aztec) capital (Map 1). At its peak, this city was one of Mesoamerica's most prominent urban centers, and it was carefully planned with four main sectors, each one for a cardinal point in their cosmological system. At the center was the Main Precinct with seventy-eight buildings to represent the central axis point that joins the different realms together. In a short period, the city evolved from a vacant island into a town populated with between one hundred fifty thousand and two hundred thousand people, and at the time of the conquest in the early sixteenth century, Tenochtitlan reached around twelve square kilometers (González López 2019).

We explore important key features of the Flower World from the vantage point of the Mexica by focusing on the articulation of the solar war cult with a militaristic ideology, sacrifice, and the use of fire as a transformative element to access this sacred place. The ruling class created, promoted, and reproduced an official manifestation of this realm interwoven with religious ideals, including representations of belligerent power intersecting with the economic interests of the Aztec empire. However, the imagery generated was also a reflection of the real conditions of existence during the Late Postclassic that included violence and human sacrifice. This chapter focuses on iconographic information and contextual analyses of 212 sculptures from the Templo Mayor, the adjacent West Plaza, and historical sources to demonstrate how and to what degree the Flower World realm was interpreted and understood by the head of the Aztec empire.

This chapter is divided into three parts, each showing the conceptualization of the flower world in this urban center with the point of origin and source as the Templo Mayor, the center of the Mexica universe. On the human scale, material culture examined here sheds light on regular behaviors practiced by the users of this space for ninety years (A.D. 1430 to 1519) through the reign of five emperors: Motecuhzoma I, Axayacatl, Tizoc, Ahuitzotl, and Motecuhzoma II.

FLOWER WORLD IN THE TEMPLO MAYOR OFFERINGS

In addition to the central placement of offerings inside Templo Mayor, Mexica people incorporated a set of elements to re-create their particular version of the flower world. Indigenous artists evoked this spirit domain by recreating a primordial place of self-sacrifice by fire, the *xiuhtetzalqualco*, which displays features of the solar war cult, and rebirth in apotheosis within the flowery paradise. The context in which these artifacts are placed reproduces the scenario and performers as they occurred at Teotihuacan and marked the origin of human sacrifice.

The Templo Mayor is interpreted here as a representation of the flower world situated at the heart of the city. This building previously has been conceptualized as Coatepec (Serpent Mountain), a sacred mountain and the axis mundi that was embedded with power, both political and supernatural. It was also considered to be the dwelling place of ancestors and the locus of origin of the natural and social order (Broda 1988; López Austin and López Luján 2009; Matos 1981). From the perspective of the sacred landscape, the pyramid was a social place created in parallel with political necessities. This construction was located not just at the center of the ancient city but at the epicenter of the Aztec empire; it served as the source of Tenochca national identity (Figure 11.1). In the Indigenous conceptions of Templo Mayor, there were several overlapping names and functions acting at the same time (López Austin and López Luján 2009:151, 230). In this chapter, we offer a new layer of meaning and pursue a better understanding of the phenomenon. Building on the identification of this building as Coatepec, we will demonstrate that it

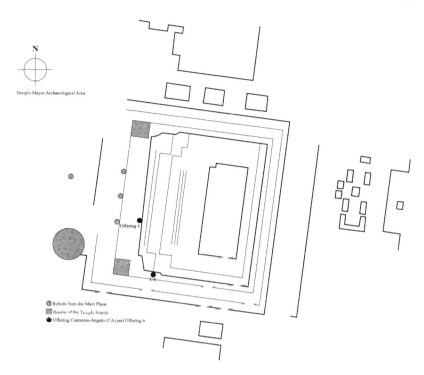

Figure 11.1 Map of Templo Mayor. Squares mark the rooms over the platform; circles mark reliefs on the Main Plaza; and solid circles mark offerings. After López Luján and González López (2014). Drawing by Ángel González López.

had several juxtaposed features that permit us to identify it as with the Mexica (Aztec) version of the flower world. The subjects of analysis in this section are offerings that included three forms of stone sculptures. These offerings are microcosmic models of the Mexica universe inside of which are found figures of Huehueteotl-Xiuhtecuhtli and Tlaloc.[1] Such sacred images long ago were recognized as the main figures inside the ritual deposits (López Luján 1993), although we incorporate stone braziers here as part of the analysis (Figure 11.2a; González López 2019:127). The arrangement of these offerings and figures, however, could express particular narratives (Navarrete 2011).

The stone figures discussed in this section were recovered from eleven ritual deposits alongside all four façades of the Templo Mayor.[2] The set of offerings is grouped by their similarities in content into the so-called

Complex A (López Luján 1993:323–30). Besides the presence of Xiuhte-cuhtli, Tlaloc, and braziers, these deposits contained the remains of fifty-seven sacrificed humans (Chávez Balderas 2017) as well as bloodletters made of eagle and jaguar bones and material imported from Teotihuacan and other ancient cultures. These microspaces re-created the universe in depicting its vertical layers, the underworld, earth, and sky as well as the horizontal layers (east, north, west, and south), and together they em-phasize the intersection of these sectors at the axis mundi. Xiuhtecuhtli and Tlaloc images were placed in a position "presiding" over the ritual, usually at the center, and surrounded by human heads, "skull masks," and a brazier.

We propose that these offerings recreate parts of the narrative of the origin of the Fifth Sun by including the essential performers and set-tings. At the same time, this act was the introduction of and the justifica-tion for human sacrifice in the Mexica cosmology. In a creation account compiled by Sahagún (2000:694–98), several deities gathered together in Teotihuacan to create the Fifth Sun. With that objective, the pustuled Nanahuatzin jumped into a hearth and then remained in the sky as the sun. But once created, the sun did not move, so the other deities then decided to sacrifice themselves to set the sun in motion. This action is used as a justification for war and human sacrifice as necessary offerings to feed the sun and earth and to maintain the universe in motion (Grau-lich 1999:30–35).

A prominent example of this idea is the arrangement of Offering Contreras-Angulo (CA), situated on the southwest corner of the Templo Mayor, where severed human heads were placed (Figure 11.2b). These seven humans were sacrificed by decapitation, while others were trans-formed into "skull masks" with flint knifes inserted in the mouth and nose (Contreras 1979:408–9). The archaeological team also recovered Mezcala and Teotihuacan material made of greenstone and turquoise disks. The clearest reference of the account of the creation of the Fifth Sun is a hu-man head, placed on the east side of the offering, attired with earspools decorated with a solar disk—an indication that this being probably was Tonatiuh, the solar deity, who died and was reborn and apotheosized as a deity. Moreover, the brazier is comparable to the hearth from which Nanahuatzin sacrificed himself and through which he became radically transformed and reborn as the new sun. Furthermore, these disks could mimic the turquoise enclosure (*xiuhtetzalqualco*) in the primordial time at Teotihuacan (Taube 2000:309–16), which was the dwelling place of the fire patron Huehueteotl-Xiuhtecuhtli. In addition, near this element was a flint knife attired with insignia of the wind deity Ehecatl (Velázquez Castro 2000:106) as well as an atlatl. This arrangement immediately recalls the myth recounted by Sahagún in that the wind god was one of the principal actors of this account (Sahagún 2000:693–98) as the being who is charged with sacrificing the rest of the deities. Using this logic, the other skulls may be the deceased warriors who accompanied the sun to zenith or the deities who died in that ritual act. At the same time, this creation event generated the necessity for captives obtained through warfare to feed the sun to maintain order in the universe. Moreover, it gave the Mexica a justification for their expansionist movement by invoking a flower world in which human sacrifice by decapitation and the exercise of warfare was a constant necessity.

Offering 6, placed in the platform of the Templo Mayor, is another example of how the recurrent social practices associated with the flower world were encapsulated in stone sculptures and related material (Figure 11.2b). We interpret this offering as a representation of the Tlalxicco (the navel of the earth, in Nahuatl) and as the place of the ancestors and the origin of the Fifth Sun by human sacrifice. This deposit was placed on the southern side of the pyramid, which was dedicated to Huitzilopochtli (López Luján 1993:327), and it includes foreign materials and relics such as Teotihuacan vessels, Mezcala masks, and greenstone figurines that were accompanied by skeletal remains of five humans, a golden eagle, and feline claws. In the *Historia general* (Sahagún 2000:694–98), these animals had a principal role as companions of the sun and moon, and they were prominent warrior emblems in Tenochtitlan. As with Offering CA, this ritual deposit contains "skull-masks" with flint knives inserted in the nose and mouth that we consider to represent warriors in the paradisiacal afterlife.

These two offerings created a symmetry with the Templo Mayor as the center of the world, or Tlalxicco, a place of abundance, metamorphosis, and the locale from where the sun rose every day after its travel through the underworld. Moreover, in Sahagún's chronicle (Sahagún 1950–1982:Book 1:84, 6:88–89), the sacrificial pyre (*xiuhtetzalqualco*) is referred to as the Tlalxicco. The *xiuhtetzalqualco* in Teotihuacan also

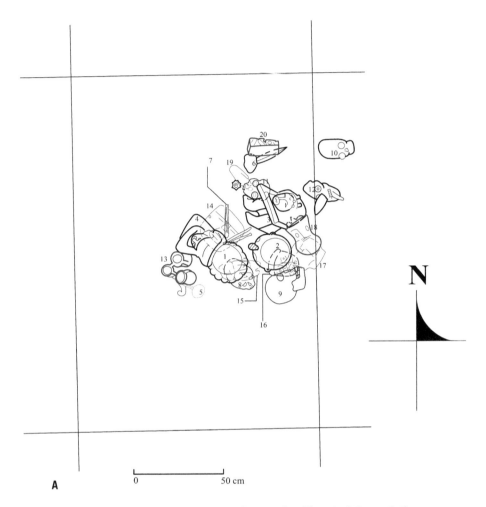

A

0   50 cm

Figure 11.2 (a) Arrangement of artifacts within Templo Mayor, Offering 6, larger objects around a stone brazier, including human skulls. After Velázquez Castro (2000:107, 108, and 117). 1. Stone brazier. 2. Tlaloc jar. 3. Xiuhtecuhtli. 4. Patecatl. 5. Knife with turquoise inlay. 6. Knife with turquoise inlay. 7. Eagle bones. 8. Human skull. 9. Human skull. 10. Human skull. 11. Human Skull with *ehecacozcatl*. 12. Skull mask. 13–20. Relics. (b, facing page) Offering Contreras-Angulo (CA). (c, facing page) Detail of the Archbishop's Stone portraying Xiuhtecuhtli conquering Chalco. Drawings by Ángel González López.

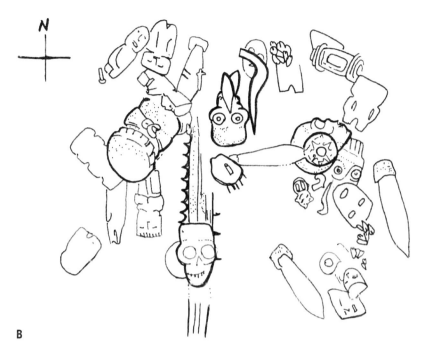

B

C

expressed a cycle of penitence, which included aspects of the solar war cult, death by fire, transformation, and rebirth in apotheosis within the flowery paradise (Taube 2000). This primordial model, from the Mexica perspective, seems to be present in these eleven ritual deposits. Furthermore, these aspects gave the Templo Mayor—identified as a sacred mountain—a component of fire. We interpret Tenochca behavior as replicating fundamental aspects of the origin account in Teotihuacan by placing relics imported from this ancient city in an attempt to control the narrative, including the practice of human sacrifice.

In Tenochtitlan, there is abundant evidence for the presence of bellicose aspects of Xiuhtecuhtli, which constituted a warfare cult at the city. Following examples from historical accounts, Tenochca late imperial imagery, the offerings, and codices, it is common for Xiuhtecuhtli to hold the Xiuhcoatl (the fire or turquoise serpent) as a weapon, which also represents his *nahualli* (animal alter ego) (Quiñones Keber 1995:3v, 24r; Anders et al. 1991:20). This animal alter ego refers to the fierce, militaristic aspect of this being, much like a caterpillar and butterfly as an embodiment of death and rebirth (Taube 2000:285). The Xiuhcoatl was also the fearsome weapon of the war god Huitzilopochtli. Monumental sculptures also expressed the bellicosity of the Mexica patron of fire Xiuhtecuhtli (Figure 11.2c).

In Mexica Flower World ideology as well as in other Mesoamerican variations, the souls of certain beings became birds or butterflies (Headrick 2003; Turner, this volume). The offerings recovered from the Templo Mayor could represent a physical reminder of this transformation, since a colonial document associates human skulls and these insects. For example, testimony by Andrés de Olmos mentions the supernatural transformation of butterflies into skulls, which may serve as an analogy for self-sacrifice and rebirth in the flower world: "As the butterfly becomes the flame, he lovingly metamorphoses into a rib cage, into a skull. Before the people, above the people, he awaits, publicly he whipped himself, he flogged himself. Then he falls inward there to suffer the stone repeatedly. Heedlessly as the moth he ascends, he falls inward" (Maxwell and Hanson 1992:178). It is possible that these human remains not only represent deities (Figure 11.3a; Chávez Balderas et al. 2015) but also butterflies, as deceased warriors in the floral realm. In the same way, one *Codex Zouche-Nuttall* scene depicts a butterfly flying at night with its head as a human

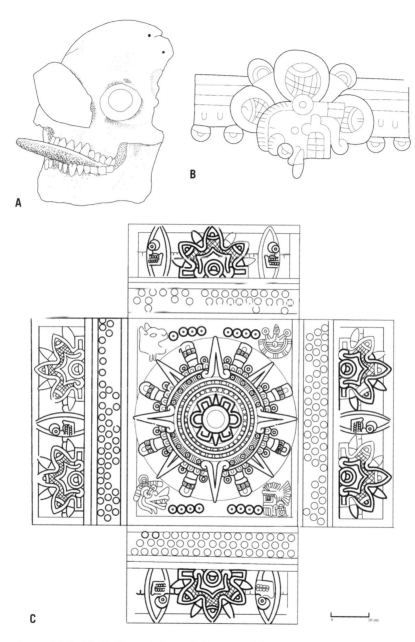

Figure 11.3 (a) Skull mask from Offering 6. (b) Probable butterfly, *Codex Zouche-Nuttall*, page 10r (Anders et al. 1992:10r). (c) Relief of the Five Ages, Yale Peabody Museum. Drawings by Ángel González López.

skull and a flint knife as its nose. Moreover, the flint in this context represents death and resurrection (Figure 11.3b) because this stone in Mexica cosmology contained radiance and life, as if it were a kind of seed.

Another probable reference to the *xiuhtetzalqualco* as the birthplace of the Fifth Sun with the presence of butterflies is present on an imperial Mexica sculpture. The Relief of the Five Ages is a cubic ritual table of unknown origin on which offerings of all sorts were placed (Figure 11.3c). The top side contains depictions of the four cosmic eras (each named after its destruction date and placed in order before the present age) and the creation of the fifth era. The sides contain reliefs with a sky band composed of stars, sacrificial flint knives, and stylized nocturnal moths. Along with representing *Lepidoptera* emerging from the sky, this stone depicts the emergence of a new sun and the sacred division of the cosmos with four directions and the center.

Returning to Offering CA and 6 from the Templo Mayor, the act of taking human lives could be understood as a polysemic act as evidence of ritual violence and as part of the narratives promoted by an expansionist state. As recent research indicates, not all of these remains present were war captives, and alternative explanations are possible (Chávez Balderas 2017:368). As mentioned above, the act of placing human heads around stone sculptures served to reenact the origin of the Sun, Moon, and warfare by self-sacrifice in Teotihuacan, an action that demonstrates continuity in the performance of ancient ideas that originated during the Classic period.

Moreover, for Tenochca people this account was the origin of the new era, their own, which was accompanied by normative actions, including the establishment of roles for warriors and the promotion of a social order tied to the creation of a group identity. These artifacts remained stored inside the building as its constitutive part. These practices illustrate how the flower world was part of imperial discourses that helped to legitimize emerging political and religious power by replicating the narrative of the birth of the Fifth Sun serving as a bridge with Teotihuacan—a primary force in Mesoamerican history—and a widespread model of the afterlife. One vital component of this narrative involves the practices and beliefs of human sacrifice through which individuals are reborn in a different reality in the floral paradise. As part of a militaristic ideology, fire ceremonies articulated several elements that enabled access to dwell in the flower world, a chromatic realm of the venerated deceased.

THE ROOMS OF THE TEMPLO MAYOR

In the second part of this chapter, we draw attention to a set of reliefs that chronologically date to the reign of Motecuhzoma I (A.D. 1440–1469), which were found on the platform of the pyramid but set in the interior of two different rooms (González López 2019:78–81; López Austin and López Luján 2009:310–20). These were more private spaces, presumably used by elite factions in the city (Figure 11.1). We propose that both portray aspects of the Mexica Flower World as the dwelling place of ancestors. Both groups are contemporaneous and are made up of long benches made of stone on which are depictions of processions that converge at the center. Their placement over the platform, inside roofed rooms, and separated from the plaza lead us to contend that the audience for this set of carvings was elite groups in Tenochtitlan, probably the king himself and his immediate royal cohort. The intended goal was to reproduce the flower world ideal and to serve as an educational tool.

On the Huitzilopochtli-affiliated side are thirty-nine reliefs (Figure 11.4a) that portray dead, victorious, and glorified Mexica warriors attired as Toltecs and chanting in the east, as indicated by the brilliant red color of the background. These beings sometimes are portrayed holding smoking weapons. The *Códice Vaticano A* (Anders et al. 1996:45) mentions a similar realm as the twelfth layer of the sky, Teotl Tlatlauhca, or "Red Heaven." This color scheme could suggest that the flower world was associated with the east as a cardinal point and as a red place (Nicholson 1971; Wrem Anderson and Helmke 2013). On top of the procession are friezes that depict undulating feathered and cloud serpents. The line of persons is led by Tezcatlipoca, who lights his spear thrower in a burning *zacatapayolli*—the plaited grass ball into which the bloodstained maguey spines used for drawing sacrificial blood were thrust—and readies himself to throw smoking darts. This procession could depict a Mexica version of Toltec warriors and ancestors who died in battle, now marching and chanting as the Tenochca army across Mesoamerica. Besides Tezcatlipoca, the rest of the warriors do not contain personal names, but the headdresses could indicate that they are the captains of the Tenochca

Figure 11.4 (a) Reliefs from the southern room. (b) Reliefs from the northern room. Drawings by Ángel González López.

army. In essence, these are the companions of the sun from sunrise to the zenith. Here, the people of Tenochtitlan created a cultural connection with the prestigious prior civilization of Tula in bolstering their claims to the legitimate right to rule over newly conquered towns.

In the north room, there are two benches with nineteen figures, which form two lines that converge (Figure 11.4b). These depictions are manifestations of Tlaloc (or perhaps Tlaloque, the multiple manifestations of the rain patron) that together are marching and chanting. Each figure holds a copal pouch, a thunderbolt, and a flowering staff. In contrast to the south room, the landscape in the north room is surrounded by mist, filled with raindrops, and the background of the scene is colored blue. The pigment may indicate that the location is symbolically placed in Tlalocan, Tlaloc's paradise, situated in the eighth level of the heavens. The *Códice Vaticano A* (Anders et al. 1996:IV) ascribes to this realm the name Ilhuicatl Xoxouhcan, or "Blue Heaven." We interpret this ceremony depicted on the stone as a petition for rain and corn, the elements necessary for maize agriculture. The *Florentine Codex* (Sahagún 1950–1982:Book 3:47) describes Tlalocan as a place full of richness, cacao, various flowers, rubber, and birds such as the spoonbill, cotinga, parrots, and quetzals. The previous descriptions may offer a glimpse into the different aspects of the Mexica Flower World and hypothetically may refer to several different flower worlds. The *Historia general* (Sahagún 2000:330) portrays this realm as one of perennial joy in which the food is never lacking—abundant maize, squash flowers, tomatoes, and marigold blossoms—but also as a place of death (Sahagún 2000:330, 572, 1037–38, 1134). In this respect, Tlaloc is linked to political power (Contel 1999) and to the economic arena with the relevant control over rain and the reproduction of agriculture practices that relate to the creation of new arable land by the Mexica. Along the southern part of the Basin of Mexico (Map 1), the drainage of swamps resulted in the transformation of 130 square km (or 10,000 acres) into highly productive farmland called *chinampas* (Armillas 1971). Thus, the promotion and reproduction of these ideas became a fundamental piece of the imperialistic agendas relating to both sources of wealth and the ritual practice of different aspects of the flower world.

Both sets of reliefs mimic to a certain degree the Toltec model, where benches depict processions and friezes are topped with undulating serpents. On the southern side, which was dedicated to Huitzilopochtli, warriors march as companions of the sun in the flower world. It is important to note that the group of agricultural deities also contains a human-sacrifice component of the paradisiacal afterlife. Within this room was found Offering 48, which contained forty-two children sacrificed in honor of Tlaloc (López Luján 2018). The Tlaloc war complex long ago was identified in Teotihuacan art (Pasztory 1974), and the Mexica incorporated it into the symbolic narrative of the Templo Mayor. Both artistic traditions were appropriated by Tenochtitlan, creating a synthesis and new expression of the flower world.

THE MAIN PLAZA AS THE FLOWER WORLD

The third part of this chapter examines a diverse group of reliefs that is contemporaneous to the previous set under the reign of Motecuhzoma I and identified historically as the Coaxalpan (López Austin and López Luján 2009:304–10; López Luján and González López 2014; Vázquez Vallín 2019). In addition to the preceding examples, the Main Plaza also contained images of the flower world as a battlefield and garden. Here, reliefs formed a pavement partly made up of seventy-eight carved stone plaques that extend westward from the foot of the pyramid. One of the main features in this construction is the clear iconographic division between the north and south side. This construction is a visual manifestation of the conception of the flower world, which covered the lower level of the pyramid and was throughout the western plaza of the Templo Mayor (González López 2019:90–92).

On the north side, images of rain patrons predominate with sixteen slabs that contain the disembodied face of Tlaloc, which may relate to the flower paradise as a place of rain and mist. The presence of a single maize plant emerging from a jade bead is appropriate because of the central role of this plant in the economic and religious life of Tenochtitlan. Intermingled reliefs also contain images of paper garments of agricultural deities. However, this landscape also contains trumpets from which emanate music and clouds with rain, a recurring characteristic of the Mesoamerican floral paradise (Figure 11.5).

On the southern sector of the plaza, some nonhumans play more active roles (Figure 11.6). The animal section shows fierce eagles singing and dancing victoriously, while a defeated jaguar cries while carrying a flag as it walks to the sacrificial stone placed on top of the Templo Mayor (Figure 11.7a). These two animals were emblems of the Tenochca

Figure 11.5 Group of reliefs from the Main Plaza, north side. After López Luján and González López (2014). Drawings by Ángel González López.

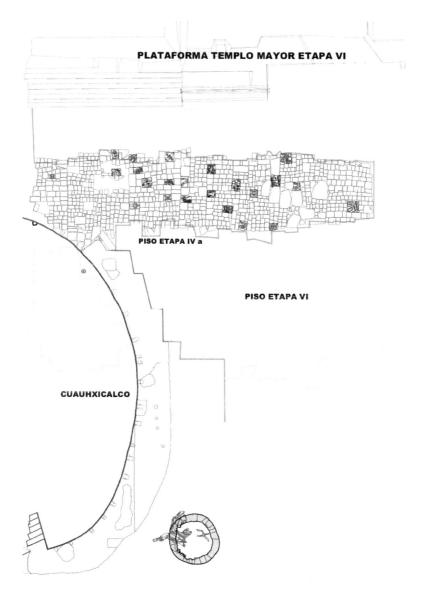

PLATAFORMA TEMPLO MAYOR ETAPA VI

PISO ETAPA IV a

PISO ETAPA VI

CUAUHXICALCO

Figure 11.6 Map of distribution from the Main Plaza, south side. Drawing by Lorena Vázquez Vallín.

Figure 11.7 Group of reliefs from the south side, which display different emblems of fire and sequences of events (presentation, decapitation, and rebirth as butterflies). Drawing by Ángel González López.

elite army and, as noted above, they played a major role in the creation of the sun at Teotihuacan. Based on the iconographic evidence and its militaristic implications, the duo here may refer to the victory of the eagles over the jaguars. In this context, there are no examples of birds with beautiful feathers as in other versions of the flower world, but in the Mexica variant they are typically birds of prey. Dance and military practices are interwoven within this scene, sometimes to the point where these two activities are inseparable. Moreover, there is a close association of dance with warfare in the initial phase of fighting, during its progress, and after its completion (Danilović 2017).

Past archaeological explorations in this area found reliefs depicting flowers with a clear connection to the subject of this chapter (Batres 1902; López Luján and González López 2014; Vázquez Vallín 2019). Some of these floral examples expel sweet aroma, while another is a combination of the glyph pinwheel and turquoise linked to the festival Tlaxochimaco (dedicated to Huitzilopochtli and deceased people). Several smoking darts are depicted, which can represent shooting stars, as a celestial and war emblem (Taube 2000:289–301). The Mexica concept of darts also includes their association with warriors who died in battle. The presence of a *zacatapayolli* reinforces these ideas because the maguey spines stuck in the ball of grass are symbolically conceptualized as captives in battle (Olivier 2004, 2006). Reinforcing these conceptions are the glyph of warfare (*atl-tlachinolli*), turquoise jewels, speech scrolls signifying smoke, and warrior garments destined for cremation.

The humans are the principal agents in this scene. There are notable differences with the warriors inside the two rooms of the Templo Mayor, although both sets are contemporaneous. While the group from the south hall are dressed as Toltecs, the set from the floor are either Mexica or captives of war. In essence, there are two groups of warriors: the victorious and the defeated. The first group dances, all while raising their spear throwers, singing, and wearing the double eagle-feather emblem (*cuauhpilolli*) and the *cuexcochtechimalli*, which possibly represents the *mimixcoa*.[3] The pleated paper attire on the back serves as a marker in the Aztec pantheon for death-related deities. In addition, this element appears on Nahua representations of mortuary bundles destined for cremation. On imperial monumental sculpture, this same attire is worn on the Archbishop's Stone and the Stone of Tizoc by Chalcan leaders (Figure 11.2c).[4] This element has a connection with the funerary ceremonies of people who perished in the war against Chalco as well as themes of political subordination, as described more fully below.

Moreover, the second group of reliefs is more descriptive (Figure 11.7). There are defeated warriors who show marks of state-sponsored violence, such as a dangling eye. Other examples include warriors on their knees with their arms tied behind their back, crying and humiliated. This set of sculptures shows the sequence of events that ends with their decapitation, transformation, and ascent to the flower world as butterflies attired with turquoise garments (Color Plate 13). This space, then, was at once a dance plaza, a symbolic battlefield, a garden of butterfly souls surrounded by flowers, and the last place that war captives glimpsed before they were marched up the stairs to be sacrificed.

There is abundant evidence for social practices in this public space in front of the Huitzilopochtli temple such as festivals, political ceremonies (González López et al. 2019), victorious parades, and funerals for warriors and kings. Historical manuscripts compiled by Diego Durán (2002:1:203–6) and Hernando de Alvarado Tezozómoc (2001:129–33) provide textual descriptions that support this scenario. The chronicles deal with the funerals of the dead warriors in the Chalco War under the command of Motecuhzoma I and concern the ceremonies that were carried out precisely within the plaza adorned with reliefs. When the army returned to Tenochtitlan, they immediately made offerings to the Templo Mayor, gathering in the Main Plaza where they deposited the spoils of war and prisoners for sacrifice. The parents of the dead came out first with weapons—adorned with precious feathers and tobacco gourds—while everyone sang. The widows took the blankets and loincloths of the fallen, the daughters took the jewels of their parents, and some relatives and friends made a large wheel with their shields and weapons. At dusk, the king and the Cihuacoatl (coruler) gave gifts to the relatives of the deceased. They made mortuary bundles of firewood (*ocoteuctin*), which represented those who had died, and the effigies were adorned with eyes, mouth, nose, weapons, flags, and feathers and were covered with precious blankets. The mourners began the so-called war dance and sang around the bundles for four days, when the bundles were burned. After a few days, the funerals continued with public burning of the clothes of the deceased while all the bereaved drank pulque until they were drunk. To honor these garments, they brought pulque and spilled it in the place where the attire of the deceased was cremated.

Chant 12 of the *Cantares mexicanos* is dedicated to admonishing those who seek honor in war, which provides a complementary description of this "battlefield" portrayed in the plaza:

> Sacred flowers of the dawn are blooming in the rainy place of flowers that belong to him the Ever Present, the Ever Near. . . . O friends, no useless flowers are the life-colored honey flowers. They that intoxicate one's soul with life lie only there, they blossom only there, within the city of the eagles, inside the circle, in the middle of the field, where flood and blaze are spreading, where the spirit eagle shines, the jaguar growls, and all the precious bracelet stones are scattered, all the precious noble lords dismembered, where the princes lie broken, lie shattered. (Bierhorst 1985:151)

The plaza of the Templo Mayor, as public space, was adorned with carved stone slabs that are clearly identified with the flower world as a space of sweet aromas, funerary and fire rituals, dance, rain, mist, music, smoke, songs, shining jewels, butterflies, and transformation as a means to access this realm. Among the periodic festivals and political gatherings in this central building, the Tenochca people, as a community, interacted face-to-face within the floral paradise with the people slain in battle, captives destined for sacrifice, and the ancestors.

The Templo Mayor, viewed as a sacred mountain at the center of the universe, was the origin and source of the citywide engagement with the Mexica Flower World realm and its related and recurrent social practices. Tenochca elites in the capital, the *pipiltin*, followed a set of shared beliefs in a floral paradise common in many parts of Mesoamerica. However, they adapted and reformulated these ideas for interests created by the empire. They encouraged the population to go to war and die, to be re-born in the flower paradise as birds (including hummingbirds, spoonbills, and eagles) or butterflies, and to ascend in social status or be part of the new expanding regions where farmers engaged in agricultural activities. The different factions on the island engaged in these activities were part of the imperial agendas of subordination and exploitation by the elite faction. In this way, it is important to recall that the first action after the war with Chalco was to distribute the best farm lands to Motecuhzoma I and Tlacaelel, the Cihuacoatl (Alvarado Tezozómoc 2001:132).

CONCLUSION

In sum, this chapter illustrates how the flower world is portrayed both in the Templo Mayor offerings: as Coatepec and displaying several aspects that led us to identify it as one of the several flower worlds, and within the two rooms on the pyramid platform. The internal arrangement of the offerings reveals the intention by the Mexica to recreate the origin of the Fifth Sun in Teotihuacan and to replicate the human sacrifices required to preserve the natural order. Mexica people arranged several artifacts to recreate the myth of the Fifth Sun, and that goes back to the divine hearth at Teotihuacan by placing effigies of Tlaloc and Xiuhtecuhtli and stone braziers mimicking the *xiuhtetzalqualco* where Nanahuatzin jumped to create the new sun and to be reborn in apotheosis. Also in-cluded were relics of older societies deposited inside the offerings as well as recreations of other essential performers, such as Ehecatl-Quetzalcoatl and two pivotal animals, jaguars and eagles. At the same time, it created a cultural connection with the largest political, religious, and ideological formation in all periods in Central Mexico. The iconographic programs located inside two rooms over the platforms are consistent with this version of the floral paradise. In the southern room, Mexica political leaders are assimilated as ancestors who march beside the sun in the east while led by Tezcatlipoca. In the northern room, a series of Tlaloque engage in procession within Tlalocan surrounded by rain, mist, and clouds. Both rooms replicate a Toltec model, creating a new link with a glorious civilization from the Tenochca perspective. Because of their placement, we propose that the set of carvings were also meant to be seen by elite groups in Tenochtitlan for educational purposes related to the conveyance of flower world ideals. The set of carved slabs at the base of Templo Mayor is one of the clearest examples of the Mexica version of the flower world depicted as a battlefield and floral garden full of jewels, sweet aromas, music, birds, and butterflies.

NOTES

1. Xiuhtecuhtli means "Turquoise Lord," and Huehueteotl is the "Old-God"; both are different aspects of fire. Tlaloc was the rain, agriculture, and lightning god.

2. Offerings 1, 6, 11, 13, 17, 20, 23, 60, 61, and 88.

3. *Mimixcoa* is the generic name of a group of celestial beings of hunting and the typical victims of sacrifice.

4. The same attire is used as a headdress on the same monuments but in the conquest of Mixtlan.

REFERENCES

Alvarado Tezozómoc, Hernando de. 2001. *Crónica mexicana*. Madrid: Dastin.

Anders, Ferdinand, and Maarten E. R. G. N. Jansen, eds. *Códice Vaticano A*. 1996. Graz: Akademische Druck- und Verlagsanstalt; Mexico City: Fondo de Cultura Económica.

Anders, Ferdinand, Maarten E. R. G. N. Jansen, and Luis Reyes García, eds. 1991. *Códice Borbónico*. Madrid: Sociedad Estatal Quinto Centenario; Graz: Akademische Druck- und Verlagsanstalt; Mexico City: Fondo de Cultura Económica.

Anders, Ferdinand, Maarten E. R. G. N. Jansen, and Luis Reyes García, eds. 1992. *Códice Zouche-Nuttall*. Mexico: Sociedad Estatal Quinto Centenario; Graz: Akademische Druck- und Verlagsanstalt; Mexico City: Fondo de Cultura Económica.

Armillas, Pedro. 1971. "Garden on Swamps." *Science* 174:653–61.

Barrera Rodríguez, Raúl, Roberto Martínez Meza, Rocío Morales Sánchez, and Lorena Vázquez Vallin. 2012. "Espacios rituals frente al Templo Mayor de Tenochtitlan." *Arqueología Mexicana* 116(July/August):18–23.

Batres, Leopoldo. 1902. *Exploraciones en las calles de las escalerillas, año de 1900.* Mexico City: Tipografía y Litografía "La Europea."

Bierhorst, John. 1985. *Cantares mexicanos: Songs of the Aztecs.* Stanford, Calif.: Stanford University Press.

Broda, Johanna. 1988. "Templo Mayor as Ritual Space." In *The Great Temple of Tenochtitlan: Center and Periphery in the Aztec World*, edited by Johanna Broda, Davíd Carrasco, and Eduardo Matos Moctezuma, 61–123. Berkeley: University of California Press.

Chávez Balderas, Ximena. 2017. *Sacrificio humano y tratamientos postsacificiales en el Templo Mayor de Tenochtitlan.* Mexico City: Instituto Nacional de Antropología e Historia.

Chávez Balderas, Ximena, Erika Robles Cortés, Alejandra Aguirre Molina, and Michelle de Anda. 2015. "Efigies de la muerte. Decapitación ritual y modificación de cráneos de la Ofrenda 141 del Templo Mayor de Tenochtitlan." *Estudios de Antropología Biológica* 17(1):53–75.

Contel, José. 1999. "Tlaloc: L'incarnation de la terre.' Naissance et metamorphoses." Unpublished Ph.D. dissertation, Université de Toulouse-Le Mirail.

Contreras, Eduardo. 1979. "Una ofrenda en los restos del Templo Mayor de Tenochtitlan." In *Trabajos arqueológicos en el centro de la ciudad de México (Antología)*, edited by Eduardo Matos Moctezuma, 403–14. Mexico City: Instituto Nacional de Antropología e Historia.

Danilović, Marjana. 2017. "Combatir bailando: Danza y guerra en el Altiplano prehispánico." *Estudios de Cultura Náhuatl* 53:142–74.

Durán, Diego. 2002. *Historia de las Indias de Nueva España e Islas de Tierra Firme.* 2 vols. Mexico City: Consejo Nacional para la Cultura y las Artes.

González López, Ángel. 2019. "The Stone Sculpture of Tenochtitlan: Changes, Discourses, and Actors." Unpublished Ph.D. dissertation, Department of Anthropology. University of California, Riverside.

González López, Ángel, Roberto Martínez Meza, and Raúl Barrera Rodríguez. 2019. "Evidencias de una ceremonia de clausura: Las esculturas encontradas frente al Templo de Huitzilopochtli." In *Al pie del Templo Mayor de Tenochtitlan: Estudios en honor de Eduardo Matos Moctezuma*, vol. 1, edited by Leonardo López Luján and Ximena Chávez Balderas, 263–88. Mexico City: El Colegio Nacional.

Graulich, Michel. 1999. *Ritos aztecas: Las fiestas de las veintenas.* Mexico City: Instituto Nacional Indigenista.

Headrick, Annabeth. 2003. "Butterfly War at Teotihuacan." In *Ancient Mesoamerican Warfare*, edited by M. Kathryn Brown and Travis W. Stanton, 149–70. Walnut Creek, Calif.: AltaMira Press.

Hill, Jane H. 1992. "The Flower World of Old Uto-Aztecan." *Journal of Anthropological Research* 48(2):117–44.

López Austin, Alfredo, and Leonardo López Luján. 2009. *Monte Sagrado-Templo Mayor: El cerro y la pirámide en la tradición religiosa mesoamericana.* Mexico City: Instituto Nacional de Antropología e Historia; Universidad Nacional Autónoma de México, Instituto de Investigaciones Antropológicas.

López Luján, Leonardo. 1993. *Las ofrendas del Templo Mayor de Tenochtitlan.* Mexico City: Instituto Nacional de Antropología e Historia.

López Luján, Leonardo. 2018. "Cuando la gente se uno-aconejó: La gran sequía de 1454 en la Cuenca de México." *Arqueología Mexicana* 35(149):36–45.

López Luján, Leonardo, and Ángel González López. 2014. "Tierra, agua y fuego al pie del Templo Mayor de Tenochtitlan: Un conjunto de bajorrelieves de la época de Motecuhzoma Ilhuicamina." *Estudios de Cultura Náhuatl* 47:7–51.

Matos, Eduardo. 1981. *Una visita al Templo Mayor.* Mexico City: Instituto Nacional de Antropología e Historia.

Maxwell, Judith, and Craig Hanson. 1992. *Of the Manners of Speaking That the Old Ones Had: The Metaphors of Andres De Olmos in the TULAL Manuscript.* Salt Lake City: University of Utah Press.

Navarrete, Federico. 2011. "Writing, Images, and Time-Space in Aztec Monuments and Books." In *Their Way of Writing: Scripts, Signs, and Pictographies in Pre-Columbian America*, edited by Elizabeth Hill Boone and Gary Urton, 175–95. Washington, D.C.: Dumbarton Oaks Research Library and Collection.

Nicholson, Henry B. 1971. "Religion in Prehispanic Central Mexico." In *Handbook of Middle American Indians*, vol. 10, *Archaeology of Northern Mesoamerica*, pt. 1, edited by Gordon F. Ekholm and Ignacio Bernal, 395–446. Austin: University of Texas Press.

Olivier, Guilhem. 2004. "De flechas, dardos, y saetas: Mixcóatl y el simbolismo de las flechas en las fuentes náhuas." In *De historiografía lingüística e historia de las lenguas*, edited by Ignacio Guzmán Betancourt, Pilar Máynez, and Ascensión H. de León-Portilla, 309–24. Mexico City: Universidad Nacional Autónoma de México/Siglo 21.

Olivier, Guilhem. 2006. "El simbolismo de las espinas de zacate en el México central posclásico." In *Arqueología e historia en el centro de México: Homenaje a Eduardo Matos Moctezuma*, edited by Leonardo López Luján, Davíd Carrasco, and Lourdes Cué, 407–24. Mexico City: Instituto Nacional de Antropología e Historia.

Pasztory, Esther. 1974. *The Iconography of the Teotihuacan Tlaloc.* Washington, D.C.: Dumbarton Oaks Research Library and Collection.

Quiñones Keber, Eloise. 1995. *Codex Telleriano-Remensis: Ritual, Divination, and History in a Pictorial Aztec Manuscript.* Austin: University of Texas Press.

Sahagún, Bernardino de. 1950–1982. *Florentine Codex: A General History of the Things of New Spain.* 12 vols. Translated by Arthur J. O. Anderson and Charles E.

Dibble. Santa Fe, N.Mex: School of American Research; Salt Lake City: University of Utah Press.

Sahagún, Bernardino de. 2000. *Historia general de las cosas de Nueva España*, 3 vols. Mexico City, Mex.: Consejo Nacional para la Cultura y las Artes.

Taube, Karl A. 2000. "The Turquoise Hearth: Fire, Self-Sacrifice, and the Central Mexican Cult of War." In *Mesoamerica's Classic Heritage: From Teotihuacan to the Aztecs*, edited by Davíd Carrasco, Lindsay Jones, and Scott Sessions, 269–340. Boulder: University of Colorado Press.

Taube, Karl A. 2001. "The Breath of Life: The Symbolism of Wind in Mesoamerica and the American Southwest." In *The Road to Aztlan: Art from a Mythic Homeland*, edited by Virginia M. Fields and Victor Zamudio-Taylor, 102–23. Los Angeles: Los Angeles County Museum of Art.

Taube, Karl A. 2005. "Representaciones del paraíso en el arte cerámico del Clásico Temprano de Escuintla, Guatemala." In *Iconografía y escritura teotihuacana en la Costa Sur de Guatemala y Chiapas*, edited by Oswaldo Chinchilla Mazariegos and Bárbara Arroyo, 35–54. U Tz'ib, Serie Reportes, vol. 1, no. 5. Guatemala City: Asociación Tikal.

Taube, Karl A. 2006. "Climbing Flower Mountain: Concepts of Resurrection and the Afterlife at Teotihuacan." In *Arqueología e historia del Centro de Mexico: Homenaje a Eduardo Matos Moctezuma*, edited by Leonardo López Luján, Davíd Carrasco, and Lourdes Cué, 153–70. Mexico City: Instituto Nacional de Antropología e Historia.

Vázquez Vallín, Lorena. 2019. "Análisis iconográfico de los relieves de la Plaza Manuel Gamio." In *Al pie del Templo Mayor de Tenochtitlan: Estudios en honor de Eduardo Matos Moctezuma*, vol. 1, edited by Leonardo López Luján and Ximena Chávez Balderas, 237–62. Mexico City: El Colegio Nacional.

Velázquez Castro, Adrián. 2000. *El simbolismo de los objetos de concha encontrados en las ofrendas del Templo Mayor de Tenochtitlan*. Mexico: Instituto Nacional de Antropología e Historia.

Wrem Anderson, Kasper, and Christophe Helmke. 2013. "The Personification of Celestial Water: The Many Guises of the Storm God in the Pantheon and Cosmology of Teotihuacan." *Contributions in New World Archaeology* 5:165–96.

12

The Flowery Matter of Chant

The Use of Organic Colors in Pre-Hispanic Mesoamerican Codex Painting

Davide Domenici

Building on Jane Hill's seminal article (Hill 1992), various contributors to this volume stress that Indigenous peoples of Mesoamerica and the Southwest did not, and still do not, conceive of flower world(s) as symbolic or metaphorical entities, as products of human imagination. Rather, flower worlds are conceived as actual dimensions of reality that reveal themselves to humans mostly during ritual activities, when they can be physically and sensorially experienced. This experiential character of the flower worlds makes it possible to explore what I would define as their aesthetic dimension, where the term *aesthetic* must not be understood as a specific product of Western philosophical thinking but rather—in a stricter etymological sense—as a body of values and meanings invested into sensory experiences through a process of "socialization of the senses" (Morphy 1996:209).

One of the most powerful aesthetic dimensions of the flower world as represented in pre-Hispanic pictorial depictions and early colonial literary sources is related to light and color. More specifically, brilliancy and chromatic richness are perceived as the most striking visual expressions of that "burst" of generative power that is inherent to the flower world and that is often described by means of a synesthetic overlapping between the blossoming of fragrant, colorful flowers and the oral enunciation of sacred chants.

A similarly strict relationship between color and speech characterizes ancient Mesoamerican codices, whose colorful pages were ritually enunciated during ceremonial performances. Basing my discussion on data collected by means of scientific noninvasive analyses, I will explore the technical dimension of codex painting in pre-Hispanic Mesoamerica in order to investigate how the selection of certain painting materials was driven by their physical and optical properties in order to create ritual items imbued with aesthetic values somehow related to the experiential perception of the flower worlds. I will argue that the preferential use of materials based on organic chromophores, characterized by a stunning polychromy and luminosity, was based on deeply entrenched aesthetic notions linking the fragrance, colorfulness, and brilliance of flowers with the generative power of ritual speech.

THE MATERIALITY OF MESOAMERICAN PICTORIAL MANUSCRIPTS

Mesoamerican pictorial manuscripts—recording a variety of topics such as sacred histories, genealogical records, calendric almanacs, ritual formulas, and astronomical tables—were perceived as quintessential instantiations of Mesoamerican cultural memory (Color Plate 14).[1] The knowledge recorded in manuscripts was often metaphorically alluded to by the difrasismo *in tlilli in tlapalli* (the black soot, the colored pigment), that is, the colors employed to paint the codices. The cultural relevance of the material dimension of codex painting is also attested in this famous early colonial description of the *tlacuilo*, the scribe-painter, recorded in the *Florentine Codex*, book 10: "The scribe; the black soot, the colored pigment, the black ink are his duty. An artist [lit. Toltec], he creates ornaments, uses charcoal, uses charcoal, uses soot, dilutes soot, grinds pigments, uses pigments" (Sahagún 1950–1982:Book 11:28).[2]

Our knowledge of the material dimension of the colors employed to create pictorial manuscripts has long been based mostly on colonial sources, foremost among them book 11, chapter 11 of the *Historia general de las cosas de la Nueva España* (1576–1577) by Bernardino de Sahagún (1950–1982:Book 12:11; see Dupey García 2015b).[3] Even if the preciousness of the few extant pre-Hispanic manuscripts strongly limited the possibility of performing proper scientific studies that required the collection of actual samples from the codices, from 1912 onward various destructive studies were performed. At the beginning of the present century, a veritable technological threshold was then marked by the introduction of nondestructive spectroscopic analytical techniques.[4] The following sketch of the technology of codex painting in pre-Hispanic and colonial Mesoamerica is mostly based on the results of a research project based on the MOLAB Mobile Laboratory of the National Center of Excellence SMAArt (Scientific Methodologies applied to Archaeology and Art,

University of Perugia/CNR, Italy).[5] Indeed, the portable character of the MOLAB allowed the performance of scientific analyses on a large group of pre-Hispanic manuscripts held in various European libraries: *Codex Cospi* at the Biblioteca Universitaria in Bologna, *Codex Madrid* at the Museo de América in Madrid, *Codex Fejérváry-Mayer* at the World Museum in Liverpool, *Codex Nuttall* at the British Museum in London, codices *Laud* and *Bodley* at the Bodleian Library in Oxford, and codices *Borgia* and *Vaticanus B* at the Biblioteca Apostolica Vaticana in Rome. Our team also analyzed some colonial manuscripts: *Codex Tudela* at the Museo de América in Madrid, codices *Mendoza*, *Selden*, and the *Selden Roll* at the Bodleian Library in Oxford, and *Codex Vaticanus A* at the Biblioteca Apostolica Vaticana in Rome.

The painting surfaces of all pre-Hispanic codices, whether they are paper or skin, consist of a white layer, or imprimiture. Scientific analyses showed that these imprimatures were composed of various forms of calcium sulfate or calcium carbonate. Black color has been identified on all pre-Hispanic manuscripts as vegetal carbon black, a material that in different grades of dilution was used to produce black and grey areas. Red colors can be grouped into two main families: the iron oxides (hematite)—only employed on Maya codices (*Madrid* and *Códice Maya de México*, formerly *Grolier*)—and those extracted from cochineal insects (*Dactylopius coccus*)—used both on Maya manuscripts (even if quite rarely) and on all Nahua and Mixtec codices. In most cases the analyses revealed that the cochineal extract was mixed with a mordant—usually alum—in order to obtain a lake pigment.[6] On various codices the cochineal lake was mixed with a clay, probably employed as a filler to thicken the liquid red lake (Domenici et al. 2017:93). Blue colors are among the most famous products of ancient Mesoamerican technology. Actually, on most codices the analyses detected the use of intercalated hybrid pigments, such as the famous Maya Blue. "Typical" Maya Blue—that is, composed of indigo as chromophore and palygorskite as inorganic base—has been detected on a large number of pre-Hispanic manuscripts, such as codices *Cospi, Borgia, Laud, Fejérváry-Mayer, Nuttall, Colombino*, and *Madrid* as well as in small repaintings on *Codex Bodley*. On *Codex Vaticanus B* we identified a variant composed of indigo and sepiolite, while in some pages of *Codex Borgia* the blue intercalated hybrid is composed of indigo and a mixture of palygorskite and sepiolite.

"Generic" blue hybrids were detected on Mixtec codices such as *Codex Bodley* and the colonial *Codex Selden*, employing a form where the chromophore is *Commelina coelestis* fixed on a nonidentified silicate. This suggests that in some regions of pre-Hispanic Mesoamerica painters were experimenting with alternative forms of "Maya Blue," perhaps to overcome difficulties in obtaining the rare palygorskite clay only found in the Yucatán peninsula.

The yellow/orange/brown range of colors is the most varied and complex. In extreme synthesis, we can state that in Nahua and Mixtec codices (yellows are extremely rare in Maya codices), they can be divided into three main families. A first one is represented by lake pigments obtained by mixing vegetal dyes with mordants like alum. A second family comprises "generic" hybrid pigments where the organic dyes were fixed on clay bases. The use of pure yellow dyes—that is, not used as components of lakes or hybrids—is extremely rare and only occurs in codices *Fejérváry-Mayer* and *Vaticanus B*. The third kind of yellow color is orpiment, or arsenic trisulfide, the single inorganic color so far detected on pre-Hispanic manuscripts, which was employed on a rather small group of manuscripts (codices *Laud*, *Fejérváry-Mayer*, *Cospi* verso, and *Nuttall* recto). Its restricted usage, as well as its appearance on the later sides of two manuscripts (*Cospi* and *Nuttall*), suggests that its introduction in the painters' palette was a quite late innovation, probably limited to a specific area in the Southern Puebla/Northwestern Oaxaca region.

The last chromatic range is that of greens, whose extreme complexity is due to the fact that green colors were usually produced by mixing or superimposing blue and yellow ones. In most cases, one of the above-mentioned yellow dyes (or orpiment) was mixed with a blue hybrid pigment. A different group of greens includes colors showing a brownish or mustard-like appearance that we recognize as green for semantic reasons, that is, because they were used to paint green items such as feathers, crocodiles, etc. Strangely enough, in these greens the blue component is often elusive if present at all. The exact composition of these mustard-looking greens, as well as the degradation processes that seem to have affected their visual appearance, is one of the most intriguing open problems to be tackled in the future.

The data so far summarized are useful, especially if adopting a comparative approach, to pursue different research lines. Indeed, the cooccurence of specific painting materials in palettes shared by various codices can lead to the identification of manuscripts' technological groups and traditions, each one with its own specific spatial and chronological dimensions. Despite the limited number of extant pre-Hispanic manuscripts, interesting results of this kind have been attained. Having measured all the five core members of the so-called *Borgia Group*, for example, we were provided with a fresh look at the long-standing problem of their mutual relationships, and we also identified a specific technological subgroup composed of codices *Fejérváry-Mayer* and *Laud* that probably reflect painting practices of a specific region in Southern Puebla/Northwestern Oaxaca. Interestingly enough, *Codex Cospi* shows technological traits that suggest that its recto was painted in the same region where *Codex Borgia* was created, while its verso was painted with a palette typical of *the Fejérváry-Mayer/Laud* subgroup. This suggests that *Codex Cospi* traveled through different regions of the Nahua world, a movement that can be added to the already complex biography of that manuscript. On the other hand, a clear Mixtec subgroup is formed by codices *Bodley* and *Selden* (colonial but highly traditional in its palette), sharing so many technological traits that can be ascribed to the same Mixtec technological tradition. The technologically "intermediate" position of *Codex Nuttall*, in between this Mixtec tradition and the *Fejérváry-Mayer/Laud* subgroup, suggests some kind of Nahua-Mixtec interaction that is also attested by the painting style of the codex. The Maya codices do show unique traits that clearly belong to a separate, southeastern technological sphere.[7]

BRILLIANCE, LUMINOSITY, AND THE FLOWERY MATTER OF CHANT

I want to pursue a different interpretive venue based on the materiality of color, since one of the clearer results of the chemical analyses is that Nahua and Mixtec pre-Hispanic codices were painted using mostly—if not exclusively—materials that included an organic component. This required the development of techniques to produce lakes and other kinds of hybrids, that is, pigments that, while exploiting the chromatic diversity of the vegetal (and animal) realm, were nevertheless as durable and resistant as mineral ones. What is especially surprising is the almost complete absence of inorganic pigments, the only exception being the orpiment that as we saw was probably a quite late and regionally restricted phenomenon. The complete absence of ochres and iron oxides is actually striking, since such materials were widely employed to paint murals and polychrome sculptures in the Nahua world (Dupey García 2018:193–99; López and Chiari 2012). Similarly, the absence of materials such as cinnabar, manganese, azurite, or limonite—all of which were available to Mesoamerican artists—is notable among pre-Hispanic codices.

The relevance of these choices made by pre-Hispanic painters is even clearer when we observe the technological changes that occurred in colonial times. While early manuscripts such as *Codex Borbonicus* (Pottier et al. 2018, 2019) or *Codex Selden* display very traditional palettes, from the mid-sixteenth century new materials were used to paint manuscripts that in most cases assumed the format of European books. Interestingly enough, the most relevant technological innovations were not so much related to the introduction of new materials of European origin but rather to the sudden introduction of painting materials such as ochres, manganese, azurite, limonite, and so forth, that is, those colors that had always been available in Mesoamerica but that had been purposefully excluded from the painters' palettes (Domenici et al. 2020). Both pre-Hispanic and colonial codex painting practices seem to reflect processes of cultural selection of painting materials by the Indigenous painters, and their choices, which were not merely driven by the availability of pigments and colorants, merit further inquiry.[8]

Various authors noticed that the preferential use of organic colors on pre-Hispanic codices could depend on the fact that they produce very brilliant, bright color hues, especially if compared with the duller tones of most mineral pigments (Domenici 2016, 2017; Dupey García 2010:I:92–97, III–17, 2018; González Tirado 1998:7; Magaloni Kerpel 2011:55, 2014:127). Both Diana Magaloni Kerpel (2011, 2014) and Élodie Dupey García (2015a, 2018) showed that the distinction between organic and inorganic painting materials was emically so relevant in Nahua culture that it became the organizing principle of *Florentine Codex*, book 11, chapter 11, where the colors used by painters are listed and where it is clear that the colors employed for codex painting are mostly derived from flowers, plants, and animals. As we saw, scientific analyses showed that orpiment represents an exception to this rule since it is an inorganic pigment employed in codex painting. Nevertheless, as also noticed by Dupey García

(2015a:161–62), arsenic trisulfide produces a particularly bright and luminous yellow. I suggest that it is precisely this material property that induced Mesoamerican painters to introduce this mineral into their palette.

Brightness, iridescence, and luminosity played a key role in Mesoamerican aesthetics (e.g., Caplan 2014; Domenici 2017; Dupey García 2010, 2018), where specific optical properties of the materials were signified, or valued—through a process that Howard Morphy would have called socialization of the senses (Morphy 1996:209)—as expressions of a life force, of a generative energy that has recently been termed "the life within" things (Houston 2014). According to both Diana Magaloni Kerpel (2014:38) and Élodie Dupey García (2018:203), the preferential use of organic colors by codex painters would have endowed codices with a brilliance linked to the Nahuatl notion of *tonalli*, a life essence manifested in the form of light and heat, so that colors based on organic chromophores would have "allowed artists to imbue the codices with life and with divinity" (Dupey García 2018:204). It is not surprising, then, that dullness and lack of luster characterize the work of the "bad" scribe in a famous colonial Nahuatl text: "The bad scribe [is] dull, detestable, irritating, a fraud, a cheat. He paints without luster, ruins colors, blurs them, paint askew, acts impetuously, hastily, without reflection" (Sahagún 1950–1982:Book 11:28).

The cultural implications of the use of brilliant, luminous colors would have been further enhanced by the fact that most of them were not only organic but were literally extracted from flowers to the extent that painting materials were perceived as flowery matter and were often employed to paint flowery images: "The scribe . . . paints flowers, with flowers paints things, as a Toltec" (Sahagún 1950–1982:Book 11:28).[9] This same characteristic was also noticed by European observers such as Toribio de Benavente Motolinía, who wrote that "Indians make many colors with flowers, and when they want to change color, they clean the brush in their mouths, since colors are made out of flowers" (Benavente 1971:218).

The flowery quality of painting materials would have been further signified on the basis of the deep-rooted relationship that Mesoamericans established between flowers and elegant speech. Flowery speech scrolls were painted at least since the Early Classic period and well into colonial times (Houston and Taube 2000), and the same association is expressed by the famous Nahuatl difrasismo *in xochitl, in cuicatl*, "the flower, the chant." In the same vein, the Nahua god of singing, dance, and artistic expression was Xochipilli, "The Flower Prince," and the destiny of those who were born on a day Flower (*Xochitl*) of the 260-day divinatory calendar was to excel in arts, in poetry, or in chant. All these elements are manifestations of the Uto-Aztecan "flower complex" discussed by Jane Hill (1992), who first noticed the existence of a ritual system centered on flowers and their chromatism. And singing, often describing flowery heavenly places, was in her words "the domain par excellence of chromatic symbolism" as well as "the appropriate verbal genre for invoking the symbol of the flower" (Hill 1992:119, 122). Similarly, Louise Burkhart (1992) wrote about a "cult of brilliance," stressing the conceptual analogy between the blossoming of flowers and the emission of light expressed by Nahuatl verbs such as *celiya*: "to blossom," "to bloom," "to green," but also "to burst" (Burkhart 1992). Further, meaningful hints regarding the conceptual association between the sprouting of flowers and the emission of speech can be found in early colonial Nahua songs and especially in those ascribable to the *xopancuicatl* ("Song of the Green Place/Season")/ *xochicuicatl* ("Flower Song") genre (León-Portilla 1983:73–74), which are among the most renowned manifestations of the Nahua Flower World. A song in the *Cantares mexicanos*, for example, says "My songs are greening [*celia*]. My word-fruit sprouts" (Bierhorst 1985:221). The brilliance of the flowery chant is at times paired with the shining of jades: "As jewel mats, shot with jade and emerald sunray, the Green Place flower songs [*xopanxochicuicatl*] are radiating green" (Bierhorst 1985:141). Significantly, the *Cantares mexicanos* also contain a lengthy dialogue between Tecayehuatzin, lord of Huexotzinco, and various singers exploring the deepest meanings of the *xochicuicatl*, "flower song" (Bierhorst 1985:160–69).

The relationship between the chromatic brilliance of flowers and the emission of elegant speech becomes relevant for our discussion if we consider how codices were used and "read." Even if our knowledge of the performative contexts in which codices were used is rather limited, they clearly implied some kind of oral enunciation. This is rather obvious in the case of Maya codices such as the *Dresden* and *Madrid*, containing hieroglyphic inscriptions that record ritual formulas, most probably enunciated aloud. Mixtec and Nahua codices, even if employing proper writing systems in a more limited way, also entertained a complex relation with some kind of highly formalized oral enunciation (e.g., Bleichmar, forthcoming; Jansen and Pérez Jiménez 2009; King 1994; Monaghan 1990; Oudijk 2002). Indeed, early colonial, alphabetically recorded Nahuatl texts closely matching the content of pictorial manuscripts do show a parallelistic and formulaic structure probably more akin to chanting than to plain reading (e.g., Johansson 2004). Other colonial texts clearly mention forms of reading aloud, such as a passage in the *Libro de los Coloquios*, where the *tlamatinime* (plural of *tlamatini*) are described as "those who observe the codices, those who recite. Those who noisily turn the pages of the illustrated manuscripts. Those who have possession of the black and the colored and of that which is pictured" (Sahagún 1980:108–10). The relationship between painted books and songs is also made explicit in a passage of the *Florentine Codex*, book 3, where it is said that in the *calmecac* (the "school" for noble young men) there was "teaching of songs which they called the gods' songs [*teocuicatl*] inscribed in books [*amoxotoca*]" (Sahagún 1950–1982:Book 4:67). Referring to a different cultural context, the Dominican friar Francisco de Burgoa wrote in his *Palestra Historial* (1670) that the Mixtecs "used to hang [codices] as cosmographic tables in their lords' rooms, for greatness and vanity, proud to treat those matters during their meeting and visits" (Burgoa 1989:210). It is not difficult to imagine orators and singers elegantly retelling genealogies, marriages, and conquests of their lords and ancestors, that is, those deeds that are recorded in extant Mixtec historical manuscripts.[10]

In light of these data, it is interesting to note that colonial Nahuatl songs such as those recorded in the *Cantares mexicanos* or in the *Romances de los Señores de la Nueva España* also provide hints about a culturally established relationship between "flowery painting" and "flowery chanting" to the point that Miguel León-Portilla listed paintings among the precious materials most often paired with flowery symbolism (León-Portilla 1983:73). In such texts, the sprouting of creative oral enunciation is described in chromatic terms: "Life Giver, you're coloring-reciting your songs" (Bierhorst 2009:127); "With flowers you paint them, O Life Giver, with songs you color them. You color-recite them who'll live on earth" (Bierhorst 2009:148–49). In both cases, "coloring-reciting" translates the Nahuatl verb *tlapalpohua*, including the radical *tlapal-* ("red," "color") and the verb *pohua*, "to count," "to tell a story," "to read" (Molina 1571). Thus, the creative divine speech is metaphorically expressed as something that conjoins painting with flowers and emitting colorful, flowery words, as also expressed in this passage: "His holy songs are like paintings, like delicious flowers, fragrant ones" (Bierhorst 1985:385). The pairing of chanting and painting also leads to explicit mentions of *amoxtin*, or painted manuscripts: "It's raining feather-flower songs in Your home. They're painted as picture paintings [*tlacuiloamoxticaya*] in Your house of crimson: as red feather flowers they're emitting fragrance" (Bierhorst 1985:353).

CONCLUSION

The data so far discussed suggest that the preferential use of organic colors extracted from flowers by pre-Hispanic codex painters should be understood as a way to produce manuscripts constituted by flowery matter and imbued with chromatic richness and brilliance that would have been signified as manifestations not only of a *tonalli*-like life-force but, more specifically, of the creative, generative power of ritual speech. Indeed, their optical properties would have been enhanced, according to a powerful "cultural synesthesia" (Houston and Taube 2000), the "bursting" or the "blossoming" (*celiya*) of a colorful, fragrant, flowery speech, thus eliciting a sensorial, synesthetic perception of the highly valued aesthetic and moral principles of the flower world (see Sandstrom, this volume, on the related notion of *xochisonis* among contemporary Nahua groups).

Seen in this light, the complex technologies that Mesoamericans developed in order to obtain permanent, resistant pigments such as lakes and hybrids from organic dyes could even be understood as appropriate ways to pursue the typically Mesoamerican aesthetic impulse to transform ephemeral phenomena into permanent ones (Houston 2014). Rather than mere representations of ontologically separate entities and phenomena, Mesoamerican works of "art" were perceived as sharing the same essence of what they depicted, so that a pictorial manuscript would have physically embodied its own oral enunciation. Thanks to the artists' technological skills, the precious but volatile words of ritual speech (songs, spells, calendric divinations, etc., i.e., most of the genres falling into the emic Nahuatl categories of *cuicatl* and *tlahtolli*; see León-Portilla 1983) would have been materialized in the enduring, colorful pages that we can still appreciate today.

The production of colors and the painting of pictorial manuscripts, far from being a "mere" technical enterprise, was thus a culturally charged activity strictly related to the codices' performative contexts. And when these contexts were dramatically transformed by the Spanish conquest, far from passively adopting European painting practices and materials, Indigenous painters purposefully adapted their palette to the colonial situation, now including those inorganic colors that, inadmissible on native *amoxtin*, were perfectly adequate to paint European-like books. Nevertheless, the deep-rooted notions that guided the actions of pre-Hispanic artists were not forgotten: as shown by James Córdova (this volume) in a chapter that strongly resounds with the present one, the miraculous creation of the powerful colonial religious icon of the Virgin of Guadalupe still required a divine, flower-laden palette.

ACKNOWLEDGMENTS

My deepest thanks to Michael D. Mathiowetz and Andrew D. Turner for inviting me to be part of the present volume and of the earlier SAA symposium from which it "blossomed." I also want to thank all the other contributors to the volume for sharing their insights during a thought-challenging week of brainstorming at the Amerind Foundation (AZ). To Christine Szuter and all the staff of the Amerind Foundation, my warmest thoughts for welcoming us in their facilities and providing all of us with a wonderful occasion of intellectual exchange. Thanks to Antonio Sgamellotti, Costanza Miliani, David Buti, and all the personnel of the MOLAB for the fruitful research project we carried out together as well as to all the institutions that allowed us to perform scientific analyses on the manuscripts they held. Last but not least, my warmest thanks to Élodie Dupey García, a friend and colleague who shared with me her knowledge during various steps of the research that led to this text; many of the ideas here expressed took form during our exciting discussions; she also commented on a draft of the present chapter. The responsibility for any error or misinterpretation is solely mine.

NOTES

1. Useful introductory works to the rich literature on Mesoamerican codices are Boone (2000, 2007), Escalante Gonzalbo (2010), Glass (1975), Jansen and Pérez Jiménez (2010), and Vail (2006).

2. The English translation I am providing differs from the one given by Anderson and Dibble and is based on the Spanish version given to me by Élodie Dupey García (personal communication), who made a detailed analysis of the Náhuatl text and of the versions previously provided by various scholars. The couplet *in tlilli in tlapalli* is often translated as "the black, the red," since *tlapalli* literally means "red." Nevertheless, Sahagún explicitly wrote that *tlapalli* was the "collective term for any color," specifically referring to painting materials (Sahagún 1950–1982:Book 12:254; see Dupey García 2016:248), and this more general meaning is obviously the one intended in the couplet, pairing black soot with all the other colors employed on manuscripts.

3. For a synthesis of the scholarly tradition of historical studies devoted to the materiality of manuscripts' colors, see Dupey García and Domenici (forthcoming).

4. For a history of the scientific analyses of Mesoamerican codices, including relevant bibliographic references, see Domenici and Dupey García (forthcoming).

5. For detailed presentations of the MOLAB results, see Buti et al. (2014, 2018), Domenici (2016, 2017, 2018), Domenici et al. (2014, 2017, 2018, 2019a, 2019b, 2020), Grazia et al. (2019, 2020), Higgitt (2013), and Miliani et al. (2012). In various important works, Élodie Dupey García compared the results of the scientific analyses with information drawn from historical sources (Dupey García 2015a, 2017, 2018).

6. A terminological clarification is in order here. Lakes are pigments where a soluble dyestuff—which acts as chromophore, that is, the element that provides the color to the pigment—is precipitated and/or absorbed onto an insoluble inorganic substrate, often called "mordant." During the process, the complexation between the dye molecules and a metal cation as well as the precipitation of the complex together with an inorganic substrate occurs. Alum (hydrated double sulfate of aluminum and potassium) was among the most common "mordants" used in ancient Mesoamerica. Intercalated hybrids are pigments where the dye molecules are intercalated within the tubular molecular structure of a fibrous clay, usually palygorskite or sepiolite, as in the case of the famous Maya Blue. When instrumental analyses detect some kind of interaction between the dye and the clay but it is not possible to demonstrate either a chemical bond (as in lakes) or an intercalation (as in Maya Blue), we speak about "generic" hybrids. This is the case of various yellow and blue pigments employing clays different from palygorskite and sepiolite.

7. For a more detailed treatment of this comparative approach, see Domenici et al. (2014, 2018, 2019b).

8. Specific cultural practices governing the selective use of colors have also been detected in other Mesoamerican cases, such as the Late Preclassic Maya mural paintings of San Bartolo, Guatemala (Hurst and O'Grady 2015) or the colonial *Florentine Codex* (Magaloni Kerpel 2011, 2014).

9. Dibble and Anderson translated the expression *suchitlacuiloa, tlasuchiicuiloa, toltecati* as "draws gardens, paints flowers, creates works of art." I choose the more literal version "paints flowers, with flowers paints things, as a Toltec," also based on the Spanish translation given by M. León-Portilla (2013:150–51).

10. On Mesoamerican speech and song, see Houston et al. (2006:153–63).

REFERENCES

Benavente, Toribio de (Motolinía). 1971. *Historia de los Indios de Nueva España.* Mexico City: Porrúa.

Bierhorst, John. 1985. *Cantares mexicanos: Songs of the Aztecs.* Stanford, Calif.: Stanford University Press.

Bierhorst, John. 2009. *Ballads of the Lords of New Spain: The Romances de los Señores de la Nueva España.* Austin: University of Texas Press.

Bleichmar, Daniela. Forthcoming. "The Legible Image: Painting in Translation." *Renaissance Quarterly.*

Boone, Elizabeth Hill. 2000. *Stories in Red and Black: Pictorial Histories of the Aztec and Mixtec.* Austin: University of Texas Press.

Boone, Elizabeth Hill. 2007. *Cycles of Time and Meaning in the Mexican Books of Fate.* Austin: University of Texas Press.

Burgoa, Francisco de. 1989. *Palestra Historial.* Mexico City: Porrúa.

Burkhart, Louise M. 1992. "Flowery Heaven: The Aesthetic of Paradise in Nahuatl Devotional Literature." *RES: Anthropology and Aesthetics* 21:88–109.

Buti, David, Davide Domenici, Chiara Grazia, Johanna Ostapkowicz, S. Watts, Aldo Romani, Federica Presciutti, Brunetto Giovanni Brunetti, Antonio Sgamellotti, and Costanza Miliani. 2018. "Further Insight into the Mesoamerican Paint Technology: Unveiling the Colour Palette of Pre-Columbian Codex Fejérváry-Mayer by Means of Non-invasive Analysis." *Archaeometry* 60:797–814.

Buti, David, Davide Domenici, Costanza Miliani, Concepción García Sáiz, Teresa Gómez Espinoza, Félix Jímenez Villalba, Ana Verde Casanova, Ana Sabía de la Mata, Aldo Romani, Federica Presciutti, Brenda Doherty, Brunetto Giovanni Brunetti, and Antonio Sgamellotti. 2014. "Non-invasive Investigation of a Pre-Hispanic Maya Screenfold Book: The Madrid Codex." *Journal of Archaeological Science* 42:166–78.

Caplan, Allison. 2014. "So It Blossoms, So It Shines: Precious Feathers and Gold in Pre- and Post-Conquest Nahua Aesthetics." Unpublished M.A. thesis, Department of Art History, Tulane University.

Domenici, Davide. 2016. "La memoria fiorita: Scrittura, memoria e materialità del colore nell'antica Mesoamerica; Confluenze." *Rivista di Studi Iberoamericani* 8:161–80.

Domenici, Davide. 2017. *Il senso delle cose: Materialità ed estetica nell'arte mesoamericana.* Bologna: Bononia University Press.

Domenici, Davide. 2018. "Codex Painting Practices and Scribal Interactions in Postclassic Mesoamerica: A View from Color's Materiality in the Madrid Codex." In *Gedenkschrift in Honor of Alfonso Lacadena*, edited by Harri Kettunen, María Josefa Iglesias Ponce de Leon, Felix Kupprat, Gaspar Muñoz Cosme, Verónica Amellali Vázquez López, and Cristina Vidal Lorenzo, 865–89. Madrid: Universidad Complutense.

Domenici, Davide, David Buti, Chiara Grazia, Élodie Dupey García, Aldo Romani, Laura Cartechini, Antonio Sgamellotti, and Costanza Miliani. 2019a. "Noninvasive Chemical Characterization of Painting Materials of Mesoamerican Codices Borgia (*Borg. mess.* 1) and Vaticanus B (*Vat. lat.* 3773) of the Biblioteca Apostolica Vaticana." *Miscellanea Bibliothecae Apostolicae Vaticanae* 25:201–28.

Domenici, Davide, David Buti, Costanza Miliani, Brunetto Giovanni Brunetti, and Antonio Sgamellotti. 2014. "The Colours of Indigenous Memory: Noninvasive Analyses of Pre-Hispanic Mesoamerican Codices." In *Science and Art: The Painted Surface*, edited by Antonio Sgamellotti, Bruno Brunetti, and Costanza Miliani, 94–119. Cambridge: Royal Society of Chemistry.

Domenici, Davide, David Buti, Costanza Miliani, and Antonio Sgamellotti. 2020. "Changing Colours in a Changing World: The Technology of Codex Painting in Post-Classic and Early Colonial Mesoamerica." In *Materia Americana: The 'Body of Spanish American Images (16th to Mid-19th Centuries)*, edited by Gabriela Siracusano, 45–57. Mexico City: Consejo Nacional para la Cultura y las Artes; Los Angeles: Getty Foundation.

Domenici, Davide, and Élodie Dupey García. Forthcoming. "Estudios de la materialidad de los códices mesoamericanos. I. Apuntes para una historia de los análisis científicos." In *Materiality, Sense and Meaning in Pre-Columbian Art*, edited by Ma. Luisa Vázquez de Ágredos Pascual, Ana García Barrios, and Megan O´Neil. London: Archaeopress.

Domenici, Davide, Chiara Grazia, David Buti, Aldo Romani, Costanza Miliani, and Antonio Sgamellotti. 2017. "La cochinilla en la pintura de códices prehispánicos y colonials." In *Rojo mexicano: La grana cochinilla en el arte*, edited by Miguel Ángel Fernández Félix, 88–99. Mexico City: Instituto Nacional de Bellas Artes, Museo del Palacio de Bellas Artes.

Domenici, Davide, Costanza Miliani, David Buti, Bruno Brunetti, and Antonio Sgamellotti. 2018. "Coloring Materials, Technological Practices, and Painting Traditions: Cultural and Historical Implications of Non-destructive Chemical Analyses of Pre-Hispanic Mesoamerican Codices." In *Painting the Skin: Studies on the Pigments Applied on Bodies and Codices in Pre-Columbian Mesoamerica*, edited by Élodie Dupey García and María Luisa Vázquez de Ágredos Pascual, 129–43. Tucson: University of Arizona Press; Mexico City: Universidad Nacional Autónoma de México, Instituto de Investigaciones Históricas.

Domenici, Davide, Costanza Miliani, and Antonio Sgamellotti. 2019b. "Cultural and Historical Implications of Non-destructive Analyses on Mesoamerican

Codices in the Bodleian Libraries." In *Mesoamerican Manuscripts: New Scientific Approaches and Interpretations*, edited by Maarten Jansen, Virginia M. Llado-Buisán, and Ludo Snijders, 160–74. Leiden: Brill.

Dupey García, Élodie. 2010. "Les couleurs dans les pratiques et les représentations des Nahuas du Mexique Central (XIVe–XVIe siècles)." Unpublished Ph.D. dissertation, 2 vols., Section des sciences religieuses, École Pratique des Hautes Études, Paris.

Dupey García, Élodie. 2015a. "El color en los códices prehispánicos del México Central: Identificación material, cualidad plástica y valor estético." *Revista Española de Antropología Americana* 45:149–66.

Dupey García, Élodie. 2015b. "Traducción del náhuatl al español del capítulo once del libro XI del Códice florentino." *Estudios de Cultura Náhuatl* 49:223–49.

Dupey García, Élodie. 2016. "Aztec Reds: Investigating the Materiality of Color and Meaning in a Pre-Columbian Society." In *Essays in Global Color History: Interpreting the Ancient Spectrum*, edited by Rachel B. Goldman, 245–64. Piscataway, N.J.: Gorgias Press.

Dupey García, Élodie. 2017. "The Materiality of Color in Pre-Columbian Codices: Insights from Cultural History." *Ancient Mesoamerica* 28:21–40.

Dupey García, Élodie. 2018. "Making and Using Colors in the Manufacture of Nahua Codices: Aesthetic Standards, Symbolic Purposes." In *Painting the Skin: Pigments on Bodies and Codices in Pre-Columbian Mesoamerica*, edited by Élodie Dupey García and María Luisa Vázquez de Ágredos Pascual, 186–205. Tucson: University of Arizona Press; Mexico City: Universidad Nacional Autónoma de México, Instituto de Investigaciones Históricas.

Dupey García, Élodie, and Davide Domenici. Forthcoming. "Estudios de la materialidad de los códices mesoamericanos. II. Acercamientos desde la historia y perspectivas para el futuro." In *Materiality, Sense and Meaning in Pre-Columbian Art*, edited by Ma. Luisa Vázquez de Ágredos Pascual, Ana García Barrios, and Megan O´Neil. London: Archaeopress.

Escalante Gonzalbo, Pablo. 2010. *Los códices mesoamericanos antes y después de la conquista española*. Mexico City: Fondo de Cultura Económica.

Glass, John B. 1975. "A Census of Native Middle American Pictorial Manuscripts." In *Handbook of Middle American Indians*, vol. 14, *Guide to Ethnohistorical Sources*, edited by Howard Cline, 81–252. Austin: University of Texas Press.

González Tirado, Rocío Carolusa. 1998. "Análisis de pigmentos en ocho códices mexicanos sobre piel." Unpublished M.A. thesis, Faculty of Applied Sciences, Department of Chemistry and Physics, Leicester: De Montfort University.

Grazia, Chiara, David Buti, Anna Amat, Francesca Rosi, Aldo Romani, Davide Domenici, Antonio Sgamellotti, and Costanza Miliani. 2020. "Shades of Blue: Non-invasive Spectroscopic Investigations of Maya Blue Pigments: From Laboratory Mock-Ups to Mesoamerican Codices." *Heritage Science* 8(1). https://doi.org/10.1186/s40494-019-0345-z

Grazia, Chiara, David Buti, Laura Cartechini, Francesca Rosi, Francesca Ga-
    brieli, Virginia Lladò-Buisàn, Davide Domenici, Antonio Sgamellotti, and
    Costanza Miliani. 2019. "Exploring the Materiality of Mesoamerican Manu-
    scripts by Non-invasive Spectroscopic Methods: Codex Laud, Bodley, Selden,
    Mendoza and Selden Roll at the Bodleian Library." In *Mesoamerican Manu-
    scripts: New Scientific Approaches and Interpretations*, edited by Maarten Jansen,
    Virginia M. Llado-Buisán, and Ludo Snijders, 134–59. Leiden: Brill.
Higgitt, Catherine. 2013. *Molab User Report*. London: British Museum.
Hill, Jane H. 1992. "The Flower World of Old Uto-Aztecan." *Journal of Anthro-
    pological Research* 48(2):117–44.
Houston, Stephen D. 2014. *The Life Within: Classic Maya and the Matter of Per-
    manence*. New Haven, Conn.: Yale University Press.
Houston, Stephen D., David Stuart, and Karl Taube. 2006. *The Memory of Bones:
    Body, Being, and Experience Among the Classic Maya*. Austin: University of
    Texas Press.
Houston, Stephen D., and Karl Taube. 2000. "An Archeology of the Senses:
    Perception and Cultural Expression in Ancient Mesoamerica." *Cambridge
    Archaeological Journal* 10:261–94.
Hurst, Heather, and Caitlin O'Grady. 2015. "Maya Mural Art as Collabora-
    tion: Verifying Artists' Hands at San Bartolo, Guatemala Through Pigment
    and Plaster Composition." In *Beyond Iconography: Materials, Methods, and
    Meaning in Ancient Surface Decoration; Selected Papers in Ancient Art and Ar-
    chitecture*, edited by Sarah Lepinski, 35–56. Boston: Archaeological Institute
    of America.
Jansen, Maarten, and Gabina Aurora Pérez Jiménez. 2009. "Lenguaje ceremonial
    en ıos codices mixtecos." In *Image and Ritual in the Aztec World*, edited by
    Sylvie Peperstraete, 7–18. British Archaeological Reports International Series,
    vol. 1896. Oxford: British Archaeological Reports.
Jansen, Maarten, and Gabina Aurora Pérez Jiménez. 2010. *The Mixtec Pictorial
    Manuscripts: Time, Agency and Memory in Ancient Mexico*. Leiden: Brill.
Johansson, Patrick. 2004. *La palabra, la imagen y el manuscrito: Lecturas indíge-
    nas de un texto pictórico en el siglo XVI*. Mexico City: Universidad Nacional
    Autónoma de México.
King, Marc B. 1994. "Hearing the Echoes of Verbal Art in Mixtec Writing." In
    Writing Without Words: Alternative Literacies in Mesoamerica and the Andes,
    edited by Elizabeth H. Boone and Walter Mignolo, 102–36. Durham, N.C.:
    Duke University Press.
León-Portilla, Miguel. 1983. "'Cuicatl' y 'Tlahtolli': Las formas de expresión en
    náhuatl." *Estudios de cultura Nahuatl* 16:13–108.
León-Portilla, Miguel. 2013. *La tinta negra y roja: Antología de poesía náhuatl.
    Edición bilingüe*. Mexico City: Era.
López Luján, Leonardo, and Giacomo Chiari. 2012. "Color in Monumental
    Mexica Sculpture." *RES: Anthropology and Aesthetics* 61/62:330–42.

Magaloni Kerpel, Diana. 2011. "Painters of the New World: The Process of Making the Florentine Codex." In *Colors Between Two Worlds: The Florentine Codex of Bernardino de Sahagún*, edited by Gerhard Wolf and Joseph Connors, 46–76. Florence: Kunsthistorisches Institut in Florenz, Max-Planck-Institut, Villa I Tatti, and the Harvard University Center for Italian Renaissance Studies.

Magaloni Kerpel, Diana. 2014. *The Colors of the New World: Artists, Materials, and the Creation of the Florentine Codex.* Los Angeles: Getty Publications.

Miliani, Costanza, Davide Domenici, Catia Clementi, Federica Presciutti, Francesca Rosi, David Buti, Aldo Romani, Laura Laurencich Minelli, and Antonio Sgamellotti. 2012. "Colouring Materials of Pre-Columbian Codices: Non-invasive In Situ Spectroscopic Analysis of the Codex Cospi." *Journal of Archaeological Science* 39:672–79.

Molina, Alonso de. 1571. *Vocabulario en lengua castellana y mexicana.* Mexico City: Antonio de Spinosa.

Monaghan, John D. 1990. "Verbal Performance and the Mixtec Codices." *Ancient Mesoamerica* 1:133–40.

Morphy, Howard. 1996. "For the Motion (1)." In *Key Debates in Anthropology*, edited by Tim Ingold, 206–9. London: Routledge.

Oudijk, Michel. 2002. "La toma de posesión: Un tema mesoamericano para la legitimación del poder." *Relaciones* 91:96–131.

Pottier, Fabien, Anne Michelin, Anne Genachte-Le Bail, Aurélie Tournié, Christine Andraud, Fabrice Goubard, Aymeric Histace, and Bertrand Lavédrine. 2018. "Preliminary Investigation on the Codex Borbonicus: Macroscopic Examination and Coloring Material Characterization." In *Painting the Skin: Pigments on Bodies and Codices in Pre-Columbian Mesoamerica*, edited by Élodie Dupey García and María Luisa Vázquez de Ágredos Pascual, 157–74. Tucson: University of Arizona Press.

Pottier, Fabien, Anne Michelin, Salomon Kwimang, Christine Andraud, Fabrice Goubard, and Bertrand Lavédrine. 2019. "Macroscopic Reflectance Spectral Imaging to Reveal Multiple and Complementary Types of Information for the Non-invasive Study of an Entire Polychromatic Manuscript." *Journal of Cultural Heritage* 35:1–15.

Sahagún, Bernardino de. 1950–1982. *Florentine Codex: General History of the Things of New Spain.* 12 vols. Translated by Arthur J. O. Anderson and Charles E. Dibble. Santa Fe, N.Mex.: School of American Research: Salt Lake City: University of Utah Press.

Sahagún, Bernardino de. 1980. "The Aztec-Spanish Dialogues of 1524." Translated by J. Jorge Klor de Alva. *Alcheringa: Ethnopoetics* 4:52–193.

Vail, Gabrielle. 2006. "The Maya Codices." *Annual Review of Anthropology* 35: 497–519.

13

The Flowers of Our Lady of Guadalupe

Marian Devotional Painting and Nahua Cosmology After the Conquest

James M. Córdova

To the modern eye colonial Mexican paintings of the Virgin of Guadalupe may not immediately educe familiar Mesoamerican aesthetics or cosmology. This is due not only to their Christian content and apparent Europeanized stylization but also to the fact that they are largely oil-on-canvas works, that is, products of European-based artistic technology that took root in the Americas after the conquest. Consequently, they may be seen as markers of the success of European artistic practices and technologies at the expense of Indigenous ones, and, relatedly, as signs of Christianity's triumph over Indigenous belief systems (Elizondo 2001:xvii, 31; Kubler 1985:66 [1961]). Another perspective relates certain aspects of Guadalupe with those of Aztec goddesses (Kroger and Granziera 2012:232), and in its most radical form regards her as a Christianized version of a preconquest deity (Nebel 1995).[1] More recent approaches take into account the complex interworking of early modern European Marian devotions, religious literature, and iconography with Indigenous writings, sacred geography, and ritual practices (Burkhart 2001; Peterson 2014). In this vein, the present work investigates colonial Mexican visual and literary productions of the Virgin of Guadalupe that bridge key aspects of Indigenous cosmology with early modern Christian notions of the sacred. I posit that a group of colonial Mexican images of the Virgin of Guadalupe and the literary sources on which they were partially premised evince a creative dialogue between Counter Reformation theology and key aspects of the Indigenous flower world, the latter of which was first articulated by Jane Hill in her influential essay "The Flower World of Old Uto-Aztecan." According to Hill (1992:117, 127–28) and Hays-Gilpin and Hill (1999:2) the flower world is a multidimensional realm of ancestral origin and return related to the sun, heat, music, and luminous colors, and it is an integral piece of Indigenous cosmology in Mesoamerica and parts of the American Southwest. As the essays of this volume make evident, this realm is fundamental to preconquest and modern-day Mesoamerican cosmology, ritual, and material culture. This essay analyzes its integration with colonial-period Christian devotionalism though a group of images of the Virgin of Guadalupe that would have resonated with Indigenous, Spanish, Creole, and mixed audiences in colonial Mexico.

THE IMAGE AND ITS NARRATIVE

The original painting of the Virgin of Guadalupe (Figure 13.1), now enshrined in the Basilica of Guadalupe in Mexico City, is the model on which successive colonial images of this subject are premised. In it the Virgin appears as a young, beautiful woman standing on a darkened crescent moon and supported by an angel. She wears a blue-green mantle with gold trimming and star designs as well as a rose-colored robe with floral and vegetal patterns. Solemnly bowing her head with eyes lowered, she firmly clasps her hands together in prayer. Her skin is olive toned, her dark hair is neatly parted down the middle of her head, and a burst of light with individualized sun rays that were originally composed of gold leaf surrounds her entire figure.[2]

Despite Franciscan devotion to the Virgin Mary and specifically her Immaculate Conception at the time of the painting's production, some in the order opposed Guadalupe's local cult and image. For example, the sixteenth-century friar and historian of Indigenous Central Mexico Bernardino de Sahagún (1950–1982:1:90) suspected that her cult was an idolatrous continuation of the preconquest worship of *tonantzin*, an Indigenous deity whose temple, he pointed out, once existed on the same grounds as Guadalupe's principal shrine. A contemporary of Sahagún's, Fray Francisco de Bustamante, provincial of the Franciscans in Mexico, apparently expressed his concerns in a sermon about a falsely miraculous but popular image of the Virgin located in a shrine at Tepeyac, the site of Guadalupe's apparitions (Map 1; Torre Villar and Navarro de Anda 1982:59). According to Alonso Sánchez de Cisneros, who was present in an investigation of this sermon, Bustamante claimed the image was produced by an Indigenous painter whom he simply identified as Marcos.[3] Clara Bargellini (2011:6) notes this painter was probably trained at the Colegio de San José de los Naturales, a school for Indigenous nobles who

Figure 13.1 Virgin of Guadalupe. Sixteenth century. Tempera and oil on cloth. Básilica of Guadalupe, Mexico City. D.R. © Archivo del Museo de la Básilica de Guadalupe.

were given a classic humanist education that included drawing, painting, and other artistic practices. Underscoring his artistic mastery and popularity, Jeanette Peterson (2014:116) suggests that the same Marcos was probably the principal artist charged with constructing the main altarpiece (*retablo mayor*) for the chapel of San José de los Naturales, which was actually connected to the Franciscan motherhouse in Mexico City.

Subsequent artists in colonial Mexico modeled their paintings of Guadalupe on the original image, and by the mid-seventeenth century they also began to consult with published accounts of her apparition narrative, the first of these being Miguel Sánchez's *Imagen de la Virgen María, Madre de Dios de Guadalupe* (1648), which the author apparently premised on Indigenous oral tradition, although he clearly directed it to the local Creole population (Poole 2017:109). Another contemporary source was Luis Laso de la Vega's *Nican mopohua* from the larger work *Huei tlamahuiçoltica* (1649), published in Nahuatl but apparently exerting little influence on colonial Mexico's Spanish and Creole inhabitants (Poole 2017:123). Later publications variably premised on these initial accounts as well as other related sources also circulated locally and abroad to disseminate the Guadalupe narrative and propagate her cult.[4]

José Juárez, a prominent Mexico City artist, painted the first known single canvas that includes scenes of her apparitions, which he probably based in part on Sánchez's account (Figure 13.2). Inscriptions accompany each scene to inform the viewers of this still relatively new narrative. Four vignettes surround the central image of the Virgin and picture her interactions with Juan Diego, the Indigenous man to whom she appeared, as well as his presentation of her image to the bishop. In the first scene (upper left), the Virgin, in a cloudburst, extends her hand out to a visibly startled Juan Diego. The second one (upper right) shows her instructing him to collect flowers on top of the sacred hill, Tepeyac. In the next scene (lower left), Juan Diego presents to the Virgin the miraculous flowers that he has collected in his cloak (*tilma*). And finally, in the lower right, we witness the moment in which he presents to the bishop-elect, Juan de Zumárraga, the original image of Guadalupe imprinted on the same garment in which he collected the flowers, which are strewn on the floor where he stands. Juárez includes flowers in all but the first vignette.

Subsequent colonial paintings of Guadalupe prominently feature flowers either as part of the apparition narrative, as a framing device,

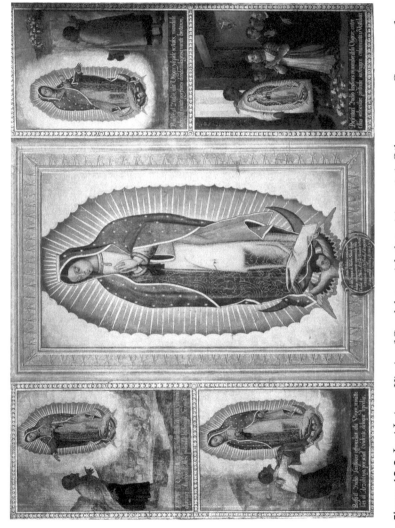

Figure 13.2 José Juárez. *Virgin of Guadalupe with Apparitions.* 1656. Oil on canvas. Convent of the Conceptionists, Ágreda, Soria, Spain. Photo by Alejandro Plaza.

or both, as Juan Correa's 1667 painting *History of the Apparitions of the Virgin of Guadalupe* demonstrates (Figure 13.3). Correa arranges four vignettes in roundels that are arranged around a central rectangular scene. Each vignette is numbered to indicate the sequence in which the narrative unfolds. Scene one depicts the Virgin's first apparition to Juan Diego in the upper-left corner of the composition, and it is followed by another episode in the upper-right corner. Scenes three and four are to be read from left to right in the bottom portion of the painting, and the final episode, which pictures the narrative climax, appears in the center. It is the moment in which Juan Diego reveals to Zumárraga the Virgin's image on his cloak as the flowers he collected in the last scene at Tepeyac spill down to his feet. The imagery and sequence are similar to Juárez's painting, but new are the angels that flank the center scene and hold or sprinkle flowers along the composition's borders. These angels are not a part of the official apparition narrative but rather elements that Correa added to the composition. An inscription in the painting's bottom portion narrates the story and calls attention to the role of the flowers.

Roughly a century later, the prominent Mexico City artist Miguel Cabrera published *Maravilla americana y conjunto de raras maravillas* (1756), an examination of the original Guadalupe painting in which he declared it to be beyond the technical ability of any human artist and a statement on the nobility of the profession of painting. He produced many replicas of the original painting in which he was careful to match the original's proportions, scale, line, and so forth so as not to deviate from that sacred model. In some cases, Cabrera, like Correa before him, took some artistic license, although not with the central figure, which accurately replicates the original painting, but instead with the vignette scenes and the colorful floral arrangements that flank Guadalupe (Color Plate 15). Bargellini (2011:17) has argued that flowers framing the central image of Guadalupe are not simply decorative, they are actually rooted in the official Guadalupe narrative, which establishes the generative role of flowers. Significantly, Cabrera matched the hues of the central image with those of the surrounding flowers, thereby visually tying the two. He makes this relation even more explicit in the lower-right vignette, where Juan Diego reveals to Zumárraga the image on his mantle, which chromatically matches the flowers that have fallen to the floor.

Figure 13.3 Juan Correa. *History of the Apparitions of the Virgin of Guadalupe*. 1667. Oil on canvas. © Museo Nacional de Escultura, Valladolid, Spain. Photo by Javier Muñoz y Paz Pastor. CE 1679.

FLOWERY SHRINES IN PRE- AND POSTCONQUEST MEXICO

Flowers are featured not only in colonial paintings of Guadalupe. Actual colonial-era celebrations dedicated to her included flowery frames or shrines for the original image, as seen in the grand scale painting *Transfer of the Image and Inauguration of the Sanctuary of the Virgin of*

Guadalupe (ca. 1709) (Figure 13.4a), attributed to Manuel Arellano. This work commemorates the festivities surrounding the installation of the original *tilma* image in Guadalupe's newly erected church designed by Pedro de Arrieta and featured in the center of the composition. On April 30, 1709, lay people, government officials, and members of various religious orders and confraternities gathered to witness the transfer. The main event, the procession of Guadalupe to her newly erected shrine, appears just below the courtyard to the left of the church, near the lower-left portion of the canvas. A closer look reveals the *tilma* set upright on

Figure 13.4 (a) Attributed to Manuel Arellano. *Transfer of the Image and Inauguration of the Sanctuary of the Virgin of Guadalupe.* ca. 1709. Oil on canvas. Collection of Marqués de los Balbases, Spain. Photo courtesy of the Archivo Fotográfico Manuel Toussaint, Instituto de Investigaciones Estéticas, Universidad Nacional Autónoma de México, Mexico City. (b) Attributed to Manuel Arellano. *Transfer of the Image and Inauguration of the Sanctuary of the Virgin of Guadalupe* (detail). Photo by Jeff Wells.

a platform and surrounded by an elaborate framework of flowers as it makes its way through the crowd (Figure 13.4b). This arrangement, which enshrines a sacred image in a floral framework, is strikingly reminiscent of Diego Durán's (1971:88) description of a floral shrine in which Aztec priests would place the figure of Huitzilopochtli, the Mexica tribal deity, during this god's feast. Earlier figural objects from the Classic period (A.D. 300–900)—like the anthropomorphic censers of Teotihuacan and Escuintla, Guatemala, which incorporate floral, feather, and butterfly motifs—may have also conjured the flower world, especially in ritual, when they would have emitted their fragrant incense (introduction, this volume). Doris Heyden (1983:101) reminds us that numerous Mesoamerican deities were ritually honored with flowers, indicating that floral displays featuring sacred objects and images had a local history that antedated the conquest.

Bridging the past to the present, Alan Sandstrom (this volume) notes that in contemporary southern Huastec communities in Mexico, flowers are requisite embellishments for shrines and ritual events. In fact, the sacred energy or substance that binds together all of creation, which Nahuatl speakers in this region call *totiotzin* (from the term *teotl*, signifying divinity and life force), can show itself through *tlamantli*, that is, properly arranged things like a painting or an altar ornamented with flowers. Sandstrom (this volume) also notes that *tlamantli* should not be interpreted as metaphoric or symbolic but rather as objects that "[disclose] the sacred substrate" and "open to view what is normally hidden." Because they embody aspects of *teotl-totiotzin*, they possess agency and thereby can cause things to happen. This calls to mind the renowned agentic quality of the original Guadalupe image, which has been credited with producing many miracles such as alleviating floods, healing people, and even reviving the dead (Poole 2017:125–29). Such wondrous deeds are a part of the realm of *teotl-totiotzin* and reveal the animacy of things that, to the modern Western mind, are simply inanimate and representative objects or images incapable of acting (Bassett 2015; Dean and Leibsohn 2017:416–18).

THE FLOWERS OF GUADALUPE IN WORD AND IMAGE

There is no evidence that colonial artists included floral imagery in their paintings of Guadalupe in order to conjure or reference *teotl-totiotzin*.

Instead, they probably based this imagery on local apparition narratives, like Sánchez's publication, which stresses the crucial role of flowers in the story of Guadalupe. For example, Sánchez (Sousa et al. 1998:138) states that when Juan Diego opened his mantle, the bishop saw in it "a holy forest, a miraculous spring, an abbreviated garden of roses, white lilies, carnations, other lilies, broom, jasmines, and violets, which on all falling from the cloak left painted on it the Virgin Mary mother of God in the holy image that today is preserved, kept, and venerated in her sanctuary of Guadalupe of Mexico City."

Both colonial literary and pictorial works explicitly identify the original image of Guadalupe as the product of divine intervention, thereby establishing it as a local thaumaturgic object of veneration.[5] For example, Mateo de la Cruz's *Relación de la milagrosa aparición de la imagen de la Santa Virgen de Guadalupe* (1781:24 [1660]), an abridged version of Sánchez's publication, explicitly states that God or the Virgin herself or perhaps the angels painted the *tilma* image. He (11) also notes that the original image of Guadalupe was painted with flowers. As if combining these statements, an unsigned eighteenth-century Mexican painting pictures God the Father painting the image of Guadalupe on Juan Diego's cloak, which angels hold up (Figure 13.5). His palette is spotted with flowers instead of paint, and two angels below him hold up roses, while Christ, who is positioned between the Father and his painting, cradles a flower close to his chest. In a similar contemporaneous work, attributed to Joaquín Villegas (Figure 13.6), Juan Diego kneels at the top of a flowery hill, probably Tepeyac, and offers up to the Trinity a bouquet of flowers. Meanwhile God the Father paints the Virgin while angels stretch out and support the canvas. A scrolled inscription near the figure of Juan Diego reads, "flowers appeared in our land," a quotation taken from the Song of Songs.[6] The escutcheon Juan Diego balances indicates that God the Divine Painter desired these flowers and painted the beautiful image of the Virgin on the modest cloak of Juan Diego.[7] Meanwhile, a garden-like valley with a circular body of water appears beneath the painting of Guadalupe, possibly referencing the fertile basin of Mexico and the Earthly Paradise (Peterson 2014:197). I would add that it also evokes the Enclosed Garden (*hortus conclusus*), a traditional symbol of the Virgin Mary taken from the Song of Songs 4:10–15.[8] This symbol was not lost on the Nahuas, as Mary is identified as the *hortus conclusus* in the Nahuatl

Figure 13.5 Artist unknown. *God the Father Painting the Virgin of Guadalupe.* Eighteenth century. Oil on canvas. Whereabouts unknown. Photo courtesy of the Archivo Fotográfico Manuel Toussaint, Instituto de Investigaciones Estéticas, Universidad Nacional Autónoma de México, Mexico City.

Sermoniario en lengua mexicana (1606): "And now may you know, oh my precious children, that the flower garden, the flowery enclosure, our lord God's place of consolation, his place of repose, is really she, the precious noblewoman, Saint Mary" (Burkhart 2001:15).

Colonial Mexican paintings that depict a member of the Holy Trinity—God the Father, the Son, and the Holy Spirit—as the artist of the original Guadalupe image are most closely related to early modern Spanish depictions of *Deus Pictor*—God the Divine Painter—which, in Spain, related the monarchy to the Virgin of the Immaculate Conception and

Figure 13.6 Attributed to Joaquín Villegas. *God the Father Painting the Virgin of Guadalupe*. ca. 1750. Oil on canvas. Museo Nacional de Arte, Mexico City. Photograph © Art Resource.

also made a statement on painting as an intellectual pursuit that God first exercised in his primordial conceptualization of the Virgin Mary (Cuadriello 2009; Moreno Cuadro 2019; Pórtus Pérez 2017). In addition to Spanish images of *Deus Pictor* and colonial hagiographies of Guadalupe, contemporaneous Mexican images of God painting the Virgin of Guadalupe are also connected to a substantial body of concurrent religious literature that expounded on God's privilege as inventor and creator, a theme that Counter Reformation theologians made in regard to the visual arts and a cause that New Spain's artists took up in the eighteenth century (Brading 2001:96–99, 146–68; Córdova and Farago 2012; Cuadriello 2001:66, 141–42; Mues-Orts 2002).

However, unlike Spanish paintings of this subject, some analogous Mexican works bridge *Deus Pictor* with the creative and wondrous role of flowers as they are expounded in Guadalupe's apparition narratives and also in Nahuatl devotional literature of the early colonial period. Louise Burkhart (1992:89) has noted that this Indigenous literary genre references flowers—along with birds, butterflies, and precious stones—as a means to constitute "a rhetorical mode by which Christianity was rendered meaningful" for Nahuas. Specific references to the Virgin Mary as a flower are common in these works. For example, the *Oración de la concepción de Nuestra Señora* states, "You, oh noblewoman, you are the spout of the fine heart-flower tree, you are quite slender, you are the straight lily flower." And this from an unsigned Jesuit manuscript now in the Biblioteca Nacional de México: "Oh, may you be joyful, oh Saint Mary, oh fresh and pure one who is in a sacred way a flower!" (Burkhart 2001:20).

Before and after the conquest, flowers were rife with multivalent meanings and ritual functions in Mesoamerica. The *Romances de los Señores de la Nueva España* and the *Cantares mexicanos* frequently identify local flowers, including the *izquisuchil* (*Bourreria*, or "popcorn flower"), as sacred (McNeil, this volume). The *Nican mopohua* (Sousa et al. 1998:91) specifically references this flower in its description of Guadalupe's garments: "On the surface, her outfit appears to be rose-colored, and in the shadowy parts, it almost seems crimson, embroidered with various kinds of flowers, dinted with popcorn flowers [*izquixochimimìnqui*]; and it has gold edges all around." Similarly, flowers figure into the Virgin's appearance in Sahagún's *Psalmodia Christiana* (1993:251 [1583]), a book of Christian devotional literature composed in Nahuatl. In the fourth psalm of the prayer dedicated to the Assumption of the Virgin Mary, "When in four days her [Mary's] precious soul went up to Heaven, many angels took her there. Her precious body entered. She lived; she was risen from the dead. Then her previous body was adorned, attired in heavenly array. She shone brightly she gleamed brightly. She was very beautiful. She was clothed in heavenly flowers."

Flowers and luminescence are tied up with the chromaticism of the flower world, whose signs include colored flowers, iridescent natural phenomena (e.g., dawn, sunset, and rainbows), birds, colored lights, flames, and solar heat (Burkhart 2001:20; Hill 1992:117). Significantly, Guadalupe's first apparition narratives note that the Virgin appeared to Juan

Diego at sunrise and also at sunset (Sousa et al. 1998:61, 133). Also, Juan Diego found himself bathed in light (131), and he saw that the Virgin's "clothes were like the sun the way they gleamed and shone" (65). Emphatic chromaticism is also present in colonial images of Guadalupe, which picture her in a sunburst, clad in brilliant blue and red garments with gold edging and supported by a feathered and brightly colored angel. Images that feature her radiant apparitions and/or incorporate floral decorations around her central figure further emphasize the chromatic aspect of Guadalupe.

Flowers have also long been a facet of Christianity, and, in some cases, they can specifically reference the Virgin. For example, the lily is a symbol of Mary's purity and commonly appears in medieval and early modern images of the *Annunciation*, in which the Archangel Gabriel holds it before a youthful Mary. Red roses are linked to the blood of martyrs as well as the divine love shared between Christ, the Virgin, select female saints, and nuns, who were regarded as Christ's brides (Córdova 2014:69–92). Additionally, flowers could represent particular Christian virtues such as chastity, penitence, obedience, and charity (Córdova 2014:75). Despite the distinct cosmologies of Mesoamerica and Europe, the relation of flowers to the sacred would have resonated with both groups and acted as a bridge for ritual practices and artistic expression in the colonial period.

FLOWERS AND PAINTING IN NAHUA COSMOLOGY

Bargellini (2011:17) has noted that the association between flowers, painting, and the sacred in some of the pictorial works examined in this chapter has its roots in "indigenous sixteenth-century painting practices and ideas, in which the making of pigments and dyes with flowers and plants is the norm, and in which flowers were an integral part of relating to the divine."[9] The sixteenth-century Spanish friar Motolinía (1971:218 [1858]) corroborates this in noting that Indigenous artists in Mexico produced a myriad of flower-based colors for their paintings. And the *Florentine Codex* (Sahagún 1950–1982:10:28) defines the good artist as one who "paints, applies colors, makes shadows, draws gardens, paints flowers, creates works of art."[10] Recently, Davide Domenici (2019:112, this volume) has argued that the almost exclusive use of flowery, organic pigments in preconquest manuscripts was linked to the ritual context in which those manuscripts were read. He notes that after the conquest, Indigenous manuscript artists began to incorporate more inorganic pigments into their work as the ritual aspect of performing/orating the manuscripts changed.

Early colonial Nahuatl literature expounds on the relation of flowers and painting to song in a ritual setting. According to the *Cantares mexicanos* (Bierhorst 1985:231): "With flowers he is making paintings, he, Life Giver." Humans express their joy and gratitude to Life Giver by responding in song, which is likened to flowers and painting: "Your heart is pleasured, it imbibes the painted flowers. Songs are painted!" (Bierhorst 1985:206–7). In the *Romances de los Señores de la Nueva España*, the author waxes poetically about Tamoanchan, the realm of the gods and the place of creation, and emphasizes its paradisiacal setting full of flowers: "I come quickly to weave the flowering tree with blooming flowers in Tamoanchan, there are perfect flowers on the flowery carpet, flowers without roots" (Garibay 1993:29 [1582]).[11] And again, "The flowering tree is entwined: still there opening its corollas in your house, oh God. Various birds come there, they suck the honey there: and they also chatter there in your house, oh God" (32). "It's raining feather-flower songs in Your home. They are painted as picture paintings in Your house of crimson: as red feather flowers they are emitting fragrance" (Bierhorst 1985:353).

In Guadalupe's published narratives and in the colonial Mexican *Deus Pictor* works examined here, flowers explicitly provide the colors used to make the image of the Virgin on Juan Diego's cloak, a crucial element absent in early modern Spanish paintings of this subject. This strongly suggests that Mexican artists were drawing on these local accounts, which emphasized the creative and wondrous role of flowers in a sacred context, a well-established precedent among the Nahuas as *Cantares mexicanos* and *Romances de los Señores de la Nueva España* substantiate. In this manner, the garden-like setting in Villegas's painting conjures a paradisiacal sacred space that is both local and cosmic. That space opened up to Juan Diego on Tepeyac and provided him with beautiful flowers to present to Zumárraga. Peterson (2014:73–81) has noted that the sacred geography to which Tepeyac belonged provided a rich context for Guadalupe's story. Sánchez and Laso de la Vega specifically identify it as the site where the Virgin chose to appear radiantly to Juan Diego and also the place where flowers miraculously grew and birds and angels played precious, heavenly music. Significantly, the hill, brilliant light, flowers, birds, and angels are present in Correa's painting (Figure 13.3). Note the translucent choirs of angels above Guadalupe's head in each apparition scene as well as the brightly colored birds between her and Juan Diego in the first scene. The same elements are variably present in the other works examined here, indicating that colonial artists were familiar with these important publications and explicitly drew from them.

Another Nahua reference to the bearing that flowers had is present in the scene where Juan Diego presents to Zumárraga the flowers and image of Guadalupe on his cloak. Heyden (1983:49–50) notes that certain flowers were reserved for nobles and warriors, and the *Florentine Codex* elaborates on the kind of floral arrangements that were given as gifts to nobles in preconquest Mexico. The corresponding image from the codex (Figure 13.7) pictures a standing individual handing floral garlands and bouquets to a lord who receives them and wears them on his body while sitting on his reed mat.[12] This gesture calls to mind the figure of Juan Diego offering flowers to the bishop-elect, who was the highest and most noble religious official in colonial Mexico. Not until

Figure 13.7 Artist unknown. Nobleman receiving flowers, from the *Florentine Codex*, Book 11, ca. 1580. Ink and pigments on paper. Biblioteca Medicea Laurenzana, Florence. Drawing by James M. Córdova.

Juan Diego presented these flowers and their miraculous image did Zumárraga properly receive him and believe his story about Guadalupe. Burkhart (2001:150) has noted that in addition to the Virgin's association with flowers in Nahuatl devotional texts, her nobility would have also resounded with Nahua notions of sacredness. We have already seen in the *Oración de la concepción de Nuestra Señora* and the anonymous Jesuit manuscript in the Biblioteca Nacional that Mary is identified both as flower and noblewoman.

CONCLUSION

Since Jane Hill's seminal first study of the Mesoamerican flower world, other studies on this topic have expanded and refined our knowledge of this important aspect of Mesoamerican cosmology as it relates to colonial visual culture (Alcántara Rojas 2011; Córdova 2014; Wake 2010). We know well that the Virgin of Guadalupe was not simply a sign of the Christian conquest of Indigenous Mexico, for the extinction paradigm to which this thinking belongs does not adequately account for the dynamism and complexity of Nahua cosmology after the conquest. Nor was Guadalupe simply regarded as an Aztec goddess disguised as the Virgin Mary in colonial times—colonial cosmologies are much too nuanced for such a monolithic interpretation. Rather, Mesoamericans' intricate knowledge of creation, divinity, nobility, and beauty as related through flowers made meaningful the story and image of Guadalupe in a way that Spaniards and others not versed in the Indigenous flower world could certainly appreciate but not fully comprehend as an Indigenous audience might. However, many Nahuas would have been able to reconcile Euro-Christian and Mesoamerican belief systems and their notions of a flowery paradise, which together contributed to the cross-cultural currency of this beloved religious icon now recognized the world over.

ACKNOWLEDGMENTS

My thanks to Andrew Turner and Michael Mathiowetz for inviting me to be a part of this edited volume. I am also grateful to my fellow volume contributors from whom I learned much and to the Amerind Foundation for generously hosting our seminar on a most vital topic in a most beautiful setting. Special thanks to Clara Bargellini, Jeanette Peterson, and Donna Pierce, who graciously helped me locate and acquire some of the images for this essay.

NOTES

1. *Aztec* and *Nahua* are used interchangeably here. The Nahuas are a Central Mexican Indigenous group who speak Nahuatl and established themselves in the basin of Mexico in the late Postclassic (A.D. 1200–1520).

2. Guadalupe's image is closely tied to the Marian advocations of the Immaculate Conception, *Mulier amicta solaris* (woman clothed with the sun), *Tota Pulchra* (all beautiful), and the Assumption of the Virgin (Peterson 2014:119–29).

3. The *información* on which this statement is premised has been lost. See Poole (2006) for a discussion of the circumstances involving it. Also see Poole (2017:62–68) for a cogent analysis of the context of Bustamante's sermon.

4. Among these publications, Becerra Tanco's 1675 *Felicidad de México* (Becerra Tanco 1979 [1675]) and Francisco de Florencio's 1688 *Estrella del norte* were preeminent. Mateo de la Cruz's 1660 *Relación de la milagrosa aparición de la Santa Imagen de la Virgen de Guadalupe*, published earlier than these, is an abridged version of Sánchez's *Imagen de la Virgen María*.

5. In addition to works examined in this essay, contemporaneous paintings with strikingly similar subject matter include an anonymous oil-on-canvas work depicting God the Son painting the Virgin of Guadalupe on the sacristy retablo in the church of la Congregación in the city of Querétaro and an anonymous oil-on-canvas work depicting the Holy Spirit painting the Virgin of Guadalupe on the main altar of the church of San Juan Tilapa, Estado de México. See laminas 87 and 88 in *Imagenes Guadalupanas*, 110. Cuadriello (1994:105) states, "there are no more than a dozen examples [like this] in Mexican collections."

6. "*Florés appauerunt in terra nostra Cantar, 2.*" Cuadriello (2001:256, no. 49).

7. Cuadriello (2001:256 no. 49). "Dios qual Pintor soberano / gastar quiso lindas flores, / y a María con mil primores / copió como de su mano: Lienso ministró el Indiano / de tosco humilde sayal / en su capa y sin igual / se veé con tanta hermosura, que indica ser tal pintura; obra sobre Natural."

8. Alcántara Rojas (2011:130) notes the analogous relation between the Enclosed Garden and the flower world in early colonial Mexico. See Córdova (2014:72–92) for this same relation in images of the Virgin as well as the profession and death portraits of nuns in colonial Mexico.

9. The sixteenth-century Spanish friar Motolinía (1971:218 [1858]) noted that Indigenous artists in Mexico produced a myriad of flower-based colors for their paintings.

10. Domenici (this volume) offers a more literal translation of this passage: "paints flowers, with flowers paints things, as a Toltec."

11. Translation by author. See López Austin (1997:49–122) for a detailed examination of Tamoanchan.

12. Additionally, Alcántara Rojas (2011:113–14) notes that in the *Florentine Codex*, flower designs appear as part of the insignia and apparel of nobles, leaders, and other participants in flower-dance ceremonies.

REFERENCES

Alcántara Rojas, Berenice. 2011. "*In Nepapan Xochitl*: The Power of Flowers in the Works of Sahagún." In *Colors Between Two Worlds: The Florentine Codex of Bernardino de Sahagún*, edited by Louise Waldman, 106–32. Florence: Kunsthistorisches Institut in Florenz, Max Planck Institut, Villa I Tatti, and the Harvard University Center for Italian Renaissance Studies.

Bargellini, Clara. 2011. "The Colors of the Virgin of Guadalupe." In *Colors Between Two Worlds: The Florentine Codex of Bernardino de Sahagún*, edited by Louise Waldman, 2–25. Florence: Kunsthistorisches Institut in Florenz, Max-Planck-Institut, Villa I Tatti, and the Harvard University Center for Italian Renaissance Studies.

Bassett, Molly. 2015. *The Fate of Earthly Things: Aztec Gods and God-Bodies*. Austin: University of Texas Press.

Becerra Tanco, Luis. 1979 [1675]. *Felicidad de México en el principio y milagroso origen que tubo el santuario de la Virgen Maria Nuestra Señora de Guadalupe*. Facsimile ed. Mexico City: Editorial Jus.

Bierhorst, John, ed. 1985. *Cantares mexicanos: Songs of the Aztecs*. Stanford, Calif.: Stanford University Press.

Brading, David. 2001. *Mexican Phoenix: Our Lady of Guadalupe; Image and Tradition Across Five Centuries*. New York: Cambridge University Press.

Burkhart, Louise. 1992. "Flowery Heaven: The Aesthetics of Paradise in Nahuatl Devotional Literature." *RES: Anthropology and Aesthetics* 21:88–106.

Burkhart, Louise. 2001. *Before Guadalupe: The Virgin Mary in Early Colonial Nahuatl Literature*. Albany, N.Y.: Institute of Mesoamerican Studies, University of Albany.

Cabrera, Miguel. 1977 [1756]. *Maravilla americana y conjunto de raras maravillas . . . en la prodigiosa imagen de Nuestra Señora de Guadalupe de México*. Facsimile ed. Mexico City: Editorial Jus.

Córdova, James M. 2014. *The Art of Professing in Bourbon Mexico: Crowned-Nun Portraits and Reform in the Convent*. Austin: University of Texas Press.

Córdova, James M., and Claire Farago. 2012. "*Casta* Paintings and Self-Fashioning Artists in New Spain." In *At the Crossroads: The Arts of Spanish America and Early Global Trade, 1492–1850*, edited by Donna Pierce and Ronald Otsuka, 129–54. Denver, Colo.: Frederick and Jan Meyer Center for Pre-Columbian and Spanish Colonial Art.

Cuadriello, Jaime. 1994. "La propagación de las devociones novohispanas: Las guadalupanas y otras imágenes preferentes." In *México den el mundo de las colecciones de arte, Nueva España*. Mexico City: Universidad Nacional Autónoma de México.

Cuadriello, Jaime. 2001. "El obrador trinitario o María de Guadalupe creada en idea, imagen y materia." In *El Divino Pintor: La creación de María de Guadalupe en el taller celestial*, edited by Paula Mues Orts, 61–205. Mexico City: Museo de la Basílica de Guadalupe.

Cuadriello, Jaime. 2009. "The Theopolitical Visualization of the Virgin of the Immaculate Conception: Intentionality and Socialization of Images." In *Sacred Spain: Art and Belief in the Spanish World*, edited by Ronda Kasl, 121–45. Indianapolis, Ind.: Indianapolis Museum of Art.

Dean, Carolyn, and Dana Leibsohn. 2017. "Scorned Subjects in Colonial Objects." *Material Religion* 13(4):414–36.

De la Cruz, Mateo. 1781 (1660). *Relación de la milagrosa aparición de la imagen de la Santa Virgen de Guadalupe*. Mexico City: Felipe de Zuniga y Ontiveros.

Domenici, Davide. 2019. "Codex Mendoza and the Material Agency of Indigenous Artists in Early Colonial New Spain." *Latin American and Latinx Visual Culture* 1(2):107–12.

Durán, Diego. 1971. *The Book of Gods and Rites and the Ancient Calendar*. Translated by Fernando Horcasitas and Doris Heyden. Norman: University of Oklahoma Press.

Elizondo, Virgil. 2001. *Guadalupe: Mother of the New Creation*. Maryknoll, N.Y.: Orbis Books.

Garibay, Angel, ed. 1993 [1582]. *Poesía Náhuatl I: Romances de los Señores de la Nueva España; Manuscrito de Juan Bautista de Pomar, Tezcoco, 1582*. Mexico City: Universidad Nacional Autónoma de México.

Hays-Gilpin, Kelley, and Jane H. Hill. 1999. "The Flower World in Material Culture: An Iconographic Complex in the Southwest and Mesoamerica." *Journal of Anthropological Research* 55(1):1–37.

Heyden, Doris. 1983. *Mitología y simbolismo de la flora en el México prehispánico*. Mexico City: Universidad Nacional Autónoma de México.

Hill, Jane H. 1992. "The Flower World of Old Uto-Aztecan." *Journal of Anthropological Research* 48(2):117–44.

Kroger, Joseph, and Patrizia Granziera. 2012. *Aztec Goddesses and Christian Madonnas: Images of the Divine Feminine in Mexico*. Farnham: Ashgate.

Kubler, George. 1985 [1961]. "On the Colonial Extinction of the Motifs of Precolumbian Art." In *The Collected Essays of George Kubler*, edited by Thomas F. Reese, 66–74. New Haven, Conn.: Yale University Press.

López Austin, Alfredo. 1997. *Tamoanchan, Tlalocan: Places of Mist*. Niwot: University Press of Colorado.

Moreno Cuadro, Fernando. 2019. "El tipo iconográfico del *Deus Pictor*: A propósito de José García Hidalgo." *Archivo Español de Arte* 92(365):25–36.

Motolinía, Toribio de Benavente. 1971 [1858]. *Motolinía's History of the Indians of New Spain*. Translated by Francis Borgia Steck. Washington, D.C.: Academy of American Franciscan History.

Mues-Orts, Paula. 2002. "Merezca ser hidalgo y libre el que pintó lo santo y respetado: La defensa novohispana del arte de la pintura." In *El Divino Pintor: La creación de María de Guadalupe en el taller celestial*, edited by Paula Mues Orts, 29–59. Mexico City: Museo de la Basílica de Guadalupe.

Nebel, Richard. 1995. *Santa María Tonantzin, Virgin de Guadalupe: Continuidad y transformación religiosa en México*. Translated from the German by Father Dr. Carlos Warnholz Bustilos, Archpriest of the Distinguished National Basilica of Guadalupe, with the collaboration of Mrs. Irma Ochoa de Nebel. Mexico City: Fondo de Cultura Económica.

Peterson, Jeanette Favrot. 2014. *Visualizing Guadalupe: From Black Madonna to Queen of the Americas*. Austin: University of Texas Press.

Poole, Stafford. 2006. *The Guadalupan Controversies in Mexico*. Stanford, Calif.: Stanford University Press.

Poole, Stafford. 2017. *Our Lady of Guadalupe: The Origins and Sources of a Mexican National Symbol, 1531–1797*. Tucson. University of Arizona Press.

Pórtus Pérez, Javier. 2017. "La Inmaculada como pintura perfecta de Dios." In *Intacta María: Politica y religiosidad en la España Barroca*, 45–53. Valencia: Museo de Bellas Artes de Valencia.

Sahagún, Bernardino de. 1950–1982. *Florentine Codex: A General History of the Things of New Spain*. 12 vols. Translated by Arthur J. O. Anderson and Charles E. Dibble. Santa Fe, N.Mex.: School of American Research; Salt Lake City: University of Utah Press.

Sahagún, Bernardino de. 1993 [1583]. *Bernardino de Sahagún's Psalmodia Christiana (Christian Psalmody)*. Translated by Arthur J. O. Anderson. Salt Lake City: University of Utah Press.

Sánchez, Miguel. 1648. *Imagen de la Virgen Maria, Madre de Dios de Guadalupe: Milagrosamente aparecida en la ciudad de Mexico; Celebrada en su historia, con la profecia del capitulo doce del Apocalipsis*. Mexico City: Imprenta de la Viuda de Bernardo Calderon.

Sousa, Lisa, Stafford Poole, and James Lockhart. 1998. *The Story of Guadalupe: Luis Laso de la Vega's "Huei tlamahuiçoltica" of 1649*. UCLA Latin American Center Publications, vol. 84. Stanford, Calif.: Stanford University Press; Los Angeles: UCLA Latin American Center Publications.

Torre Villar, Ernesto de la, and Ramiro Navarro de Anda, eds. 1982. *Testimonios históricos guadalupanos*. Mexico City: Fondo de Cultura Económica.

Wake, Eleanor. 2010. *Framing the Sacred: The Indian Churches of Early Colonial Mexico*. Norman: University of Oklahoma Press.

"It's Raining Feather-Flower Songs"

Commentary on Current Flower Worlds Research

Kelley Hays-Gilpin

I take my title from a line in a Nahuatl poem cited in the previous chapter by James Córdova. It seems more exciting than simply "Discussion," and my ensuing text will not provide definitive conclusions to what is an ongoing process of exploration. People have been singing flowery songs for at least two thousand years throughout Mesoamerica and the Northwest Mexico/Southwest U.S. region. Academic research on their flowery worlds is perhaps three decades deep. The participants in the flower worlds symposium said from the beginning of our collaboration that "the flower world" is not a place or a thing and quickly moved to a plural mode of thinking, "flower worlds." To say that this is just an analytical concept is true for many scholars, but that does not do justice to the lived experiences of Indigenous people who created and continue to create the images and texts we discuss here. At least one of the authors, and many we identify herein as mentors and collaborators, have direct experience of a flower world. To study flower worlds comparatively, we have identified images, attributes, patterns, and relationships that form a fuzzy set—no single attribute defines the concept, but there are strong associations that have persisted for millennia over a very large region I will call greater Mesoamerica, an imperfect shorthand meant to include all of Mexico and Central America with northwestern Mexico and the southwestern United States. In this volume, we highlight cultural, linguistic, and economic integration that waxed and waned over millennia throughout this region without, however, implying political integration, the distribution of state-level societies, or other ways that the term *Mesoamerica* has been used.

Our aim is not just to identify when and where people practice(d) rituals and image making that express flower worlds. We also explore and aim to understand a broader and deeper sense of Indigenous ontologies, or "how the world is." The authors' various research and writing skills were honed in the halls of academia, museum collections, participant observation in Indigenous communities, archaeological field excavations, and specialized laboratories for peering into micromysteries from pigments to pollen. How to bring these often narrow and focused skills to the exploration of Indigenous ontologies in respectful ways is one of the great challenges of anthropology and related disciplines. We take the position that traditional anthropological "outsider" approaches are valid and productive, particularly for large-scale comparative projects like the one reported here, but "insider" understandings contribute deeper insights that are in the long term more "real." As we learn more from cultural insiders, we hope to be more respectful to those whose living heritage is represented.

The outsider/insider dichotomy is enshrined in anthropological practice as the etic/emic contrast. When Jane Hill began her work on the "Flower World of Old Uto-Aztecan" in language and song (Hill 1992), and when I joined in later on to link in imagery in ancient material culture (Hays-Gilpin and Hill 1999), we were working with an etic framework, and many of the archaeological chapters in this volume continue with etic approaches. Jane's 1992 article came out a year before the publication of Jack Goody's book, the *Culture of Flowers* (Goody 1993). Goody identified nearly universal flower imagery, usually with feminine associations, and often with ritual contexts. He flagged Mesoamerica as an unusual case in which flower images were associated with masculine pursuits such as warfare; Aztec flower wars (*xochiyaoyotl*) were of course the most dramatic example. That piqued Jane's interest, of course, as a scholar of Nahuatl language and one who always enjoyed exploring contrasting approaches to a subject. Jane's regional comparative study resulted in a definition of the Uto-Aztecan flower world as a pattern of verbal and graphic images, behaviors, and practices; Goody's global study produced a broader, more general pattern to which the Aztec, at least, did not seem to conform. Both studies are significant for archaeology because they give us a baseline pattern of regular associations of images and contexts that we can look for in the material record of past behavior and then use as a line of evidence for historical relationships. We can explore flower worlds' articulation with social and political strategies in polities at various scales. We can explain as outsiders how the leaders of the Aztec

Empire deployed imagery of flowers, butterflies, and fire to promote participation in flower wars and perpetual human sacrifice, including self-sacrifice, to keep the sun moving in the sky—a very different use of flower imagery from previous and later cultural practices. We do not need to understand the "inside" meanings of imagery and ritual practices to draw some valuable historical conclusions about politics and state religions, for example.

And yet some of us are compelled to understand more deeply, or at least to make attempts. Our intentions are not to violate the cultural protections usually afforded esoteric information, but inevitably we do. We intend to afford Indigenous culture, artworks, and history the same focused attention and respect that scholars have long devoted to the Western canon. We want to demonstrate that greater Mesoamerican art, culture, and history are just as important, sophisticated, complex, and interesting as those of Europe and Asia, about which vast libraries have been stocked for centuries. Perhaps more important, insights gained from monistic, animistic, and pantheist worldviews such as that of the flower worlds may prove to be a basis—the basis?—for a rejection of the Western culture/nature dichotomy that when enacted through settler colonialism, industrialism, and now predator capitalism has radically degraded our global environment to the brink of disaster.

FROM SYMBOLS TO LIVED REALITY

The primary criticism that many authors in the volume leveled against the etic approach in Hill's original flower world study is that it is not merely a set of symbols or metaphors, images that "stand for" something other than themselves. Instead, in lived reality, there is no separation of signifier and signified. That dichotomy may be helpful in linguistics (sometimes), but it is a Western "outsider" construct that diminishes the original intentions, contexts, and experiences of these images, songs, and practices.

Several of the preceding chapters (Molina and Shorter, Neurath, and Sandstrom) make the case that the expression of flowery worlds in contemporary Indigenous practice reveals a monistic understanding of the world contrary to the Western dualisms of sacred/secular, good/evil, spirit/body, and so on. Sacredness pervades everything—pantheism, not polytheist cataloging of various deities. In Nahua, Yoeme, and Wixárika understandings of the world, sacredness is revealed or unconcealed according to its own volition in collaboration with human actions and orientations. Because the term *sacred* implies its opposite, *secular*, in Western thought, this term is problematic. *Spiritual* might be suitable—but a spirit world/material world contrast needs to include the interpenetration of these worlds. Both are always present, but the spirit world is usually concealed. As we intend flower worlds to be understood, they are made visible, or are unconcealed, in contexts enacted in the ethnographic contexts described here as rituals. Ritual, as observable behavior, is often amenable to archaeological study because ritual acts often leave material traces. Like many rituals, flower worlds embody reciprocal relationships among humans and all the other agential beings of the cosmos. Worlds in this sense are active, agential. *Worldings* might be a better term. Ritual performances that are not only sacred but entangled with all life activities—from hunting to feasting to weaving—are called "doings" in the Pueblos (Fowles 2013; Kealiinihomoku 1989). These activities and their images, materials, and technologies, are generative. As Sandstrom's Nahua collaborators explain, one sings the flower world into this world. One sings people into relationships with the world (chap. 1). Wixárika pilgrims become peyote flowers (chap. 2). Felipe Molina, as a Yoeme deer singer, brings the *sea ania*, flower world, into this world (chap. 3). When he enters the village plaza, it becomes a flowery patio of the *sea ania*, where space and time, people and animals, are deeply connected in dynamic balance.

BALANCE AND ORDER

The world (particularly its human components) is constantly moving, adjusting, slipping out of balance, being brought back toward balance, and shifting or drifting off again. In greater Mesoamerica, ritual practices and paraphernalia, with all their deeply meaningful imagery and materials, are about ordering things properly, arranging things in the world to achieve balance. The flower world imagery we are examining here is part of this ordering and arranging. Sandstrom (chap. 1) demonstrates an Indigenous ontology with a Nahua perspective. From this view, flowers do not symbolize the flower world: they give form to it. Flowers are "proof of the ordered beauty that transcends human beings' fragmented experiences of reality." We cannot understand the flower world by study-ing its imagery alone but only in the context of a back and forth moving duality, not static dualism.

The flowery worlds are generative. They bring themselves into being in this world through human work. Córdova (chap. 13) noted that in Na-hua thought, flowers were the very sacred materials that the Creator, as Life-Giver, used to create beauty in the universe and in life. Anthropolo-gists often focus on how ritual practice renews community values. In the cases described here by Córdova, Sandstrom, Molina and Shorter, and other authors, flower worlds manifest values of cosmic balance, respect for ancestors and family relationships, and relationships with other-than-human persons including plants, animals, mountains, lakes, and streams. Ritual practices get the attention of divine powers and bring them into communion with humans. Bringing the world of flowers into this world is hard work. Preparing and enacting the flower worlds require collective labor. Washburn (chap. 4) explains one of the primary themes of Hopi katsina songs—to remind people of their shared values of hard work, humility, and reciprocity.

But the flower worlds are not all goodness and light. Neurath (chap. 2) explains the danger presented to the community by those Wixárika who have become peyote. The ideal world described through songs in Wash-burn's chapter is about all the good things Hopis aspire to bring into being with the help of their katsinas, who admonish them to be humble and hardworking. But the Hopi world has light and dark sides. Its ritual calendar is divided in two—for half the year, flowery katsinas and flute ceremonies prevail, but in the other half, esoteric sodalities perform ritu-als that deal with the dead and the underworld—death that is necessary for regeneration. The ritual practices of flower worlds are also not all solemn and serious—John Pohl (chap. 10) points out the roles of ritual buffoons and clowning in Mesoamerican communities; ritual clowns also perform in the Pueblos, right alongside the serious katsinas.

ALL OUR SENSES

Flower worlds are experienced with all of the senses. Hill emphasized the linguistic aspects of the flower world and noted that Uto-Aztecan com-munities express these sets of imagery mainly through song. Washburn (chap. 4) also emphasizes songs. Hopi katsinas sing their songs while dancing, adorned with colorful regalia. The ethnographers among us describe multisensory expressions in ritual altars and performances—color, light, images, song, sound, scent, and movement, including dance. From ethnographic descriptions, archaeologists are inspired to look for material correlates of multisensory practice and experience. Chinchilla Mazariegos (chap. 5), Turner (chap. 7), and others find this evidence in the form of censers, elaborate pottery vessels adorned with flowery images used to burn *copal* and other incense. McNeil (chap. 6) analyzes plant pollen on floor surfaces that would have been the sites for ritual performance in the Maya city of Copan. Flower pollen distribution is strongly patterned and reveals the use of "popcorn flowers" with strong fragrance and other affordances (such as medicinal properties and resemblance to clouds) that evoke the spirit world, the watery place of origin, or the life cycle of maize and humans. Flowers and flowering plants were used here not as "just" symbols but to "actualize paradisiacal places of creation" to repeatedly remake Copan as a place of creation. Taube (chap. 9) associates images of flute players and cicadas with the role of music and song in promoting the growth of plants, from maize, the essential food of greater Mesoamerica, to the reed in Pueblo and Navajo origin narratives that the ancestors climbed from the underworld to emerge into this world.

Domenici (chap. 12) deploys material science to answer questions about Nahua art and ritual practice. He examines the paints used to create Mesoamerican codices and finds botanical ingredients. He links the acts of creating paint from flowers, painting the codices, and the actions of oral performance of sacred texts that were chanted or sung. These are explained by the chain of meanings that Hill describes in her 1992 article—the importance of songs, the floweriness of song, and the depiction of song in Mesoamerican codices as speech scrolls adorned with flowers. Naturally, then, actual flowers and plants infused into paint created the vibrant colors in the imagery that probably guided oration in actual performance. Flower paint expresses life force, generative energy, and the life within things. Scribes moistened their brushes in their mouths, bringing flower-based paint into their bodies and infusing some of their own substance into the paint and onto the page. Molina and Shorter (chap. 3) note that for the Yoeme, songs are a type of medicine.

They make people feel healthier. Again, flowers are not "just" metaphors but embodiment, performance, and multisensory experiences.

FLOWER WORLDS ARE GENDERED

In most of our studies, we can recognize that flower worlds are generative, and as such they or their components are often gendered. But gender configurations are complicated. In Chinchilla Mazariegos's study (chap. 5), flowery imagery in the Pacific Coast of Guatemala appears early on in our historical sequence. There, flowers seem to refer to female deities and fertility—flowers inseminate women, perhaps. The flower world there was not associated with the sun, males, and war as it was for the Mexica in Central Mexico later on. The Wixárika case (chap. 2) shows some gender complementarity but also some ambiguity—Wixárika men can become feminine deities as well as masculine ones, but not the reverse—women can only embody feminine deities. The Hopi katsina songs that Washburn (chap. 4) presents here not only admonish listeners to work hard but also enforce gender roles. In this matrilineal and matrilocal society, gender roles are complementary rather than hierarchical, but women's roles are narrower and more restricted.

FLOWER WORLDS' STRATEGIC POTENTIAL

Flower worlds also facilitate access to ancestors, and for some, to the time-place of emergence from the world below into this world. Evoking flowering worlds involves geographies and temporal dimensions in which time and place can be collapsed so that Flower Mountain, from Teotihuacan to Hopi, is both origin and destination. How do the different communities we engage with use these rich ideological constructs in their social and political lives? Anthropologists are good at broad and comparative views. Several chapters, taken together, highlight the contrast between deployment of flower worlds in small-scale communities versus Mesoamerican cities, states, and empires.

Hopis, for example, tamp down economic inequality in various ways, including the katsinas' admonishments to everybody to work together for a common good and to be humble (Washburn, chap. 4). Their unpredictable desert environment leaves little opportunity to accumulate surplus food, land, or labor. At the same time, theirs is a hierarchical society, with ranking based on clan identity, order of clan arrival, clan ownership of ceremonies, and lineage ranking within clans. There is little opportunity for social or economic mobility. Dissenters "vote with their feet" by migrating out to join other communities. In the Wixárika case, *peyoteros* make extraordinary personal sacrifices to undertake pilgrimage, uphold cargo responsibilities, and bring the blessings of the flower world back home. They become powerful ancestors. Yet their friends and neighbors greet them with ridicule and suspicion. "As the creators of everything important, initiated people have an enormous potential to accumulate and to abuse power" (Neurath, chap. 2). And accumulation of power must be countered; power must be leveled or balanced.

In hierarchical Mesoamerican communities, elites accumulate and wield power. They can deploy, focus, or invert elements of flower world imagery and ritual practice for their own purposes, and they do, in examples developed here by González López and Vázquez Vallín (chap. 11), Turner (chap. 7), and Pohl (chap. 10). Mesoamericans at various times and places engaged in violent struggles for social status with remarkable continuity in imagery from Teotihuacan to Tenochtitlan and from Maya to Huastec to Nahua. The most striking example that emerged from our seminar discussion is the Aztec (Mexica) deployment of flower imagery from a context of fertility to sacrifice/militarism/masculinity. The Aztec flower world was both garden and battlefield. Flowers evoked blood and sacrifice. Birds and butterflies were understood to be the souls of warriors. The flower world was deployed as justification for war and empire expansion, tribute to the Aztec elite center.

The most compelling case for strategic deployment of the ancient concept of flower worlds is presented by Córdova in chapter 13 with the bridging of Indigenous Mesoamerican and Spanish Catholic worlds through the Virgin of Guadalupe, who came into being through flowers. She painted herself with flowers on Juan Diego's cape—not just European flowers (e.g., lilies and roses) but also the fragrant "popcorn flowers" already used in the region for millennia as described by McNeil in chapter 6. The Virgin wears not just a brightly colored cloak; her clothes gleamed and shimmered like the sun—like the iridescent birds, feathers, and jewels of Mexica temple offerings. Córdova demonstrates that the Virgin of Guadalupe was not just a replacement for an ancient goddess with a new one but an admixture, a transcultural bridge across time and cultures.

HISTORY OF FLOWER WORLDS

Most of the seminar participants assume that the sets of imagery and practices we are examining began somewhere in southern Mesoamerica and spread north to Arizona and New Mexico. Hill proposed that the flower world spread with Uto-Aztecan languages carried by migrant farmers thousands of years ago, persisted in verbal expressions, and was sometimes expressed in visual arts. Mathiowetz (chap. 8) argues here for a later spread (although perhaps facilitated in part by an Uto-Aztecan dialect chain) from Mesoamerica to west Mexico to the southwestern United States. Either way, how were these sets of ideas and practices transmitted? Were they carried in esoteric rituals with prescribed liturgies or by emulation and refiguration in each instance? What were the roles of individual creativity, variation, and innovation? Similarities can connect elites in different communities, but trade, migration, sodality initiation, intermarriage, and many other human connections can move ideas, images, techniques, tools, raw materials, songs, and artifacts from person to person over long distances.

One way to think of the fuzzy set of flower world elements is as a loose constellation of flexible "part ideologies" that can be deployed for different purposes in different contexts but validated by continuity through time and long-distance connections and interactions. Different kinds of long-distance connections probably account for the patterns documented by Mathiowetz (chap. 8). Transmission of the flower, bird, serpent, and cloud imagery occurred from central to west Mexico; from west Mexico to Chaco and Mimbres in one interval of time; from west Mexico to Casas Grandes over a century later; and from Casas Grandes to the New Mexico Pueblos and Hopi in perhaps the fifteenth century. Each segment of this journey probably involved different modes of transmission and different configurations of specific icons. For example, how do serpents fit in the flower world ideologies? Mathiowetz links serpents with other flower world icons in the Casas Grandes region. For the Wixárika of west Mexico, people who have become peyote flowers transform into feathered cloud snakes, the breath of the world that contains all the ancestors—so there is a clear connection there. Neither of these serpents are rattlesnakes, as is more common for imagery of the feathered serpent Quetzalcoatl in Mesoamerica. In contrast, in Hopi katsina practice—the main vessel for flower world imagery—serpents and snakes are virtually absent. The Hopi Water Serpent is a very different being from the Rattlesnake. The two are owned by different clans, appear in different ceremonies, and although both are rain bringers, their histories and functions differ. Neither is particularly flowery. Hopi ritual knowledge and practice is partitioned to maintain separation of powers and distribution of obligations and resources. Matrilineal clans have distinct migration histories and sodality ownership of ceremonies. All come together in the katsina half of the year, but more esoteric ceremonies including Water Serpent- and Rattlesnake-focused ceremonies are separate. We could enumerate many other examples of partial symbol sets. There is no "whole package," but some packages are more developed than others, perhaps when elites consolidate partial ideologies and symbol sets.

This concept of part ideologies coupled with monism or pantheism (rather than polytheism) explains why it is impossible to sort out all of the Mesoamerican and Puebloan deities, name them, classify them, and find cross-cultural equivalents. Asking "Is the Hopi Water Serpent the same as Quetzalcoatl?" is not exactly a helpful question. Deities are not fixed; their roles and names change and vary. This is not a problem because in a monistic worldview the whole manifests itself in various ways, as Sandstrom explains in chapter 1. Thus, early on in the seminar project, I very much appreciated Chinchilla Mazariegos's use of the term *flower worlds* in the plural. Expression is diverse. In seminar discussions, several participants pointed out that multiple culturally distinct epistemologies and worldviews coexisted and comingled in Mexico in the past, and still do. Neurath (chap. 2) notes that Amerindian peoples like diversity—they deliberately differentiate themselves from their neighbors. Creativity and innovation add to diversity. New songs are composed all of the time. Hopi composers write new katsina songs, and groups perform them, sometimes only once. Wixárika ritual practitioners dream new songs, and each of their yarn paintings represents a unique vision. Yet Turner and Pohl (chaps. 7 and 10) show how flower world imagery bridged polities in the Epiclassic and Late Postclassic worlds, respectively, in the creation of an international-style symbol set that facilitated economic exchange and elite marriage alliances over a wide region and across political and linguistic boundaries.

Catholicism provided another push to uniformity in the Colonial period, but some Mesoamericans were already familiar with texts and liturgies. Domenici (chap. 12) focuses on pre-Hispanic painted codices containing liturgies that were read and chanted. Even the oral transmission of songs and prayers and ritual liturgy probably were passed along precisely across many generations. In both the passing along of traditions and processes of innovation, the roles of specialist practitioners must be recognized in all of the societies explored here: scribes, mural painters, sculptors, potters, dyers, weavers, embroiderers, composers, priests, and pilgrims. These are the people, whether in a village or a state capitol, who know how things should be properly arranged, who can direct building and adorning altars, who can provide songs for every occasion. We cannot overstate the importance of apprenticeship and mentoring in transmitting the elaborate images and contexts of flowery worlds.

NOT CONCLUDING, BUT CONTINUING

As I took part in the flower worlds seminar, I kept thinking about the way one of my mentors, Hopi artist Mike Kabotie, talked with me about mentoring. He referred to the Water Serpent as a mentor as well as a Water Clan ancestor and deity. Honoring mentors came up in our seminar often—Jane Hill was a mentor for all of us. Emory Sekaquaptewa mentored Dorothy Washburn and me. Kenneth Morrison mentored David Shorter. Karl Taube mentored Michael Mathiowetz, Andrew Turner, and Ángel González López. And so on. As in ritual sodalities and their patrons and participants, ideas don't just "arrive" somewhere but are offered and accepted, often by specialists/mentors/masters to apprentices/protégés. Hard work is involved. Reciprocity or payment is necessary. And we feel gratitude!

I conclude with a contemporary Hopi mural painting by Michael Kabotie and Delbridge Honanie (Color Plate 16) created in 2001 when they were artists in residence at the Museum of Northern Arizona. Titled *Pottery Mound: Germination*, the mural depicts the life cycle of humans and maize with images reinterpreted from fifteenth-century kiva murals at Pottery Mound, a Pueblo site located not far southwest of

Albuquerque that was excavated by the University of New Mexico in the late 1950s (Hibben 1975). What you see here is the dynamic duality of the underworld and this world in the summer growing season. The abstract, flowing fragments of bird and flower imagery in the underworld represent death and decay, Mike told me. But these are also the materials from which new life is emerging. The corn grows because the butterflies, flowers, and people encourage it to do so with song and prayer that bring rain and warmth. They all are bringing each other into being with focused effort and good hearts.

REFERENCES

Fowles, Severin M. 2013. *An Archaeology of Doings: Secularism and the Study of Pueblo Religion*. Santa Fe, N.Mex.: School of American Research Press.

Goody, Jack. 1993. *The Culture of Flowers*. Cambridge: Cambridge University Press.

Hays-Gilpin, Kelley, and Jane H. Hill. 1999. "The Flower World in Material Culture: An Iconographic Complex in the Southwest and Mesoamerica." *Journal of Anthropological Research* 55(1):1–37.

Hibben, Frank C. 1975. *Kiva Art of the Anasazi at Pottery Mound*. Las Vegas, Nev.: KC Publications.

Hill, Jane H. 1992. "The Flower World of Old Uto-Aztecan." *Journal of Anthropological Research* 48(2):117–44.

Kealiinohomoku, J. W. 1989. "The Hopi Katsina Dance Event 'Doings.'" In *Seasons of the Kachina*, edited by L. J. Bean, 51–64. Hayward, Calif.: Ballena Press.

CONTRIBUTORS

Oswaldo Chinchilla Mazariegos (Ph.D., Vanderbilt University) is an associate professor in the anthropology department at Yale University and was formerly professor at the Universidad de San Carlos de Guatemala and curator at the Museo Popol Vuh in Guatemala City. His research interests include Mesoamerican art, religion, and writing; the study of ancient urbanism and social complexity with a special focus on the Pacific Coast of Guatemala; and the history of archaeology in Guatemala. In 2011 he was awarded a John Simon Guggenheim Fellowship for his work on Cotzumalhuapa art and archaeology. His books *Art and Myth of the Ancient Maya* (2017) and *Imágenes de la Mitología Maya* (2011) offer innovative views and methodological breakthroughs in the study of ancient Maya religion and art. He is the author of *Corpus of Maya Hieroglyphic Inscriptions* (2017), *Cotzumalguapa, la Ciudad Arqueológica: El Baúl-Bilbao-El Castillo* (2012), editor of *Arqueología Subacuática: Amatitlán, Atitlán* (2011), and coeditor of *The Decipherment of Ancient Maya Writing* (2001) and *The Technology of Maya Civilization: Political Economy and Beyond in Lithic Studies* (2011).

James M. Córdova (Ph.D., Tulane University) is associate professor of art history at the University of Colorado, Boulder. His research delves into issues of gender, materiality, hybridity, and text/image relations in colonial Mexican visual culture. Currently he is working on the role of sacred materials and images in colonial Mexico's conquest narrative. His publications include *The Art of Professing in Bourbon Mexico: Crowned Nun Portraits and Reform in the Convent* (2014), for which he received the Miller Meiss Publication Award from the College Art Association, as well as a number of articles that have appeared in academic journals and edited volumes.

Davide Domenici is associate professor of anthropology at the Department of History and Cultures, University of Bologna (Italy). His past research has mainly focused on Mesoamerican and Mississippian archaeology; he directed the Rio La Venta Archaeological Project (Chiapas, Mexico 1999–2010) and the Cahokia Project (Illinois, United States, 2011–2016). He is currently researching the collection history of Mesoamerican objects brought to Italy and Europe in early modern times, reconstructing their cultural biographies on the basis of archival research. Since 2005, in collaboration with the MOLAB mobile laboratory, he has conducted a long-term project of noninvasive chemical analyses of pre-Hispanic and colonial Mesoamerican pictorial manuscripts in order to characterize their painting materials, to identify different technological traditions, and to investigate Indigenous conceptions of the materiality of colors. He is the author and coauthor of several articles and monographs.

Ángel González López (Ph.D., University of California, Riverside) is a postdoctoral research fellow at the North Carolina Museum of Art. The primary focus of his research is on iconographic analyses of Late Postclassic art in Central Mexico (A.D. 1200–1519). He founded the Aztec Stone Sculpture from the Basin of Mexico Project (AZSSBMP) to create a standardized database of stone sculptures that are currently found in various educational institutions in the United States, Mexico, and Europe to facilitate comparative analyses. He is the author of *Imágenes sagradas: Iconografía en esculturas de piedra del recinto sagrado de Tenochtitlan y el Museo Etnográfico* (2015). González López was previously a junior fellow at the Dumbarton Oaks Research Library and a full-time excavation specialist with the Proyecto Templo Mayor for ten years before beginning his graduate studies.

Kelley Hays-Gilpin (Ph.D., University of Arizona) is professor of anthropology at Northern Arizona University and curator of anthropology at the Museum of Northern Arizona. She has researched pottery, rock art, murals, textiles, and other visual arts in the Southwest, including expressions of flowery worlds, for over thirty-five years and has published numerous books and articles. Her current research focuses on long-term histories of Hopi and Zuni communities and contemporary artists' expressions of relationships with land, water, and ancient sites.

Michael D. Mathiowetz (Ph.D., University of California, Riverside) is a lecturer in anthropology at the University of California, Riverside. Since 2002, his research has focused on the archaeology, ethnohistory, ethnology, and oral histories of Indigenous groups in west Mexico, northern Mexico, and the American Southwest. His archaeological field research is primarily centered in the Aztatlán core zone of Pacific-coastal Nayarit and northern Jalisco with an emphasis on the interrelationship of Aztatlán, Casas Grandes, and Puebloan societies between A.D. 850/900–1350+. He is the author of a number of articles on the art, religion, and sociopolitical organization of pre-Hispanic cultures in these regions and the living legacies among descendant societies. Mathiowetz was a 2014/2015 UC MEXUS-CONACYT Postdoctoral Fellow at Centro Instituto Nacional de Antropología e Historia, Nayarit, and currently he is coediting a volume with Dr. John M. D. Pohl on the Aztatlán culture titled *Reassessing the Aztatlán World: Cultural Dynamics in Postclassic Northwest Mesoamerica*.

Cameron L. McNeil (Ph.D., Graduate Center, City University of New York) is an associate professor in anthropology at Lehman College and the Graduate Center, City University of New York. She has worked in the Copan Valley in Honduras for over twenty years investigating ancient ritual plant use and human-environmental interactions. McNeil is an archaeobotanist specializing in palynology and a field archaeologist. Since 2011, she has directed excavations in two areas of the Copan Valley investigating landscape transformation in both the Early Classic period and the Late Classic to Postclassic period transition. McNeil's work focuses on plant use among the Maya, including pre-Columbian and modern cacao consumption.

Felipe S. Molina (Yoem Pueblo, Marana, Arizona) is a retired public school teacher. He currently works at the Pascua Yaqui Tribe Social Service Department and is the Yoeme cultural history instructor at the Center for Employment Training. He has coauthored two books with Dr. Larry Evers. He also coauthored the *Yoeme-English Dictionary* with Dr. David Shaul and Herminia Valenzuela. He is now working with Dr. Richard Felger on the forthcoming book *Yoeme Ethnoecology*.

Johannes Neurath (Ph.D., Universidad Nacional Autónoma de México, México) is a researcher at the Museo Nacional de Antropología and a lecturer at the Universidad Nacional Autónoma de México. Since 1992 he has conducted ethnographic fieldwork among Wixáritari, Náyari, and other Mexican Indigenous groups. His main research interests are ritual and cosmopolitics. Currently he studies pre-Columbian and contemporary Indigenous art in a comparative perspective. His most important publications are *La vida de las imágenes: Arte huichola* (2013) and *Las fiestas de la Casa Grande: Procesos rituales, cosmovisión y estructura social en una comunidad huichola* (2002).

John M. D. Pohl (Ph.D., University of California, Los Angeles) is adjunct professor in art history at the University of California, Los Angeles, and lecturer in anthropology at California State University, Los Angeles. He has received numerous fellowships and grants for his research on the Nahua, Mixtec, and Zapotec civilizations of southern Mexico and is investigating the roles they played in a Pacific-coastal exchange system that linked Oaxaca directly with West Mexico and the greater American Southwest. In addition to his academic pursuits, Dr. Pohl has had a prolific career as a writer, designer, and curator for major museums and exhibitions around the country, including "Sorcerers of the Fifth Heaven: Art and Ritual in Ancient Southern Mexico" for Princeton University, "The Aztec Pantheon and the Art of Empire" for the Getty Villa Museum, and "Children of the Plumed Serpent: The Legacy of Quetzalcoatl in Ancient Mexico" for the Los Angeles County Museum of Art and the Dallas Museum of Art.

Alan R. Sandstrom (Ph.D., Indiana University), professor emeritus of anthropology at Purdue University, Fort Wayne, is a sociocultural anthropologist with interests in cultural ecology, cultural materialism, economic anthropology, history and theory of anthropology, Native Americans, and religion and ritual. He conducted field research among Tibetans in exile in Himachal Pradesh, northern India, and has worked for nearly fifty years in a single Nahua community in northern Veracruz, Mexico. His five published monographs, three coedited volumes, and numerous journal articles and book chapters have focused broadly on the ethnography of the Indigenous peoples of Mexico. A recently completed book manuscript documenting Nahua religious pilgrimage to venerated mountains written with coauthor Pamela Effrein Sandstrom is currently being evaluated for publication.

David Delgado Shorter (Ph.D., University of California, Santa Cruz) is professor of world arts and cultures at the University of California, Los Angeles. His 2009 book *We Will Dance Our Truth: Yaqui History in Yoeme Performances* won the Chicago Prize for best book in folklore. In 2011 he developed the Wiki for Indigenous Languages, an online language vitalization tool. His 2013 film *Lutu Chuktiwa/Cutting the Cord* features the first ever recording of the sorrow-releasing ceremony in a Yoeme pueblo featuring Yoeme language and narration. Dr. Shorter now directs the *Archive of Healing*, a digitized archive of healing approaches from around the world. He is a distinguished teaching award recipient who researches and teaches the borderlands of science, methodologies of knowledge production, and cross-cultural healing.

Karl A. Taube (Ph.D., Yale University) is a distinguished professor of anthropology at the University of California, Riverside, and is an archaeologist specializing in religious traditions and writing systems of Ancient Mesoamerica, including the Olmec, Maya, Teotihuacan, and the Aztec. In addition he also studies religious traditions of the ancient and contemporary greater Southwest and cultural relations between this region and Mesoamerica. Much of his research focuses on the symbolism of maize in Mesoamerica and the greater Southwest as well as concepts of paradise and the afterlife in both regions. Along with numerous articles and book chapters, he has published twelve books, including six monographs. In 2015 he received the Proskouriakoff Award from the Peabody Museum at Harvard University. Along with engaging in extensive linguistic and ethnographic fieldwork in Quintana Roo, he has participated in archaeological projects at Chichén Itzá, San Angel and Naranjal in the states of Yucatan and Quintana Roo, Mexico, as well as at Copán, Honduras, and in Guatemala at San Bartolo as well as sites pertaining to jadeite sources in the Middle Motagua region.

Andrew D. Turner (Ph.D., University of California, Riverside) is a senior research specialist at the Getty Research Institute. The primary focus of his research is art, identity, and cross-cultural interaction in Central

Mexico during the Epiclassic period (A.D. 600–900), and he has also written articles on the art of the Olmec, Teotihuacan, the Mexica, the ancient Maya, the Moche, and colonial Andes. In addition to numerous journal articles and chapters, Turner authored the book *Sex, Metaphor, and Ideology in Moche Pottery of Ancient Peru* (2015). Turner is currently engaged in an extensive project that traces the looting and collection of pre-Hispanic antiquities from Mexico. Before joining the Getty, Turner held positions at the Yale University Art Gallery and the University of Cambridge in the Museum of Archaeology and Anthropology and the McDonald Institute for Archaeological Research.

Lorena Vázquez Vallín (Licenciatura, Escuela Nacional de Antropología) is a researcher with the Programa de Arqueología Urbana in Mexico City. Her research focuses on Aztec archaeology, and current excavations explore the area surrounding the Templo Mayor and adjacent buildings in the Main Precinct of Tenochtitlan. She is the project manager in charge of the excavation of the recently discovered *tzompantli* skull rack, the Main Plaza, and the ballcourt. Vázquez Vallín also has excavated in other regions of Mesoamerica, including Chihuahua, Sinaloa, and the southern part of Mexico City.

Dorothy Washburn (Ph.D., Columbia University) is a consulting scholar in the American Section at the Penn Museum, University of Pennsylvania. Her analysis of geometric design with plane pattern symmetries has revealed that symmetry choice is culture specific and moreover that the symmetries of pattern are structural metaphors for social relationships within a culture. She has focused on the ceramic designs from the pre-Hispanic American Southwest, but to test her method and results, she has analyzed repeated patterns from California baskets, southern Laotian textiles, Bakuba raffia cloth, Basketmaker sandals, and Ica Valley ceramics as well as studied the perception of pattern with experimental psychologists and the voicing of key social relationships in ritual song with native speakers. She was a fellow in the Miller Institute for Basic Research in Science at the University of California, Berkeley, and an associate curator and chairman in the department of anthropology at the California Academy of Sciences, San Francisco. She is the author and coauthor of twelve books and over eighty-five articles.

INDEX